End-of-Life Decisions in Medical Care

Those involved in end-of-life decision making must take into account both legal and ethical issues. This book starts with a critical reflection of ethical principles including ideas such as moral status, the value of life, acts and omissions, harm, autonomy, dignity and paternalism. It then explores the practical difficulties of regulating end-of-life decisions, focusing on patients, health-care professionals, the wider community and issues surrounding 'slippery slope' arguments. By evaluating the available empirical evidence, the author identifies preferred ways to regulate decisions and minimise abuses at the end of life, and outlines an ethical theory which can provide practical guidance for those engaged in end-of-life decisions.

STEPHEN W. SMITH is a Lecturer in Law at the Birmingham Law School, where he teaches Bioethics, Criminal Law and Medicine and Jurisprudence.

Cambridge Bioethics and Law

This series of books was founded by Cambridge University Press with Alexander McCall Smith as its first editor in 2003. It focuses on the law's complex and troubled relationship with medicine across both the developed and the developing world. In the past twenty years, we have seen in many countries increasing resort to the courts by dissatisfied patients and a growing use of the courts to attempt to resolve intractable ethical dilemmas. At the same time, legislatures across the world have struggled to address the questions posed by both the successes and the failures of modern medicine, while international organisations such as the WHO and UNESCO now regularly address issues of medical law.

It follows that we would expect ethical and policy questions to be integral to the analysis of the legal issues discussed in this series. The series responds to the high profile of medical law in universities, in legal and medical practice, as well as in public and political affairs. We seek to reflect the evidence that many major health-related policy debates in the UK, Europe and the international community over the past two decades have involved a strong medical law dimension. With that in mind, we seek to address how legal analysis might have a trans-jurisdictional and international relevance. Organ retention, embryonic stem cell research, physician assisted suicide and the allocation of resources to fund health care are but a few examples among many. The emphasis of this series is thus on matters of public concern and/or practical significance. We look for books that could make a difference to the development of medical law and enhance the role of medico-legal debate in policy circles. That is not to say that we lack interest in the important theoretical dimensions of the subject, but we aim to ensure that theoretical debate is grounded in the realities of how the law does and should interact with medicine and health care.

Series Editors
Professor Margaret Brazier, *University of Manchester*
Professor Graeme Laurie, *University of Edinburgh*
Professor Richard Ashcroft, *Queen Mary, University of London*
Professor Eric M. Meslin, *Indiana University*

Marcus Radetzki, Marian Radetzki, Niklas Juth
Genes and Insurance: Ethical, Legal and Economic Issues

Ruth Macklin
Double Standards in Medical Research in Developing Countries

Donna Dickenson
Property in the Body: Feminist Perspectives

Matti Häyry, Ruth Chadwick, Vilhjálmur Árnason, Gardar Árnason
The Ethics and Governance of Human Genetic Databases: European Perspectives

Ken Mason
The Troubled Pregnancy: Legal Wrongs and Rights in Reproduction

Daniel Sperling
Posthumous Interests: Legal and Ethical Perspectives

Keith Syrett
Law, Legitimacy and the Rationing of Health Care

Alastair Maclean
Autonomy, Informed Consent and the Law: A Relational Change

Heather Widdows, Caroline Mullen
The Governance of Genetic Information: Who Decides?

David Price
Human Tissue in Transplantation and Research

Matti Häyry
Rationality and the Genetic Challenge: Making People Better?

Mary Donnelly
*Healthcare Decision-Making and the Law: Autonomy, Capacity and the
Limits of Liberalism*

Anne-Maree Farrell, David Price, Muireann Quigley
Organ Shortage: Ethics, Law and Pragmatism

Sara Fovargue
Xenotransplantation and Risk: Regulating a Developing Biotechnology

John Coggon
*What Makes Health Public?: A Critical Evaluation of Moral, Legal, and
Political Claims in Public Health*

Anne-Maree Farrell
The Politics of Blood: Ethics, Innovation and the Regulation of Risk

Mark Taylor
Genetic Data and the Law: A Critical Perspective on Privacy Protection

Stephen W. Smith
*End-of-Life Decisions in Medical Care: Principles and Policies for
Regulating the Dying Process*

End-of-Life Decisions in Medical Care

Principles and Policies for Regulating the Dying Process

Stephen W. Smith

Birmingham Law School, University of Birmingham

CAMBRIDGE
UNIVERSITY PRESS

CAMBRIDGE UNIVERSITY PRESS
Cambridge, New York, Melbourne, Madrid, Cape Town,
Singapore, São Paulo, Delhi, Tokyo, Mexico City

Cambridge University Press
The Edinburgh Building, Cambridge CB2 8RU, UK

Published in the United States of America by Cambridge University Press,
New York

www.cambridge.org
Information on this title: www.cambridge.org/9781107005389

First published 2012

Printed in the United Kingdom at the University Press, Cambridge

A catalogue record for this publication is available from the British Library

Library of Congress Cataloguing in Publication data
Smith, Stephen W., 1973–
    End-of-life decisions in medical care : principles and policies for
    regulating the dying process / Stephen W. Smith.
        p. ; cm. – (Cambridge bioethics and law)
    Includes bibliographical references and index.
    ISBN 978-1-107-00538-9 (hardback)
    I. Title. II. Series: Cambridge bioethics and law.
    [DNLM: 1. Right to Die–ethics. 2. Right to Die–legislation &
    jurisprudence. 3. Ethics, Medical. 4. Euthanasia–ethics.
    5. Suicide, Assisted–ethics. W 50]
    179.7–dc23
    2011044366

ISBN 978-1-107-00538-9 Hardback

\#757147651

To my parents, because the acorn doesn't fall far from the tree.
(Although that doesn't mean they should be blamed for anything I've written in the book.)

Contents

Table of cases

OTHER CASES

Acknowledgements

With any project like this, there are a number of people who have helped me along the way. This includes the normal group of family and friends who have provided immense help and support over the years. In addition, there have been a number of fellow academics, lawyers, doctors, etc., with whom I have discussed these issues over the years at conferences and similar occasions. Several people are worthy of specific mention, however. First, several friends and colleagues have read various parts of the book in draft form and made helpful critical comments. They include: Gavin Byrne, Rob Cryer, Liz Wicks and Mary Neal. Their comments on drafts have greatly improved the final book, although, of course, all errors should still be laid at my feet and not theirs. The Birmingham Law School provided valuable study leave at the start of the process. Luke Price, the research assistant at the Birmingham Law School, provided extremely valuable research and editing support.

Those involved at Cambridge University Press have also been wonderful supporters of the project and I could not have completed the book without their help. This includes Margot Brazier and Graeme Laurie, the general editors of the series, in addition to Finola O'Sullivan, the Editorial Director for Law.

Finally, Sherman deserves a special thank you for being an excellent example.

The law is accurate as of 27 June 2011.

1 Introduction

1 Introduction

Death and dying in today's managed care society are messy. I do not mean messy physically (although that may be the case as well), but messy emotionally and philosophically. This is particularly true when considering issues such as physician-assisted suicide and euthanasia. It is impossible to engage in the debates on these twinned issues without feeling that any answer reached will not be completely satisfactory. If it is decided that these practices should be allowed or at least decriminalised, then you have to accept the very real possibility that abuses may exist. If you take the contrary position – that these practices should not be allowed – then you have to deal with the fact that medical care at the end of life is often a painful, debilitating, dehumanising experience, despite the wonderful advances in palliative care and the care provided by medical staff.

I am not convinced, however, that this messiness is necessarily a bad thing. This should not be an easy issue. We are dealing with lives, both in a biological and in a narrative sense, which may be in conflict. We are dealing with fundamental philosophical ideas such as autonomy, choice, respect, dignity, paternalism, personhood and life, which may often pull in different directions. We are dealing with complex arguments that span philosophy, ethics, law and medical practice. Finally, we are dealing with empirical arguments when the information is not always readily available or easily analysable. These are basic human questions that do not readily lend themselves to easy answers. Nor should they.

In addition, of course, there is a plethora of academic (and non-academic) work in the area, much of it taking a specific perspective on, or focusing on a particular aspect within, the debates around the end of life.[1] Even if it were desirable to read everything that has been

---

[1] While the literature on the subject is too vast to list all of the possible academic sources on the subject, some of the most important books in the area are: R. Dworkin, *Life's*

written about the subject, which is doubtful, to do so would be practically impossible. You may be required to look at materials from a particular jurisdiction only; alternatively, you may be limited to materials
from a certain perspective (e.g. either legal, ethical or medical). You
may simply read as widely as possible and hope for the best – i.e. to have
read sufficient material to be able to provide a good general assessment
of the issues, even at the risk of ending up staring blankly at someone
who has quoted the latest obscure text about some aspect of the end-
of-life debate.

If it is already impossible to read everything within this morass of
information, argument and opinion, what can one more work in the
area possibly add? One answer is that it can attempt to be comprehensive. In other words, it can attempt to make it easier for those seeking
to learn about the topic to be able to navigate the large collection of
material and inform themselves about the debates on the end of life.
There are two ways it is possible to accomplish this goal. First, one way
that a book can be comprehensive is to look at the issues surrounding
end-of-life treatment from more than one perspective.

Second, there is a tendency to focus on only one aspect of end-of-life
decisions. Some academic works will focus, for example, on euthanasia and assisted suicide; others on particular aspects of one subject.[2]
End-of-life decisions, however, are a set of possible options available to
doctors and medical staff when patients are dying. They are not isolated
decisions, but part of a range of possibilities that the doctor or other
health-care practitioner might consider. As such, there is an interrelation that can be missed if one only considers different possible actions
(or inactions) in isolation. The simplest way these particular decisions

---

Dominion (New York: Vintage Books, 1994); J. Keown (ed.), *Euthanasia Examined*
(Cambridge University Press, 1995); J. Griffiths, A. Bood and H. Weyers, *Euthanasia
and Law in the Netherlands* (Amsterdam University Press, 1998); H. Hendin, *Seduced by
Death: Doctors, Patients and Assisted Suicide* (New York: W. W. Norton and Co., 1998);
M. Otlowski, *Voluntary Euthanasia and the Common Law* (Oxford University Press,
2000); J. Keown, *Euthanasia, Ethics and Public Policy: An Argument against Legalisation*
(Cambridge University Press, 2002); R. Magnusson, *Angels of Death: Exploring the
Euthanasia Underground* (New Haven, CT: Yale University Press, 2002); M. P. Battin,
Ending Life: Ethics and the Way We Die (Oxford University Press, 2005); R. Huxtable,
Euthanasia, Ethics and the Law: From Conflict to Compromise (Abingdon: Routledge-
Cavendish, 2007); P. Lewis, *Assisted Dying and Legal Change* (Oxford University Press,
2007); and J. Griffiths, H. Weyers and M. Adams, *Euthanasia and Law in Europe*
(Oxford: Hart Publishing, 2008).

[2] For example, Keown, *Euthanasia, Ethics and Public Policy* and Lewis, *Assisted Dying
and Legal Change*, both focus on euthanasia and assisted suicide generally. Griffiths *et
al.*, *Euthanasia and Law in the Netherlands*, focuses on assisted dying practices in the
Netherlands. Magnusson, *Angels of Death*, focuses on a particular empirical study that
he performed.

may interact is if one particular action is removed from the list of possibilities for legal reasons, then it may become more difficult for the doctor or health-care worker to act in what he or she might consider to be the most appropriate manner. The doctor may then feel that another option must be shoe-horned to fit what is believed to be most appropriate. Treatment options may then begin to resemble other options even if they did not do so originally. This may cause conflicts legally or ethically when trying to differentiate between certain practices, making it harder for health-care practitioners, lawyers and ordinary members of the community to decide which actions are acceptable and which ones are not. There is, thus, an important reason to consider these types of treatment decisions as a range of possibilities instead of isolated practices. It provides us with a greater consistency among practices, helps us to understand the relations between various practices and allows us to measure the impact one treatment has on other treatment possibilities.

Comprehensiveness is important, but it is not the only (or even the main) goal of this book. It is also my intention here to examine end-of-life issues in a way that reveals and illuminates the role of bioethics in modern life. Bioethics, like any form of ethics, is a philosophical pursuit designed to examine issues so as to allow us to live more moral lives. Its goal, then, is to make our lives better by providing a framework for making better (more moral) decisions. Indeed, some of the decisions bioethics is particularly concerned with can be some of the most difficult decisions we could ever face, and we might expect that advice and input from people more accustomed to thinking through the various dilemmas and complexities involved in such decisions may often be very welcome. But that is not always the case with bioethics. Disability rights groups protest against bioethicists either in person or online.[3] Peter Singer, one of the world's most famous bioethicists, is all but barred from speaking in Germany.[4] The Catholic Church has even recently suggested that some of the most dangerous types of 'new sins' occur in bioethics.[5] Not medical science, biology or science in general – but bioethics.

As a result, we have a field of study that is supposed to improve our moral lives which has been characterised as a malign influence. We have

---

[3] See, for example, the website of the disability rights group, Not Dead Yet, http:// notdeadyetnewscommentary.blogspot.com/search/label/bioethics (accessed 21 June 2011) or P. Singer, *Practical Ethics* (2nd edn) (Cambridge University Press, 1993), pp. 337–359, where he discusses protests against him.
[4] Singer, *Practical Ethics*.
[5] D. Willey, 'Fewer Confessions and New Sins', http://news.bbc.co.uk/1/hi/world/ europe/7287071.stm (accessed 21 June 2011).

a field of study designed to help determine what is morally right which is often criticised for getting it so morally wrong. How then to explain this disconnect? In some ways, of course, this is not the fault of bioethicists or bioethics. Statements made by bioethicists can often be misinterpreted, misquoted or misunderstood. Quotations may be attributed to bioethicists which might be incomplete expressions of what they said. They may even be statements which are not representative at all of what the specific bioethicist has said. Peter Singer, in particular, seems to be routinely criticised for positions he either does not actually hold or to positions which are, at best, caricatures of his actual position.[6]

That this occurs so often should not necessarily surprise us. Bioethicists, like all philosophers, may care more about things such as the logical foundations of arguments or consistency of ethical positions than the ordinary member of the moral community.[7] For bioethicists, it is less a concern of being able to live with the consequences of a decision than being able to defend that position in a published work – largely because bioethicists may not be confronting these issues directly (or at least not directly when they are writing the journal article or book). Ordinary members of the moral community, who are likely to face these decisions only when they have a direct impact on their lives, are much more likely to be concerned about being able to sleep at night or look loved ones in the eye after making a decision than they are about the logical consistency or reasonable defensibility of that decision. So, the risk of making a decision which is contrary (or apparently contrary) to another, earlier decision probably matters less to an ordinary member of the moral community than to a bioethicist.

An acceptance that these are two separate projects – resolving ethical dilemmas in our own lives, and engaging in academic debate about ethics – does not mean that the dichotomy goes away. While some blame belongs to those who misrepresent, intentionally or otherwise, the positions or aims of bioethics, there is also fault on the part of bioethicists themselves. That is because bioethicists do sometimes say some rather counter-intuitive things. Some bioethicists claim that apes are entitled

---

[6] Peter Singer's responses to most of the common misunderstandings of his theory can be found at his website: www.princeton.edu/~psinger/faq.html (accessed 21 June 2011).
[7] I am going to use the phrase 'ordinary member of the moral community' throughout this book as a shorthand for those individuals who would not consider themselves or be considered by others to be an expert on bioethics. So, essentially, someone who does not spend their professional life researching issues of medical law and ethics. Another possible term for this might be the oft-quoted UK legal phrase of the 'man on the Clapham omnibus'. For reasons that will become apparent in the chapter on moral status, I will avoid that particular phrase.

to more moral status than human infants, especially, but not exclusively, those which could be classified as severely disabled.[8] We may make the same sorts of claims about those with dementia, or in persistent vegetative states.[9] Alternatively, we may claim that even patients who have no chance of recovery or improvement should be continued to be maintained by medical science, despite what doctors advise or what the family of the patient or indeed anyone else actually connected with the patient wants.[10] We might argue that all life should be protected and therefore we are committing mass murder when we brush our teeth.[11] Add to this a plethora of terms that appear familiar but are used in highly technical and often confusing ways (for example, 'personhood', 'quality of life', 'autonomy', 'dignity', 'harm' and even – as we will see in Chapter 3 – 'innocent') and the whole thing can be impossible to work through.

What we seem to have, then, is a similar problem to the one in legal theory exposed by H. L. A. Hart in the first few pages of *The Concept of Law*.[12] We have an ever decreasing circle of people called 'bioethicists' who talk among themselves about ideas which are not only confusing to ordinary members of the moral community, but are seen as wrong, absurd or clearly wrong-headed. Even more importantly, we seem to have a situation where the ordinary member of the moral community appears to be unable to use these particular ethical frameworks. Nowhere is this starker than in the case of Peter Singer. Singer has long championed the idea that those who are not persons[13] are not entitled to full moral consideration, particularly in relation to whether or not

---

[8] See, e.g., J. Glover, *Causing Death and Saving Lives* (Penguin Books: London, 1977); J. Harris, *The Value of Life* (Routledge: London, 1985); H. Kuhse and P. Singer, *Should the Baby Live?* (Oxford University Press, 1985); and M. Tooley, *Abortion and Infanticide* (Oxford: Clarendon Press, 1983).

[9] J. Harris, 'The Philosophical Case against the Philosophical Case against Euthanasia', in Keown (ed.), *Euthanasia Examined*, pp. 36–45.

[10] J. Keown, 'Restoring Moral and Intellectual Shape to the Law after *Bland*' (1997) 113 *LQR* 482–503. J. Finnis, '*Bland*: Crossing the Rubicon' (1993) 109 *LQR* 329–337. In both cases, the argument presented is more complex than the one listed above. Both Keown and Finnis argue that intentional killing of a patient because the life of the patient is determined to be 'worthless' is unacceptable, but that some withdrawal of treatment in cases where it is futile is acceptable. However, it is clear that in the case in question, *Airedale NHS Trust* v. *Bland* [1993] 1 All ER 821, the doctors and family did intend to kill Anthony Bland and did so precisely because they saw the value of his continued existence as being 'worthless'.

[11] M. A. Warren, *Moral Status* (Oxford University Press, 1997), p. 37, discussing the viewpoint of Albert Schweitzer.

[12] H. L. A. Hart, *The Concept of Law* (2nd edn) (Oxford University Press, 1994), pp. 1–2.

[13] A term discussed in greater detail in Chapter 2.

they can be killed.[14] Those who are not persons include patients with dementia. When his own mother was struck with dementia as a result of Alzheimer's disease, Singer admits that he did not treat his mother in the way which his theory recommends.[15] But, if Singer cannot abide by his own theory, why should the rest of us (who have no investment in the theory) be guided by it either if faced with similar circumstances?

The critical concept in bioethics, then, may be about usefulness. Despite its logical cohesiveness or internal consistency, a theory about ethics which is completely impractical may be of no more use than one based upon the teachings of the flying spaghetti monster.[16] What is useful, however, is a theory of ethics that ordinary members of the moral community can put into practice. It is important to remember that ethics is, by and large, a personal thing. What matters is that the ethical system one adopts has to be a useful one for the individual. If an individual cannot see how an ethical system can be put into practice, they are likely to deride it as useless and ignore it. When evaluating an ethical system, then, perhaps we ought not to be focusing on whether it is a universally acceptable system, or one characterised by logical consistency or internal coherence. Rather, perhaps we should, when we evaluate the merits of an ethical system, place more emphasis on how readily it might be used by individuals in real-life situations. This is not to suggest that things like internal coherence and logical consistency are unimportant. It is very important that ethical systems be able to produce consistent results across a number of situations and display internal coherence. Otherwise, moral decisions may well be made on whims or random chance. Nevertheless, if you cannot put a theory into practice, all of its logical consistency and internal coherence count for nothing.

Chapters 2 and 3 of this book provide examples of what this means in practice. Chapter 2 concerns ideas about moral status and about how we determine who matters morally and who does not. This debate has long been dominated by two theories as to how we make these sorts of determinations. One theory holds that species membership is of primary importance. Human beings, quite obviously, are at the top of the chain and therefore are deserving of full moral status. Other species are entitled to less moral status and as such we may do things to them

---

[14] Singer, *Practical Ethics*, pp. 89–95.
[15] M. Specter, 'The Dangerous Philosopher', *The New Yorker*, 6 September 1999, pp. 46–55.
[16] For those interested, the flying spaghetti monster is a deliberately absurd creation intended to make a point about the difference between scientific evidence and religious belief. For further information about the flying spaghetti monster, see www.venganza.org (accessed 21 June 2011).

which we may not do to human beings. The problem with this is that it is incredibly difficult to be able to show why human beings are entitled to this special status without relying on theological or self-serving arguments. But the alternative creates its own problems. The alternative to regarding species membership as the primary determinant for moral status is to focus on an entity's possession of specific characteristics. These can be anything, but are most often things like rationality or sentience. However, this can mean that not all human beings are entitled to full moral status. Adopting a more easily satisfied characteristic (life, for example) only seems to create further problems; we may end up regarding bacteria as being as morally relevant as human beings, for instance. Consequently, we end up spending time debating these two different approaches while ordinary members of the moral community remain as confused as before or conclude that the whole debate is nothing more than some sort of elaborate joke.

Chapter 3 deals with the concept of the value of life and presents similar problems. Again, the debate in bioethics revolves around two positions. The first, referred to as the sanctity or inviolability of life, argues that life has an inherent value. The alternative position, known as the quality of life position, holds that life does not have an inherent value but is only valuable because of the things that it allows us to do. These two positions are said to be mutually exclusive – in other words, it is necessary to choose between them. Many ordinary members of the moral community, however, seem to prefer a compromise position between the two. They may want to insist, for some purposes, that life is inviolable, but to treat quality of life as being relevant at other times. Bioethicists, however, indicate that such selectivity is not possible without logical inconsistency.

Under the traditional bioethics formulations above, such issues may seem irresolvable. But the traditional formulations are not the only ones. This book will show that a different way is possible by providing, in Part I, a practical ethical formulation for end-of-life concerns. In order to do so, it will be necessary to return to the first principles involved in these particular issues. In other words, we have to start at the beginning in terms of the basic ethical and legal concepts and the broad frameworks they inhabit. In the cases of some of the ethical concepts, this will mean a re-examination of key ideas and a clearing out of some of the intellectual clutter that has arisen. What will remain, however, will be ethical concepts which are more readily available to and applicable by ordinary members of the moral community. These will then be worked together into an overall ethical framework from which we can make decisions about end-of-life treatment in a way which is intellectually coherent but still capable of providing practical moral guidance that it is actually possible to follow in our daily lives. This does not mean that the resulting ethical framework created in Part I will be universally acceptable. Not everyone who reads the framework will find it convincing or right. I make no claims, therefore, that the answers suggested here are the only valid ones. Instead, I aim only to suggest a useable, coherent framework which, I believe, offers a helpful way of negotiating the complexities of decision-making at the end of life.

But ethics is only part of the story when considering end-of-life treatment. It is also essential to ask whether and how the ethical framework created in Part I can be implemented by legal regulation. It is not a simple matter of merely taking the ethical conclusion and making that decision legally acceptable. Ethics is primarily about ideals – what we think that people ought to do, ideally, in certain circumstances. Often, the law cannot insist on ideals, but can only deal with the reality of particular situations. That means that even if we consider a decision to be ethically acceptable, problems in regulating behaviour may mean that the practice must be legally sanctioned. Concerns such as the impact on others unrelated to the action, the prevention of abuses, so-called 'slippery slope' arguments and procedural safeguards may all be stronger considerations in legal frameworks than in ethical ones. It is therefore necessary to consider to what extent the ethical answers arrived at in Part I of the book can be implemented in any legal framework and what type of legal framework is best suited to address not only the ethical questions but practical and legal questions as well. This will involve an examination not only of the legal structures available, but also of the empirical evidence that is available about these practices.

Part II of the book will therefore focus on the legal regulation of end-of-life decisions. As with Part I, there is considerable clutter that should be addressed. First, as with the ethical approaches, there is a tendency to regulate individual aspects of end-of-life decision-making in isolation, without regard to their interaction with other issues. So, for example, attempts may be made to legalise physician-assisted suicide or voluntary euthanasia or to change the manner in which we make withdrawal of treatment decisions for incompetent patients without wider discussion about the overall regulation of death and dying. Considering the interrelation between these various end-of-life issues, this is a significant oversight and one this book will seek to address. As such, the sections in Part II will not just focus on isolated aspects of end-of-life decisions, but rather will consider how the conclusions reached about the regulation of one practice will impact upon the regulation of other practices at the end of life. It will be possible at the end of Part II, therefore, to envisage a coherent regulatory scheme for all end-of-life decision-making, not just one or two practices.

In addition to the creation of a comprehensive regulation scheme, another focus of Part II of the book will be on clarification about how we should best evaluate the effectiveness of any such scheme. There are two points which are vital to any evaluation. The first thing to keep in mind is the appropriate standard for evaluation. For example, in many cases where people are examining whether to legalise assisted suicide or euthanasia they look at the possibility of breaking the law. Since the number of incidents where the law is broken is clearly not zero, they determine that assisted suicide and euthanasia should not be legalised. But looking for a rate of zero is extremely unhelpful in evaluating whether these practices should be legalised. No statute or legal rule is ever completely effective. Even if we consider the most trivial regulation (say a parking regulation) and couple it with the harshest penalty, we are unlikely to get complete success, presuming that success is compliance with the law. Why then should we expect this to be any different? One argument may be that we are dealing with human lives and therefore the stakes are much higher than in parking regulations or other trivial matters. This is, of course, true. That just means we ought to make sure that we get it right. To do so, we have to make the success rate as close to 100 per cent as we can. We should also try to create a law that is as foolproof as possible and therefore strive for complete success as an ideal. Even with all that, though, we need to keep in mind that despite our best efforts, we will not reach that ideal. So, basing decisions about regulation schemes for end-of-life decisions on whether they reach that ideal is fruitless.

Often, such unrealistic expectations of our regulatory schemes are accompanied by the failure to notice that all jurisdictions currently have a regulatory scheme in relation to end-of-life practices, whether they be statutory-based or based in the common law. The evaluation of any proposed new regulation must therefore include an appraisal of how the existing regulation works. When comparing regulatory schemes, we need to keep in mind the question of metrics. If our biggest concern is the rate of compliance with the law, it does no good to expect the new regulation to achieve a 100 per cent success rate if we are not expecting the same of the current regulation. In other words, we must compare like with like. Otherwise, we risk determining that the current regulation is the most appropriate despite it having a much lower success rate than an alternative.

Considerations about the slippery slope argument[17] present an example of unrealistic expectations coupled with a failure to recognise the existence of a current regulatory scheme. When evaluating regulations which would legalise or decriminalise voluntary euthanasia or assisted suicide, much is made of the possibility of a slide towards non-voluntary or involuntary euthanasia.[18] In order to show this, commentators often rely on the evidence from the Netherlands which shows that there are instances of non-voluntary/involuntary euthanasia following the legalisation of voluntary euthanasia.[19] This does not prove the point as convincingly as some commentators wish, however. All the Netherlands information proves (at least in isolation) is that the Dutch have not been completely successful in preventing non-voluntary and involuntary euthanasia. In other words, the Dutch system, like every other regulatory system including our own, does not command perfect obedience. As stated already, perfect obedience is an illusory goal anyway, and the lack of it should not be taken as evidence of any fundamental unsuitability of the regulation (or scheme of regulation) in question. Instead, these considerations only serve to underline the need to make comparisons on an equal footing in order that realistic assessments about the value of the various regulatory schemes available can be valid ones.

In summary, then, Part I will provide an examination of the ethical concepts which are relevant in decision-making about medical treatment at the end of life. The purpose of this part of the book is not only to present the current arguments about these ethical concerns but to critically analyse whether they actually provide a useful method for determining how we ought to act. From this, it will be possible to create an ethical framework at the end of Part I which will be able to provide one method for determining how we ought to treat patients at the end of life. Part II will take the conclusions reached in Part I and explore how best to legally regulate end-of-life decisions consistent with those conclusions, taking account not only of proposals for change, but also the currently regulatory system. From this, it will be possible to draw general conclusions about the ethical and the legal frameworks we should adopt to help us determine the acceptability of treatment at the end of life.

---

[17] Slippery slope arguments will be explained in greater detail in Chapter 13.
[18] See, e.g., Keown, *Euthanasia, Ethics and Public Policy*.
[19] *Ibid.*

2   Some definitional concerns

Before embarking upon the task, however, some definitional matters should be addressed. Despite the amount of debate and the volume of commentary on end-of-life issues and the various practices involved in end-of-life care, there is often not a universal definition for these practices. Some people, for example, consider assisted suicide to be part of euthanasia.[20] Some call all withdrawing of treatment from patients to be passive euthanasia.[21] The Dutch, when discussing their own practices, refer only to active voluntary euthanasia as euthanasia.[22] All other forms of euthanasia are given other names. Considering this definitional fluidity, it may sometimes be difficult to decide whether the author truly intended the argument to apply to a particular form of end-of-life decision-making or not. In order to avoid this problem in the arguments presented in this book, I will now provide a set of definitions, the use of which will be consistent throughout this discussion, unless otherwise stated. Some of these concepts are more prone to definitional fluidity than others, but for the sake of completeness, they will all be defined.

Palliative care is the treatment of the symptoms of a disease without addressing the underlying disease. In the end-of-life context, this usually refers to the provision of pain-relieving medication. The provision of palliative care only usually causes problems when the dosage of medication given to relieve pain reaches a level which might also depress respiration (and thus cause, or hasten, death). This may also cause problems when palliative care rises to the level of *terminal sedation*, which is when a patient is provided with medical treatment designed to put the patient in a coma-like state.

Withholding and withdrawing treatment are often considered to be linked forms of end-of-life treatment but there are important differences. The *withholding of treatment* applies to situations where doctors or

---

[20] See, e.g., E. Gailey, *Write to Death: News Framing of the Right to Die Conflict, from Quinlan's Coma to Kevorkian's Conviction* (Westport, CT: Praeger Publishers, 2003).

[21] See, e.g., J. Rachels, 'Active and Passive Euthanasia' (1975) 292 *New England Journal of Medicine* 78–80, reprinted in M. P. Battin, L. P. Francis and B. M. Landesman (eds.), *Death, Dying and the Ending of Life* (Aldershot: Ashgate Publishing, 2007), vol. II, pp. 5–8, which appears to consider all cases of withdrawal and withholding as passive euthanasia. B. Steinbock, 'The Intentional Termination of Life' (1979) 6 *Ethics in Science and Medicine* 59–64, reprinted in Battin *et al.* (eds.), *Death, Dying and the Ending of Life*, pp. 9–14. It should be specifically noted, of course, that Rachels' seminal article was first published in 1975 and the precise definition of euthanasia was far from clear at that time.

[22] Griffiths *et al.*, *Euthanasia and Law in the Netherlands*, p. 17.

other medical staff do not provide treatment to a patient, particularly in cases where the treatment would have sustained the life of the patient. For example, if doctors comply with a Do Not Resuscitate Order with a patient in an emergency situation by not providing CPR, then they have withheld treatment from that patient. *Withdrawal of treatment*, on the other hand, is when doctors or other medical staff remove treatment which has previously been provided to a patient. Again, in the context of the present discussion, it will be particularly pertinent to consider cases where the treatment would have sustained the patient's life. The removal of a patient from a ventilator would be a relevant instance of treatment withdrawal. Both withdrawal and withholding of treatment are sometimes referred to as *passive euthanasia*.[23] However, this is misleading. Euthanasia, as we shall see below, has specific definitional characteristics which not all cases of withdrawal and withholding of treatment would fit. Failing to provide a blood transfusion to a Jehovah's Witness is withholding treatment (the doctor is failing to provide treatment which might otherwise sustain the life of the patient). It is difficult to argue, however, that it is euthanasia. Passive euthanasia, therefore, would only be a subset of the wider group of withdrawing and/or withholding of treatment. However, even if a distinction can be made, it is rarely made in fact. UK courts, for example, do not distinguish (at least post-*Bland*[24]) between those cases of withholding and withdrawing treatment which count as passive euthanasia from those which do not. Thus, for the purposes of this discussion, all such treatment will be referred to either as withholding or withdrawing treatment, rather than as forms of passive euthanasia.

Euthanasia is where someone is helped to die by another person. Unlike assisted suicide, however, euthanasia occurs when the final action that brings about death is not performed by the person who is dying but by someone else. In the case of medical treatment, this would include situations where a doctor or other member of hospital staff injects a patient with a lethal dose of drugs with the intention of bringing about the death of the patient. There can be several different types of euthanasia. *Active euthanasia* is where the doctor (or other person) takes positive action (such as injecting a patient) which brings about death. *Passive euthanasia* would include cases where death is caused by the withdrawal or withholding of treatment. As noted above, there are those who refer to all instances of withdrawal and withholding of treatment as passive euthanasia. If euthanasia is to mean deliberate acts of killing, however,

---

[23] See, e.g., Rachels, 'Active and Passive Euthanasia'.
[24] *Airedale NHS Trust* v. *Bland* [1993] 1 All ER 821.

passive euthanasia would only include those cases where the withdrawal and withholding of treatment is done intentionally to bring about the death of the patient which would count as passive euthanasia. As stated before, it is therefore easier to avoid the definitional difficulty provided by the term passive euthanasia and refer to such practices simply as 'the withdrawal or withholding of treatment'. In addition to the distinction between active and passive euthanasia, euthanasia can also be voluntary, involuntary or non-voluntary. *Voluntary euthanasia* covers cases of euthanasia which are done at the request of a competent patient. *Involuntary euthanasia* covers cases of euthanasia where a patient is capable of requesting euthanasia but has not done so. It is therefore a case of euthanasia against the consent of the patient. *Non-voluntary euthanasia* covers cases of euthanasia where the patient is unable (either due to age, incompetence or unconsciousness) to consent. It is possible to combine cases using the first distinction (between active and passive) with cases using the second distinction (voluntary, involuntary or non-voluntary) so we can speak about *active voluntary euthanasia* (AVE) or passive non-voluntary euthanasia. When people discuss the legalisation of euthanasia, the most common form discussed is active voluntary euthanasia.

In the UK, suicide is not illegal but assisting a suicide is illegal.[25] *Assisted suicide* is where one person helps another to commit suicide. When a patient is assisted by a doctor acting in a professional capacity (as opposed to acting as a relative or friend) then it is called *physician-assisted suicide* (PAS). Whatever the method of assistance provided by the doctor, in assisted suicide it is the patient who must make the final action which brings about death. PAS most often involves the doctor providing a prescription for a lethal dose of drugs which the patient then takes, although it is not necessary that this be the case. In the case of drugs, it is the patient who must take the medication, it cannot be injected by the doctor to fit within the definition of assisted suicide. This, unlike the withdrawal or withholding of treatment which ends in death, is a deliberate killing of the patient. When discussing PAS and AVE together, these practices collectively may be referred to as *assisted dying*.

These definitions will be used throughout the book. Other definitions will be added as and when they become necessary.

---

[25] Suicide Act 1961, s. 2(1); *R (on the application of Pretty)* v. *DPP* [2001] UKHL 61.

Part I

2   Moral status

1   Introduction

In this first substantive chapter, the primary focus will be on the concept of moral status. Moral status is an important foundational concept for ethics because it is only those entities which have moral status that it is necessary to consider when making decisions about our actions. Thus, when deciding whether a particular action is ethically acceptable, it is important for me to consider the impact that action may have on other humans; it is less likely that I need to consider the impact my actions may have on rocks.[1] This chapter, then, will explore a concept of moral status so that when we move on to the relevant individuals involved in discussions about end-of-life treatment, we can more properly analyse whose interests matter and whose do not. The use of the phrase 'a concept of moral status' as opposed to 'the concept of moral status' is deliberate and worth emphasising at this point. What follows below is one possible attempt to develop a concept of moral status which is both philosophically sound and protects all of those things I think worthy of protection. That does not mean that other concepts of moral status are not equally valid. I will, of course, consider and reject certain other versions of moral status during the discussion of this chapter. Some readers might think it unwise that I reject certain ones (which they might argue would have greater usefulness than I have indicated) but, to my mind, the one put forth in this chapter is the most defensible. However, the fact that I believe that this approach is the most defensible does not mean necessarily that I think all of those who disagree with me are automatically doing something morally wrong.

Before delving into that analysis though, it will be useful to look at specific examples in this chapter. I will therefore provide two entities[2]

---

[1] There are, of course, possible exceptions to both of these rules which we shall consider below.

[2] Because this chapter will discuss not only human beings but other things such as dogs, microbes, rocks, etc., it is useful to use a term to indicate a broad range of things which fall under the category of 'thing which we are deciding if it is morally worthwhile or

at the start who will be relevant to a number of the discussions. The first is Anthony Bland. Anthony Bland was the central figure in the case *Airedale NHS Trust* v. *Bland*.[3] He was, from all accounts, a normal 17-and-a-half-year-old when he went to attend the FA Cup semi-final at Hillsborough stadium between Liverpool, the team he supported, and Nottingham Forest on 15 April 1989. A victim of the tragedy that day, Anthony Bland suffered crushed ribs and punctured lungs and stopped breathing. Due to the efforts of the paramedics and other emergency personnel at the scene, they were able to get him stabilised. However, as a result of oxygen deprivation, his higher brain functions did not work, although his brain stem still did. In fact, the judges in the case make specific reference to there being 'more space than substance in the relevant parts of Anthony Bland's brain'[4] or to his brain being a 'mass of watery fluid'.[5] He was diagnosed as being in a persistent vegetative state (PVS). For three-and-a-half years he stayed in this condition, under the care of Airedale NHS Trust. He did not regain consciousness nor did he interact with the medical staff or his family in any way during this time. Furthermore, he did not appear to feel pain as the medical staff performed surgery on him without anaesthesia.[6] Finally, the doctors at Airedale NHS Trust, with the support of his family, petitioned the court to allow them to remove the naso-gastric tube which they used to provide nutrition and hydration to him. The House of Lords approved of the decisions of the lower courts granting the petition and the doctors were allowed to remove the tube.[7] Anthony Bland died as a result on 3 March 1993.

The second entity which will be relevant is Sherman, who is my adult pet dog. There is nothing particularly special about him and he seems to be a fairly typical example of his species. He has four legs, a tail, barks at the mailman and seems to spend most of his time sleeping on the couch, playing with his toys or trying to convince me to give him more food. Sherman has been picked as an example merely to fill the function of a domestic pet in our discussions. The only benefit he has

---

not', although that particular phrase is fairly cumbersome to write or read. To that end, then, I will use the term 'entity' for such a purpose.

[3] [1993] 1 All ER 821.

[4] *Ibid.* at 825 (*per* Sir Stephen Brown P).

[5] *Ibid.* at 860 (*per* Lord Keith).

[6] *Ibid.* at 825 (*per* Sir Stephen Brown P). Specifically, according to the case, 'He is fitted with a catheter which has given rise to infection necessitating surgical intervention. It is to be noted that the necessary surgical incision was made without any anaesthetic because Anthony Bland is utterly devoid of feeling of any kind.'

[7] *Ibid.* at 821.

over other possible examples is that he happens to be the one I can observe most often.

In addition to Anthony Bland and Sherman, a number of other examples will be used throughout the chapter. These two, however, will be the most frequent examples when we analyse the general concept of moral status.

2   Some initial thoughts

There are two initial statements about moral worth that can be made, according to Mary Anne Warren. First, she states that most believe that there is such a thing as moral worth or moral status. Second, she suggests that there is a 'substantial consensus about some of the things that have it and about some of the things that do not'.[8] The first concern is to consider whether this substantial consensus is important.

For example, if we were to survey ordinary members of the moral community about the actions that are morally acceptable to perform in reference to entities such as Anthony Bland and Sherman, a majority will probably hold similar views. Most people, I would presume, would think that Anthony Bland was owed certain moral rights and should have been treated in a particular way. In fact, while there has been significant discussion about what treatment Anthony Bland should have received, none of the parties involved thought that he should have been entitled to no moral standing. Quite the contrary, both sides needed him to be morally worthwhile for the arguments about his treatment to make sense. This would likely (although not necessarily) contain the view that Anthony Bland could not have been intentionally killed by a lethal injection. In fact, Lord Browne-Wilkinson in *Bland* makes just this point. He says:

How can it be lawful to allow a patient to die slowly, though painlessly, over a period of weeks from lack of food but unlawful to produce his immediate death by a lethal injection, thereby saving his family from yet another ordeal to add to the tragedy that has already struck him? I find it difficult to find a moral answer to that question. But it is undoubtedly the law and nothing I have said casts doubt on the proposition that the doing of a positive act with the intention of ending life is and remains murder.[9]

Were Sherman, on the other hand, to be seriously injured, the opinions of ordinary members of the moral community might be considerably different. Even if Sherman were not injured to anywhere near the extent

---

[8] Warren, *Moral Status*, p. 9.
[9] *Airedale NHS Trust* v. *Bland* [1993] 1 All ER 821 at 884.

of Anthony Bland, it might still be considered acceptable to give him a lethal injection. Merely because that may be the general consensus (if it is) does not mean that those opinions are correct. It may be that the general consensus results from a common misconception about the nature of either Anthony Bland or Sherman or is based on other biases or prejudices which ought to have no place within moral reasoning.

With that in mind, however, the fact that there is a general consensus about certain entities being clearly morally relevant or clearly not should not be discarded entirely without further reflection. This is not to add support to the claim that intuitions are a reliable tool for moral discussions.[10] They may not be and, in any case, it is not a discussion I think particularly fruitful to pursue at this time. Instead, I wish to make a more limited point first set out in the introduction. Any system of moral status needs to be used by members of the moral community in that it must be able to guide and constrain conduct on particular ethical issues. If that is not possible, then the essential reason for creating the system is lost. As such, any system which wants to claim usefulness needs to engage with those moral issues in which members of the moral community are interested. This does not mean, of course, that it need provide the same results as the (perhaps unreflective) viewpoint of the members of that particular moral community but it should, at a minimum, address those concerns. Then, if a decision reached by a moral system is different, there can at least be a dialogue about why the answer reached by the moral system is different from the normal viewpoint. Thus, engagement with the views of ordinary members of the moral community (whether or not one believes moral intuitions to be a convincing foundation for moral decisions) is a vital component of any moral system. Therefore, in this chapter, we will presume that there are worthwhile reasons to engage with those sentiments of the ordinary member of the moral community.[11]

But, there will be times when I am concerned with more than simple engagement with the views of ordinary members of the moral community. Instead, I will assume that a viewpoint which is consistent with those views is better than one that is not. By this, I wish to be clear about the impact of this assumption on the project. It is only in those

---

[10] For a general discussion about the use of intuition in moral theory, see J. Dancy, 'Intuitionism', in P. Singer (ed.), *A Companion to Ethics* (Malden, MA: Blackwell Publishing, 1991), pp. 411–420.

[11] It is worth noting that this is not an unusual approach in examining ethical concerns. See, e.g., P. Unger, *Living High and Letting Die* (Oxford University Press, 1996), where he examines the issue of whether it is wrong to fail to donate a percentage of one's income to protecting vulnerable groups such as children.

cases where a coherent ethical view can be created which is consistent with the viewpoints of ordinary members of the moral community that this will be an issue. If there is no possibility of a coherent viewpoint, then the fact that it is consistent with the viewpoints of even a majority of the members of a moral community will not be sufficient. However, if there are two possible views and both are philosophically justified but only one is consistent with the general opinions of ordinary members of the moral community, then the view which is consistent will be preferred. As such, if it is possible to do so, I will examine ways in which the views of ordinary members of the moral community can be considered philosophically valid as opposed to necessarily constructing a view which is philosophically justifiable and then seeing whether it conflicts with our normal views.

Returning to the main discussion, we may consider why moral status should be relevant at all.[12] It would certainly be easier prima facie to apply moral standards if there was no reason to worry about the moral status of relevant entities first. However, despite how it may look at first blush, it is actually easier to apply moral standards if we can ascribe moral status to entities. If moral status was not important, it would become very difficult to act in any way. This is because it would be necessary for moral actors to consider the effects of their actions on not only those entities such as other adult human beings usually considered to be morally worthwhile, but also other entities which are not normally so considered, such as rocks, soil, water, microbes, animals, etc.[13] The need to consider the adverse impact of actions on such a broad range of entities would make moral actors incapable of actions as any action will have an adverse impact on some other entity in the world. For example, even actions such as walking, cleaning the house or brushing our teeth have a tremendously adverse impact on microscopic entities. So, unless there is some way to determine which entities matter when deciding on which actions are appropriate, we would be left incapable of acting.

Deciding that we need a method for determining moral status, however, is only part of the issue. And, as it turns out, it also happens to be the relatively easy part. The much more difficult problem is deciding how to determine which entities are morally worthwhile and which are not. Assuming that we want principled, justifiable reasons for deciding

---

[12] The initial statement from Warren above merely indicates that we do believe there is such a thing as moral status; there is no indication that such a belief is actually justified.

[13] The environment as a whole has become more of a general ethical issue, so it may be that the environment is entitled to some sort of moral status. It is unlikely, though, that an individual rock or piece of soil is entitled to any moral status.

that certain entities are morally worthwhile and certain other entities are not, we may have difficulties in keeping all of those things we want within the morally relevant category without expanding it too far to cover those things we do not. Alternatively, we may find that the use of relevant criteria means that certain entities which we do not want to make morally irrelevant become so. The difficulty, then, is to use justifiable criteria to determine that those things we want to be morally worthwhile are considered to be so without expanding the group too far and making any action immoral.

3   Species and speciesism

Historically, of course, moral worth was determined by species membership. Those things which were classed as human beings were morally relevant and those things that were not were not morally relevant. Actually, that is being generous. Large populations of entities which were human beings (e.g. women, slaves and minorities, whether based on racial, ethnic or other classifications, etc.) were not classed as morally relevant so it was not as easy as being human. What was an essential part, however, was that the entity must be human in order to be morally relevant. So, while not all human beings may have always been morally relevant, only human beings were ever morally relevant.[14] That idea, however, came to be questioned. Once society became more secularised, it was harder to justify the special place human beings had in any moral system. No longer could the idea of ensoulment or 'human beings given domain over animals to treat as they wish' in the Book of Genesis[15] be a reliable justification for the treatment of other entities.

Consequently, a justification was necessary, to avoid the increasingly greater concern about speciesism. Speciesism is the idea that one has preferred one's own species merely because it is one's own species. Speciesism, many commentators began to argue, was like other -isms such as racism or sexism. It could not be justified merely on a personal preference. If the only reason for preferring human beings over other animals – indeed, over any other entity – was the fact that we were human, then it was no more capable of justification than ideas such as

---

[14] For philosophers, this is the difference between a necessary condition and a sufficient one. A necessary condition is something which is required for a certain state of affairs to be created but is not all that is required for that state of affairs to be created. A sufficient condition is something which can, by itself, create a certain state of affairs. We shall return to this important difference when we consider slippery slope arguments in Chapter 13.

[15] Genesis 1: 26–30.

racism or sexism, which we consider to be clearly wrong.[16] Thus, if we wish to prefer human beings over other entities, there needs to be a reason for such a preference.

4   Preference based on characteristics

This led a number of academic commentators and philosophers to consider that moral relevance was not based upon membership in any particular species, but in the possession of certain characteristics. The three characteristics most commonly used were life (i.e. all living things were morally relevant);[17] sentience (those things which could feel pain were morally relevant);[18] and personhood (those things which were capable of rational thought were morally relevant).[19] All of these characteristics came with their own set of problems, however. If moral relevance is based upon the entity being alive, then the problems about the ability to act at all are not significantly reduced. Again, as mentioned previously, many actions such as brushing our teeth are considered to be minor actions in our day-to-day life, but destroy countless numbers of microbes.[20] As microbes are undoubtedly living things, their moral relevance would need to be considered when engaging in such mundane activities. In fact, Albert Schweitzer, a prominent theorist advocating the characteristic of life, argues that brushing our teeth was the equivalent of mass homicide.[21]

If a moral theory based on life caused these types of problems, then, the search began for other ways to determine moral status which were less problematic. These began to centre on particular qualities that the entity possessed. In particular, it became apparent that one needed

---

[16] J. Harris and S. Holm, 'Abortion', in H. LaFollette (ed.), *The Oxford Handbook of Practical Ethics* (Oxford University Press, 2003), pp. 112–135, 118–119; Singer, *Practical Ethics*, pp. 75–76.

[17] Warren, *Moral Status*, pp. 24–49, discusses some of the more important systems for moral status based upon a life criteria.

[18] Singer, *Practical Ethics*, pp. 57–58.

[19] Glover, *Causing Death and Saving Lives*; Tooley, *Abortion and Infanticide*; Harris, *The Value of Life*; Kuhse and Singer, *Should the Baby Live?*; Harris and Holm, 'Abortion', pp. 112–135, 115–117. It should also be noted that there are other systems similar to personhood, although they are based upon slightly different criteria. For example, Deryck Beyleveld and Roger Brownsword have presented a view of moral status which is based upon Alan Gewirth's agency principles. While there are important distinctions between agents and persons under Beyleveld and Brownsword's view, they are not too dissimilar for our purposes. Those interested should consult Beyleveld and Brownsword's book, *Human Dignity in Bioethics and Biolaw* (Oxford University Press, 2002).

[20] Warren, *Moral Status*, p. 37.

[21] *Ibid.*

to focus on those things which presented an entity with the capacity to have interests, especially interests in how it was treated. Again, life seems a particularly relevant concept. It is only (by and large) those things which are (or at least at some point have been) alive which appear to have the capacity to have interests or to care about how they are treated. Those things, like rocks, which have never been alive do not appear to worry about how they are treated. There may be concerns about things such as rocks in special cases (e.g. Uluru/Ayers Rock in Australia or parts of the Grand Canyon, Arizona, USA, which have special significance to indigenous peoples),[22] but the rocks themselves do not ever appear to express any opinion about how they are treated. That, however, just leads back to the idea of mass homicide of microbes so something more restrictive is needed to generate a useful theory of moral status.

The first possibility for a more restrictive concept is the ability to feel pain. Not everything that is alive seems to be able to feel pain. Plants and microscopic entities do not appear to feel pain. They do not cry out in pain in the same way or even a remotely similar way to the way in which, for example, Sherman would if I were to accidentally step on his tail. Importantly, the causing of pain to something which can feel pain but does not deserve or want that pain is generally seen as being unacceptable. Utilitarians, virtue ethicists and deontologists would all seem likely to agree that the causing of unnecessary pain on an entity which does not want it is something that should be avoided. Consequently, it may be possible to limit the conception of moral status to those entities which feel pain.

That, however, only seems to help to a very limited extent. Plants and microscopic entities might not feel pain, but a lot of other entities would be sentient, including a number of small insects, worms, spiders, etc., in addition to entities like humans, apes, cows and dogs. So, there is still a large number of entities that must be considered when performing any action. Additionally, some of these entities may not be ones generally considered to be worth much from a moral point of view. Presumably, any number of small insects can feel pain (they do have a nervous system, after all) but I am not aware of many people who think it is morally wrong to squash one sitting on a windowsill. Furthermore, it would be difficult to argue against the death of large numbers of sentient organisms that occur through the act of farming.[23] That is not to suggest that all farming practices are ethical, but merely to suggest that the act of farming per se is something normally considered to be

---

[22] *Ibid.*, p. 171.   [23] *Ibid.*, p. 79.

morally acceptable. In fact, many who propose a sentience view of moral status suggest that we should all become vegetarians as a result of such a stance on moral status.[24] One result of that, presumably, would be an increased need for farming. We could argue in an attempt to resolve the problem that entities' moral status ought to be dependent on their relative abilities to feel pain. So, entities with a greater capacity to feel pain (either in amount or intensity) should be considered to be more morally relevant than those with a lesser capacity. There is no guarantee, though, that those entities which we would consider to be less morally relevant initially are the ones which feel less pain. More importantly, there does not appear to be a valid metric for deciding whether a cow or a worm can feel more pain. Moreover, there are cases where we consider that moral harm has been done to the entity even if it is not capable of feeling the pain associated with it. Thus, those under anaesthesia, some lepers and those in comas may not feel pain but can still be caused moral harm. Sentience, then, causes a number of problems for a moral theory as well. It, like using life as a basis for a system of moral status, appears to let in too many entities to be a particularly satisfactory system for moral status. It not only greatly increases the number of entities that must be considered, it seems to preclude a number of activities which are not considered to be generally morally problematic.

Because of these difficulties, a number of academic commentators focus not on life or sentience, but on personhood as the relevant criteria for moral status.[25] To some, this may seem like a return to the species-dependent theories rejected previously. Person, however, is not the same thing as a human being. Person is an entity which has certain cognitive or mental characteristics. Among them are: self-awareness, self-control, a sense of the future, a sense of the past, the capacity to relate to others, concern for others, communication, curiosity, rationality, the use of language or autonomy.[26] It is worth emphasising that it is not the discernable presence of the specific criteria that is necessary for personhood but the capacity to exercise such criteria. Thus, a competent human adult (usually the quintessential example of a person) may still be a person even if that adult never seems to utilise a particular characteristic necessary for personhood or if the adult is currently unable to exercise that particular characteristic such as when asleep. There may also be differences between versions of personhood theories

---

[24] See, e.g., P. Singer, *Animal Liberation: Towards an End to Man's Inhumanity to Animals* (London: Paladin, 1977).

[25] For examples, see the works cited at n. 19.

[26] Kuhse and Singer, *Should the Baby Live?*, pp. 130–131. See also J. Harris, 'Euthanasia and the Value of Life', in Keown (ed.), *Euthanasia Examined*, pp. 6–22, 9.

about the relevant criteria, whether one must possess all of the criteria or only a percentage of them (e.g. can someone suffering from permanent amnesia be a person?) and other issues but, by and large, the basics of personhood theory are relatively stable.

To some, this would require that the entity in question must be human in order to be a person, but that is not necessarily the case. For example, a number of non-human animals satisfy the common test for self-awareness, which is referred to as the 'mirror test' or 'mirror self-recognition (MSR)'.[27] The test is relatively simple. A mark is placed on the entity in question in a spot which is not visible under ordinary circumstances and then the entity is put in front of mirror. If the entity indicates the ability to realise that the mark on the mirror image is also on it (by attempting to find the mark on itself, touch itself where the mark is, etc.) then the entity is determined to be self-aware.[28] Importantly, it is not only humans who pass this test. Apes, dolphins, and elephants all have passed the self-awareness test.[29] So, it does not necessarily require that the entity in question has to be a human.

Even with non-human persons being a possibility, one of the benefits of a personhood theory of moral status is that the entities which qualify for personhood are much smaller than those which would qualify under either a life or sentience basis. For example, Sherman, even if he does have self-awareness, does not appear to qualify. Additionally, most other animals, plants or microbes do not seem to satisfy this test, making oral hygiene, farming and a number of other practices morally unproblematic. All of that should be considered a plus. Additionally, it does eliminate concerns about speciesism. Anything which fits the criteria is morally relevant whether or not it is human; everything which does not is not morally relevant.

Which, unfortunately, is the considerable problem with the theory. Since human beings are not entitled to particular moral relevance, it is

---

[27] J. M. Plotnik, F. B. M. de Waal and D. Reiss, 'Self-recognition in an Asian Elephant' (2006) 103 *Proceedings of the National Academy of Sciences of the United States of America* 17053–17057, 17053.

[28] *Ibid.*

[29] *Ibid.*; D. Reiss and L. Marino, 'Mirror Self-recognition in the Bottlenose Dolphin: A Case of Cognitive Convergence' (2001) 98 *Proceedings of the National Academy of Sciences of the United States of America* 5937–5942; J. Anderson and G. Gallup, 'Self Recognition in *Saguinus*? A Critical Essay' (1997) 54 *Animal Behaviour* 1563–1567. I am not aware of any tests being done on dogs, which of course may not be great for poor Sherman. Nor have I done the test myself. I can report, however, that Sherman does not react to his mirror image in the same way that he reacts to other dogs, even in situations where smell appears not to be an issue. This, obviously, does not mean he is self-aware; at best, it can be said to be minimal evidence that further tests would have to be done.

possible that human beings which do not fit the criteria are not morally relevant. Anthony Bland, for example, does not appear to qualify. Thus, while he is human, he is not a person and is therefore not entitled to moral status. Just as importantly, many other human beings which do not qualify as persons include those with dementia as a result of Alzheimer's disease, those in PVS, and children under the age of two.[30] So, it is not just the Anthony Blands of the world who lose their moral status, but a significant proportion of the human population.

To some, that might be perfectly acceptable. If species preference and the problems it causes are a real concern, there may be substantial benefits in a theory which takes a very hard line on that score. But, for many people, the results of personhood theory may be too much to take. We want Anthony Bland to be morally relevant.[31] We also want children under two to be morally relevant.[32] We therefore want a theory of moral relevance which includes them. Additionally, those who explore this idea in any depth are likely to come across the Peter Singer issue mentioned in the Introduction. As noted in the Introduction, Singer has been a champion of the idea of full moral status being granted only to those things which satisfy the criteria of personhood.[33] As noted in the paragraph above, among those who do not qualify for personhood, and thus full moral status, are those with dementia. When his mother, however, was struck with Alzheimer's disease and developed dementia as a result, Singer did not treat her in the way that the theory suggests. Instead, he wanted her to be treated just as one would likely expect. Despite the fact that his arguments would have to conclude that she was not a person, he hired a team of home health-care workers to look after her, spending tens of thousands of dollars a year in the process.[34]

By mentioning this, I want to make clear that I do not consider what Singer did in relation to his mother to be something wrong. Nor do I

[30] Children under the age of two are not sufficiently rational to qualify as persons. They, for example, do not pass the mirror test for self-awareness. M. De Veer and R. van den Bos, 'A Critical Review of Methodology and Interpretation of Mirror Self-recognition Research in Nonhuman Primates' (1999) 58 *Animal Behaviour* 459–468, 459, 460.

[31] Again, the best evidence for this is that both sides in the dispute about his treatment made arguments based in part on him being a morally worthwhile individual.

[32] Evidence for this can be gleaned from the response of ordinary members of the moral community to suggestions that parents of newborns suffering from severe disabilities should be allowed to terminate the newborn's life by lethal injection. For the various arguments involved, see Kuhse and Singer, *Should the Baby Live?*; Harris, *The Value of Life*; and Tooley, *Abortion and Infanticide*.

[33] Singer, *Practical Ethics*, p. 100. He also advocates lesser moral rights for sentient beings, which forms the basis for his arguments for moral rights for animals. *Ibid.*, p. 55–82.

[34] Specter, 'The Dangerous Philosopher', p. 55.

think he has shown himself to be a hypocrite for not being able to prac-
tise what he has often preached. The purpose for bringing up the story
of Peter Singer and his mother is to show how difficult it is to adhere to
such a moral view. Singer is one of the foremost champions of this sort
of view. He has lived a life which is, in many ways, as close to his ideal
view as possible. He does not eat meat or wear leather because it has too
detrimental an impact on the animals involved. He donates a large proportion of his earnings to charity (including the entirety of the royalties
for one of his most famous books, *Practical Ethics*). So, certainly more
than most of us, he adheres to his philosophy. But, in this particular
case, he was unable to do so despite knowing what counted as the right
action under the theory. He did so 'because it is different when it's your
mother'.[35] If someone like Singer could have so many problems putting
this into practice, though, the chances the rest of us (who may not be as
wedded to the notion as Singer) have will be even more slim.

A first way out of this issue is to rely not on capacities but on radical
capacities of the entity in question.[36] A capacity is the ability to exercise
something – for example, a skill such as speaking a foreign language.
A radical capacity is the ability to develop the ability to exercise something. Someone has a radical capacity if, despite not being presently
able to perform the relevant action, skill, etc., they could learn. Neither
Sherman nor I are capable of speaking German and thus neither of us
has the capacity. I, however, have the radical capacity because I could
develop the ability to speak German. Sherman does not because, irrespective of what training I provide to him, he will be unable to speak
German. This will provide some benefit for us but not, unfortunately,
enough of one. While most of us have the radical capacities necessary
for personhood, some such as Anthony Bland simply do not have the
ability to develop the capacities necessary. No matter what training or
help is provided to Anthony Bland, he will forever remain incapable
of rational thought after the Hillsborough disaster. So, radical capacities cannot provide us with sufficient grounds to include all humans as
persons.

Another way out of this particular quandary is to examine more closely
what lawyers would refer to as burden of proof issues. There are probably
three that are of major concern in our case. First, who has the burden of
proof? In other words, who is expected to show that a particular entity
has the requisite criteria for moral status? Is it up to the entity it-/her-/

---

[35] *Ibid.*
[36] See J. Finnis, 'A Philosophical Case against Euthanasia', in Keown (ed.), *Euthanasia Examined*, pp. 30–33; J. Finnis, 'The Fragile Case for Euthanasia: A Reply to John Harris', in Keown (ed.), *Euthanasia Examined*, pp. 47–50.

himself or is it the individual wishing to act in a certain way towards that entity? While it is not necessarily clear all the time, the general trend is for those arguing for these sorts of characteristic-based theories of moral status to place the burden of proof on the entity.[37] Thus, if I was trying to determine whether Sherman had significant characteristics for person-hood, it would be on Sherman or one acting on his behalf to prove that he had those capabilities. It would not be my role to show that Sherman does not have those capabilities. Why the burden of proof is exercised in such a way is less clear. There seems to be no compelling reason why Sherman must prove to me he is a person instead of me proving he is not. After all, I am the one who wishes to act in a particular way. Whatever that action is would seem to be done for some purpose which benefits me.[38] If that is the case, then I should be the one who has to prove that I am able to do whatever the act is, including showing how it is morally acceptable.[39] So, really, the burden of proof should lie with the one wish-ing to act as opposed to the entity itself.

Assigning the burden of proof, however, is only part of the issue. There are two more remaining issues related to the burden of proof. What sorts of evidence are necessary and how strong should that evi-dence be? For example, can it be considered sufficient evidence of com-munication that Sherman appears to understand that the word 'food' means he should come into the kitchen because I am going to put edible substances in his bowl? Is it sufficient that he appears to see his mir-ror image as something other than another dog? Or, in both cases, is more (and clearer) evidence of the possession of those characteristics needed before Sherman is entitled to sufficient moral status? Would it be necessary, instead, to show that Sherman does not merely know that when I make the collection of sounds and other related non-verbal things relating to the word 'food' that he is getting fed, but to under-stand that those collection of sounds means food? Likewise with the mirror. It may not be enough for Sherman merely to see that the shape in the mirror is not another dog. Instead, it may be necessary to show that Sherman understands that the shape in the mirror is him instead of something else.

---

[37] See, e.g., Harris and Holm, 'Abortion', pp. 112–135, 116, where they indicate that we want not only reliable criteria but 'detectable evidence' of personhood.
[38] It is perhaps not absolutely necessary that it does so, but probably in a large number of cases, my actions are likely to be things which I perceive to benefit some purpose that I have.
[39] For a more detailed explanation of these views, see S. W. Smith, 'Precautionary Reasoning in Determining Moral Worth', in M. Freeman (ed.), *Law and Bioethics, Current Legal Issues* (Oxford University Press, 2008), vol. XI, pp. 197–212.

What this involves, of course, is a method for dealing with doubt, particularly doubts about our knowledge of other minds. This is a long-standing problem in philosophy. It is difficult to show that we can ever have knowledge of other minds due to the fact that our senses do not allow us to perceive other minds. It may be, for example, that the thing I think is a rational entity talking to me is actually a computer program (like in the *Matrix* films), an automaton or some other entity which merely pretends to be a rational thinking entity. The best we can do, then, is guess based upon the available evidence. This does not mean that we should consider that there are no other minds; ethics would be a largely useless endeavour if there were no other morally worthwhile entities around. We do, however, need to accept that our beliefs may turn out to be wrong and have some way to minimise those doubts. So, we must have some idea what evidence is necessary to prove the characteristics necessary for moral status and how strong that evidence needs to be.

Despite all that, however, it will not solve all of our problems. Unless our beliefs about the world are seriously incorrect, it does not seem like merely changing the burden of proof is going to help with the case of Anthony Bland. As noted, he appears to have had no physical brain besides a brain stem and thus no consciousness. There is also no evidence of any sort that he felt pain and some reasonably strong evidence that he did not as the doctors performed surgery on him without anaesthesia. So, while clarification about the burden of proof might help move, for instance, children under the age of two towards the morally relevant categories, it appears to do nothing for Anthony Bland. It may help, but will not help as much as it would need to.

5   Central cases

All of which leads back to species membership. It is important to realise, however, that concerns about speciesism do not indicate that preferences on the grounds of species membership are *always* morally bad. It is only ones which are not justifiable; ones for which the only reasons for the particular preference is because it happens to be a species we like (or are a member of ourselves). It is therefore just like preferences based on gender or race. While there may be many moral reasons which would prohibit preferences for males when hiring for a job, there may be significantly less concerns for systems which provided treatment for breast cancer to women only. That is because in the one case, it is likely that the gender preference has no relevance to the determination whereas in the other there is a clear reason to provide benefits to only one gender (as, by and large, it is only women who develop breast cancer).[40] So, if there is a reason for preferring human beings over other species, then it would be morally acceptable.

As a consequence, it is worth returning to species membership as a legitimate criterion for moral status. In particular, it is worth examining the concept of a central case. To use a central case to analyse the concept of moral status, the primary concern is the central case for a particular entity. For a central case to be valid, it does not have to be the case for every member of a particular group; it does not even have to be the case for a 'statistically preponderant' group of cases. All that is required is that the central case be the standard example of what a member of a particular group ought to be. Entities are therefore granted moral status not based upon the individual criteria that they possess, but what is considered to be the criteria possessed by the central case.[41] We would not, therefore, consider Sherman in particular, but the central case for a dog. Sherman's moral status would be based on the characteristics possessed by the "central" case dog, not based upon what he might individually possess. While this might appear to be more than a bit strange (Sherman, after all, is available to look at, so reference to some sort of 'central case' dog seems unnecessary), there are benefits to these sorts of arguments. First, a central case can be simpler to apply because it will have less of what economists would call transaction costs. Instead of attempting to determine the presence of the characteristics for moral status in every dog, it is only necessary to do so once for a central case. It would therefore save time and other resources necessary to consider every individual member of a particular group on its own. Justifications based on central cases also might prevent sloppy analysis resulting from misleading examples. Perhaps one of the most illustrative examples of this phenomenon is the justification for torture based upon 'ticking time bomb' scenarios where governmental agents are attempting to extract

[40] It may be that our moral judgements may be subject to claims about legal rights which various parties may have. At the moment, however, I wish to put these concerns to one side and focus only on the moral acceptability of particular actions.
[41] For an example of this approach, see J. Gardner, 'Nearly Natural Law' (2007) 52 *American Journal of Jurisprudence* 1–22. However, there is some misunderstanding about persons and humans in the article. Gardner, for example, cites Michael Tooley when suggesting that 'some' are tempted to say that a human in PVS is not a human. While Gardner correctly states that Tooley is talking about 'persons' and not 'humans' (and also neonates and not PVS patients), he fails to understand that Tooley is using 'person' in the way we have considered previously. It is thus a philosophical category for rational entities, not a synonym for human beings. Thus, while Tooley would most likely argue that a PVS patient is not a person and would do so consistently with other personhood theorists like Harris and Singer, none of them would indicate that the PVS patient was not human.

information from a potential subject in a limited time frame.[42] In such a case, an outlandish scenario which is factually implausible is used to justify a practice in a number of other circumstances. If we focused on a central case of torture – torturing a prisoner to gain information in 'ordinary' circumstances – we would see the justification does not work. So, central cases can have their uses.[43]

When applying this central case idea to moral status, it provides benefits for the Anthony Bland situation that has caused us considerable problems. Anthony Bland is a human being. If the central case for human being has the criteria necessary for personhood (and hence, full moral status), then Anthony Bland gets treated as if he also has those characteristics. We would therefore treat him as being entitled to full moral status whether or not the evidence we have on his behalf about those characteristics is certain. Indeed, even in his case, where the evidence strongly indicates the reverse, he is still entitled to be treated as if he possesses those characteristics.[44] This is why he is entitled to a moral status that Sherman is not. Sherman is only entitled to the moral status of a dog, which, since the central case does not have the criteria necessary for personhood, does not gain that status. What we therefore have is a system which is not based upon species membership (if dogs had the criteria necessary for personhood, they too would be entitled to full moral status) but which also protects individuals such as Anthony Bland. It is, we could argue, not based upon undeserved species preferences and thus not speciesist.

At first glance, this looks like it solves all of the issues we have been considering. An individual such as Anthony Bland is entitled to full moral status under this approach. There is an explanation for why he ought to be treated in a particular way even if the characteristics he possesses (or at least what the best available evidence shows he possesses) would only seem to entitle him to lesser moral status. The same can be said for other human entities (children under two, those with dementia, etc.). However, entities such as Sherman are not entitled to full moral status and therefore certain actions are acceptable in regards to them (e.g. putting him to sleep if he gets badly injured) that are not acceptable in the case of Anthony Bland, despite the fact that Sherman is sentient and Anthony Bland is not. More importantly, claims of speciesism

---

[42] K. Lasson, 'Torture, Truth Serum, and Ticking Bombs: Toward a Pragmatic Perspective on Coercive Interrogation' (2008) 39 *Loyola University Chicago Law Journal* 329–360.

[43] I am thankful to Robert Cryer for discussions on this point.

[44] This is, of course, Gardner's specific point. See Gardner, 'Nearly Natural Law'. Anthony Bland is a PVS patient like the example he uses.

can be avoided as the relevant moral criteria are not species-based, but based upon characteristics. It therefore seems to solve any remaining concerns we have.

Closer inspection, however, shows three major problems with this sort of approach. First, this approach just seems to wilfully disregard the available evidence. I already have experience as to whether Sherman can or cannot feel pain. I already have experience about his capabilities in other areas. Removing those individual characteristics from the equation when deciding how to treat him adds a dimension of distance to the ethical standards which is neither particularly necessary nor sufficiently appropriate. I am not necessarily deciding how to treat dogs generally – I am trying to determine how to treat Sherman in particular. I should therefore treat Sherman as himself and not as some 'dog'. Indeed, this is some of the concern expressed about Singer's approach to moral reasoning. Singer has been criticised because he argues that no individual ought to be treated differently from another – every morally relevant being is treated in a similar fashion. So, if I think it is morally acceptable to let one human being die to save thousands, then it should not matter if that person is a member of my family, close friend, acquaintance or someone I do not know at all. But these connections do matter to a great many of us. As such, Singer's theory is flawed because it does not account for those connections. That criticism must apply equally to this approach as well since Sherman is not treated as an individual but merely the embodiment of a class. Additionally, of course, even if we move beyond Sherman, we have granted characteristics to an entity, Anthony Bland, which, from all available evidence that we have, he does not possess. In his case, it is not just an attempt to disregard evidence, but to actively act against that knowledge.

Second, this approach may not be able to escape claims of speciesism as easily as it may appear. That is because there must be a reason why the relevant moral category for Anthony Bland is that of a human being. Anthony Bland is a member of many groups. He is a Yorkshireman, a Liverpool supporter, male, a PVS patient, a human being, a mammal, a member of the animal kingdom, a living thing, so on and so forth. Why is human the relevant group for determining his moral status? This is an important question because the central case for different groups might lead to very different conclusions about his moral status. The first three (Yorkshireman, Liverpool supporter and male), of course, are going to give us central cases which are similar to the one for human (at least on the grounds relevant at the moment) but others will be vastly different. Some of these differences will be in broader cases but the central case for a PVS patient is not necessarily sentient or rational. In fact, Anthony Bland probably is as close to the central case for a PVS patient as we are likely to find. There therefore needs to be a compelling reason for why species membership is the relevant category, but none has been presented. Obviously, in some cases, such as discussions about human rights or human dignity, it is clear that the classification of something as human is particularly important. However, we are discussing moral status in general and here the classification along species criteria is less important. Remember, all a species classification means is that one has a particular genetic pattern. That does not necessarily provide any rational reason to prefer any genetic grouping over any other or indeed any reason why genetic groups ought to matter at all. Consequently, this approach does not eliminate claims about speciesism at all. It merely moves such concerns back a step.

The final problem with this central case theory concerns the actual application of the theory itself. At the moment, it seems to work quite well. Notice, though, that all of the changes to moral status happen when an entity which might not possess characteristics gets to assume those characteristics. Sherman, for example, stays relatively the same (he is probably not that far on relevant grounds from the central case of a dog) but Anthony Bland, who is not rational or sentient, receives moral status as if he was. So, in both of the cases so far, the central case idea has pulled an entity up to a greater moral status or left it where it was. This may not happen in all situations. In fact, there may be cases where, instead of pulling an entity up in our moral hierarchy, the central case theory pushes that entity down. I shall call this the Einstein problem due to the example I am going to use to explain it. I should make it clear from the start that the Einstein used in this example is not the Nobel Prize-winning physicist, although the Einstein in our example is named after him. In fact, our Einstein is not even real. He is a character in the novel *Watchers* by American thriller author Dean Koontz.[45] What makes this Einstein particularly relevant for our purposes is that Einstein is a dog, in particular a roughly one-year-old golden retriever. However, due to genetic experiments, Einstein does not just possess the attributes normally associated with canines, but also possesses a human (or at least human-like) intelligence. At various parts of the book, Einstein clearly indicates an ability to think. He can formulate rational plans, discern between fiction and reality, understand that he is a unique individual, feel empathy for others and make decisions on his own place in the universe. Crucially, he is also able to read and to communicate – either through simple actions like wagging

[45] D. Koontz, *Watchers* (New York: Berkley Books, 1988).

his tail or barking to indicate simple statements (like yes or no) or by the use of written form (i.e. scrabble tiles) to indicate more complex or abstract ideas. He is also clearly not human, although he is what one might consider a 'naturally occurring' species of animal. Taken on his own, then, as an individual life-form, Einstein would be entitled to full moral status under any of our characteristic-based methods. He is alive, sentient and rational and is so seemingly to the same level as any human being. But even with the genetic modifications, he is still a dog and still associates himself with that species.

Therein lies the problem. Using the central case method, Einstein would only be entitled to the same level of moral status as the central case dog, which is closer to Sherman's level. Sherman, unlike Einstein, is not rational and neither is the central case dog. Since dogs are not entitled to full moral status (as shown by our treatment decisions about Sherman), Einstein would also not be entitled to full moral status. He would receive some lesser standard despite fulfilling the basic criteria necessary for full moral status. This is quite unfair to Einstein. It is hardly his fault he was born a dog. Why, then, he should be effectively punished for being so is not entirely clear. Instead, I am sure Einstein would argue (if he were real) that he ought to be treated as him, as Einstein, as opposed to being treated just as 'some dog'.[46]

There may be two responses to the Einstein problem. The first is simply to suggest it hardly matters what we do about Einstein. Einstein is not real. He's a fictional character. More importantly, unless there are some incredible scientific breakthroughs which have not been made public, Einstein is not even a character that could exist in our world at the moment. That, however, brushes too quickly past the point which makes Einstein relevant for the discussion. Obviously, he is not real. If science progresses the way it is going, though, an Einstein may eventually exist. As a result, there is very little reason to refuse to consider how to treat such entities now before the problem arises. More importantly, Einstein has only been used to put a face on a specific type of evolutionary outlier – an entity which has important relevant criteria which others of its genetic species do not possess. And, as long as evolutionary theory is correct, those have existed and will continue to exist. The first humans who evolved from apes (whenever and whoever that was) would

---

[46] Indeed, the character of Einstein does object to being treating as a mere dog in the novel. As he was a lab animal, he had been tattooed for identification purposes and some of the people attempting to find Einstein focus on the tattoo as a means of locating him so they can return him to the lab. Einstein objects to the entire purpose of the tattoo, indicating that he 'is not a cow'. *Ibid.*, p. 434. Other characters also refer to Einstein as being 'a person with a soul'. *Ibid.*

have been in a similar position to Einstein. There may yet be others (for example, the apes in captivity who speak in sign language). As a result, it does matter how we deal with entities in similar situations to Einstein and thus the issue does bear pondering.

If consideration of the Einstein problem is important, there is still another response that can be made. We might argue that the Einstein problem leaves us in a very uncomfortable situation. It is one thing to consider a nice, cute, genetically engineered dog who can communicate with humans, but it also opens the door to arguments that we can treat certain segments of human beings better than others because some of them are 'advanced' in ways in which others are not. In other words, could we not use the Einstein argument as part of an attempt to generate a Nietzschean superman problem?[47] Such issues should always be taken extremely seriously and there are similarities between Einstein's relation to other dogs and the possible relation between the superman and other human beings. There is also an important difference between Einstein and the Nietzschean superman scenario. The difference is the groups to which they belong and the moral status of those groups. The difference between Einstein and the central case for dog (or even Sherman) matters because it shifts Einstein from a lesser moral category to a higher one. He moves from whatever moral category we put dogs into to the full moral status category. On the other hand, we as humans, already have full moral status. There is therefore no higher category that the so-called superman could belong to. There is no, for instance, full moral status plus category with additional benefits to those who belong to that group. Additionally, even if such a category did exist, all it would be capable of doing would be to raise up those 'supermen'; it could not lower our own moral status. Sherman's moral status does not lessen because of Einstein. All that happens is that Einstein's is elevated to a more appropriate level. Thus, even if Nietzschean supermen were possible (and they were entitled to some

---

[47] The Nietzschean superman problem is one created in part by Friedrich Nietzsche's assertion that man was only a stage (or, as he himself puts it, 'a rope over the abyss') between animals and the 'superman' – an improved human being. See F. Nietzsche, *Thus Spoke Zarathustra* (London: Penguin Books, 1961 [original publication 1883–1885]). The Nietzschean superman, then, is a more advanced human being and, consistent with the views of morality that Nietzsche proposed, presumably not subject to the common morality (or notions of moral status) to which the normal human being would be subject. That, of course, does not mean (necessarily) that the superman is free to treat other human beings as he or she wishes, but this concept of the superman has sometimes been changed and altered by others so that it could be used as a justification for terrible practices, such as those that occurred in Nazi Germany during the Second World War.

greater moral status), any additional rights granted to them would not negate the ones that we already possess as full moral actors.

So, in summary, the central case method is no better at solving the problems of moral status than the characteristic-based methods or the species-based methods previously considered. It too will treat some entities as either being more morally relevant than they perhaps are entitled to be or will treat some entities as being less morally relevant than they are entitled to be. This may lead some readers to wonder what the point of this chapter has been. I stated at the beginning that I was going to offer a theory of moral status in this chapter which can ground the ethical framework used throughout the book. So far, all I have done is show why the standard moral frameworks cannot be used to ground our decisions about moral status. Indeed, all I have probably done so far is sow doubt as to whether some sort of general ethical framework for moral status is possible at all. But I do think that a general ethical framework for moral status is possible. I also believe that it is possible to create one which provides better answers to the complex problems of moral status that arise. In order to move onto that theory, though, it has been necessary to expose the fatal flaw in the previous theories we have considered. What those theories have in common is that they all rely on only one test for moral status. Whatever that test may be (species membership, personhood, sentience, etc.), if the entity satisfies that test, it is entitled to a specific level of moral status. If it does not, then it is not entitled to that level of moral status. It is true that certain systems may have a hierarchy. In systems such as Peter Singer's, there is more than one level of moral status. Persons are entitled to full moral status; those entities which are sentient are entitled to a lesser standard; those which are neither persons nor sentient are not really entitled to any moral status. But, there is still only one test per category. The entity either satisfies the test for personhood or the entity does not. Likewise with the test for sentience. And it is the results of those tests which determine the outcome.

However, our reasons for wanting particular entities to be morally relevant do not depend only on one criterion. Assuming that my own moral thoughts are even in the slightest generalisable, there are a number of different reasons why something may be morally relevant. I think that I, as an individual, ought to be morally relevant because I can make rational judgements (particularly about my own existence), can feel pain, can create and nurture relationships and a host of other reasons. Einstein, were he real, would be entitled to be considered morally relevant for similar reasons. Anthony Bland, on the other hand, should be morally relevant as well, but not necessarily for those reasons.

He was a person (whether defined as merely a human being or in the philosophical sense) and is entitled to respect on that basis, even if he can no longer make rational judgements about his life. Children under two who do not satisfy the criteria necessary for philosophical personhood should be morally relevant because of their place within society as developing moral actors, for their connection to other human beings and for their place in our social groups. Sherman, I believe, is entitled to some moral status because he can feel pain and because we have formed a bond and I think it would be wrong to not act as if that bond mattered. He does not gain his moral status only from these, however, as I think that stray dogs to which I do not have any real bond should be treated in similar ways. So, I cannot be cruel to them (I cannot needlessly kill or harm them) and it may be that I have some positive duties towards them, although those are not as significant as those I have voluntarily undertaken in Sherman's case. I feel less concerned about rats even if I do think one should not be needlessly cruel to them. I may even feel that something like Mount Rushmore or Uluru/Ayers Rock in Australia is worthy of some sort of moral status (it would be wrong to blow them up, for example), although those reasons might be more derivative of other entities.[48] In short, then, there may be many reasons for why a particular entity or thing ought to be relevant when we make moral decisions. If that is the case, then it is no wonder that any system of moral relevance based upon one criterion is bound to fail. They have to because there is not just one criterion for determining moral status. Instead, there are many. A system of moral status, then, should likewise consider many ways in which an entity can gain moral status. A unicriterial system has the benefit of simplicity, but it is a simplicity that comes at the cost of usefulness and usability.

6   A multi-criterial system for moral status

If a uni-criterial approach will not provide an effective mechanism for deciding on the moral status of particular entities, then a system which has a basis in more than one criteria may be preferable. Such an approach will not have the benefit of simplicity, but it may provide a stronger foundation for our ethical decisions. Of course, the mere

---

[48] Although that may not be entirely the case. The destruction of the Bamiyan Buddhas in Afghanistan may provide an illustrative example. There is no specific group for which the Buddhas were sacred in the same way that Uluru/Ayers Rock is sacred to aboriginal people in Australia. Even so, their destruction by Taliban forces in 2001 was met with considerable international outrage and the belief by many that it was wrong to have destroyed them.

change to a multi-criterial approach to moral status will not, in and of itself, solve the problems posed by entities such as Anthony Bland or Einstein. The only way a multi-criterial approach will be more effective is if the most effective criteria are part of the system. The essential task, then, is to determine which criteria are necessary for this approach.

Fortunately, while multi-criterial approaches are rarer than their uni-criterial counterparts, they are not non-existent. One in particular merits mention and will form the basis for the multi-criterial approach that will be used here. That approach is the one presented by Mary Anne Warren in *Moral Status*. Warren has argued, as I have done here, that a uni-criterial approach does not accurately reflect our beliefs about the moral status of a number of entities.[49] Instead, she presents a list of seven criteria about moral status which she believes will provide a firmer basis for moral decisions about particular entities. The principles are:

1. **The Respect for Life Principle**
   Living organisms are not to be killed or otherwise harmed, without good reasons that do not violate principles 2–7.
2. **The Anti-Cruelty Principle**
   Sentient beings are not to be killed or subjected to pain or suffering, unless there is no other feasible way of furthering goals that are (1) consistent with principles 3–7; and (2) important to human beings, or other entities that have a stronger moral status than could be based upon sentience alone.
3. **The Agent's Rights Principle**
   Moral agents have full and equal basic moral rights, including the rights to life and liberty.
4. **The Human Rights Principle**
   Within the limits of their own capacities and of principle 3, human beings who are capable of sentience but not of moral agency have the same moral rights as do moral agents.
5. **The Ecological Principle**
   Living things that are not moral agents, but that are important to the ecosystems of which they are part, have, within the limits of principles 1–4, a stronger moral status than could be based upon their intrinsic properties alone; ecologically important entities that are not themselves alive, such as species and habitats, may legitimately be accorded a stronger moral status than their intrinsic properties would indicate.

---

[49] Warren, *Moral Status*, p. 147.

6. **The Interspecific Principle**

Within the limits of principles 1–5, non-human members of mixed social communities have a stronger moral status than could be based upon their intrinsic properties alone.

7. **The Transitivity of Respect Principle**

Within the limits of principles 1–6, and to the extent that it is feasible and morally permissible, moral agents should respect one another's attributions of moral status.[50]

As it takes Warren about 150 pages to get to the point where she can put forth those principles, it is likely they take some explanation. Warren argues that principles are meant to 'operate interactively', meaning that the principles are determined in part by the way they interact with the other principles.[51] Furthermore, one needs to consider as many of the principles as are relevant in a particular decision.[52] It is not simply a task of finding one principle which applies and using that to the exclusion of the other principles.

Additionally, not all of the principles are of the same sort. The first three are based upon intrinsic properties possessed by members of a particular class.[53] In fact, they are the same as the three we have looked at previously, as moral agency is roughly the same as personhood. The fifth principle, however, is based upon ecological principles. This would allow us to ascribe some sort of moral status to ecologically important entities and even to things such as soil, water and other things which we would not even consider entities.[54] The important value in this case is therefore not intrinsic but the value of the entity or thing to the environment and our world.[55] The sixth and seventh principles are also not based on inherent characteristics of the entity in question. Instead, they are based upon social values ascribed by other individuals.[56] Such methods for ascribing moral status are different from ones we have considered previously but many feminist viewpoints of ethics are built on these methods.[57] They ascribe value based upon the relationships created between individuals or the caring attitudes that particular entities might create in others. Such approaches to ethics can sometimes be difficult to use as the moral status of entities is largely defined by our

---

[50] *Ibid.*, pp. 148–172.   [51] *Ibid.*, p. 148.   [52] *Ibid.*
[53] *Ibid.*, p. 182.   [54] *Ibid.*, pp. 166–168.   [55] *Ibid.*
[56] *Ibid.*, pp. 168–172.
[57] Two of the seminal texts about feminist ethics are C. Gilligan, *In a Different Voice: Psychological Theory and Women's Development* (Cambridge, MA: Harvard University Press, 1982) and N. Noddings, *Caring: A Feminine Approach to Ethics and Education* (Berkeley: University of California Press, 1978). For an overview, see J. Grimshaw 'The Idea of a Female Ethic', in Singer (ed.), *A Companion to Ethics*, pp. 491–499.

ability to empathise with those entities.[58] It would thus seem that when we are unable to empathise with a particular entity, then it lacks moral status, even if the failure is ours. So, if we cannot empathise with an entity because we do not consider it to be cute or friendly or useful or whatever, then that entity's moral status goes down.[59]

To many, this hardly seems to be a fair result. As a result, some may give such ethical approaches short shrift. There is, however, an important benefit to these sorts of approaches which makes it useful to incorporate them into our multi-criterial approach. As stated previously, we are looking to create an ethical system of moral status which is useable by ordinary members of the moral community. One thing that is of particular importance to us is the relationships we form, both with other moral agents and with things which might not be moral agents.[60] I, for example, place a specific value on my interactions with Sherman and I think there is an importance in how I treat him. It does not matter to me that others may not see Sherman in the same way. We have many such relationships in our life and while the values we ascribe to such relationships may be difficult to validate on rationalistic grounds, it does not mean those values have disappeared. In other words, these types of relationships matter to us. As such, it says a great deal about us as individuals when we treat the entities for which we have developed such bonds in a particular manner. If I were to treat Sherman badly, despite the affection that he shows me, then this would reflect badly on my moral reasoning. If I treat him as if he is valuable, then even those people who do not have any particular affection for dogs as a species or Sherman in particular are likely to at least understand my actions. Our moral system should reflect such values.

The same goes for principle 7, which can be shown by our actions towards things like Uluru/Ayers Rock.[61] I, myself, have no particular interest in the landmark. To me, it is simply a unique geological formation in the middle of Australia. I therefore place no particular moral or ethical worth on it. Even so, I realise that others (notably the native aboriginal tribes of Australia) do place an important value upon it. As such, it does say something about me as a moral individual if I were to disregard those views merely because I do not share them. So, even though I do not share the particular viewpoint about the worth of Uluru/Ayers Rock that others do, I should still act in a certain way in relation to it. If, for example, I were to travel to Uluru/Ayers Rock and climb it (even though I know that is against the views of the aboriginal

[58] Warren, *Moral Status*, p. 143.   [59] *Ibid.*   [60] *Ibid.*, p. 146.
[61] *Ibid.*, p. 171.

tribes), then people can rightly question my moral views. A response that I do not share the views of those aboriginal tribes does not seem to be sufficient as it does not indicate the proper respect for those who do hold those views. Again, our moral system should reflect a respect for viewpoints other than our own.

Does principle 7 also cause difficulties in regard to the moral status of some human beings? Certain groups, for example, may argue that their perspective on other groups (racial or ethnic minorities, women, etc.) should be taken into account when we make moral judgements and that we ought to respect their attribution of lesser rights to those groups. Does the Transitive Principle really require us to do so? Warren is a bit unclear on this point. She states that:

> The Transitivity of Respect principle requires that we give fair hearing to other people's reasons for ascribing to certain entities a stronger *or a weaker* moral status than we think appropriate. It also requires that, to the extent that is feasible and morally acceptable, we must seek to avoid harming entities to which other persons ascribe a high moral status.[62]

As Warren seems to include human beings within the category of entities (as we have here), this would indicate that we are required to give those people a fair hearing about why certain human beings should be entitled to a lesser moral status. Nevertheless, the second sentence only asserts that we seek to avoid harming those ascribed a higher moral status by others. It says nothing about those entities to which others may want to ascribe a lower moral status. Indeed, if we look specifically at the wording of the principle, respect for others' opinions must still satisfy principles 1–6. Thus, we need not accept that the multi-criterial approach in general and principle 7 in particular requires that we give respect to the decisions of moral agents which seek to provide certain entities with a lower moral status. We are entitled to give them a fair hearing, but especially due to principle 4, it does not seem possible for us to accept that moral viewpoint as binding.[63]

Principle 4, the Human Rights Principle, thus becomes vitally important. It not only protects human beings in our moral systems, it prevents

---

[62] *Ibid.*, p. 170 (emphasis added).
[63] The question does arise, then, what the point of the 'fair hearing' might be if it does not appear possible to change our viewpoints on these issues. It is also possible to wonder what 'fair' means in that context. What I believe that Warren is getting at, though, is that we should give others the opportunity to change their minds about, for example, the intrinsic capacities that a particular entity has. This does present difficulties for anyone arguing that other human beings are owed some lesser moral standard due to principle 4, which only requires that other human beings belong to that group.

others from using the Transitivity of Respect principle to lower their moral status in other ways. Unfortunately, the Human Rights Principle that Warren presents may not have the most firm grounding as a principle. Her reasons for why we ought to include a human rights principle are: (1) because we need to develop future moral agents, which we do by allowing them to be morally relevant themselves, and (2) because sentient humans are part of our social communities.[64]

Both of those justifications seem to require further explanation. The first is true if we consider the bare fact that we receive much of our moral training from parents and other authority figures early in life[65] but using that fact to protect future moral agents (in children) seems more of a pragmatic response to continuing the species than a moral principle. It seems to be the idea that the development of more moral agents in the world is better than fewer moral agents. Or at least, a greater percentage of entities which might possibly be moral agents actually becoming moral agents should be preferred.[66] That makes sense as the more moral agents we have in the world, the better that world would seem to be (provided, of course, that those agents were acting morally). Nevertheless, that does not seem to include all human beings. Instead, it only seems to cover those human beings who are in the early stages of their moral development. It seems like it would not cover, for example, those with advanced Alzheimer's. Moreover, it would seem that, if this is a moral principle, then it could just as easily be applied to other entities which are not human. So, if Sherman were capable of receiving such moral instruction, the same principle would seem to require that we treat him as fully morally relevant when he was a puppy. As such, limiting the principle to human beings seems unnecessary.

Additionally, while Warren calls it the Human Rights Principle, it still does not cover all human beings. Anthony Bland, who, we must remember is not sentient, is not covered under the principle. Warren's rationale for this is that one needs to be sentient (even minimally) in order to be a part of the social community. She argues:

To be part of a social community in more than name, a being must be capable of sentience; a permanently unconscious organism has no capacity for social response. Thus, anencephalic infants, who will never be capable of conscious

---

[64] Warren, *Moral Status*, pp. 164–166.
[65] *Ibid.*, p. 164.
[66] By this, I mean the greater number of current potential moral agents. So, if we have a certain number of possible moral agents currently in the world, it is better that a greater number of that potential class of agents become moral agents as opposed to the notion that we need to create as many moral agents as possible. This would inevitably lead to population control questions which are beyond the scope of this book.

experience, cannot really be part of a social community and neither can persons whose brains have been so severely damaged that no return to consciousness is even remotely possible. But even with a minimal level of sentience, a human being can often love and be loved.[67]

The essential phrase in this passage is 'to be part of a social community' and what exactly that entails. Warren argues that one must have a minimal level of sentience because one must be able to respond socially, in some way, in order to be part of a social community. I do not doubt that the ability to respond socially is required for optimal membership in a social community. Social communities almost by definition require a social element and a social community could not exist without members of that community engaging in social interactions. Notwithstanding this, the question we must consider is whether it is necessary for a social community to only contain members who have the capacity for a social response. Again, our clearest example of this is probably Anthony Bland. He did not have the capacity for a social response nor was he, to the best of our knowledge, sentient. Deciding, however, that he was not part of a social community seems more difficult. His family and friends and the hospital staff at Airedale NHS Trust certainly treated him as if he was part of a community of some sort. In fact, everyone concerned with the case appears to have considered him part of some social community, otherwise there would have been no need to discuss his treatment at all (as we do not in the case of other living but non-sentient or rational entities). In other words, one of the primary ways you become a part of a social community is for others in that community to treat you as a member. That usually happens to those who are at least sentient but also may contain others who are not (as in Anthony Bland's case).

More importantly, it is not clear why this sort of relational ground is relevant to principle 4 anyway. It seems like this idea of being a member of a social group fits in much more closely with principle 6. As it is currently constituted, principle 6 only applies to non-human members of moral communities. Warren, however, has already removed non-sentient human beings from the confines of principles 3 and 4. As a result, it would appear that Anthony Bland (who would not be covered) would be considered to be worth less morally than Sherman.

One way out of this is to expand principle 4 to cover these sorts of cases. However, I think it is more consistent to put these cases within principle 6. Some might argue that this would lessen the moral protection that we give anencephalic infants, those with severe dementia or those in PVS. A closer look at principle 6 does not reveal this to be true.

[67] Warren, *Moral Status*, p. 166.

All principle 6 states is that those within mixed social groups are entitled to a higher status than their intrinsic properties alone may indicate. In other words, it simply states that we can treat these entities better than we might otherwise be able to because of their connection with a mixed social group. It is silent as to the extent of that treatment. Thus, we could, consistent with principle 6, treat Anthony Bland as fully morally relevant because he is a member of a social group as opposed to how we might treat him otherwise.

Principles 4 and 6 therefore will need to be revised in the following way:

4. Developing Agents Principle
Within the limits of their own capacities and of principle 3, all developing moral agents who are capable of sentience but not of moral agency should be treated as if they were full moral agents.

6. The Interspecific Principle
Within the limits of their own capacities and consistent with other principles, human members who do not qualify as moral agents or developing moral agents and non-human members of mixed social communities have a stronger moral status than could be based upon their intrinsic properties alone.

A different addition to the Warren multi-criterial approach deals with the issues surrounding the burden of proof concerns I raised earlier. These specifically relate to principles 1–3. As noted above, these surround the questions we can raise regarding our knowledge of other minds. This is of particular interest to us in relation to the first three principles because they all rely on intrinsic characteristics of the entity. But, if we cannot ever totally be sure about our knowledge of other entities (and those characteristics in particular), then it is hard to claim that we can be completely accurate about our assessment of those entities. However, as the determination of moral status is so important to how we decide to treat numerous entities, we should do all we can to ensure that we are as accurate and fair in our assessments as possible. To my mind, the best method for doing so is to start with the knowledge that those determinations are not infallible. This does not mean that we jettison our available knowledge about entities, but that we consider ways to minimise the risks associated with knowledge failures. Two rules then seem to be an effective way to minimise these risks. First, we should assign the burden of proof upon encountering new entities to those seeking to interact with the entity as opposed to the entity itself. Thus, in the familiar 'aliens from another planet' scenario, it would be beholden on us to provide evidence if we wished to put those aliens in a particular category (especially if the category is something less than full moral status). Second, when there is reasonable doubt about the moral status of a particular entity, we should treat that entity as being in the highest available class instead of a lower class. Thus, if our aliens seemed to fall between the classes of sentient beings and rational beings, we would treat them as rational beings. The added principle, principle 8, would then look as follows:

8. The Precautionary Principle

Within the limits of principles 1–7, when determining the moral status of a particular entity, the burden of proof should lie with those seeking to assign the status of the entity instead of the entity itself. If there is reasonable doubt about a particular entity, it should be treated as far as possible as being within the highest available class of moral status.

The language 'as far as possible' is of particular importance. Because the number of morally relevant entities increases using the precautionary principle, there is a greater likelihood that the interests of entities may come in conflict. This will cause specific problems when we have one entity which falls definitively within a particular category and another entity which only gains moral status through the precautionary principle. In such cases, we should treat those entities as being morally relevant as far as we can. In cases of intractable conflicts, we will need to prioritise and should go with the entity which is more likely an agent than ones which are less likely an agent. Cases of intractable conflict, however, will be quite rare and none are likely to be an issue for us here. For instance, even if one considers Anthony Bland to only gain moral status under principle 8, it would not mean that we could harvest his organs to give to someone we think worthy of moral status under principle 3 because they are a moral agent. In such cases, there would be other methods available from which we could gain the organs necessary for the moral agent.[68]

With this set of eight principles, we should be able to deal with most questions of moral status in a reliable way. We can test that hypothesis by returning to some of the examples we have used throughout this chapter. Sherman, for example, would be sentient (even considering principle 8, there is likely not enough evidence to push him into the full moral status envisioned in principle 3) and thus entitled to greater moral status than those entities which are merely alive. However, he is also part of a 'mixed social community' under principle 6 so can be considered to

---

[68] The most difficult, however, of these cases of intractable conflict is in disputes between a mother and a foetus. While a full discussion about how to resolve such conflicts is beyond the scope of this book, I have discussed these issues previously. See S. W. Smith, 'Precautionary Reasoning in Determining Moral Worth', pp. 197–212 and S. W. Smith, 'Dignity: The Difference between Abortion and Neonaticide for Severe Disability', in C. Erin and S. Ost (eds.), *The Criminal Justice System and Health Care* (Oxford University Press, 2007), pp. 175–188.

have a higher moral status than other entities which are sentient but not part of our mixed social communities – entities like rats, worms and the like. Adult human beings would be considered full moral actors under principle 3; children and newborns, while not capable of being considered full moral actors under that principle would be entitled to that status under principle 4 (as developing moral actors). Einstein, the genetically modified golden retriever, would also receive full moral status under principle 3. Entities such as chimpanzees and other great apes would likely be entitled to full moral status. While there would be doubt as to whether they completely satisfy the criteria of principle 3, under principle 8, they would be entitled to that status due to doubts about their status and full moral status being the highest class of moral status available for them. What of our most difficult example, Anthony Bland? He, again, would only be entitled to moral status under principle 1 to begin with, as he is neither sentient nor rational (and thus not eligible under principles 2 and 3). However, he is a member of a social community and, as such, available for a higher moral status under principle 6 that he might receive just from his characteristics alone and, as stated previously, this can include treating him as being entitled to full moral status. Consequently, the system provided appears to do a reasonable job of determining the appropriate moral status of a number of entities, including ones which are notoriously difficult under other methods.

7   Conclusion

In conclusion, this chapter has primarily focused on the concept of moral status and how we determine moral status. It has examined many of the uni-criterial methods for determining moral status and found that they do not necessarily provide appropriate moral status for all the entities we may wish to consider. It was thus decided that a multi-criterial approach was a preferred method for moral status. To that end, a set of eight principles was proposed. Those principles are as follows:

1. **The Respect for Life Principle**
   Living organisms are not to be killed or otherwise harmed, without good reasons that do not violate principles 2–7.
2. **The Anti-Cruelty Principle**
   Sentient beings are not to be killed or subjected to pain or suffering, unless there is no other feasible way of furthering goals that are (1) consistent with principles 3–7; and (2) important to human beings, or other entities that have a stronger moral status than could be based upon sentience alone.

3. **The Agent's Rights Principle**
   Moral agents have full and equal basic moral rights, including the rights to life and liberty.
4. **Developing Agents Principle**
   Within the limits of their own capacities and of principle 3, all developing moral agents who are capable of sentience but not of moral agency should be treated as if they were full moral agents.
5. **The Ecological Principle**
   Living things that are not moral agents, but that are important to the ecosystems of which they are part, have, within the limits of principles 1–4, a stronger moral status than could be based upon the intrinsic properties alone; ecologically important entities that are not themselves alive, such as species and habitats, may legitimately be accorded a stronger moral status than their intrinsic properties would indicate.
6. **The Interspecific Principle**
   Within the limits of their own capacities and consistent with other principles, human members who do not qualify as moral agents or developing moral agents and non-human members of mixed social communities have a stronger moral status than could be based upon their intrinsic properties alone.
7. **The Transitivity of Respect Principle**
   Within the limits of principles 1–6, and to the extent that it is feasible and morally permissible, moral agents should respect one another's attributions of moral status.
8. **The Precautionary Principle**
   Within the limits of principles 1–7, when determining the moral status of a particular entity, the burden of proof should lie with those seeking to assign the status of the entity instead of the entity itself. If there is reasonable doubt about a particular entity, it should be treated as being within the highest available class of moral status.

But these principles are only the beginning. We still need to determine what moral rights we wish to grant to morally relevant entities. We shall begin that discussion with the issues surrounding the value of life in the next chapter.

3   The value of life

1   Introduction

The focus of the previous chapter was on who matters morally. While that is a crucially important question, it is only the beginning of our ethical discussion about end-of-life decisions. For once we know who we are talking about (ethically), we need to decide what it is we owe those individuals who matter morally. In other words, what moral rights do those we have decided have moral status actually possess? Of course, all of the moral rights we give those individuals with moral status are not necessarily at issue in end-of-life decisions. Some may have no inherent impact upon the kinds of decisions that must be made when a patient presents with a terminal disease. Others, however, will have vital importance in how we determine ethically what kind of treatment options are available to the patient. Thus, while we will be discussing specific moral issues and rights in the next several chapters, it is not my intention to provide a full list of the moral rights we may wish to grant to those we have determined have moral status. Instead, we will focus only on those moral rights that have a direct impact on end-of-life decision-making. And, of those, the first issue that must be addressed is the value we place on life, both on our own life and the lives of those to whom we have decided moral status should be accorded.

As we shall see, the issue of the value of life has long been concerned with the argument between those who argue in a position called 'the sanctity of life' and those who argue for a position called 'the quality of life' (discussed below). I shall argue, however, that neither position in the debate truly captures the view of ordinary members of the moral community. Instead, I shall offer a different position, outside the debate on quality versus sanctity of life, which better approximates the thinking of at least a number of ordinary members of the moral community. It is this third position, I shall argue, which provides us with the most useful way forward when deciding on how best to value life when we are making decisions about the end of life.

2   The sanctity versus quality of life debate

Before discussing alternative views, however, it is best to start with the standard formulations of how we value life. As stated above, this generally takes the form of a debate between two sides. One side refers to its position as the 'sanctity of life' and the other refers to its position as the 'quality of life'. These two positions are seen as being mutually exclusive, meaning one must accept one of the two positions as being accurate but cannot accept both. This debate has been characterised most clearly by John Keown, who has discussed this debate in a number of publications.[1] According to Keown, though, there are actually three distinct positions one can take. It is worth discussing these three positions in detail.

The first position is one he calls Vitalism. Vitalism holds that life is an absolute value. Consequently, it should never be taken or even lessened.[2] Thus, if it is possible to extend the life of a morally relevant individual for a second it should be done, no matter the cost in resources, time or energy. Keown considers this to be an extreme position and, in fact, says that 'it is as ethically untenable as its attempt to maintain life indefinitely is physically impossible'.[3] On the other side of the spectrum from Vitalism is the Quality of Life position.[4] The Quality of Life position holds that there is no value inherent in life.[5] Instead, life is only valuable because it allows you to do things which are valuable.[6] Thus, it is not my being alive which is valuable, it is the fact that I am able to do all of those things which I find worthwhile that is valuable. It is not because I am alive, but because I can read books, form friendships, play baseball, watch movies, eat good food, and so on and so forth. Since it is only the experiences I have which are valuable and not life itself, then it is possible for my life to have a negative value if the negative experiences in my life outweigh the positive experiences.[7] Again, Keown considers this to be an extreme position. Instead, he advocates what he calls the

---

[1] See, e.g., Keown, 'Restoring Moral and Intellectual Shape to the Law after *Bland*'; Keown, *Euthanasia, Ethics and Public Policy*; J. Keown, 'Restoring the Sanctity of Life and Replacing the Caricature: A Reply to David Price' (2006) 26 *Legal Studies* 109–119.

[2] Keown, *Euthanasia, Ethics and Public Policy*, p. 39.

[3] Keown, 'Restoring Moral and Intellectual Shape to the Law after *Bland*', 482. Other commentators have also suggested that no theorist adheres to this position. See S. Pattinson, *Medical Law and Ethics* (London: Sweet and Maxwell, 2006), p. 18.

[4] Keown, *Euthanasia, Ethics and Public Policy*, pp. 43–44. Keown makes sure to put this position in capital letters for reasons which will become clear shortly.

[5] *Ibid.*, p. 45.   [6] *Ibid.*, pp. 43–44.

[7] *Ibid.*

middle position of Sanctity of Life.[8] The Sanctity of Life position holds that life is a basic or inherent good, but not an absolute one.[9] It therefore should not be intentionally taken away, although one need not do everything possible to extend life when treatment is futile.[10] What those taking the Sanctity of Life position do instead is to look at whether the value of the treatment is worthwhile.[11]

To further illustrate the differences between these three positions, Keown gives us two examples, both of which involve newborns. The first is Agatha. Agatha is a baby born with Down syndrome and an intestinal blockage.[12] The Down syndrome is not immediately fatal, although it will have developmental and mental consequences for Agatha. The intestinal blockage is fatal but easily treatable through surgery; thus, if she has the surgery, she will have a normal life span.[13] According to Keown, both Vitalism and the Sanctity of Life approach would require that the surgery go ahead. For Vitalism, this is an easy case as Agatha is alive and the surgery will help to keep her alive.[14] It therefore must go ahead. For the Sanctity of Life position, it is also an easy judgement as Agatha's life has an inherent value and the surgery is not futile.[15] The Quality of Life approach, however, is more difficult. In this case, those who take a Quality of Life approach must decide whether Agatha's life would be so worthless as to be worse than non-existence. In other words, would it be better for Agatha to continue to exist as a Down syndrome child or better to simply not exist at all? Thus, for those advocating a Quality of Life approach, it may be (although it is not necessary) that Agatha should not have the surgery and should be allowed to die instead.[16]

---

[8] *Ibid.*, pp. 40–41, 46.

[9] *Ibid.*, p. 47. The use of the term 'basic good' is particularly instructive. This is borrowed from John Finnis's natural law position which argues that there are seven basic goods which we want whatever else we might want. See J. Finnis, *Natural Law and Natural Rights* (Oxford University Press, 1980), pp. 85–90.

[10] Keown, *Euthanasia, Ethics and Public Policy*, pp. 40–41.

[11] *Ibid.*, pp. 42–43.

[12] Keown, 'Restoring Moral and Intellectual Shape to the Law after *Bland*', 485.

[13] *Ibid.*, 486. The inspiration for this example appears to be the UK case of *Re B* which has identical facts to Agatha's situation. See *Re B (a minor)* [1990] 3 All ER 927, [1981] WLR 1421 (CA).

[14] Keown, *Euthanasia, Ethics and Public Policy*, p. 48.

[15] *Ibid.*, p. 49; Keown, 'Restoring Moral and Intellectual Shape to the Law after *Bland*', 486.

[16] Keown, *Euthanasia, Ethics and Public Policy*, p. 49. It may be that Keown is overstating the difference between the positions here, at least in the present day. While it is true that for some years it was considered acceptable for doctors to allow Down syndrome children to die in these conditions (of which the *Baby Doe* case in the US and the *R* v. *Arthur* case in the UK are merely two examples), it is much less likely that would be the case today. Even so, the illustrative example shows us that the method

A second example further explains the differences between the three approaches. This second example involves Bertha, a newborn child with a terminal illness which will 'inevitably lead to death in a matter of hours'.[17] She is also suffering from breathing difficulties. The issue for the medical staff (and her parents) is what to do in case it is necessary to provide CPR or other respiratory treatments for Bertha, which might put her in pain but provide very little benefit to her.[18] Again, under a Vitalism approach, treatment should go ahead even if it puts Bertha in pain and provides little in the way of therapeutic benefit.[19] Under a Quality of Life approach, it probably should not. Bertha's life is not worth enough to counteract the pain she will be in and it is therefore better for her to be allowed to die.[20] The Sanctity of Life approach, however, leads to a different conclusion from the previous case of Agatha.[21] Since the treatment provides no real therapeutic benefit[22] and there is the real possibility of pain, the quality of life of Bertha (which is not the same as the Quality of Life) means that treatment should not go ahead.[23] It would be futile. As such, she can be allowed to die. It is because of the differences in the treatment between Agatha and Bertha that Keown argues that the Sanctity of Life approach is a middle way.

While the argument that the Sanctity of Life is a middle way requires further consideration, there are some important points which need to be highlighted about Keown's descriptions. First, they are reasonably standard descriptions of, at least, the Sanctity of Life and Quality of Life approaches. Second, they are mutually exclusive categories. One cannot hold any two of these positions at the same time while still being logically consistent. Finally, they are exhaustive of the field. One must

---

for determining the outcome is different, even if the result of that determination is the same.

[17] Keown, 'Restoring Moral and Intellectual Shape to the Law after *Bland*', 486.

[18] *Ibid.*

[19] Keown does not specifically mention how Vitalism would deal with this case, but it seems evident from his description that a vitalist would argue that Bertha should be treated.

[20] Again, Keown does not specifically mention how a Quality of Life position would deal with this case, but he does not dispute David Price's assertion that her treatment should be withdrawn and Price is an advocate of the Quality of Life position. Keown, 'Restoring the Sanctity of Life and Replacing The Caricature'. David Price's position can be found at D. Price, 'Fairly *Bland*: An Alternative View of a Supposed New "Death Ethic" and the BMA Guidelines' (2001) 21 *Legal Studies* 618–643.

[21] Keown, 'Restoring Moral and Intellectual Shape to the Law after *Bland*', 486.

[22] Questions about the use of the term 'therapeutic benefit' will be considered below. For the moment, we can simply give the term its common meaning of benefit to Bertha's health.

[23] Keown, 'Restoring Moral and Intellectual Shape to the Law after *Bland*'.

hold one of these positions.[24] There are no other possible approaches to the way in which we value life. A graphical representation of these three approaches would therefore look like this:

Vitalism // Sanctity of Life approach // Quality of Life approach

There are some important concerns that arise because of this formulation. The first is this idea about the Sanctity of Life approach being the middle ground. As noted above, Keown argues that it is a middle way because it does not accept the extremism of either Vitalism or Quality of Life.[25] However, it is important to note that Vitalism is hardly a viable option in the first place. As Keown correctly indicates, hardly anyone could really be a Vitalist.[26] It therefore seems more than a bit odd to put it on a par with the Sanctity of Life and Quality of Life positions, both of which contain many adherents.[27] In fact, Vitalism appears to be more a position created so that Keown can claim a middle ground than one with any real possibility of being considered. More importantly, though, it actually seems that a middle ground is not possible in Keown's description. The reason for this can best be illustrated by his emphasis on why the Quality of Life approach is an extreme one. What exactly makes it extreme? Unlike Vitalism, it does have its adherents. It is therefore not extreme because no one agrees with the position. Nor is it extreme because it reaches absurd conclusions. As stated previously, Keown concedes that the Quality of Life position reaches the same conclusion as the Sanctity of Life position in Bertha's case and the result likely would be the same in Agatha's case as well.[28] If it reaches the same results (although it does so for different reasons) and happens to be a viewpoint shared by a number of academic commentators, then it is worth wondering why it is an extreme position.

[24] Or at least it appears that they are exhaustive of the field. Keown originally stated in an article in the *LQR* that 'there are *at least* three competing alternatives' (emphasis added). 'Restoring Moral and Intellectual Shape to the Law after *Bland*', 482. Subsequent formulations, including in *Euthanasia, Ethics and Public Policy*, remove the qualifying language 'at least' and just mention the three competing schools of thought. *Euthanasia, Ethics and Public Policy*, p. 39. This does not mean, necessarily, that Keown has now come to believe that there are only the three possible schools of thought. It is important to note, however, that he has never discussed, to my knowledge, any other possible way to value life other than the three schools of thought presented here.

[25] Keown, *Euthanasia, Ethics and Public Policy*, p. 46.

[26] Keown, 'Restoring Moral and Intellectual Shape to the Law after *Bland*', 482. The only exception is an Indian religion called Jainism which does adhere to Vitalism.

[27] John Keown himself is a proponent of the Sanctity of Life position, as is John Finnis. Peter Singer, John Harris and David Price would all be examples of people who would take the Quality of Life position.

[28] Keown, 'Restoring the Sanctity of Life and Replacing the Caricature', 112.

The answer seems to be that the Quality of Life approach argues from a position where life itself is not valuable. In other words, there is no inherent value to life according to the Quality of Life perspective. Life is only valuable because of what you get from it. The extremism, thus, comes from the point that the Quality of Life approach differs on the answer to the question of whether life is inherently valuable. The conclusion seems to be, then, that the essential question for Keown is whether a position agrees with the inherent value to life. If that is the case, then there cannot be a middle-ground position because it is a yes or no question. Those positions which hold that there is an inherent value in life (Vitalism and Sanctity of Life) are one side; those which do not (Quality of Life) are on the other. Vitalism and Sanctity of Life disagree, of course, as to what that value is, but neither disagrees with the idea that there is value. It seems then that there is not as sharp a divide between the two as Keown would like us to believe. Instead, they are on two sides of a spectrum. Thus, graphically, Keown's formulation of the debate actually looks more like the following:

Vitalism <--> Sanctity of Life / / Quality of Life

If this is the case, then it simply is not possible for any of his stated positions to operate in a middle-ground way. That is because a middle-ground position would have to include elements of the more extreme positions. But, neither Vitalism nor Sanctity of Life can incorporate the essential elements of the Quality of Life position because they are diametrically opposed in relation to the foundational question. More importantly, the question requires either a yes or a no answer in Keown's formulation. So, to summarise, Keown's Sanctity of Life position cannot be a middle ground. This does not mean that Quality of Life is a middle-ground position. It is not a middle ground either. Under the formulation Keown presents, there can be no middle ground.

Perhaps more importantly, this question about the inherent value of life seems difficult to resolve. As stated above, Keown borrows his language about basic goods from John Finnis, who states that there are seven basic goods, one of which is life.[29] However, crucially, Finnis has never provided an argument in support of life as a basic good (or indeed any of the basic goods). Instead, he has stated that they are self-evident.[30] As such, Finnis suggests they are incapable of being proved

---

[29] Finnis, *Natural Law and Natural Rights*, pp. 86–90.
[30] *Ibid.*, p. 69. This particular discussion in *Natural Law and Natural Rights* is about knowledge, but Finnis makes it clear that the concept of self-evidence pertains to all of the basic goods.

because they are first principles.[31] There is therefore nothing prior to these basic goods from which one can construct the premises necessary for an argument supporting them. What he suggests is that anyone thinking rationally will know that these are the basic goods because they, in essence, provide the supporting arguments for themselves.[32] Whatever the merits of Finnis's position in relation to truth about the basic goods, it has not been uncontroversial.[33] There has been much dispute about whether there are basic goods as he describes them, and, even if they are, whether Finnis's list is an accurate one. As long as this concern about Finnis's natural law position is unresolved, then it appears that it will continue to be a problem for Keown as well.[34]

3   The fundamental problem

Even if these concerns could be alleviated, however, there is a much more difficult problem for Keown to resolve. To illustrate that problem, we should consider an example he provides. Keown gives us the example of a 99-year-old, irreversibly and imminently dying patient who has suffered a massive cardio-pulmonary arrest.[35] The issue for the medical staff is whether they should resuscitate this patient. Keown does not give the patient a name (as he does with Agatha and Bertha), but we shall give him the name of Chris. What do the relevant positions say about the resuscitation of Chris?[36] The Quality of Life position would likely hold that Chris should be allowed to die because the value of his remaining time does not outweigh the burdens of that time (which would only be a few hours).[37] The Sanctity of Life position 'would regard such resuscitation as futile because, despite the fact that resuscitation may be physiologically feasible, it would offer no hope of therapeutic benefit to the patient'.[38] Thus, the Sanctity of Life position

---

[31] *Ibid.*   [32] *Ibid.*
[33] See, e.g., M. Kramer, 'What Good is Truth?' (1992) 5 *Canadian Journal of Law and Jurisprudence* 309–319, which discusses some of these issues in relation to the basic good of knowledge.
[34] Keown could, presumably, decide to jettison the Finnis connection and thus Finnis's definition of a basic good. However, were he to do that, Keown would then have to provide us with an argument in support of why life is a basic good.
[35] Keown, 'Restoring the Sanctity of Life and Replacing the Caricature', 112.
[36] By relevant positions, I mean those positions people may actually hold. I am therefore dropping any consideration of what a vitalist might say about Chris.
[37] Keown again gives us no explicit statement about what would be possible under a Quality of Life approach in Chris's case, but it seems likely that at least some would argue that treatment should be withdrawn for the reasons I have specified.
[38] Keown, 'Restoring the Sanctity of Life and Replacing the Caricature', 112.

would also allow for Chris to die. So far there does not seem to be any problems. Now let us compare Chris with Dan. Dan is also a 99-year-old, irreversibly and imminently dying patient who has suffered a massive cardio-pulmonary arrest. The question for the medical staff is also whether to resuscitate Dan. In essence, Dan is exactly like Chris – except for one major difference. Dan has children who live two hours away. They have just been informed about Dan's emergency condition and are travelling as quickly as they can to his bedside to say goodbye. If Dan is resuscitated, then his family would be able to get to his beside in time; if he is not, he will die before they arrive.

Should Dan be treated any differently from Chris? The Quality of Life approach at least provides us with an argument that we can treat him differently. Since the question is about the value of the experiences that Dan has, it may be the case that allowing him (and his family) to have the chance to say goodbye makes his life valuable enough that resuscitation is now the more ethical decision than letting him die.[39] There are, of course, a number of factors which may impact this decision (Dan might not like his children, for example), but the Quality of Life approach at least allows us to consider this new information.[40] Does the Sanctity of Life also allow us to consider this new information? This is more complicated. The decision on whether to provide treatment is dependent on whether the treatment is worthwhile, while not considering whether the patient's life has any worth.[41] We decide whether treatment is worthwhile if it satisfies the purposes of medicine. Keown states there are two purposes to medicine: (1) to restore the patient to a condition of health and well-functioning (or some approximation of it), and (2) when that is no longer possible, to palliate symptoms.[42] Unfortunately, and here is the rub, providing treatment to Dan satisfies neither of those purposes. It does not restore Dan to a condition of health or well-functioning. It certainly does not do so to any greater

---

[39] Price seems to argue for this. He suggests that 'If the patient had a good quality of life in any brief remaining time, one would be obliged to at least consider the benefits of treatment, resource implications aside'. D. Price, 'My View of the Sanctity of Life: A Rebuttal of John Keown's Critique' (2007) 27 *Legal Studies* 549–565, 553.

[40] It will also allow us to decide to what extent we should consider the viewpoint of other people. It may be, for example, that Dan is not particularly bothered about saying goodbye to his children (as he would be dead) but he knows that his children would value that opportunity highly. In such a case, if Dan considers the value that his children would place on the experience to be important to what should happen, then we too should value the impact upon his children. However, if Dan is not concerned about those views, then we should not use the views of his family to override Dan's valuation of the situation.

[41] Keown, *Euthanasia, Ethics and Public Policy*, pp. 40–41.

[42] Keown, 'Restoring the Sanctity of Life and Replacing the Caricature', 113.

extent than it would Chris (who Keown has already said should not be resuscitated). In fact, this is why Keown suggests that the main concern is whether it provides any 'therapeutic benefit' to Chris. Nor does it palliate symptoms. It seems, then, that Keown would have to suggest that the Sanctity of Life doctrine would require that Dan be treated exactly the same as Chris. In other words, that he should not be resuscitated.

Maybe there is another way out of this particular dilemma for Keown. Perhaps he could argue that there are additional purposes to medicine which he had not previously considered or that I have taken too narrow a definition of the ones he has provided. Even if he wished to do so, I do not think that Keown can take that line. The reason is as follows. If we start with the idea that the treatment for Dan is worthwhile (while it is not for Chris), we are left with the question of why. More specifically, what value does it provide to Dan that it would not provide to Chris? It does not extend Dan's life for any longer period than it does Chris. It does not provide palliation of symptoms. All it does is allow his family to reach his bedside in time. In other words, it is not that the treatment provides any greater benefit to Dan at all. What has changed is that the value of that benefit has changed. Those hours *now matter* to Dan in a way they do not to Chris. The treatment is valuable because those additional few hours have value. But, according to Keown, we should not consider the value of the life itself. So, unless he is willing to concede that sometimes (at least) the value of a particular part of a patient's life is an important consideration, he cannot provide a reason to treat Dan differently. If he does that, though, the difference between the Sanctity of Life position and Quality of Life appears to be largely illusory.

The problem seems even more serious when we consider the fact that it does actually appear necessary for us to reach a different decision about Chris and Dan. All that seems to matter is that we consider the cases differently. So, even if we decide that Dan, like Chris, should not be resuscitated, as long as we took the time to consider how this new information impacted the decision, we have considered inappropriate information.

What then is left? Do we all need to accept that the Quality of Life approach is the right one? Are we stuck with accepting that there is no inherent value in existence? Not quite yet. But, to do so, we need to accept that there is a fundamental flaw in Keown's system. Not just in his formulation of the Sanctity of Life position, but in the entire discussion. We need to accept that finding a way out of this problem does not necessitate taking one of his positions at all. How we do so will be considered below.

4   Returning to basics

Let us start our re-examination with a basic statement about the Sanctity of Life position. A standard formulation of that position is as follows: 'It is wrong to intentionally terminate the life of an innocent human being.' From the previous chapter, we would have to change 'human being' to 'moral actor' in conjunction with our full moral status category (it would be as wrong to intentionally kill Einstein, our genetically engineered intelligent dog, as it would a human being), but that can be done with little change to the overall integrity of the statement. That minor change, however, is not the focus of our discussion. As with almost all supposedly simple philosophical statements, most of the words in that sentence are doing a considerable amount of work. The word 'intentionally', for example, provides some justification for Keown's Sanctity of Life position in the first place. It allows him to argue that the removal of life-support systems in cases of futility is not wrong because it is not an 'intentional' termination of life. The purpose of the removal of treatment is not because it kills the patient, but because such treatment provides no benefit. As such, it lacks the intentional element that other potential options (such as assisting a suicide) would have and is therefore acceptable under the principle.[43]

Intention is not the only word in that sentence which requires further discussion. Specifically, we should look at two of the other words in greater detail. The first is the word 'innocent'. Unfortunately, the word is often dropped from the sentence, but that is a great disservice to the role it plays in the ethical principle. Even more unfortunately, there is a considerable problem with the word as it does not have its ordinary meaning. Innocent, thus, does not necessarily have the definition an ordinary member of the moral community would likely give it. Instead, innocent in this context means 'has not given up the right that others ought not to kill him or her'. So, depending on the context, even the most evil person who would not count as innocent in any other context might still be classed as an innocent under this terminology. In fact, those who are not classed as innocent are decidedly narrow. They include those involved in armed conflict, cases of self-defence and execution resulting from a lawful sentence. The specific instances of those who are not classed as innocents may go a long way towards explaining why the word 'innocent' gets left out in discussions about the value of life in medical law and ethics. Simply put, none of them appears to be

---

[43] We will look at this particular distinction based on intention in more detail in Chapter 4, when we discuss the difference between killing and letting die.

relevant. Medical law and ethics are not especially relevant in cases of self-defence, armed conflict or capital punishment.[44] This, however, is too easy a way out. There are reasons why these sorts of actions are acceptable, even if they end in another's death. We could learn a lot from further consideration about why they are acceptable in these cases if not in others. So, merely assuming that because none of the standard categories of innocent cover the sorts of cases which concern us they are thus irrelevant to the discussion may not be the best option.

Be that as it may, there is another important word that requires further examination. That word is 'life'. Out of all of the possible ambiguous words in that sentence, it hardly seems to be top of the list. I want to argue, nevertheless, that 'life' is a very ambiguous word in this context. The ambiguity is also extremely important as, in reality, the debate over the sanctity versus the quality of life is really a debate over the meaning of the word 'life'. How we understand it, then, provides a vital starting point in how we value life. So, we need to consider the different ways in which we might define the concept of life. We can see some of the different ways we define the concept by some of the statements made in the *Bland* case. Some of the judges involved in the case refer either explicitly or otherwise to the idea of Anthony Bland 'being alive' but not 'having a life'. The only way that idea can be something other than gibberish is if we have different ways of defining life. Otherwise, anything which was alive would necessarily have a life. Ronald Dworkin, in *Life's Dominion*, provides us with two possible ways in which we might define life, which he traces back to the Greeks. The first way, which the Greeks called *zoe*, is physical or biological life.[45] The second, called *bios*, means a life as lived.[46] In other words, the 'actions, decisions, motives and events that compose what we now call a biography'.[47] He correlates the biological value of life to 'nature'.[48] The second, which he likens to art, is 'less evident but equally crucial'.[49] As he explains:

---

[44] See, e.g., Keown's dismissal of such concerns in *Euthanasia, Ethics and Public Policy* at p. 40. They are not, of course, completely irrelevant. Doctors and other medical staff may be involved in armed conflict even if only as medical staff and the *UN Convention (I) for the Amelioration of the Condition of the Wounded and Sick in Armed Forces in the Field* sets out the rights and duties of those medical staff. That includes, in Article 22 of the Convention, the right to bear arms and use those arms in self-defence or the defence of those in their care without losing the protection of the Convention. Recently some doctors have also refused to participate in capital punishment in California because of ethical reasons. So, even under these limited cases of 'non-innocence', doctors may still have a vital ethical role, but those discussions are beyond the scope of this chapter and, indeed, this book.
[45] Dworkin, *Life's Dominion*, p. 82.   [46] *Ibid.*, pp. 82–83.
[47] *Ibid.*   [48] *Ibid.*, p. 82.   [49] *Ibid.*

each developed human being is the product not just of natural creation, but also of the kind of deliberate human creative force that we honor in honoring art. A mature woman, for example, is in her personality, training, capacity, interests, ambitions, and emotions, something like a work of art because in those respects she is the product of human creative intelligence, partly that of her parents and other people, partly that our of her culture, and also, through the choices she has made, her *own* creation.[50]

We could also call these two concepts biological life and biographical life.[51]

---

[50] *Ibid* (emphasis in original).

[51] Keown has, on at least two occasions, commented on the formulation presented by Dworkin in *Life's Dominion*. One is a review article of the book published in the *Law Quarterly Review*, (1994) 110 *LQR* 671–675, and the second is in n. 37 of the article 'Restoring Moral and Intellectual Shape to the Law after *Bland*', 493. Keown has presented two main criticisms of Dworkin's position. He asserts that the position Dworkin takes misstates the Sanctity of Life position and also that Dworkin espouses dualism. The first criticism is, as, hopefully, I have shown above, is based upon a misunderstanding of Dworkin's formulation. Dworkin is not presenting an argument within the three-category system Keown espouses and therefore it is not that his formulation misrepresents the Sanctity of Life position as Keown understands it. Instead, Dworkin's formulation is completely outside that system. The second claim is harder to discuss, not least because it is not entirely clear as to the argument Keown is attempting. In the book review, he merely states that 'He [Dworkin] also distinguishes between those with "biological life" and "persons", but the philosophical objections to such dualism are nowhere addressed'. Note 37 provides even less information and merely states that Dworkin 'espouses dualism'. It is part of a section about the *Bland* decision which also indicates the judges are espousing dualism, however, which might give us a better idea of the concern. The concern he has with the judgments made by the various courts in the *Bland* decision is with statements such as Sir Stephen Brown's that '[Anthony Bland's] spirit has left him and all that remains is the shell of his body'. This suggests that Keown is concerned with a mind–body dualism problem (i.e. whether the mind and body are separate things). In Dworkin's argument, the body is 'biological life' and the mind is 'persons'. Dworkin, however, does not require a mind–body dualism. As discussed in the previous chapter, 'person' can often mean not a human being but a moral agent, and it is clear that Dworkin is using it in this way in *Life's Dominion*. As such, it is simply another category to which an entity might belong. Oftentimes, an entity which belongs to one of these categories belongs to the other, but we may have entities which are persons but not humans (such as Einstein) and vice versa. All Dworkin's statement is, then, is an assertion that certain entities, such as Anthony Bland, are humans but not persons. One need not accept mind–body dualism to argue that a particular individual belongs to one category of thing but not to some other category of thing. It would be no different to me maintaining belonging to the category of academic lawyers even if I left my current university employer. Additionally, even those who would strongly argue against mind–body dualism would locate the centre of consciousness in the brain. Those with very severe brain damage (such as Anthony Bland) will therefore have limitations in their consciousness. Of course, this may be so extreme as to mean that the individual in question does not have consciousness at all (again, such as Anthony Bland whose brain had been reduced to a 'mass of watery fluid'). One need not argue for a non-physical mind to argue that a patient such as Anthony Bland has lost consciousness and nothing in Dworkin's argument requires it.

It may seem that this does not get us very far. Biological life is probably not significantly different from the Sanctity of Life position we considered earlier. We can see this if we add the phrase 'biological life' to our statement about the sanctity of life: 'It is wrong to intentionally terminate the biological life of an innocent moral actor.' Likewise, a focus on biographical life probably does not lead us very far from the standard perception about the Quality of Life position. It focuses on 'actions, decisions, motives and events' all of which are important to a Quality of Life judgement. In some ways, it appears that we have just added different synonyms and the same problem remains. Dworkin's formulation, however, has an additional benefit which may not be readily apparent. Under this system of valuing life either biologically or biographically, there is no mutual exclusivity. In other words, it is possible to value life both biologically and biographically and to do so at the same time. In fact, Dworkin asserts that both values are important to what he refers to as the sacredness or inviolability of life. He states: 'That combination of nature and art – two traditions of the sacred – supports the further more dramatic claim that each individual human life, on its own, can be understood as the product of both creative traditions.'[52] The emphasis for Dworkin, then, is that both have value and it is not a case of determining that either *zoe* or *bios* is the only criteria for value but how best to value both when we seek to value life. In other words, we can value something both inherently and instrumentally at the same time. If we think critically about valuing life, we can see how Dworkin can come to this conclusion. Really, all that a belief in the value of biological life means is to think that the statement 'it is valuable (in terms of my life) that I exist' is true. All that a belief in biographical life means is that the statement 'it is valuable (in terms of my life) that I can do X' is true. There is no compelling reason why only one of those statements needs to be true; indeed, there is no reason why one of those statements even needs to be more true than the other one. Our existence matters. It is what allows us to have any experiences at all. It allows us to participate in the universe in some way. Anyone who has watched *It's a Wonderful Life* during the Christmas holidays would be hard pressed to argue that existence does not matter.[53] But just because my existence matters it does not mean that my life is not even more valuable because of the things I am allowed to do because of that existence. The fact that I can do those things I enjoy (read philosophy, give talks and seminars, play

---

[52] Dworkin, *Life's Dominion*, p. 82.
[53] I shall discuss *It's a Wonderful Life* in more detail below for those unfamiliar with the film.

with Sherman, etc.) means that my life has even more value than simply the value of existence. Again, this is easy enough to verify when we consider how much time, money and energy we may expend on things which we feel matter, even if they matter only to us.

If we wanted to look at another way to examine this point, we can consider something else which may have both instrumental and inherent value. While we could probably use any of Finnis's seven basic goods, it may be easiest to focus on friendship. According to Finnis, friendship is one of those things we value whatever else we value.[54] And, at least on its face, it is difficult to disagree. Most of us probably think it is valuable to have friends. We like the idea of friends and, even if we may not be particularly good at developing friendships, we are very likely to see the idea of friendship (even as just an abstract idea) as being valuable. Friendship thus has inherent value. That does not mean, however, that it only has inherent value. Friendships may also have instrumental value, which augments and supports that inherent value. So, while I can agree that friendships generally are valuable, it does not mean that I do not place additional value on certain ones (such as with those friends who can take care of Sherman on those days when I am away). As such, there is no reason why inherent and instrumental values cannot coexist.

If it is true, then, that both statements are true, then we need not accept that Keown has presented all of the possibilities for us. In fact, Dworkin's characterisation appears to offer us a true middle ground between the two possibilities that Keown offers. Thus, we have a way to explore a viewpoint which provides a greater understanding of our ability to accept both of those statements as true. We, consequently, do not have to force our opinions into either side of the sanctity versus quality of life debate because there are a number of other options available to us.

5   A new way of valuing life

What, then, would our new approach to valuing life look like? Well, as stated above, we must first take notice of the fact that existence (or our biological life) is valuable. As a result, our biological life has a value greater than zero.[55] This means that, in general, existence is better than

---

[54] Finnis, *Natural Law and Natural Rights*, p. 88. He also refers to this as sociability.
[55] I want to be clear that while I am going to use a quasi-mathematical approach in this section, it does not mean that I believe our lives can be so easily quantified. It merely happens to be the easiest way to describe how we value life.

non-existence. This value, however, may be modified based upon the life story (or biographical life) which is being told. Because of the differences in life stories that people tell, certain aspects of life will be valued more highly than others and at different points in time during that story. So, there may be aspects to my life which are more important at certain points in the biographical narrative I am telling than they are in others. Most importantly, the value of life for my particular story is determined by the author of that story – me. The story one tells is a personal one and thus decisions made about the value of that story are to be made by the person living it. This is similar to the way that only the author of a novel can decide whether to continue the story or throw it out. We might all decide, of course, not to purchase or read a particular novel, but that cannot stop the author from actually writing it.

From the perspective of this book, the most important aspect of this method for valuing life is how it deals with end-of-life issues. Consequently, it is useful for our purposes to examine in detail how this approach might help us to determine the value of a person's life when it is ending. As stated in the previous paragraph, we would start with the fact that the person's existence has value. It matters that the patient exists. That only gets us part of the way to a conclusion, however, because we must also consider whether there are any modifications to that value. We would thus need to decide on the value of all of the additional elements of the patient's biographical life. This may include (but is not limited to) questions about family that still exist and participate in the patient's life, life projects which have not been fulfilled, personal relationships, events the patient wishes to see happen, so on and so forth. Importantly, though, these additional elements do not have an objective value; the value placed on those elements is the value placed on those elements by the patient. This is vitally important because those things which the rest of us might place minimal value on have a great value to the individual, and those decisions about value are worthy of respect. This will, in a great majority of cases, mean that the value of the patient's life goes up further. By and large, the actions, events, relationships and other things in our life add value, and that does not change when one is dying. In a small number of cases, though, this will not be true and the value of our life will be less than bare existence; in an even smaller number, the value of our life will be worse than not existing at all.[56]

---

[56] Again, we can return to the example of friendship. Even if we agree that friendships in general are valuable, it does not mean that we think all individual friendships are valuable. There may be friendships which are not worthwhile for any number of

To some, such an argument may seem nonsensical. How can non-existence ever be better than existence? Existence is something; non-existence is nothing. If we further explore the concept of our lives as a story, however, things are not that simple. Consider all of the novels, movies, etc. that you may have seen. Some of them are likely to have memorable endings. These memorable endings may be surprise endings or twists in movies, but that does not necessarily have to be the case. Some make the work artistic, turning what might be an ordinary piece into something greater.[57] Others, unfortunately, may lessen the overall value of the work.[58] Some may even go so far as to destroy any value that the work might have had.[59] If the endings of books and movies can have such a large impact on the value of those artistic works, it seems unlikely that the endings of our own lives would not do the same. This can be particularly an issue when we have an ending which goes against everything that has happened previously. This does not mean, of course, that merely because a particular dying process may be at odds with a previous life shows that it should not happen. Deathbed conversions, religious or otherwise, do happen and they can have tremendous value. But the value that has to matter is the value to the individual, even if we are discussing deathbed conversions. Our insistence that a particular series of events, when dying or otherwise, must have a particular value does great disservice to the events that have occurred previously and to the person who has lived them.

All of this leads to the question of what should happen in the case of individuals who are unable to tell us the value they place on their lives. This may include a number of different sorts of problems. We may have cases of people like Anthony Bland who were once capable of giving us information about value but now are not capable of doing

reasons. Finnis, of course, may argue that such friendships are not 'true' friendships but this seems to create further problems for him. First, the fact that a particular friendship may cease to be valuable now does not mean it was not a true one. It may be that the friendship has simply run its course. Furthermore, if comparisons to friendship are correct, then Finnis presumably has to have a concept of 'true' life, another of his basic goods. Ones which are not deemed to be inherently valuable, although there does not appear to be any definitive way to determine which friendships (or lives) are 'true' and which are not. If that is correct, then it seems that this approach will provide less protection than the one I have been suggesting

[57] At least to my individual taste, the movie *The Usual Suspects* is a good example of an artistic work where the ending added considerable worth to the movie as a whole.

[58] Some criticisms of Dostoevsky's *Crime and Punishment* claim the Epilogue for the book detracts from the overall worth of it generally. See, e.g., S. Cassidy, 'The Formal Problem of the Epilogue in "Crime and Punishment": The Logic of Tragic and Christian Failures' (1982) 3 *Dostoevsky Studies* 171.

[59] Most literary or cinematic examples of this type have been deservedly confined to the dustbin.

so. It may also include people in dementia who may be able to give us limited ideas about the value of their life. It may also include those who were never capable of expressing an opinion about the value of their life (such as severely disabled newborns). In all of these cases, gauging the current value of the patient's life will be difficult, but these sorts of cases cannot all be treated exactly the same. In the case of a person like Anthony Bland (who may have been once capable of expressing a view but could not after the Hillsborough disaster), the best option would be to see what indications he might have made in the past about what he would like to see done in such a situation. If that is not possible (as it is in a number of cases, including Anthony Bland himself), things are more difficult but every effort should be made to discern (as much as possible) what the opinion of the patient would have been in such circumstances.[60]

There is an added complication in cases such as those suffering from dementia. These would be cases where the patient may be able to give us limited ideas about the value of their life but it might not be the same as previously (when the patient did not have dementia) and the patient is not likely to be considered competent to make decisions. Thus, we may have a situation where the patient had made statements about the value of his or her life with dementia before having it and this may conflict with the patient's limited expressions about the value of his or her life at the current time. Thus, the question which must be decided is whether to use the (possibly) long-standing commitment to a particular value or to accept a new valuation which might be completely at odds with that view. We, consequently, have a conflict between past and present lives. In such cases, preference should be given to the present life as opposed to previous ones. This is predominately because the past life experiences of a person have ended, while the present ones continue. As such, the present ones receive priority as current decisions will continue to have an impact upon them; they will not have the same impact upon previous experiences.

The final group are those, primarily severely disabled newborns, who have not in the past been capable of expressing an opinion on the value of their lives and will not develop the capability of doing so. In these

---

[60] Again, it may be that here is where the views of others may become important. For example, it may be that Anthony Bland would have had no opinion about living his life in PVS. It may be that he places great value, however, in how his family and friends see him. As such, it may be those views which become important in deciding how best to treat Anthony Bland. What is crucial, however, is that those views are only used to help us construct a best understanding of the story as Anthony Bland would have wanted it to be told, not necessarily the story others may have wanted.

cases, it is impossible to find out what sort of value the individual would have placed on his or her life. Nor is it even really possible to guess what kind of value the individual might have placed on his or her life. There is simply no information available to us about how the individual patient values anything. In these cases, it seems morally best to treat the patient as being morally worthwhile and worthy of respect, but that the value of the life of these individuals is likely to be determined by other methods. In such cases, we are required (as there are no other available options) to treat the patient without any true reference to the biographical value which that individual might place on his or her life. This will generally mean the patient is treated by proxy. In other words, others such as parents or medical staff will likely make any decision about treatment based upon the values they believe that the life of the newborn has. While this may seem like an overall abdication of responsibility, it is important to realise that the patient is still considered to be morally worthwhile under the principles developed in the previous chapter. In addition, other important ethical principles that we will discuss in subsequent chapters will also come into play. So, while the way we value life may not create concrete solutions in the case of those who could not and will not be able to value their own life, there will still be significant ethical principles which can be used to guarantee that those individuals are treated with respect.

6   Benefits of the new approach

One of our primary concerns when discussing these ethical claims has been the value of such claims to those who have to make these sorts of decisions. As a consequence, it behooves us to discuss the possible benefits of the new approach I have been considering. It is not necessarily any simpler to apply than any of the three categories Keown has previously considered. Conversely, it may end up being more complex and difficult to apply than the three categories. This does not mean that there are not significant benefits to the approach, however. First, it may be a more accurate representation of at least some of the actual viewpoints of actual members of the moral community. Such statements can be hard to verify without empirical support. Without some sort of questionnaire response, it is difficult to gauge how many individuals hold a particular view. Instead, what often happens is that philosophers may use words like 'many' to indicate a significant number without having to provide any empirical data to substantiate that view. I am not going to try to substantiate the view that the approach I have presented is a majority one. I do believe that at least a substantial number of people would agree with the position, but I do not have the empirical data to verify that.

The point I wish to make is a more limited one. I have, hopefully, shown previously that it is logically consistent to hold that both biological and biographical life have value. I now want to make the point that it is not only a logically possible position to hold but that at least some people actually do hold this position. Those whom I am particularly concerned with are the judges involved in the *Bland* decision. Keown has long criticised the judges for misunderstanding the Sanctity of Life position.[61] If one follows his articulation of that position, then Keown and others are correct. The position the judges take in the case does not follow his formulation of the Sanctity of Life position. However, I do not believe the position of the judges was actually an attempt at that position. Instead, the fact that the judges did indicate a belief that life was intrinsically valuable but still thought that Anthony Bland 'had no life' is an indication that their position seems more akin to the one I have presented here. Additionally, one of the judges, Lord Hoffman, makes specific mention of having been influenced by Dworkin's *Life's Dominion*.[62] If, as I have suggested, Dworkin's argument about the value of life is entirely outside the three-category system Keown develops, then it seems more likely that Hoffman's approach, which does not appear substantially different from any of the other judges, is more likely to be something similar to what I have presented here. If this is true, then the approach I have provided is not just logically possible, but one that others, including judges, have actually used in making ethical and/or legal decisions. This more nuanced approach to valuing life (the Sanctity of Life and Quality of Life positions addressed by Keown would be merely at the end of the spectrum under this approach, not eliminated entirely) would thus provide us with a more consistent approach to valuing life which would allow us to address the views of ordinary members of the moral community without distorting their views.

Additionally, a benefit of this new approach will address issues about the protections afforded by our principles for valuing life. One of the criticisms of the Sanctity of Life position that Keown articulates is that it protects too much, in the sense that it keeps those alive when there seems to be little benefit for doing so. My concerns are actually the opposite – I believe that Keown's Sanctity of Life position protects too little. An explanation for that is most likely in order. Keown's Sanctity of Life position only really protects one's existence. It has to do that

---

[61] Keown, 'Restoring Moral and Intellectual Shape to the Law after *Bland*'.
[62] *Airedale NHS Trust* v. *Bland* [1993] All ER 821 at 851.

because, quite simply, that is its only requirement. Once you are alive, you are guaranteed protection of your existence but additional qualities provide no added benefits or protections. While that may create some benefits, it also creates certain problems. If your existence is the only thing that is protected, then it is possible to remove everything but your existence without falling foul of the principle.[63] Thus, if we were to think about the common science fiction plot device where an individual's consciousness is either suppressed (such as in *The Matrix* trilogy where human beings are used as batteries) or supplanted (such as in Peter Hamilton's *Night's Dawn* trilogy where the dead possess the bodies of living human beings), we could have a situation where an individual still exists but nothing else. The actions of the interlopers do not appear to violate the Sanctity of Life principle articulated by Keown. If we are looking for a less science fiction example, we could imagine the situation where an individual is placed in a coma, reducing their life to bare existence. Again, it does not appear as if it would violate Keown's Sanctity of Life principle. We could, of course, bolt on ideas such as autonomy, dignity or self-determination which would provide ways to argue that those actions are wrong, but there is nothing inherent in the Sanctity of Life principle which does so. Additionally, supplementing the value of life with additional principles does not necessarily resolve the dispute, as any time there is more than one principle in play, they are almost guaranteed to conflict at some point. Furthermore, it is worth mentioning that when they do conflict, Keown seems to subvert them all to the Sanctity of Life principle anyway.[64] So, even if there are possible additions, they look like they would generally lose out.

Those who are not particularly interested in hypothetical situations or examples pulled from science fiction are likely to wonder whether the whole concern is not simply meaningless. As far as we are aware, we are not living as batteries to some conspiracy from machines, the dead are not coming back to life to control our bodies and we do not routinely put people into comas for no particular reason. There is a more fundamental point at the heart of this concern and that point is uniqueness. If only my existence is protected, then there does not appear to be anything which protects my uniqueness as an individual. There is,

---

[63] I am not suggesting that Keown would necessarily agree with this assessment. However, it seems to me to be the logical extension of his views on the value of life.

[64] For example, Keown argues that the autonomous decisions which are 'immoral' are not worthy of moral respect. *Euthanasia, Ethics and Public Policy*, pp. 53–54. We shall discuss how even immoral choices (or those deemed to be immoral by others) which are autonomous can be worthy of respect in Chapter 5.

in fact, no individual at all – just an entity which exists.[65] There is, then, no protection for *me* as a unique individual. Again, because this is the fundamental test for the Sanctity of Life position, it is all it can protect, even if we wish it could do more. So, there is no protection for my experiences, my relationships, my interests, my plans – anything which allows me to be a unique individual instead of some blank example of 'human'. None of those things which have contributed to making my life unique have any value to this approach; indeed, they cannot possibly have any value. To see why this is important, though, let us return to the movie example I used to show that existence matters: *It's a Wonderful Life*. The movie, for those who have not seen it, deals with the question of the value of one human life, in this case, the life of George Bailey. George Bailey runs a building and loan company in the small town of Bedford Falls. When his uncle loses $8,000 of the company's money (the movie was set shortly after the Second World War), George contemplates suicide. The only reason he does not is that Clarence, an angel sent down to help George, appears (well, falls into a river and needs saving). George wishes to Clarence, his guardian angel, that he had never been born. Clarence then shows George what life would have been like had he not been. What is crucial, however, is how Clarence goes about showing George how much his life matters. He does not do so by attempting to compare the difference to George between existence and non-existence.[66] Instead, what he does is to show George a series of events – those things that would have happened to his family, friends and town without him. So, he is shown the grave of his brother who died because George is not there to save him; he is shown his wife Mary's life as a bitter spinster because George does not marry her; he is shown Bedford Falls turned into a sleazy slum named

---

[65] There is an additional point that needs to be considered about Keown's formulation. Because there is no value to the uniqueness of a morally relevant individual, we need a clear idea of what counts as a morally relevant individual. Otherwise, all things which might have moral relevance should be treated equally. Unfortunately, all Keown has ever presented us with is a short footnote in an article in the *Law Quarterly Review* where he states that 'This is not the place to canvass the important reasons for distinguishing human from other animal life' (Keown, 'Restoring Moral and Intellectual Shape to the Law after *Bland*', 483). This will, however, create substantial problems if there are different accounts of moral worth. One may agree with Keown's Sanctity of Life principle but decide that his idea of moral worth is incorrect. So, if one were to believe that sentience is the only relevant criteria for moral worth, we would have a situation where the existence of a worm is the same as the existence of a human being. At the very least, we need a more considered version of moral worth, which has not been provided.

[66] Clarence could, for instance, have shown George what non-existence would have entailed.

Pottersville by the evil Mr Potter because he is not there to oppose him. What Clarence does, then, is show George the impact he has had on the lives of people and how much he needs to be around. Now, part of this is that George Bailey has to be born – he has to exist. But what Clarence shows him is more complex than that. It is not just that a George Bailey has to exist. It is *this* George Bailey that has to exist. A George who had let his brother drown or had failed to marry his wife or had left Bedford Falls to seek his fame and fortune (as George had actually wanted to do) will not suffice. It is the George Bailey that he has become that is so important. That is why, at the end of the movie, George Bailey is returned, not to the life he might have wanted, but to the one where he is already.[67] Keown's Sanctity of Life only provides protection for the life of *a* George Bailey. What we need instead is protection for *this* George Bailey.[68] That can be supplied by the approach I have provided. Consequently, the Sanctity of Life principle as put forth by Keown actually provides us with too little protection. It does not provide sufficient reason to protect the experiences, relationships and interests that are so important to our lives.

We can see this further if we look back at Keown's example of Agatha, Bertha and Chris. While I have not directly quoted the passages from the articles those examples are taken from, I have not left out any information. Which is a large part of the problem. What do we actually know about these three people? We know Agatha is a newborn child born with Down syndrome and an intestinal blockage. We do not really have any further information about her. As all three schools of thought would appear to argue for treating Agatha, it may not be a particular problem. However, there may be additional facts which are important to our considerations. We seem to know even less about Bertha. We know she has a respiratory problem and current breathing difficulties. But that is it. There is more to learn about everyone, even newborn children. What, for example, is Bertha's reaction when her parents are in the room? Does she seem to derive pleasure from their presence in the way the severely disabled newborn child did in *An NHS*

---

[67] Compare what happens to George Bailey to what happens to Marty McFly in *Back to the Future*, for example.

[68] It is true that part of the appeal of the film is that the things which George Bailey ultimately values are things we believe he ought to value. The nature of the film changes if Mr Potter is the main character. What is important to realise, though, is that Value of Life questions do not end our ethical inquiry. They just tell us the value that the individual places on his or her life. It may be that there are compelling ethical (or legal) reasons why, even if a person values a particular life, we should not let someone lead that life. We will consider some of those concerns in later chapters.

Trust v. *MB*?[69] Does she consistently seem to defy the prognosis of doctors as Charlotte Wyatt seems to do?[70] We know none of this information, even though cases in law have sometimes turned on these sorts of facts. Finally, we seem to know the least about Chris, despite the fact he would have a more extensive life story than either Agatha or Bertha. We do not even know his name. We do not know if he has any family (it may be, for example, that there is no difference between him and Dan); we know nothing about his life plans, what he has accomplished, his hopes, dreams or anything else which is specifically relevant to him. We do not even know what Chris wants as far as cardio-pulmonary resuscitation. It may be that this is all moot because Chris has a signed advance directive refusing treatment in such a situation. That may not be the case, but it is information we ought to have in front of us when making the decision.

One response to this concern may be to argue that these are examples provided in articles. They are not going to be able to provide us with all of the information that we might have available to us in a real-life situation. In some senses, there can be no argument to such a response. I have not told you everything I could about Sherman. I have not mentioned anything about his history, his breed or even what colour fur he has. But that only further illustrates the problem with Keown's examples. I have not given you any further information about Sherman because those facts are not relevant to our purposes. It does not matter whether Sherman is a pure-breed dog or a mix between Black Labrador and Staffordshire Bull Terrier. It does not matter whether his fur is black or not. Those facts are not relevant to why Sherman is important for our discussions. But, Chris's life story is relevant. It is important to know those things about Chris, Agatha and Bertha. We are deciding whether to end those lives. We ought to know more than a bare minimum about them when we do so. The reason we do not, of course, is because those facts are not relevant to how Keown's schools of thought deal with these issues. But, they are (or at least can be) important to the courts. And, as we have seen by examining the difference between Chris and Dan, they may be important to our decision-making systems as well. Any school of thought which fails to take these into account cannot provide us with the answers we will desperately need when we have to make these decisions in real-life situations.

---

[69] *An NHS Trust* v. *MB* [2006] EWHC 507 (Fam.). It should be noted that David Price uses this case for similar purposes. See 'My View of the Sanctity of Life', 555.
[70] *Wyatt* v. *Portsmouth NHS Trust* [2005] EWCA Civ 1181, [2005] 3 F.C.R. 263.

The importance of this sort of approach can be best shown by examining questions surrounding those with disabilities. It has long been argued that the Quality of Life approach ends up being biased against those with disabilities. No doubt this viewpoint has been fuelled by the comments of some of the biggest proponents of a Quality of Life position, such as Peter Singer or John Harris, both of whom have advocated that newborns with disabilities can be killed based only on their disability.[71] Consequently, it is argued that the Sanctity of Life position needs to be taken to protect those with disabilities. Some may wonder whether the approach I have championed here will provide support for those with disabilities or whether it would also advocate a position which provided a lesser value for those lives. I would argue that the position I have supported here will in fact provide stronger protection for those with disabilities than either of the other positions. This is due not only to the focus on the life story of the individual, but to the fact that the value of that life story is determined by the individual him or herself. This emphasis on value to the individual means that decisions are not made for the patient based upon notions of value which are not shared by the patient. Instead, it is the value that life has to the patient which determines the worth of particular treatment. It is thus not a situation, like the one with Chris, where we can avoid knowing what the individual thinks about his illness, treatment options and life in general. We must know and, more importantly, we must consider that viewpoint to be our primary concern, meaning that those with disabilities will be best suited to determine the value of their own existence. It is therefore not a situation where those with disabilities will have their lives devalued because others would not want to live their lives in that way.

Consistent with this idea is the benefit that the approach I have outlined above sits better with other values which we find important. It is more mutually complementary with notions of autonomy and dignity, both of which will be considered in more detail in subsequent chapters. It does so because notions of dignity and autonomy are wrapped up in the notions of a biographical life. These are aspects of the idea that one's life has meaning because of what one does with it, not merely because one exists.

7   Conclusion

Questions about the value we place on the lives of morally relevant beings are vitally important to our moral considerations. It is even more

---

[71] See Singer and Kuhse, *Should the Baby Live?*; Harris, *The Value of Life*.

important when we consider how best to respect those beings which are at the end of life. Treatment and other options provide a multitude of choices, not all of which are appropriate in every case. When we make these sorts of determinations, it is necessary to have a valid system for determining the value of lives. Our lives are valuable; they are also difficult to quantify. There are so many choices, so many life plans which we can either contribute to or partake of which make it nearly impossible to determine in advance what kind of life is most valuable. But, the biggest mistake we can make in these types of cases is to try to simplify matters too much. Life is inherently valuable. Life is also valuable because of all of the things that go into it. It behoves us, then, to find a system for valuation which takes account of all of these different things. I have attempted to provide a system here which does so and, in so doing, have hopefully provided us with a way to value life in all of its forms.

But that does not end our ethical journey. There are still a number of other ethical principles which will need to be considered, examined and analysed before we can properly decide on the ethical way to deal with decisions at the end of life.

4 Killing versus letting die and moral responsibility

1   Introduction

When considering which end-of-life decisions to allow and which to prohibit, one concern which seems to have always created controversy is the distinction between those deaths which are referred to as killings and those which are referred to as ones where the doctors and medical staff let the patient die. These concerns are not only limited to end-of-life decision-making concerns but also include other moral problems such as abortion and whether and how much we ought to give to charity. Despite this, no real consensus has emerged about this distinction between killing and letting die. Indeed, if anything, the debate appears to be even more polarised at this point.

This is unfortunate as the difference between killing and letting die (if there is one) will be a crucial factor when deciding which actions doctors should take at the end of life. However, in order to properly determine its value, we need clarification about the distinction in the first place. This chapter, then, will explore the concepts of killing and letting die to see if any real distinguishing features exist between them. This will mean an examination of ideas used to ground that distinction including the contrast between acts and omissions and the one between intention and foresight. The purpose of this will be to be able to come to some conclusions about whether there is any real way to distinguish morally between killing and letting die and, if so, in what cases that distinction matters.

One possibility which should be discounted at the start (at least for now) is that the difference between killing and letting die is based upon their use as semantic categories. In other words, those actions which we disapprove of go into the category called 'killing'. Those which we want to allow go into the category called 'letting die'. If this is the case, then there is nothing about the distinction between killing and letting die which accounts for our permissiveness about these actions. Instead, they are only shorthand for conclusions we have reached prior to their determination as a 'killing' or a 'letting die'.[1] While it may be that this is the conclusion we ultimately reach, it is worth exploring the idea of more principled distinguishing criteria between the two categories before accepting their use as only a semantic distinction.

2   The act/omission distinction

The first possible relevant difference between killing and letting die is the one between acts and omissions.[2] Killings are morally prohibited, so the argument goes, because they result from an action, whereas one only omits to act when letting someone die. We are more morally responsible for those actions we commit than those things we simply fail to do. As such, killing is morally prohibited (in most circumstances) but letting someone die is not. Philosophers, when discussing this possibility, will sometimes refer to it as the difference between doing and allowing.[3]

As an initial claim, this has some appeal. We do normally consider that we are morally responsible for our actions but that we cannot be held to be morally responsible for those things we do not do (at least in the absence of other duties). This can be true even if the results of our actions/inactions are the same. For example, we would not normally consider it morally wrong to fail to send a sum of money to a charity which would, in turn, save the lives of a certain number of disadvantaged persons. However, if instead of sending money, we sent some sort of poison which killed the same number of people, we would be considered morally bad.[4] At first glance, then, this appears to be promising.

---

[1] One example of this appears to be the decision of the House of Lords in *Bland*. The actions of the doctors in the case are considered to be a letting die even though the Lords admit that their actions fit within the category of things we normally consider to be acts. Additionally, at least one of the Lords (Lord Goff) admits the problems their decision might cause with an unlawful interloper. *Airedale NHS Trust* v. *Bland* [1993] 1 All ER 868 [per Lord Goff].

[2] Sometimes when we discuss omissions, we do not mean all things which might be classified as 'not doing something'. Instead, we limit the discussion about omissions to those things where we could have done something which would have impacted upon the result. However, for the purposes of this chapter, I will be using omission to include all instances where we have not done something regardless of whether we could have influenced the result. The reasons for this will, hopefully, become clear in section 5.

[3] See, e.g., P. Foot, 'The Problem of Abortion' (1967) *Oxford Review* No. 5, reprinted in B. Steinbock and A. Norcross (eds.), *Killing and Letting Die* (2nd edn) (New York: Fordham University Press, 1994), pp. 266–279; P. Foot, 'Killing and Letting Die', in J. L. Garfield and P. Hennessey (eds.), *Abortion: Moral and Legal Perspectives* (Amherst, MA: University of Massachusetts Press, 1984), pp. 177–185.

[4] This is a standard example in the philosophical literature. See, e.g., Foot, 'Killing and Letting Die', p. 177; Unger, *Living High and Letting Die*. It is worth emphasising,

Unfortunately, that promise disappears quite quickly. First, the difference between an act and an omission may be more difficult than we originally think. An example in the philosophical literature provides us with an illustration.[5] Suppose we have someone sitting in a chair in a particular room. The dust in the room has been designed to work with a certain explosive. If the person stays perfectly still, then the dust will settle in such a way as to diffuse the bomb and no one will be hurt. However, if the person moves in any way, then the bomb will go off and many people will be hurt or killed. It could be argued that the person staying still for long enough is failing to act and therefore allowing the dust to settle. On the other hand, if the person does move, then that person has acted. Others might disagree and would point to the fact that, if the person had to struggle to remain still, then that person has acted.[6] Alternatively, if, because of a spasm, the individual in question moved without volition, then it would not be a case of doing.

This may be an overstatement of the problem as it is created only because of the addition of other facts which are not part of the original hypothetical. Adding a factor of having to struggle to remain motionless is a different scenario than simply sitting still and the original hypothetical only involved the latter. Nor does a spasm necessarily correspond to a 'normal' moving of the arm. The difference would seem to be some concern about what we would generally call effort. If I do not move (such as when I am asleep) and it takes no effort, then it would be hard to say that I have done anything. If, however, I have to concentrate and strive to remain still, then it seems more problematic to claim that I have done nothing. Instead, I appear to have exerted effort and the process of staying still becomes something closer to an action, despite what it may be normally. It would seem that in order to properly understand the difference between 'doing' and 'allowing', we need to consider them based not only on whether something has been done or not, but whether there was effort in the doing of something or not. So, an act becomes a situation where we have done something with an

though, that not all would see these as being morally different. See, e.g., Unger, *Living High and Letting Die*; P. Singer, 'Famine, Affluence and Morality' (1972) 1 *Philosophy and Public Affairs* 229–243.

[5] The basic example comes from J. Bennett, 'Morality and Consequences', in *The Tanner Lectures on Human Values II* (Salt Lake City, UT: University of Utah Press, 1981), pp. 66–68. Bennett himself does not add the explosion. That is added by W. S. Quine in his article 'Actions, Intentions and Consequences: The Doctrine of Doing and Allowing' (1989) 98 *Philosophical Review* 287–312, reprinted in Steinbock and Norcross (eds.), *Killing and Letting Die*, pp. 355–382.

[6] Bennett in fact appears to take this view. J. Bennett, 'Negation and Abstention: Two Theories of Allowing' (1993) 104 *Ethics* 75–96, reprinted in Steinbock and Norcross (eds.), *Killing and Letting Die*, pp. 230–256, 247–248.

exercise of effort, whereas an omission is a case where we have not done something or have exercised no effort in the doing of something (like in the case of a spasm).

Even if this sorted out the definitional problem between 'doing' and 'allowing' (and I am not convinced that it does), there are additional concerns which are more significant. The most significant concern is that the difference between doing and allowing does not appear to create a difference in every case. Again, we can point to an example from the philosophical literature to illustrate this. In his seminal article, 'Active and Passive Euthanasia',[7] James Rachels presents the following hypothetical considering two similar cases:

In the first, Smith stands to gain a large inheritance if anything should happen to his six-year-old cousin. One evening while the child is taking his bath, Smith sneaks into the bathroom and drowns the child and then arranges things so that it will look like an accident.

In the second, Jones also stands to gain if anything should happen to his six-year-old cousin. Like Smith, Jones sneaks in planning to drown the child in his bath. However, just as he enters the bathroom, Jones sees the child slip and hit his head, and fall face down in the water. Jones is delighted; he stands by, ready to push the child's head back under if it is necessary, but it is not necessary. With only a little thrashing about, the child drowns all by himself, 'accidentally' as Jones watches and does nothing.[8]

Rachels asks if we really think that Smith's actions are worse than Jones, merely because Smith has 'killed' his cousin while Jones has '"merely" let the child die'.[9] In other words, Smith has acted while Jones has allowed something to happen. If this difference between doing and allowing was important, then it should lead to a discernible difference between Smith and Jones's actions. But Rachels believes that we would not come to this conclusion. For example, if their actions became known, Jones should be able to rely on the following defence: 'After all, I didn't do anything except stand there and watch the child drown. I didn't kill him; I only let him die.'[10] Rachels considers this 'a grotesque perversion

---

[7] Rachels, 'Active and Passive Euthanasia', 79. The specific target of Rachels' article is a statement made by the American Medical Association House of Delegates on 4 December 1973, which approved of the distinction between active and passive euthanasia (or, in our terminology, the difference between active euthanasia and the withdrawal/withholding of medical treatment). Some of the criticisms made of the article are on the basis that Rachels' hypothetical is not actually analogous to the statement made by the Delegates. See, e.g., Steinbock, 'The Intentional Termination of Life'. Considering the focus of this chapter is on the distinction between killing and letting die and not the specific statement involved, we shall not consider those concerns.

[8] Rachels, 'Active and Passive Euthanasia', 79.

[9] *Ibid.*   [10] *Ibid.*

of moral reasoning'.[11] Jones, then, is not any better than Smith because fortuitous events intervened which made his actions unnecessary. He still wanted his cousin dead. He was ready to do something in case he needed to. In such a case, to assert that he should not be considered morally responsible for the death of his cousin because his body did not move in a particular manner seems to be deciding that form matters more than function.

Consequently, the contrast between acts and omissions (or between doing and allowing) cannot ground the difference between killing and letting die. All omissions are not better (in some moral sense) than all acts. This is not to deny that it may sometimes provide distinguishing criteria as it does with the cases of failing to contribute to charity and sending poison detailed at the beginning of this section. But, as it does not provide a reason to differentiate them in every case, it does not appear sufficient, on its own, to ground a moral distinction between killing and letting die.

3   Intention and foresight

If the difference between doing and allowing is insufficient to create a reason for distinguishing between killing and letting die, there are other possibilities which have been proposed. One of the most important can be derived from the Smith and Jones hypothetical that Rachels presents. The argument is that while the act/omission distinction cannot create an explanation for our moral reasoning in these two cases, there is one if we look at some other possibilities. In both Smith and Jones's case, the individual in question *intended* to drown the child. It is this intention which creates the moral responsibility and thus explains why we do not consider Jones to be any better morally than Smith. On the other hand, if we consider the failing to contribute to the charity/ poisoning example above, a failure to contribute to a charity does not normally include an intention to kill disadvantaged individuals, whereas sending them poison (provided there is knowledge that one is sending poison) does include such an intention. Instead, a failure to contribute to charity may be done with the foreseeability that it will have adverse affects for others, but that is not what we intend when we throw away the letter instead of sending in our money. So, it is claimed that the distinction between killing and letting die is based not on the contrast between acts and omissions, but between those things we intend and those which we only foresee.[12]

---

[11] *Ibid.*
[12] See, e.g., J. Finnis, 'A Philosophical Case against Euthanasia', pp. 28–30.

We can begin a more detailed exploration by looking at one of the standard examples used to highlight this difference.[13] Suppose I decide one night to go out with friends and drink alcoholic beverages to excess. I intend to drink and have a good time with friends. I may even intend to get drunk. I do not intend, however, to get a hangover the next morning, despite the fact that it is the foreseeable result of my actions the previous evening. It may even be foreseeable to a virtual certainty (e.g. I always have a hangover if I have a certain amount of drinks or drink a certain beverage). Thus, my drunkenness may be intentional; my resulting hangover is not, but is only foreseeable.

While this simple example may provide us with a clear way of differentiating between intention and foresight, it creates problems that need to be addressed if this is going to ground our claims about the distinction between killing and letting die. First, it is far from clear that this creates the moral difference that we need. I may not have intended my hangover, but it does not seem that I can avoid moral responsibility for it.[14] If my hangover were to cause me to miss a meeting on the subsequent morning, my protesting that 'I'm not responsible for missing the meeting – I had a hangover' is unlikely to lead to any sympathy or exoneration. Instead, I am likely to be told that it is my own fault that I have a hangover and that it is not a sufficient excuse for missing the meeting. If I were to further protest and explain that I had not *intended* to get a hangover (and thus should not be responsible for it), I am unlikely to get any further. It is likely to be explained to me that, despite my intentions to the contrary, I am responsible for all of the reasonable results of my actions even if they are only foreseen and not intended. It is therefore not clear that intention and foresight, then, do the necessary work that we need them to do.

Even if this particular problem can be overcome, there are additional matters that need to be addressed. We need, for example, to figure out what we mean by intention and how to reliably determine what an individual intends. The common approach seems to be to assume that there is one intention that results in a particular action and that all other thoughts/beliefs/feelings regarding the actions are secondary to that. If we pay close attention, it appears that it may be more complex than this. As Timothy Quill suggests, our intentions 'may be complex, ambiguous and often contradictory'.[15] Quill is a New York doctor who came

[13] J. Harris, 'The Philosophical Case against the Philosophical Case against Euthanasia', p. 37.
[14] *Ibid.*
[15] T. Quill, 'The Ambiguity of Clinical Intentions' (1993) 329 *New England Journal of Medicine* 1039–1040, reprinted in Battin *et al.* (eds.), *Death, Dying and the Ending of Life*, vol. II, pp. 15–16.

to prominence (at least in the field of medical ethics and end-of-life decision-making) when he prescribed barbiturates for a dying patient who he called Diane so that she could end her life, and then wrote about his experiences in the *New England Journal of Medicine*.[16] As an exercise afterwards, he considered why he prescribed that medication for his patient. He did not come up with one but, instead, listed six distinct reasons. These are everything from 'to relieve her pain and suffering' to 'to cause her death (to kill her)' to 'to cause her to die alone'.[17] Quill, then, describes having a number of intentions in relation to his action. Some of them he considered laudable; others he did not.[18] But he considered all of them together to be indicative of what he meant to do when he prescribed barbiturates for Diane.

What are we to make of this assertion? There is not one coherent intention in the case. What he considered to be his true reasons constitute a multi-layered complex notion of several different, more precise intentions. If this is true of many of our decisions, what becomes the operative intention for our purposes? It seems to me that there can be several possibilities. First, we may decide that as long as one of the list of possible choices is wrongful, then the whole action is wrongful. So, in Timothy Quill's case, the fact that he intended to cause her death (if that is an unlawful intention) overrides any of the others he had which would be lawful (such as to relieve her pain and suffering). This, though, does not seem to take enough account of the different intentions that the individual has. Second, we may consider the reverse. We may decide that as long as there is one justifiable intention, then it overrides any unjustifiable ones. So, since Timothy Quill intended to relieve her pain and suffering, it does not matter if he also meant to cause her death. The action is acceptable morally. This seems to be an unsatisfactory decision for the same reasons as the first option. Despite his other reasons or motivations, Timothy Quill did intend to cause her death. If this is wrongful, then it should be considered as such, whatever else he might have intended in the process. If neither of these two seems like a sufficient option, we may attempt to come up with some sort of weighting scale and take what is considered to be the most significant intention of the individual – in other words, the one for which they would not have gone through with the action. The difficulty with this option is that it is by no means clear that we would be able

---

[16] See T. Quill, 'Death and Dignity: A Case of Individualized Decision Making' (1991) 324 *New England Journal of Medicine* 691–694.

[17] Quill, 'The Ambiguity of Clinical Intentions', 16.

[18] He mentions that the intention to 'cause her to die alone' was one he found particularly troubling and that it 'still haunts' him. *Ibid.*

to weigh up the intentions of individuals in this manner. For example, Quill himself seems to see the intention 'to relieve her pain and suffering' as most important, at least if his ordering is done on importance.[19] However, in considering the intention to cause her death (which is third in his list) he asks why he prescribes barbiturates instead of some other drug. As he indicates, 'there are safer drugs for sleep'.[20] Indeed, part of the problem with intentions in a case such as this may depend on how we designate the action in question. Is his action the prescription of pain-relieving drugs or is it the prescription of barbiturates? How we answer that particular question may go a long way to determining what we think his primary intention might have been. If it is the prescription of pain-relieving drugs, then it would seem that his primary intention was the relief of pain. If it is specific pain-relieving drugs (in this case, barbiturates), then we may consider his intention to be something completely different. This, then, seems to be no closer to giving us a useful method of determining intention. A final possibility may be to consider the different aims of the individual and try to weigh them up together to gain some sort of overall moral value to the intentions of the individual. To do this, however, we need a method and nothing appears to be certain to work. Do we consider the different weights that the individual may have put on their separate intentions? Do sheer numbers matter or not? How do we weigh and compare intentions in the first place? These questions (and undoubtedly a number of others) would have to be answered before this method of determining intention would be useful.

Two additional problems exist for this distinction in a medical context. The first has been put forward by Alastair Norcross about a further example provided by Rachels. Rachels' hypothetical provides us with two doctors – Dr White and Dr Black.[21] Both doctors are faced with a neonate who is receiving certain treatment which both doctors believe should be withdrawn. Dr White wants to cease treatment because he does not believe that the treatment is worthwhile and he thinks that continuing the treatment will lead to more suffering for the child. In the parlance we are dealing with, Dr White foresees the death of the neonate resulting from the withdrawal of treatment but does not intend it. Dr Black also wants to remove the treatment, but does so with the intention that the child die. Under the intention/foreseeability distinction we

---

[19] *Ibid.*   [20] *Ibid.*

[21] The example of Dr Black and Dr White comes from J. Rachels, 'More Impertinent Distinctions and a Defense of Active Euthanasia', in T. A. Mappes and J. S. Zembaty (eds.), *Biomedical Ethics* (New York: McGraw Hill, 1981), pp. 355–359, reprinted in Steinbock and Norcross (eds.), *Killing and Letting Die*, pp. 139–154, 141–142.

have been considering, Dr White's actions would be morally acceptable but Dr Black's actions would not be. But, both of them do exactly the same action. Both cease treating the infant. It seems very strange that the identical actions are now considered to be morally different.

The greater problem, from Norcross's position, however, is how we examine the case from the infants' perspective.[22] Actually, to make the hypothetical more understandable, let us assume that the patients are not infants but ones capable of expressing a view about their treatment. We now have a situation where Dr White is permissibly ceasing the treatment of the patient in his/her care, but that Dr Black cannot permissibly cease treatment of his/her patient. What if the patient cared for by Dr Black asks why this is the case? Why must he or she suffer while the patient in the next bed, cared for by Dr White, receives better care? The only answer we could presumably give the patient is that of bad luck – the patient cared for by Dr Black is not entitled to the treatment given to Dr White's patient due, not to anything relating to the patient, but to the mental state of Dr Black. If Dr Black had a different mental state, then the treatment would be fine; if Dr White were the doctor for our patient, then the treatment would be fine. But since neither of those things are true, the patient is stuck with being treated by Dr Black in a manner which neither Dr Black nor the patient seem to want.[23]

Practically, this seems to be an incredibly bad result. When we encounter this situation, we will need a method for determining what the individual intended to do. Presumably, we will have to go on what they tell us. In that scenario, presumably Dr Black will learn to keep his or her true intentions quiet and *pretend* to have the same intention as Dr White.[24] Morally, the answer reached here appears no better. In this case, we appear to be punishing the patient in Dr Black's care (assuming, of course, that the patient would see the continuation of treatment as being something bad) for something that his or her doctor did.

Furthermore, we may question why it is the doctor's intention that matters in these cases anyway. The patient is likewise going to have an intention, at least in those cases where the patient is able to express a view. Consider the following example. Suppose we have a patient who

---

[22] A. Norcross, 'Introduction to the Second Edition', in Steinbock and Norcross (eds.), *Killing and Letting Die*, pp. 1–23, 8.

[23] *Ibid.*

[24] *Ibid.* Practical concerns are really the purview of the second part of this book. It is useful to remember, however, that ethical decisions we make are likely to have practical implications even if we are only considering those practical effects which are non-legal. In this case, for example, one of the results of this particular method would seem to be a chance of increased deception as Dr Black now seems to have a greater impetus for concealing the truth about his or her intentions.

is ventilator-dependent. That patient asks for the ventilator to be withdrawn. In discussing the options with the doctor, the patient further explains that the reason for the request is that the patient wants to die and the patient is confident that, if the ventilator is withdrawn, he or she will suffocate to death. It is then possible to question what impact the patient's statement has on the morality of the act in question. We could suggest that it changes the morality of the action as at least one of the relevant parties now has the requisite intention. Alternatively, we might argue that, since it is the doctor who is performing the relevant action, it is only the doctor's intention that matters. Even if we presume that to be the case, it seems like the patient's intention may perhaps influence the doctor's. So, if the doctor merely intends to fulfil the wishes of the patient, it may be unclear whether this means the doctor has aided a suicide.

These thorny problems are likely to cause more practical problems. One way, of course, to avoid these concerns is for doctors to not know the patients' reasons for their requests. In other words, it would be better for the doctor above to not know that the removal of the ventilator is because of a wish to die. But that seems to require advocating a position where the doctors do not talk about troubling issues with the patient.[25] Alternatively, it would seem to be an added basis for patients to not be open and honest with their doctor. Neither of these seems ideal.

In conclusion, then, the intention/foresight issue appears not to be a sufficient basis to ground a distinction between killing and letting die, at least not for all cases in which we want the difference to matter. Intentions are neither easy to determine nor are they as simplistic as this account makes it seem. Moreover, there are cases where simply having the foresight about a particular event is sufficient to ground moral responsibility. Finally, there are problems which are specific to the health-care context which make this particular distinction an unsatisfactory one to ground our beliefs about the morality of certain actions. Again, though, like the difference between doing and allowing,

---

[25] I have made a similar argument in relation to one put forward by Luke Gormally in 'Walton, Davies, Boyd and the Legalization of Euthanasia', in Keown (ed.), *Euthanasia Examined*, pp. 113–140. Gormally argues that doctors should not override patient refusals of treatment even if they appear to be based upon suicidal ideations as it may be difficult to tell the difference between a request for suicide and a concern about the burdens of treatment. As I have stated, it seems like there would be a fairly clear way to know that – one could actually discuss it with the patient in some detail. See S. W. Smith, 'Some Realism about End of Life: The Current Prohibition and the Euthanasia Underground' (2007) 33 *American Journal of Law and Medicine* 55–95, 69–70. This problem seems to exist in the general scenarios focusing on intention above as well.

sometimes this does seem to matter. It is just insufficient on its own to provide a reason for all of the cases in which we want the distinction to hold.

4   Keeping the distinction between killing and letting die

If these concerns about the act/omission distinction and the one between intention and foresight were all that there was, we could simply accept that this supposed difference between killing and letting die is an illusion and proceed with our discussion of ethical principles. But there are cases where either the act/omission one or the intention/foresight one appear to be relevant to our ethical decision-making. For example, the ethical difference we see in failing to send a contribution to charity and the sending of poison appears to be directly relevant to the idea that in one case we have acted and in another we have not.[26] Furthermore, we can consider a hypothetical end-of-life situation where a doctor removes life-sustaining medical treatment from a patient suffering from considerable pain and loss of dignity. The doctor's actions to relieve the pain and suffering of the patient would be considered much differently than the actions of an interloper bent on killing the patient to satisfy some grudge. These distinctions, then, do matter in *some* cases. They just do not matter in *all* cases.

In other words, this provides a case based upon the difference between a necessary condition and a sufficient one.[27] A necessary condition is one which must exist for a certain state of affairs to exist. So if condition 1 must exist before state of affairs A exists, then condition 1 is a necessary condition for state of affairs A. A sufficient condition is one which can, in and of itself, create a certain state of affairs. So, in other words, if we have condition 2 that can create state of affairs B without any other conditions, that is a sufficient one. What is important to realise is that, while these two are often conflated, they are separate. Necessary conditions are not always sufficient. For example, in order to create human life, a human egg is necessary (you cannot create human life without one) but it cannot on its own create human life. Additionally, sufficient conditions might not be necessary. If we go back to our cinematic examples from Chapter 3, a surprise ending which is well done may be sufficient to turn a good movie into a great movie, but it is not the only way that can happen. In the case of the act/omission distinction and

---

[26] Again, not all agree with this assessment and would argue that we are as responsible for failing to send money as we would be for our direct actions. See n. 4.

[27] We will also return to this when discussing logical slippery slope arguments in Chapter 13.

the intention/foresight one, we have sufficient conditions which are not necessary. In other words, they may be all that is required to turn what might be considered normally an unethical event into an ethical one, but they are not always required for that to be the case.

5   Moral responsibility

The task is therefore to best explain when these distinctions matter so that useful principles can be derived. To do that, it is best to go back to the beginning and remember what it is we are actually considering when we make these sorts of decisions. When we explore whether a certain act or omission is important, we are not asking about acts and omissions at all. Instead, we are really deciding about the moral responsibility of the individual in that particular situation. We are asking, then, 'is this particular individual at this particular time responsible for this event?'[28] This entails that we have a general theory of moral responsibility as questions about acts and omissions are really just specific applications of that general theory.[29] Consequently, our understanding of the place that acts and omissions have in this area depends upon first having a theory of moral responsibility.

To determine moral responsibility generally thus becomes the important prerequisite to our understanding of the moral responsibility of events involved in end-of-life decision-making. All that does is push the questions back one stage. In general, when are we morally responsible for the events that happen in our lives? First, it would seem we need to be responsible for those events in the first place. In other words, we seem to need to be responsible in order to be considered morally responsible for a certain event. Again, though, that does not seem to help much as we now need to determine what it means to be responsible. In order to be responsible, we need a situation where there is something for which an individual takes responsibility (or at least we feel that they ought to take responsibility). While this may already feel

[28] Since we will be talking about acts and omissions from this point on, I have chosen to use 'events' as a generic phrase indicating both.
[29] One possible point of debate is whether attributing moral responsibility to a certain event only involves blame-worthy ones or whether it can also include praise-worthy ones. In other words, we might only want to attribute moral responsibility to others when we seek to show that they should have done differently than they did. While this view of moral responsibility does have its supporters, it seems more useful to hold distinct the character of the action or omission from an attribution of responsibility for that action or omission. Therefore, this chapter will consider moral responsibility to be something which can attach to morally praise-worthy events in addition to ones we might see as morally blame-worthy.

like we are creating a vicious circle, the notion of taking responsibility seems to involve a notion about control and it is here that a theory of moral responsibility can begin to take root. People are responsible when they exercise some sort of control over an event or situation. We can see this when we examine a basic example. Let us presume I am a bystander at an incident where Person A shoots Person B. In our first scenario, while I am present at the scene, there is nothing I can do which will prevent Person A from pulling the trigger and shooting Person B. It is unlikely that I would be considered to be morally responsible for the shooting. However, if I had some sort of device which would prevent Person B from being shot (perhaps I can remotely control some sort of bulletproof glass shield which will stop the bullet), then I could presumably be held to be morally responsible if I do not use it. I would not be the only person who has moral responsibility in that case (Person A would also seem to be morally responsible), but I would have moral responsibility for my failure to raise the glass shield.

Control, then, seems to be an important part of a theory of moral responsibility. But what sort of control over a situation is important? Our initial reaction may be that control requires a notion of the ability to do otherwise. In our shooting example above, I have two options – I can raise the shield or I can refrain from raising the shield.[30] I therefore seem to be able to do something different which has a direct impact on the event in question. However, it is not so certain that the ability to do otherwise is particularly important to the notion of control necessary for moral responsibility. Philosophers attempt to show this by reference to 'Frankfurt-style examples'. A Frankfurt-style example is a hypothetical example where a person seems to be morally responsible even though they could not do otherwise. It will be easiest to stick to our shooting example. As indicated above, I am morally responsible for raising or failing to raise the glass shield, assuming I have some device for doing so and can do so in time to prevent the shooting. Let us assume in this situation that I fail to raise the shield. My failure to raise the shield is because I do not want to do so. I don't like Person B and am happy for him to be shot by Person A. I therefore make a conscious decision not to raise the shield. Let us further assume that I have a microchip that has been implanted in my brain by a mad neuroscientist, of which I am unaware. The microchip allows the neuroscientist to monitor my

---

[30] There are, of course, a number of ways I can fail to raise the shield and I may perform many actions in doing so. I could eat a banana; I could dance a jig; I could cheer the shooter; I could walk away; etc. What seems important for our purposes are that there are only two important things which can happen in relation to the shooting. I can either raise the shield or I can refrain from doing so.

brainwaves so he knows what I am thinking and, in particular, the decisions that I make. The microchip also allows the neuroscientist to alter my brainwaves if he so chooses to force me to do certain actions. In this particular case, the neuroscientist also wants Person B to be shot. So, if I had decided to raise the shield, the neuroscientist would have altered my brain patterns to cause me to choose not to raise the shield. So, whatever I decide initially, the shield will, in fact, not be raised. I thus cannot do anything to avoid refraining from raising the shield although I do not actually know that. But, in the actual scenario, this changing of my brainwaves by the neuroscientist was not necessary because I freely decided not to raise the shield. According to many philosophers, I am still responsible for failure to raise the shield despite the fact that I could not have done otherwise. Now, of course, if I had initially decided to raise the shield and then the neuroscientist decided to override that decision with his microchip and forced me to refrain from doing so, I would not likely be morally responsible for that. But, in the scenario which actually happens I am morally responsible.[31] The ability to do otherwise, then, does not seem to be an essential part of whatever conception of control is necessary for moral responsibility.

If we do not have the ability to do otherwise, in what sense do we have control over a situation then? John Fischer and Mark Ravizza have suggested that the ability to do otherwise is not the only type of control we have. They distinguish between two types of control. The first, regulative control, is control *over* our behaviour. It is the kind of control in which we pick from a 'menu of generally available options'[32] and choose one particular option. In regulative control, we must have the ability to do otherwise. The other sort of control, guidance control, does not require the ability to do otherwise. Instead, guidance control is the control *of* a behaviour. Fischer explains this sort of control using the following example:

suppose you are at the controls of an airplane, a glider, and you are guiding the plane to the west. Everything is going just as you want, and the plane is making good headway. You consider whether to steer the plane to the east, but you decide to keep guiding it to the west, in part because the scenery is nicer in the

---

[31] All Frankfurt-style examples work in a similar way, although they do not all require mad neuroscientists. All that is necessary for a Frankfurt-style example is two possible choices (A and B) in a given situation. In the situation, despite the fact that these two possibilities exist, one of them (A) is guaranteed to happen in the situation. Either the individual will choose to do A or some other mechanism (M) will interfere and cause the individual to do A if the initial choice is for B. Despite M, the individual freely and willingly chooses to do A.

[32] J. M. Fischer, *My Way: Essays on Moral Responsibility* (New York: Oxford University Press, 2006), p. 6.

west. Unknown to you, the wind currents in the area are such that the plane would continue to go to the west, in just the way it actually goes, even if you had tried to steer it in some other direction. (Alternatively, we could suppose that although the plane's steering apparatus works just fine as you are guiding it to the west, it is defective, and the defect would have 'kicked in' and caused the plane to go in precisely the way it actually went if you had tried to steer it in any other direction.) In this example, you steer the plane to the west in the 'normal' way. It is not just that you cause it to go to the west (which you would equally have done had you steered the plane in the same way as a result of a sneeze or epileptic seizure). Rather, you guide the plane in a distinctive way – you exhibit a signature sort of control, which I shall call 'guidance control.'[33]

Guidance control, then, is exerting some control over an event without necessarily having the ability to do otherwise. That only tells us what guidance control does not require. It does not explain what we need to have this form of control. The first thing about guidance control and the theory of moral responsibility which derives from it is that the focus of analysis is on the actual series which led to the event in question. This idea can get lost in all the talk of alternative possibilities and Frankfurt-style examples, but the focus of our concern is not on what might have happened but on what, in fact, did happen in the event in question. So, to return to our shooting example, it does not matter that a neuroscientist would force me to refrain from raising the bulletproof shield if I freely and voluntarily decide to do that in the actual event in question. Within the context of the actual event, what happened must be both reasons-responsive and the individual's own action. Both of those require further discussion. Something is appropriately reasons-responsive under Fischer and Ravizza's view if it is moderately reasons-responsive. To be moderately reasons-responsive, the way in which the event occurs must be both *receptive to reasons* – 'that is, the agent would recognize what reasons there are'[34] and it must be *reactive to reasons* – the ability to translate reasons into choices. The receptivity to reasons present must be 'regular'. This means that the reasons-receptivity applicable in a particular case must give rise 'to a minimally comprehensive pattern' that is understandable to others and at least somewhat grounded in reality. Reactivity to reasons means that the individual in question has the ability to see at least one scenario where those reasons would have caused them to choose differently.[35] So, I would be morally responsible for failure to raise the bulletproof shield if my refraining

---

[33] *Ibid.*, p. 8.
[34] J. M. Fischer and M. Ravizza, *Responsibility and Control: A Theory of Moral Responsibility* (New York: Cambridge University Press, 1998), p. 69.
[35] Remember, though, it does not require that they actually be able to do differently, as the Frankfurt-style examples show.

was receptive to reasons – there are reasons which might convince me to raise the shield – and reactive to those reasons – that because of those reasons, there is at least one situation where I would have decided to raise the shield, even if I were not actually capable of doing so. In order for something to be the individual's own action, it must be something for which the individual would take responsibility. According to Fischer and Ravizza, taking responsibility requires three things. First, the individual in question must view him or herself as capable of causing certain things as a result of his or her actions and choices. Second, the individual must view him or herself as being an 'appropriate target' for the reactive attitudes – those feelings of blame or praise that attach to decisions about moral responsibility. Finally, the individual must see the first two as being based upon evidence available to the individual.

One of the benefits of this account of moral responsibility is that it applies not only to actions which we might do, but also applies to omissions and consequences as well. This is particularly important for our purposes as omissions and consequences are important events which are likely to occur in end-of-life decisions. Moral responsibility attaches to actions in the way specified above. Moral responsibility for omissions and consequences is slightly different, although they still result from applications of guidance control. It is easier to start with the moral responsibility for consequences. Consequences, according to philosophers, come in two different forms – consequence-particulars and consequence-universals. A consequence-particular is the consequences which result from the specific sequence of events in a particular situation.[36] They are thus a very individuated account of what has occurred in a scenario. If a different sequence of events happened then there is a different consequence-particular, even if the end result is the same. A consequence-universal, on the other hand, is more general and may result from a number of different sequences. It, then, is a focus on the end result of the sequence of events. Moral responsibility for a consequence-particular follows roughly in the same way as responsibility for actions. An individual is responsible for a consequence-particular if the individual has guidance control over the act (or omission) in question and it is reasonable to expect that action will lead to the consequence-particular. Moral responsibility for a consequence-universal is more difficult. It requires guidance control over his or her own bodily movements and the event in the external world must be suitably sensitive to that movement. In order for the event in the external world to qualify as being suitably sensitive to the individual's bodily movement,

---

[36] Fischer and Ravizza refer to this as the 'actual causal pathway'.

it should be the case that a different movement will somehow have an effect upon the event in question. So, in our example, if Person A has bulletproof-shield-piercing bullets, then I would not be responsible for the consequence-universal that Person B is shot even if I fail to raise the shield because, no matter what I do, I cannot prevent Person B from being shot.[37] Responsibility for omissions flows from the responsibility that exists for consequence-universals. A person is responsible for omissions when those failures to act are the individual's own, moderately reasons-responsive omissions (i.e. they have guidance control over the omission) and that the event in question is suitably sensitive to that omission.

We can see how this theory of moral responsibility helps to clear up the issues surrounding some of the examples presented at the start of the chapter. In the Smith and Jones hypotheticals, it seemed like moral responsibility would attach to those situations. We can now see why. In Smith's case, he has guidance control over the drowning of his nephew in that they are moderately responsive to his reasons (i.e. his desire for the money) and the drowning is his own action on the facts presented to us. Jones is also morally responsible for the death of his cousin, although he has failed to do something instead of performing an action. Since it is an omission, Jones is responsible if his bodily movements (in this case, the failure to save his cousin) are his own and moderately reasons-responsive. As they are based upon his desire for the money, it appears that they are both his own and reasons-responsive (he might, for example, have been willing to save his cousin were the saving of his cousin likely to entitle him to the money). The drowning of his cousin is also suitably sensitive to the omission as, if Jones had pulled out his cousin, he would not have drowned. It thus seems that we can attribute moral responsibility to Jones as well as Smith.

The theory of moral responsibility also helps us explain the troubling comparison between sending poison to Africa and simply refraining from sending a cheque, both of which result in the death of 30 people. Sending poison would be an easy case of moral responsibility. Again, the action is moderately reasons-responsive and the individual's own. It therefore shows guidance control over the action and the individual in question would be morally responsible for those deaths. On the other hand, failing to send a cheque does not appear to lead to moral responsibility. The failure to write and send the cheque would be subject to the guidance control of the individual. However, there are a number of

---

[37] I may, of course, be morally responsible for other things such as failing to attempt to prevent the shooting, but I cannot be responsible for the fact that Person B is shot.

other circumstances which appear likely to happen before the deaths of the victims which would reduce the moral responsibility of the individual in that case. As such, it does not appear that the deaths of those individuals are suitably sensitive for the omission to create moral responsibility. The individual, of course, may be morally responsible for failing to send the cheque, but it does not seem likely that the individual can be morally responsible for the actual deaths in question.[38]

This does bring up a point which is worth emphasising. One of the problems which arise in determining moral responsibility is that we are not always clear which of the various events in question we are attaching moral responsibility to. So, if we consider the failure to send a cheque to a charity, there may be several possibilities, including:

1. The decision to fail to send a cheque
2. The failure to decide to send a cheque
3. The failure to send a cheque
4. The failure to try to send a cheque
5. The failure to save those whom the cheque might have saved
6. The death of those who the cheque might have saved

Moral responsibility does not attach to all of those equally when one does not send a cheque to charity. The first four probably relate directly to the failure to send a cheque. The last two are more remote and therefore it is less likely that the events in question are suitably sensitive to the individual's omission.

6   A final criticism

One criticism that may be made about this approach (at least in the context of this chapter) focuses on the idea that moral responsibility contains both morally praiseworthy as well as morally blame-worthy behaviours. It might be argued that this chapter has not really answered its main concern as the issue surrounding killing and letting die is not simply about whether or not we are morally responsible, but whether we are morally blame-worthy for those things. The theory I have presented above does not provide us with an answer as to whether the actions by doctors in removing a feeding tube from a patient in a persistent vegetative state are morally blame-worthy or not. Since it does not, it may

---

[38] We might also question the connection between the omission in question and the consequence of that omission. While there is some possibility that the failure to send a cheque would lead to the death of someone, it may be hard to suggest that it be *reasonable* that the failure to send a cheque would lead to the deaths of the individuals.

be argued that the theory misses the point of the discussion about the distinction between killing and letting die.

While it is true that this chapter does not give us a firm conclusion on that score, it does provide an important first step. We must first determine whether these are the events for which an individual can be morally responsible at all before we can determine whether those events are morally blame-worthy. We cannot have a situation where the events may be morally blame-worthy but that there is no individual in question who can be held morally responsible for those events. So, we need to have a sufficient way to determine moral responsibility first. Additionally, the claims about moral blame-worthiness are not answerable on their own anyway. It is not the case that our decisions about whether to blame or praise particular actions or omissions are separate from the general discussion of ethical principles which occurs in Part I of this book. In other words, all that is possible at this point is to determine whether these are things to which moral responsibility attaches. It is only after conclusions are reached about the ethical principles in play will it be possible to make a firm determination about whether we are morally blame-worthy for those things for which we are morally responsible.

7   Conclusion

Some considerable ground has been covered and we have ended up quite a way from where we began. We started this chapter with the notion that the categorisation of something as a killing or a letting die was ethically important. To bolster that assumption, we further examined two possible methods for determining whether something was a killing or a letting die. The first possibility was that acts should be considered to be killings while omissions should be letting die. This, however, was unable to ground all of our moral intuitions about various cases and was ultimately rejected. Consideration was then given to the distinction between intention and foresight as a way to explain why killings were morally prohibited while letting die was not. This too was unable to ground our moral intuitions.

With neither of those options creating the necessary connection to ground a categorical moral difference between killing and letting die, we move back a step to the real heart of the question which is about moral responsibility. Developing a comprehensive theory of moral responsibility based upon Fischer and Ravizza's concept of guidance control allows us to determine moral responsibility without a need to categorise a particular event as a killing or a letting die. It will therefore allow a more accurate assessment of the moral responsibility for the actions, consequences and omissions of those involved in the end-of-life decisions we are exploring.

What this does not unfortunately allow us to do at this point is to make a firm conclusion about the blame-worthiness or praise-worthiness of particular acts or omissions. Instead, we need to further consider the other ethical values which are in play to determine whether the event in question was morally good or morally bad. Being able to assign moral responsibility for the event does provide us with an important first step, however, to making those final determinations. With this conception of moral responsibility in mind, then, we can begin to examine the important moral principles which will allow us to determine whether our actions or omissions are worthy of blame or not.

5   Autonomy and paternalism

1   Introduction

Having examined three of the foundational concerns about ethics –
moral status, the value of life and moral responsibility – it is time to
turn our attention to more specific ethical principles. The fact that these
principles are specific does not make them less worthwhile or important
for our discussion. They will be less general than our earlier concepts
but they will still be used in a broad number of issues. The first one we
shall examine is respect for autonomy. It should be specifically noted at
the start that autonomy, while it is a philosophical principle, is not really
an ethical one. What is an ethical principle, however, is that we respect
the autonomy of other moral actors. Therefore, even though we will
spend a considerable amount of time discussing autonomy as a concept,
the ethical principle we shall be considering is whether or not we ought
to respect the autonomous choices of others.

   To many, this may seem a particularly easy question to answer. Of
course we should protect the autonomous decisions of others. Autonomy
has become such a large part of our philosophical language that we have
reached the point where we do not question its importance. Autonomy
matters. Autonomy might not be the only thing that matters, but the
fact that a decision is autonomous is seen as justification in and of itself.
In fact, to some, it has become all-consuming.[1] We rely on it to forestall
debate or criticism of decisions because we see any disagreements or
objections as being incapable of overriding the autonomous decisions of
others or ourselves. However, we may not necessarily have a clear idea
what autonomy is. We may decide that any decision we make is autonomous as long as it is not based upon coercion or undue influence. We
may also believe that any autonomous decision is necessarily good or at
least desirable in some way. We may also not completely understand the
importance of autonomy in our decision-making processes.

---

[1] See, e.g., R. P. Wolff, *In Defense of Anarchism* (New York: Harper & Row, 1970).

The purpose of this chapter will be to examine the concept of autonomy so that we can better understand the place of the ethical concept of respect for autonomy. We will first consider what it means for something to be autonomous, using three possible conceptions of what autonomy entails. We will further consider both the reasons for respecting autonomy and the responsibilities that respecting autonomy may put on us. After that, we will consider some of the ethical problems that arise from respecting the autonomy of other moral actors and the question of paternalism.

2   The concept of autonomy

Our first task is to explore in more detail what it actually means for a decision to be autonomous. It is now trite to start with the idea that autonomy translates as 'self-rule' in Ancient Greek and related originally to city-states acting on their own without the oversight of more powerful states or cities.[2] Modified to suit individual decision-making, we may have some idea that autonomy concerns individual self-governance or self-determination.[3] Stated more vaguely, we may have some idea that autonomy means that 'I get to make the decisions for myself and no one else gets to tell me what to do'. Those ideas, however, are not sufficiently precise to help us with ethical decision-making. What does it mean to say I govern myself or that I get to decide for myself? We need something much more rigorous if it is going to be helpful in making decisions.

Therefore, let us start with an admittedly insignificant exercise of autonomy. Let us suppose that I decide to stay up until 3 a.m. one Wednesday night to watch a playoff baseball game. My reasons for making this decision are (1) baseball happens to be my favourite sport and (2) my favourite team (the Philadelphia Phillies) is playing. No one suggested to me that I watch the game. I just happened to want to do so. On the face of it, this seems like a very easy case of autonomy. I had a desire to watch a baseball game and did so. Things may become more difficult, though, if we examine my reasons in more depth. If we ask why baseball happens to be my favourite sport, I may give the following reason:

---

2 See, e.g., G. Dworkin, *The Theory and Practice of Autonomy* (Cambridge University Press, 1988), pp. 12–13; T. Beauchamp and J. Childress, *Principles of Biomedical Ethics* (6th edn) (Oxford University Press, 2009), p. 99; O. O'Neill, *Autonomy and Trust in Bioethics* (Cambridge University Press, 2002), p. 29.
3 Dworkin, *The Theory and Practice of Autonomy*, pp. 5–6.

Baseball is my favourite sport partially because of my cultural heritage as an American. Baseball has a rich history as the American pastime and a large part of American language and imagery is wrapped up with that idea of baseball as national pastime. Additionally, baseball reminds me of my childhood either playing catch with my father or watching games with him. So, he passed his love of baseball to me at an early age and I have been a fan ever since.

Again, were one to ask me why the Phillies in particular were my favourite team, I might answer in the following way:

I am a Phillies fan not because I am from Philadelphia. Nor does it have to do with a winning franchise (unfortunately, the Phillies have the opposite reputation). It is not because of colour schemes, nor is it because of players they had in my youth. Instead, the formative reason I am a Phillies fan is because my father was. As such, and in the time-honoured way such afflictions are passed down, I became a Phillies fan as a result.

With these reasons in front of us, my decision to stay up into the wee hours of the morning may seem less autonomous. After all, the formative reasons do not appear to be mine as such, but were implanted in me by my father (or my cultural heritage as an American) at a young age. I could argue, then, that I was unable to make any other decision because of indoctrinations that happened when I was too young to know better. If this is the case, how was my decision mine? What is it about the decision that makes it autonomous?

It might help us to better understand what autonomy is if we have a comparison decision. Let us suppose instead that I am a compulsive gambler. Through no fault of my own, I happen to find myself in a casino where I gamble a considerable amount of money that I do not have. I argue that I did not want to gamble the money but once I was in the casino, I was unable to stop myself from gambling. In this case, we might be more willing to listen to my argument that my decision to gamble was not autonomous. The ultimate conclusion will likely depend on a number of other factors which are unknown, but we would generally consider decisions made on the basis of compulsions we cannot change to be less autonomous than other ones.

What differentiates these two possible decisions? In both cases, I am the one who made the ultimate decision. What may be a significant difference is that in the first case, I wanted to watch the baseball game. In the second case, I did not want to gamble the money. The first case, then, is a decision I wish to own in some way that I do not wish to do in the second case. Gerald Dworkin explains this difference by reference to what he calls a second-order desire.[4] A first-order desire is those

---

[4] *Ibid.*, p. 15.

things we want.[5] In our first example, my first-order desire is to watch the baseball game; in the second, it is my desire to gamble. My second-order desires are my opinions, beliefs and attitudes towards those initial desires.[6] So, it is what I feel about my first-order desires. And there we may be able to draw a distinction between our two cases. In the first, I am happy about my first-order desire to watch the baseball game. I want to desire to watch the game. In the second, I presumably do not want to desire to gamble. I do gamble because of my compulsive inclination to do so, but I do not want to have that inclination. An autonomous decision, then, according to Dworkin, is one where our first-order and second-order desires line up. As he indicates:

> Autonomy is conceived of as a second-order capacity of persons to reflect critically upon their first-order preferences, desires, wishes and so forth and the capacity to accept or attempt to change these in light of higher-order preferences and values. By exercising such a capacity, persons define their nature, give meaning and coherence to their lives, and take responsibility for the kind of person they are.[7]

Some questions arise from this approach. First, it may be unclear why there are only two possible levels of preferences. There seem to only be first-order ones and second-order ones. However, if it is possible to have opinions about our first-order desires, it also seems possible that we could have them about our second-order desires.[8] Thus, while I may want to desire to watch baseball, I may decide that I do not want that second-order desire. That would lead to at least third-order desires, although I could presumably then have an opinion about those and so on and so forth. We could presumably blunt this particular criticism by recasting these desires as lower- and higher-order desires instead of first- and second-order preferences.[9] That leaves us with the problem of examining where these higher-order preferences come from. A higher-order preference may not necessarily come from any more autonomous source. For instance, I may want to desire to watch the Phillies, but that desire comes from a long-standing tradition that 'real fans do not switch team allegiances'. If that is my reason for maintaining an allegiance to a particular team, it may not strike some as being any more autonomous than my first-order desire was in the first place. Moreover, Beauchamp and Childress have questioned whether this particular conception of

---

[5] *Ibid.*   [6] *Ibid.*   [7] *Ibid.*, p. 20.
[8] Dworkin seems to concede this. *Ibid.*, pp. 19–20.
[9] Dworkin himself suggests calling them 'highest-order desires' in cases where that is relevant. *Ibid.*, p. 19.

autonomy requires too much of ordinary citizens.[10] They argue that
the requirement that we have reflected upon our initial desires may be
more searching an analysis of preferences than most of us do on a regular basis. They believe that Dworkin's conception of autonomy is based
more upon an idealised view that is 'beyond the reach of normal agents
and choosers'.[11]

As a result, they reject the conception presented by Dworkin in
favour of a conception which relies on three important elements. To
them, an autonomous decision is one which the chooser made '(1)
intentionally, (2) with understanding, and (3) without controlling influences that determine their action'.[12] They further specify that the first
element, intentionality, is one which is either present or not.[13] Elements
(2) and (3), however, can be something which a particular decision or
chooser has to a greater or lesser degree.[14] This leads to a sliding scale of
autonomous decisions with some being more autonomous than others,
although ones without any understanding or made due to controlling
influences cannot be considered autonomous at all. Because of this
sliding scale, Beauchamp and Childress subscribe to the notion that
full understanding and/or a complete absence of outside influences is
not necessary for a decision to be autonomous. Instead, any decision
only needs a 'substantial degree of understanding and freedom from
constraint'.[15] This conception of autonomy does eliminate the problems
with higher-order desires inherent in Dworkin's approach. However, it
may not be the most exact conception and many of the relevant terms
could be subject to greater clarity. For example, it may not be especially clear to everyone what counts as a 'controlling influence'. This
may cause particular problems in cases where we have events which
might be considered a significant influence but it is unclear how far
they contributed to the decision. The most famous case example of this
in the UK is the *Re T* case where a mother had two conversations with
her adult daughter outside the hearing of others.[16] The mother was a
devout Jehovah's Witness. The daughter was not, although she might
have possibly seen herself as a lapsed member of that church.[17] After
these conversations, the daughter sought to refuse a blood transfusion

---

[10] Beauchamp and Childress, *Principles of Biomedical Ethics*, p. 101.
[11] *Ibid.*   [12] *Ibid.*   [13] *Ibid.*   [14] *Ibid.*   [15] *Ibid.*
[16] *Re T (adult: refusal of treatment)* [1992] 4 All ER 649.
[17] *Ibid.* The evidence is not particularly clear on this point. T did have conversations
with her father where she indicated that she was not a member of that faith and indeed
the Jehovah's Witness Church indicated in a statement to the press that she was not
and never had been. However, the hospital's 'patient assessment form' indicated
under the heading of religious beliefs: 'Jehovah's Witness (Ex) but still has certain
beliefs and practices.'

for medical treatment she was going to receive as a result of a car accident. Even if we were aware of what was said in those conversations, unless we have a clear definition as to what counts as a controlling interest, we may be unable to determine whether the daughter's decision was truly autonomous or not.

Both Dworkin's and Beauchamp and Childress's conceptions of autonomy fall into a category we might wish to refer to as individual autonomy. The focus of the conception is on the choice made by the individual and not the result of that decision. They are therefore process-oriented approaches to autonomy. Onoro O'Neill, however, has argued that any of these approaches are flawed because they allow individuals to make decisions which are selfish or clearly wrong.[18] Instead of focusing on individual autonomy, which she sees as developing out of Millian philosophy, we should instead focus on 'principled autonomy' which develops out of the philosophy of Kant.[19] The fundamental difference between the two, she argues, is that Kant's notion of autonomy fits more closely into the idea of making good choices. This is because the only choices which are worthy of respect are those which we could will as a universal rule.[20] In other words, I can make an autonomous decision only to the extent that I would be happy with anyone else (and everyone else) being able to make the same decision.[21] The benefit, she argues, is that principled autonomy will lead to more ethical decision-making as we will need to have a greater concern for the consequences of our actions because what is acceptable for us is now acceptable for others.[22] One of the examples she gives is deception. Deception cannot be a universal rule because if we all deceive (or at least are allowed to deceive when we wish), then overall trust will decrease. Since overall trust will decrease, we cannot then deceive others because they will be more sceptical of what we say. It therefore cannot be a universal rule and would not be acceptable to do under principled autonomy.[23]

There is some considerable appeal to the approach that O'Neill takes. It is a definite plus for people seeking to act ethically to consider how their decisions impact upon others and the idea of a universal law is one way to achieve that goal. Even so, there are concerns whether this

---

[18] O'Neill, *Autonomy and Trust in Bioethics*, p. 73.
[19] *Ibid.*, pp. 30, 74.   [20] *Ibid.*, p. 84.
[21] *Ibid.*   [22] *Ibid.*, pp. 86–87.
[23] *Ibid.*, p. 98. I must admit that I have my doubts about the empirical claim that appears to be at the heart of this example. Simply because people deceive others does not mean that all trust would evaporate, making people unable to deceive at any future point. Even compulsive liars are bound to tell the truth every now and again even it if results from them mistakenly telling the truth when trying to tell a lie.

approach would necessarily lead to more ethical decision-making. First, it is less than clear why a universal rule conception of autonomy is the most appropriate way to measure ethical decision-making. The correct standard for ethical decisions is whether I have treated all morally relevant entities in an appropriate way, not whether in doing so, I could will my actions as a universal rule. There may be unique factors related to the particular decision (or to the entities involved, myself included) which means that while the action was ethically appropriate in this one particular circumstance, it is not something I think should be a universal rule.[24] So, it is not clear that this conception of autonomy actually does provide us with a better way to gauge our ethical decision-making.

More importantly, I am not convinced that it will necessarily lead to better ethical decisions even if we assume it could be the correct test to use. It still seemingly relies on the individual's own subjective judgement about what is best ethically. The difference is whether the individual thinks it best ethically for anyone and everyone to use as well as him or herself. But, we can be just as wrong about those sorts of decisions as we are about the ones we make relating only to our own conduct. I may have a particular ethical code which I think everyone else should agree with, but it is one which would severely curtail the actions of others. For example, I may believe that everyone ought to follow the tenets of a particular religion which required the forceful conversion of those of different religions. While I would consider that to be a universal rule, it is not one that everyone (particularly those practising a different religion) would accept, and there is no reason to believe that it suddenly becomes an acceptable rule merely because I believe anyone (or everyone) ought to be subject to it. Additionally, I may decide that I am happy for certain things to be universal rules because I believe I will benefit from them. For example, I may not mind that everyone is allowed to deceive others if I think that I am good at deception or at least good at detecting it. I may believe that such skills provide an advantage to me if deception is widespread but that I lose

---

[24] We could use the virtue of mercy as an example. The virtue of mercy seems to apply in cases where we do not want to apply a universal rule. Instead, there is some facet of the individual decision before us which indicates that we ought to treat *this* case differently from other cases. See, e.g., J. Tasioulas, 'Mercy' (2003) 103 *Proceedings of the Aristotelian Society* 101–132. We could not, therefore, seem to be able to create a universal rule in the sense that O'Neill means. If we did, we would seem to be destroying the concept of mercy because if we all acted mercifully at all times (or could do so anyway), then we would not be acting mercifully because there would be no rule from which we have deviated due to mercy. We could, I guess, create a rule which permitted us to act mercifully if we so desired and the circumstances merited it, but that seems to be significantly different from the universal rule idea that O'Neill invokes.

such an advantage if it is not. Were I to believe this to be the case, I am not sure that it means any deception that I engage in is something for which I can claim ethical justification.

Moreover, much of the justification would depend on how the universal rule is stated, and without clear rules, it may be subject to abuse. Again, let us look at the example of a member of a religious group who believes that everyone should be a member of their particular group. We could argue that the universal rule that would apply must allow for freedom of religion. We may do so on the basis that everyone would like the freedom to worship as they see fit and that this is the correct universal rule. However, the member of a religious group may argue that the correct universal rule must apply to only 'true' religions. Otherwise, we might become swamped with ethical duties that we owe to people who decide they belong to a religion which requires, for example, that they sacrifice other human beings like the Aztecs did many years ago. Of course, once we accept that claim, we are left to debate what counts as a 'true' religion and to some, there may only ever be one such religion which qualifies. So, how the rule is articulated may go a long way towards our views on whether or not the rule is ethical. Even if we decide that rules must be global it will not always be helpful. Global rules may hide particular prejudices or biases which benefit some individuals over others.[25]

O'Neill does try to address this point in part by the suggestion that we are not simply willing a universal rule. By willing an action, we must also 'commit ourselves to take any necessary and some sufficient means, taking account of the reasonably foreseeable results of the action'.[26] She argues that this will eliminate many of these concerns because things like coercion cannot be things for which we can will all of the means.[27] If we will coercion as a universal rule, then we have to will effective methods of coercion for everyone. But then at least some persons would be unable to effectively use coercion because of more effective uses of coercion by others. As a result, universal coercion cannot be a universal rule because there are no 'universally effective means to coerce'.[28]

---

[25] For an example of this in a legal context, see the US Supreme Court case of *Geduldig v. Aiello*, 417 U.S. 484 (1974). The legal rule in question involved the health-care benefits of the State of California. The state health-care plan did not cover the costs of treatment for normal complications resulting from pregnancy. State workers claimed this was discriminatory against women. The Supreme Court disagreed, arguing that the health-care plan did not discriminate against women as all patients who might suffer complications from pregnancy were not covered, regardless of whether they were a woman or a man.

[26] O'Neill, *Autonomy and Trust in Bioethics*, p. 86.

[27] *Ibid.*, p. 86–87.   [28] *Ibid.*, p. 87.

This seems to be overstating the point. There may be no universally effective means to coerce at all times in all places for all people, but that does not mean there are no universal means to coerce at all. It depends on whether we mean something that everyone can always be doing or something available to all. It may be that everyone can coerce someone else at some point but not at others (A can coerce B some of the time but not all times).[29] If that is our definition of 'universally effective means' then it seems that it is possible to will that as a universal. In other words, is the appropriate test that we have the capacity to do whatever the action is (whether means or ends) or whether it is something we can do at all times and in all places? If it is the latter, I am not sure how anything can count as a universal because there are very few ethical duties which we can do all of the time and in all places.[30]

Considering that these three conceptions of autonomy all have different strengths and weaknesses, they will likely lead to different results when we consider exercises of autonomy under these different conceptions. It would therefore be preferable to use only one of these conceptions of autonomy for our purposes. In order to choose between them, the best method is to examine which fits most closely with the reasons why autonomy is considered worthy of respect. The role of autonomy is not necessarily to help us make the right decision. Instead, the importance of autonomy is, in part, because there is unlikely to be a right decision in many cases.[31] Since there are no answers which are clearly right or clearly wrong in these cases, we need to look to other values in order to examine the decision-making process. The first value is respect for other moral actors.[32] It is believed that one of the important ways we show respect for other moral actors is to accept that they are capable of making decisions. Since they are capable of making decisions, they are also capable of forming plans involving those decisions (what we generally refer to as a life plan). Those life plans of individuals are different and the best way to ensure that people pursue their own life plans is to allow them to make autonomous decisions, even those with

---

[29] It may also depend on whether coercion is hierarchical. O'Neill seems to suggest that some people will always find themselves at the bottom of the coercion chain. This may be the case, but it hardly seems as if it must be the case. It seems possible to envisage a world where a majority of people are on the same level as far as their ability to coerce and be coerced relative to others.

[30] For example, we may have an ethical duty to care for the needy, but if I cared for all of the people we could consider to be needy, then I might run out of resources and become needy myself.

[31] J. S. Mill, *On Liberty* (Oxford University Press, 1991 [original publication 1859]), p. 17.

[32] Beauchamp and Childress, *Principles of Biomedical Ethics*, p. 103; O'Neill, *Autonomy and Trust in Bioethics*, p. 29.

which we might not agree. Additionally, and in some senses related to the above point, each individual has a different idea about what constitutes 'a good life' and the ways to pursue that life.[33] It is difficult, if not impossible, to know in advance which ones are correct or even if 'correct' good lives are possible. Since my version of a 'good life' will differ from yours, we should allow you to pursue yours in the ways you see fit and me in the ways I see fit because there are unlikely to be any right answers to these problems. This is subject, of course, to the overriding caveat about hurting others (my pursuit of a life plan can be impeded if my plan involves hurting others), but otherwise, I should be allowed to pursue that plan in whatever method I see fit.

Of the three approaches we have been considering, it appears that O'Neill's is less well suited to the purposes we have set out because it requires a greater examination of particular autonomous decisions. However, the more we examine the results of decisions, the more likely it is that others will decide that those decisions should not be allowed. But, since respect for other moral actors and pursuit of different notions of a good life are the primary benefits of respecting autonomy, those are exactly the sorts of decisions we have to allow if autonomy is to have any value. Beauchamp and Childress's approach or the one put forward by Gerald Dworkin therefore seem to be preferable to O'Neill's. We are then left to decide between the approach of Dworkin and the one Beauchamp and Childress put forward. In reality, there is not likely to be a significant difference between the two. The requirements of intentionality, with understanding and without outside controlling interests, are reasonably similar to Dworkin's conception of a second-order principle. The purpose of second-order principles in Dworkin's conception of autonomy is to provide us with some means of gauging the reflection and lack of outside controlling interests in a particular decision.[34] I would therefore suggest that in a vast majority of cases, what one would consider an autonomous decision under Beauchamp and Childress's view is likely to be an autonomous one under Dworkin's. Of the two, though, the Beauchamp and Childress approach is probably easier for ordinary members of the moral community to use. We are much more used to considering whether something is intentional or done with understanding than whether we have second-order preferences and whether our first-order ones are made in conjunction with those second-order ones. It will also eliminate the question of where those higher-order desires come from, which can be a significant problem.

[33] Mill, *On Liberty*, p. 17.
[34] Dworkin, *The Theory and Practice of Autonomy*, pp. 17, 19–20.

We may lose some definitional exactness, but in most cases that should not be a particular problem.

There are two significant problems which arise from the use of Beauchamp and Childress's approach which will require further discussion, however. First, there is a criticism of autonomy as being too individualistic or atomistic as a concept.[35] Decisions are made by the individual alone. There is no need for outside discussion or advice. If one takes notice of Beauchamp and Childress's conception of autonomy, there is no necessary connection with any other individual. I could, if I so desired, make every decision without any influence from other people and they would still be autonomous. This, however, seems to go against the way many of us make decisions. We do seek advice from others, particularly family members, friends or those we see as experts. We do see ourselves as part of a web of relationships and communities which impact our decisions in myriad ways. Why then should the concept of autonomy – one we think to be so fundamentally important – be one which goes against these truths about the way we live?

These concerns can be overstated. There is nothing in the description presented above which prohibits interaction prior to the actual decision.[36] It is merely the indication that the final decision, whatever it happens to be, is made by the individual. It is therefore a decision for which someone is ultimately responsible. More importantly, the description presented above provides us with a moral floor as opposed to a ceiling. It is not a suggestion that the best autonomous decisions are made in this manner; it just provides us with a list of necessary components for a decision to be autonomous at all. If we are able to construct a scenario where we had an autonomous individual who was separate from all other autonomous decision-makers so that there could be no impact on decision-making, the decisions made by that individual would still be autonomous if they complied with the three necessary components of an autonomous decision.[37] In other words, what the description above

---

[35] Beauchamp and Childress, *Principles of Biomedical Ethics*, p. 102. Beauchamp and Childress make specific mention that they are trying to construct a version of autonomy that is 'not excessively individualistic'. *Ibid.*, p. 99.

[36] *Ibid.*, p. 102.

[37] In constructing such a scenario, we would probably start with the standard 'person on a deserted island'. However, the scenario necessary for consideration must be more complex. An individual who is shipwrecked on a deserted island (for example) would still take with him or her the collected experiences, relationships, etc. which he or she had prior to that point. So, it would be a requirement that those not be present as well. We would therefore seem to need either a shipwrecked person with amnesia (presuming, of course, that amnesia creates a sort of blank-slate condition) or a baby born on a deserted island with no other family present (although how a baby would survive in such a condition would be a considerable mystery). Even the 'Tarzan scenario' seems

highlights is that there is no *necessary* interaction for a decision to be autonomous. That is not the same as suggesting that no interactions are appropriate for autonomous decisions. A decision does not cease being autonomous because I do not consult with my family, friends or experts. But neither does my decision fail to be autonomous because I do. And, in fact, it would be rare for any autonomous decision to be one which resulted from no interaction or input from any other person. Autonomous decisions are individualistic in the sense that there must be a final 'chooser' for that decision. Not all decisions can (or should) be made by committee. But nothing in the description from Beauchamp and Childress or in what I say here should be construed as indicating that they must be atomistic or free from outside influences.[38]

The second issue that arises is that the description given above is a process-oriented one. It gives us no understanding or information about the content of decisions. All it provides is a process for which we can arrive at autonomous decisions. This would then seem to indicate that it does not matter what the result of the decision actually is, what matters is the process which arrives at the decision. So, decisions which would seem to be wrong or bad (however we decide to define those terms) are acceptable as long as the correct process was used to make the decision. We may then be forced to approve of decisions which we may profoundly disagree with because the process in which the decision was made was an acceptable one. This is, of course, true and largely the point of autonomous decisions. We will not agree with the result of all exercises of autonomy. Those who exercise autonomy are likely to make decisions that at least some of the rest of us think are wrong or bad or just things we would not have chosen to do. In general, this hardly presents much of a problem. It does not matter most of the time if I think you should have gone to the cinema instead of watching television as you desired, or whether you think I should have read this particular fiction book as opposed to some other one.

There are some decisions, though, which we think are so bad that we do not think anyone should be allowed to make them. Some of these we will discuss further when considering paternalism. But, one of the types of decisions we think people should not ever be allowed to make are

---

like it would not help because there would be social interactions with the animal group which 'raised' the child. The fact that we have to go to such implausible lengths for a useful scenario shows not only that most of our decisions do result from some interactions with others, but also that it could not be a necessary component of any description of autonomy that decisions be made in such a manner.

[38] For Beauchamp and Childress's views, see *Principles of Biomedical Ethics*, pp. 102–103.

those decisions which result in a forfeit of autonomy. Unsurprisingly, most autonomous decisions will lead to at least some diminution of available choices. In a monogamous society, the choice to marry one person eliminates the ability to choose other potential marriage partners. A choice to eat one kind of food may eliminate other possibilities. These are not the kind of decisions which normally cause consternation, however. The ones that are objected to are those decisions which eliminate all future use of autonomy. Contained within this group are autonomous decisions to sell oneself into slavery or (of particular relevance to us) decisions to end one's life. Mill, for example, famously argued that one could not choose autonomously to sell oneself into slavery.[39]

So, we could resolve this difficulty by simply claiming that the decision made to limit all future choices was not autonomous. This would eliminate our problem because if it is not an autonomous decision, we need not protect it in the way we protect our autonomous decisions. Unfortunately, if we use the analysis presented by Beauchamp and Childress, it is hard to see why these sorts of decisions should not be characterised as autonomous ones. Autonomous decisions, as we have seen, relate to the process used to make the decision, not the final decision itself. So, conceivably, there could be a case where a decision to sell oneself into slavery was made in the correct manner. We could have an individual (A) who decides that they are particularly bad with making decisions. Every time A makes a decision, bad things result. A, however, knows of someone else (B) who seems to make good choices. As a consequence, A decides to turn over all decision-making ability to B.[40] A decides that any decisions on any matter are made by B and cannot be overruled by A due to a (perceived) lack of decision-making ability. A's decision, while it may seem completely irrational to us, appears to conform to our description of autonomy. A's decision is made intentionally. It is also made with sufficient understanding of what the decision entails. As long as the decision is not made through deception or coercion, then, we appear to have an autonomous decision by A. The fact that it forestalls future choices does not impact that.[41]

---

[39] Mill, *On Liberty*, pp. 113–114.

[40] If this sounds too implausible, it is worth remembering that we often do this in regard to particular subject areas. If we are unsure of our ability to manage money, we may hire a financial adviser and allow them to make all financial decisions, for example. In a health-care setting, we may decide to simply defer to the medical staff. So, there are at least occasions when we do hand over decision-making duties to others. The difference is that A in our hypothetical case has turned over all of them.

[41] It could be argued that A's decision is not a decision to sell oneself into slavery as B has not purchased A in any way (A just allows B to make all decisions). It could be conceivably argued then that A could presumably go back on the agreement by

The fact that A's decision is autonomous, however, does not mean we necessarily ought to allow A to do it. There are numerous reasons why we may not wish to allow people like A to make a decision to sell themselves into slavery. We might find these decisions distasteful as a society. We might believe that refusing to allow A this choice would be beneficial for A in the long run (by forcing A, perhaps, to develop decision-making skills). We may question whether A has truly made an autonomous decision and assume there is some element of coercion or deception involved. There are likely many others. All of these may be good reasons to prevent A from making this particular decision. What they do not do is change the nature of A's decision. A's decision is still autonomous even if we have compelling reasons to disallow that decision.

However, we are still left with the difficult question of how to resolve the problem of autonomous decisions which limit all future uses of autonomy. For the purposes of this book, of course, the autonomous decision we are particularly concerned with is one in which a patient in some way chooses death. A decision to take one's life is (or at least can be) an autonomous one under Beauchamp and Childress's conception of autonomy. But the larger question is still whether we should allow people to do it. Moreover, in a number of contexts, it is a more difficult problem than selling yourself into slavery. There are very few situations where even a significant minority think that selling oneself into slavery is an appropriate decision. In the case of end-of-life decisions, on the other hand, a significant number of people may think that death is an acceptable option. This does not suggest, necessarily, that autonomous decisions are ones which are plausible to either society as a whole or significant segments of it. Autonomy is not a popularity contest. But, the fact that we may see differences based upon the idea that others might agree with the decision highlights this notion of appropriate processes. The stranger a decision, the more likely it is we think the decision was not made using the correct processes, even if the decision-maker assures us that he or she has made one. In such cases, we are likely to at least require additional assurances about the decision-making process. It is not necessarily the case that the individual must provide those assurances, but we do seem to at least be able to request them.

This highlights an important concern about autonomy which is often overlooked. Autonomous decisions are not simply any sort of decision;

rescinding B's ability to make decisions for A, which is not possible in the case of slavery. I am not sure that actually matters, but, if it does, we could change the hypothetical to allow for it. We could, for example, require B to pay A for the privilege of making choices for A without A's ability to rescind.

they are a special type of decision. They are decisions which are based upon having sufficient information, a period of reflection and the capacity to make decisions, and are an attempt to make the 'best' decision for the individual under the circumstances. They are not simply decisions made on a whim or ones for which we do not have enough information. For a decision to be autonomous, certain pre-conditions must exist. If they do not, then it would be right for us to question whether they were truly autonomous. Those pre-conditions are the ones stated above: adequate information, sufficient capacity for the decision, real reflection about the decision and an attempt to make the best possible decision under the circumstances.[42]

Creating pre-conditions for uses of autonomy may cause concern. Specifically, it may be that individuals use these pre-conditions to forestall legitimate uses of autonomy by others. For example, it may be claimed that an individual has not made an autonomous decision because there is information they were not presented with or the decision does not correspond to what someone may classify as a 'best' decision. It therefore behooves us to explore this idea of pre-conditions. First, the pre-conditions, like the concept of autonomy generally, are process-oriented. They thus do not point to any specific result, but to the decision-making process. Consequently, even if certain decisions may make us more wary of accepting that the decision in question is autonomous, we still must allow the individual in question to show that the decision was made autonomously. Second, we must be aware of the limitations we operate under. It does no good to argue that individual decisions are not autonomous because of things which the individual could not possibly do. So, for example, one could not argue that a particular decision was not autonomous because the individual did not have perfect knowledge of the consequences of his or her future acts. Such knowledge is not possible and therefore we could not require autonomous decisions to have it in order to be autonomous. Third, and perhaps most importantly, a 'best' decision is not an objective measurement. It does not matter that others would have made a different decision. All that matters is that the individual in question can justify the decision as being the best one for them at that particular time and place. So, even if they would have made a different decision in different circumstances does not indicate that a particular decision was not autonomous.

---

[42] Beauchamp and Childress use a similar list. See *Principles of Biomedical Ethics*, pp. 103–105.

What these pre-conditions do accomplish, however, is to widen the remit we might have with respect to autonomous decisions by others. It is not simply our task to get out of the way of others making autonomous decisions. Instead, our role is to facilitate their autonomous decision-making process. This may provide us with positive ethical (although not necessarily legal) duties. It is our ethical duty to provide others with relevant and sufficient knowledge to be able to make autonomous decisions in cases where we possess it and they do not. It is our ethical duty to provide space for reflection about decisions, particularly those which are deemed to be vitally important. It is also our ethical duty to provide any support necessary to help individuals make the best possible choices that they can. These duties have the possibility of becoming very onerous. As such, it should be noted that I am not suggesting that we must perform these ethical duties for all people at all times. However, we should consider these to be ethical duties for those with whom we come into contact on a regular basis or for those with whom we might be in special relationships (e.g. family and friends, or patients if we are a health-care professional).

Assuming these pre-conditions are met, though, we ought to accept the autonomous decisions of others, even if it leads to the forfeit of all future autonomous decisions by that individual. There may, of course, be specific problems which we shall consider below, but in general, the respect for autonomous decisions means that we ought to accept the fact that decisions will be made which limit future autonomous choices. This is the case even if that choice limits all future autonomous choices. Again, we will need to make sure that the pre-conditions necessary for an autonomous choice have been met, but as long as that is the case, our respect for the autonomy of others requires a respect for the choices that they make, even if we disagree with them.

We now have a workable conception of autonomy. The conception of autonomy that we shall be using is the one put forth by Beauchamp and Childress. For a decision to be autonomous under their conception, the decision must be made intentionally, with sufficient understanding and without any undue controlling influences. This means that not only are there a wide range of possible decisions which may be autonomous, but there are also a number of pre-conditions necessary for a decision to be considered autonomous. As such, we may have ethical duties not only to protect the autonomous decisions of others, but also to facilitate and foster the ability of others to make autonomous decisions.

3   Regulating autonomy

Preferring Beauchamp and Childress's conception of individual autonomy over any other does not end our discussion. All discussions of autonomy (and, consequently, respect for autonomy) have to consider when
it is acceptable to regulate autonomous decision-making. We could take
the initial stance of arguing that it is never acceptable to regulate autonomous decision-making. That, however, will not pass initial scrutiny.
Many decisions are autonomous but will have serious adverse impacts
on others. This will include situations where those decisions either
impact the autonomous interests of someone else or other interests they
might have. For example, I could autonomously decide to drive on the
other side of the road from other people. Even if we assume the preconditions outlined previously, I may still believe there are good reasons for
me to drive on the wrong side. I may, for example, find it easier to get to
where I am going in places with an inconvenient set of one-way streets
in periods when there is little or no oncoming traffic. Even in such circumstances, however, it does not seem prudent to allow me to make the
choice to drive on a different side of the road from everyone else. This
is just one example of a particular type of autonomous decision which
we readily accept as being capable of regulation. Those decisions are
ones in which an autonomous decision made by one individual has an
unacceptable negative impact on another moral actor.[43] In those cases,
most accept that some regulation of autonomy is acceptable.

Additionally, regulating autonomy does not necessarily lead to less
autonomous decisions. It may be that regulation leads to greater autonomous decisions. There are two situations where this would seem to be
particularly prevalent. First, there are situations where it appears that
regulation is necessary to create the autonomous choice. For instance,
I could not choose to enter a contract or marry someone if there was
not regulation in place which allowed one to make the choice for either
of those things. Related to these types of regulation are those designed
to facilitate what Gerald Dworkin has referred to as 'autonomy by
concert'.[44] Autonomy by concert consists of cases where:

---

[43] Many if not most of our decisions are likely to have some adverse impact on others.
So, my decision to purchase a book from a particular retailer may have an adverse
impact on other retailers (since I did not buy it from them). That is not the kind
of adverse impact we are considering. We are considering cases where the negative
impact is considered unacceptable. Most cases of physical harm (although not all),
for example, are instances of unacceptable negative impacts. We will consider this
question of unacceptable harms in the next chapter.
[44] G. Dworkin, 'Paternalism' (1972) 56 *The Monist* 64–84, 69.

There are restrictions which are in the interests of a class of persons taken collectively but are such that the immediate interest of each individual is furthered by his violating the rule when others adhere to it. In such cases the individuals involved may need the use of compulsion to give effect to their collective judgment of their interest by guaranteeing each individual compliance by the others. In these cases compulsion is not used to achieve some benefit which is not recognized to be a benefit by those concerned, but rather because it is the only feasible means of achieving some benefit which *is* recognized as such by all concerned.[45]

The standard example he gives of autonomy by concert is maximum hours laws.[46] In such cases, it is not that individuals are unaware that working only a set number of hours per week will mean they are healthier, happier and more productive. Instead, what is important to realise is that individuals are in competition which prohibits us from making the decision we truly want to make. So, even if an individual knows that it is best if they work only 40 hours per week, it may be impossible to stick to that if others are willing to work longer hours, particularly in a bad economic climate. Regulation which sets a maximum number of hours would prevent individuals from undercutting others, thus allowing everyone to actually make the choice they wanted to make originally. It is not, therefore, that people need to be prevented from making choices which turn out to be bad for them, it is to provide them with the ability to make the choice they actually wanted to make.[47]

Neither of these two situations are likely to cause great concern, at least not when they are properly understood. Unfortunately, autonomy by concert is often linked with paternalism and paternalism is generally not considered an acceptable way to regulate autonomy. Paternalism is defined as cases where we regulate the autonomous decisions of individuals, not to prevent harm to others, but to prevent harm to themselves. Critics of this approach to regulating autonomous decision-making abound, with the most famous being John Stuart Mill and his 'one simple principle', where he stated:

That principle is, that the sole end for which mankind are warranted, individually or collectively, in interfering with the liberty of action of any of their number is self-protection. That the only purpose for which power can be rightfully exercised over any member of a civilized community, against his will, is to prevent harm to others. His own good, either physical or moral, is not a sufficient warrant. He cannot rightfully be compelled to do or forbear because it will be better for him to do so, because it will make him happier, because, in the opinions of others, to do so would be wise, or even right.[48]

[45] *Ibid.*   [46] *Ibid.*   [47] *Ibid.*
[48] Mill, *On Liberty*, p. 14.

As Gerald Dworkin rightly points out, however, that is neither 'one principle' nor is it 'simple'.[49] The first principle is that harm to others is an acceptable reason (at least sometimes) to interfere with 'the liberty of action' of an individual.[50] This principle is not particularly controversial and we have discussed it already at the beginning of this section. All it allows is interference with autonomous decisions when doing so will prevent harm to someone other than the decision-maker. It is the second principle which is of interest to us. That principle suggests that we cannot interfere with the liberty of action of an individual for his or her own good. It is important to realise that even Mill begins to limit that principle almost as soon as he suggests it. First, he qualifies what is meant by 'interference'. Interference means compelling the individual to make a particular decision or 'visiting him with any evil in case he do otherwise'.[51] In other words, punishment for making a particular autonomous decision is not acceptable. However, 'remonstrating with him, or reasoning with him, or persuading him or entreating him' are acceptable practices.[52] Thus, we are allowed to attempt to convince someone to change their mind, we just should not do so by force or coercion. This, perhaps, means we might be able to stop an individual temporarily to do so and, indeed, Mill hints at this. He suggests that we would be able to stop someone from crossing a bridge which we know is going to fall down but they do not.[53] We can stop them from crossing only to the extent that we provide ourselves with the opportunity to impart that knowledge about the bridge's condition.[54] Once we have told the individual, however, if they still wish to cross the bridge, we should allow them to do so. Additionally, he limits the subject of these principles. Not everyone is capable of exercising autonomy and Mill does not argue that we should allow everyone to do so.[55] He expressly limits these claims to human beings, although we could probably revise that to full moral actors without any significant change in what Mill was doing. Children, minors under the age of consent and those not capable of making decisions, however, are eliminated from Mill's principle.[56] As

[49] Dworkin, 'Paternalism', 64.   [50] *Ibid.*
[51] Mill, *On Liberty*, p. 14.   [52] *Ibid.*   [53] *Ibid.*, pp. 106–107.
[54] *Ibid.* However, Mill does indicate that if there is no possibility of warning the individual and a certainty of danger, we might stop the person altogether. For example, if a person is going to cross a bridge which is currently in the process of being demolished by dynamite we would be justified in stopping them entirely from going over the bridge.
[55] *Ibid.*, p. 14.
[56] *Ibid.* He also expressly rules out a group he refers to as 'those backward states of society in which the race itself may be considered as in its nonage' and those in 'any state of things anterior to the time when mankind have become capable of being improved

such, we can act paternalistically towards these groups. Furthermore, as discussed previously, it is worth paying attention to the fact that several things we would consider to be autonomous decisions (selling yourself into slavery) are expressly considered not to be autonomous decisions. We can also take notice of the fact that Mill was primarily concerned with legal or other political pressures as opposed to ethical ones. However, there are some interesting things which will result from an examination of Mill's principle (or principles).

Mill, for example, would seem to allow interference with autonomy for reasons consistent with the pre-conditions set out above. Those lacking capacity, for example, are not considered capable to make autonomous decisions and can therefore be treated paternalistically. Additionally, presenting evidence or arguments in support of alternative positions would seem to be consistent with our view that autonomous decisions require sufficient information and time for reflection. This can be further confirmed by the example he uses about a person crossing a falling-down bridge. In many ways, this is not surprising as our pre-conditions are based upon a conception of individual autonomy which owes a lot to Mill's ideas. But it does show that these pre-conditions are an important part of autonomy.

Of course, it also shows that interference with autonomy is not as clear cut as repeated quotations of Mill's 'one simple principle' would lead us to believe. Even Mill himself created many exceptions to the notion that all paternalism was bad. Indeed, this should hardly come as a shock as we encounter paternalistic measures every day. Mandatory seat-belt laws are paternalistic, as are warning labels on cigarette packs. We seem to accept the regulation of certain recreational drugs and requiring the wearing of helmets by motorcyclists. We have no ethical qualms about the use of regulation in these areas and may even consider it unethical not to use regulation to protect people from these particular harms. One thing that stands out about these particular uses of paternalism are that they are health and safety concerns. But not all health and safety concerns seem to be acceptable uses of paternalism. A low-salt diet is much more healthy than one that is high in salt but we would complain if our salt intake was regulated in some way. So, while health and safety concerns may be instrumental in some regulation of autonomous decisions, they are not in others.

How then do we make decisions about the interference with autonomous decisions? When is it acceptable to interfere and when is it not? If

by free and equal discussion'. *Ibid.*, pp. 14–15. We can, I think, ignore Mill's assertion that members of these groups are outside the category of responsible moral agents.

we consider a range of different paternalistic regulations, the method appears to be ad hoc. Sometimes a particular justification is sufficient, other times it is not. Sometimes autonomous decisions (even ones with which we disagree) are considered sacrosanct; other times it seems to take very little to interfere. On closer inspection, there is a method to our decisions about autonomous choices. We examine the autonomous decision in connection with the justification for the paternalistic measure. If the autonomous decision outweighs the paternalistic justification, then we believe that the paternalistic measure is unwarranted. If the paternalistic justification is considered more important, then it is a case of justifiable paternalism. In order for this to be the case, we generally consider that the justification for paternalism should be a limited set of acceptable excuses. Health and safety concerns, as noted above, are one such justification. In addition, we have ones related to the pre-conditions noted above. Paternalistic measures which are designed to solve informational deficiencies (warning labels on products or informed consent laws, for example) are acceptable. Additionally, measures which exist to allow us time for reflection (waiting periods for certain things) are considered to be justifiable. Furthermore, we accept measures which, while not perhaps expressly limiting autonomous decisions, allow us to take the time to check that the individual is capable of making a particular decision (competency hearings) and is not coerced. None of these is always an overriding justification, however. Sometimes, even if one of the justifications listed above is present, we will still consider the autonomous decision of the individual to be supreme. In legal contexts (although not necessarily in ethical contexts) we may consider the scope of the regulation of autonomy. If the regulation is very intrusive and reaches far beyond the specific justification we may wish to be addressing, it is less likely that we, as a society, will see the justification for paternalism as being sufficient to ground the regulation. Instead, we may see the autonomous decision of the individual to be more important.

What this means for us, then, is the following. Autonomy, as noted in the introduction to this section, is a very important philosophical principle which is applied to ethical decision-making. We want people to be able to make their own decisions about issues which they find important. But, while autonomy is important, it is not all-important. There are a number of ways in which autonomous decisions may be interfered with. We may interfere with them to protect others, to facilitate certain decisions or to provide a method for allowing autonomous decisions which the individual could not reach on his or her own. Sometimes, we may even interfere with the autonomous decision of an individual for his or her own good (and be justified in doing so). When considering autonomous decisions, we need to examine these things together to determine whether a particular decision should be interfered with or not. Additionally, though, we need to consider ways in which we can allow autonomy to flourish. It is not simply about interfering with decisions we do not agree with, but fostering skills and abilities which will allow others to make better and more autonomous decisions. We should therefore make sure we provide space for reflection on important issues, sufficient information and other help necessary for individuals to make the best decision they can under the circumstances.

4   Conclusion

In conclusion, we have examined the concept of autonomy in some considerable depth. There is a number of possible ways we could conceptualise what autonomy means. In the end, though, the one which will be used throughout this book is that presented by Beauchamp and Childress. To them, an autonomous decision is one made intentionally, with understanding and free from controlling interests. This conception of autonomy fits best with the stated goals of respecting autonomy – respect for moral actors and the pursuit of a 'good life'. It also, however, creates a number of pre-conditions for autonomy. If we truly wish to respect autonomy, then, it is not simply that we should protect the autonomous decisions of others, but that we should also seek to foster the ability of others to make such decisions. That may mean we have specific duties in relation to these pre-conditions. It also means that decisions which may limit any or all future choices are also worthy of respect. Even with this expansion (or what some may see as an expansion) of what we owe people in relation to autonomy, it does not mean that all autonomous decisions are sacrosanct. We can interfere with autonomous decisions in a number of ways to prevent harm to others and even harm to the individual. This, though, requires that we have a firmer grasp on what is meant by harm. That is the focus of the next chapter.

6 Beneficence, non-maleficence and harm

1   Introduction

One of the central tenets of medical ethics is the deceptively simple idea of 'First, do no harm'. It is mistakenly believed to be part of the Hippocratic Oath, but the phrase 'do no harm' does not appear anywhere in that oath, either in its original form or in the more modern form written by Louis Lasagna in 1964. The original version only states: 'I will use my power to help the sick and to the best of my ability and judgement; I will abstain from harming or wronging any man by it.'[1] The more modern version does not mention harm at all. The closest reference is the following: 'I will apply, for the benefit of the sick, all measures that are required, avoiding those twin traps of overtreatment and therapeutic nihilism.'[2] The Declaration of Geneva, as currently amended, also does not reference harm (it just states that 'the health of my patient will be my first consideration' and that 'I will practice my profession with conscience and dignity').[3] Additionally, the duties of a doctor in the General Medical Council's Good Medical Practice Guide do not reference harm,[4] nor does the phrase 'do no harm' occur in the American Medical Association's Principles of Medical Ethics.[5] Instead, it appears to be first articulated as a principle of medical ethics in the Hippocratic Corpus (*Epidemics*, Book 1, Section (ii) XI) which stated 'practice two things in your dealings with disease: either help or do not harm the patient'.[6] Regardless of its actual genesis as an

---

[1] G. E. R. Lloyd (ed.), *Hippocratic Writings* (London: Penguin Books, 1978), p. 67. It also states that 'Whenever I go into a house, I will go to help the sick and never with the intention of doing harm or injury'.
[2] www.pbs.org/wgbh/nova/doctors/oath_modern.html (accessed 21 June 2011).
[3] www.wma.net/en/30publications/10policies/g1/index.html (accessed 21 June 2011).
[4] www.gmc-uk.org/guidance/good_medical_practice/duties_of_a_doctor.asp (accessed 21 June 2011).
[5] www.ama-assn.org/ama/pub/physician-resources/medical-ethics/code-medical-ethics/principles-medical-ethics.page? (accessed 21 June 2011).
[6] Lloyd, *Hippocratic Writings*, p. 94.

ethical principle, however, the concept of doing no harm has become an important one for medical ethics.

Looking at the actual statement from the Hippocratic Corpus, though, reveals that there are two ethical principles implicit in it. The first is that doctors are supposed to help their patients. This first principle appears to be what Beauchamp and Childress refer to as the principle of 'beneficence'.[7] The second principle is that, if it is not possible to help the patient, then the doctors should at least attempt to do no harm. This principle is referred to by Beauchamp and Childress as the principle of 'non-maleficence'.[8] There are, therefore, two separate principles. Nevertheless, both principles rely on notions of harm and benefit. These two concepts, then, will be the focus of this chapter. In order to understand how to maximise the benefits to patients and to reduce the harm that patients suffer, we need to have a clear understanding of what counts as a benefit and what counts as a harm. Our first task will be to develop a robust description of harm and benefit. Once we have explored these concepts in detail, we will be better able to understand how the two principles of beneficence and non-maleficence interact not only with each other but with other important ethical principles. In the context of end-of-life decision-making, one of the most fundamental concerns is the related questions of whether life can ever be a harm and death a benefit. Consequently, the final task of this chapter will be to apply the ethical principles we have developed to answer those two related questions.

2   The concept of harm and the principle of non-maleficence

The first concept we shall consider is harm. A basic dictionary definition of harm is 'physical or mental damage: injury' or 'mischief or hurt'.[9] Neither of these definitions seem like they would be of any particular help for our conception of harm. The biggest reason for this is that almost any medical intervention would involve some sort of physical damage or injury under a strict definition of those terms. Even a simple jab involves a bit of injury. More significant medical and surgical interventions would involve more substantial injuries. For example, open-heart surgery or chemotherapy involve significant amounts of

---

[7] Beauchamp and Childress, *Principles of Biomedical Ethics*, p. 197.
[8] *Ibid.*, p. 149.
[9] *The Merriam-Webster Dictionary, New Edition* (Springfield, MA: Merriam-Webster, Inc., 2004), p. 329.

injury as one involves cracking open the patient's chest and the other involves the use of cell-killing chemicals. If either of these events happened outside a health-care context, we would not struggle to call them harmful. Within a medical context, however, we are less likely to see them as being harm, at least as far as the concept is used for the principle of non-maleficence. The simple dictionary definition of harm, therefore, is insufficient.

Two major explorations of the concept of harm – one legal by Joel Feinberg[10] and the other Beauchamp and Childress's *Principles of Biomedical Ethics*[11] – thus do not use this definition. Instead, they focus on the interests that an individual has and the setback of those interests. Something is harm, according to these conceptions of harm, if they result in an individual being prevented, frustrated or otherwise impeded in the pursuit of his or her interests.[12] This explains why a doctor opening up a patient's chest to perform open-heart surgery is different from someone else attempting to do the same thing. The doctor's actions, normally, would be aligned with the patient's interests whereas the actions of the non-doctor would not. This provides an important insight about the concept of harm. Since what counts as harm is dependent upon the interests of the individual in question, there are unlikely to be actions which are universally harmful. As a result, the concept of harm becomes individual or at least individually determined. It is also context-dependent, as what is harmful in one place at one time may not be harmful in other situations. Being confined to one's home, for example, would be harmful if there were a number of things outside the house that one wanted to accomplish. If the individual planned to read a book sitting comfortably on the sofa, it may not be seen as harmful.

Questions about what counts as an interest for the individual will therefore become particularly relevant. The first question is to determine what initially counts as an interest at all before possibly dealing with trouble cases. Beauchamp and Childress do not spend any significant time on what counts as an interest. They mention that there are broader conceptions of interests which include setbacks to 'interests in reputation, property, privacy and liberty'.[13] They do not, however, take any firm stance on whether these broader conceptions are appropriate. Instead, they focus on 'significant bodily harms and other setbacks to

---

[10] J. Feinberg, *Harm to Others: The Moral Limits of the Criminal Law* (New York: Oxford University Press, 1984), vol. I.
[11] Beauchamp and Childress, *Principles of Biomedical Ethics*, pp. 152–153.
[12] Feinberg, *Harm to Others*, ch. 1; Beauchamp and Childress, *Principles of Biomedical Ethics*, p. 152.
[13] Beauchamp and Childress, *Principles of Biomedical Ethics*, p. 152.

significant interests' which they see as being paradigm cases of harm.[14] They concentrate specifically on physical harms such as pain, death or disability,[15] which is not surprising considering the focus on general medical ethics.

Feinberg gives us a more complete conception of interests. According to Feinberg, an interest is one where an individual has a stake in something.[16] This only pushes back the inquiry because we then need some explanation of what 'having a stake' means. Feinberg states that to have a stake in something means that one 'stands to gain or lose depending on the nature or condition of X'.[17] Feinberg also wants to draw comparisons between the setback of interests per se from when a person wrongs another. Wronging, under Feinberg's definition, is when someone violates the rights of another without justification or excuse.[18] These wrongs will, in a number of cases, all consist of harms in the previous sense of setbacks of interests, but he states that 'there *can* be wrongs that are not harms *on balance*, but there are few wrongs that are not *to some extent* harms'.[19] Invasions of interests, though, may not always be wrongs. These, in particular, are the cases where the invasion of another's interest has been excusable or subject to some justification or when the interests of the individual are not worthy of respect.[20]

This does not end the inquiry into interests. We might argue that there are some interests which seem reasonably insignificant or which we have no actual power to control. As such, Feinberg differentiates between different types of interests. The first type of interests includes those he refers to as ultimate goals or aspirations.[21] These are the grand sort of projects that we have in careers and family life. But there are other interests he found just as important. He suggests:

They are rather his interests, presumably shared by nearly all his fellows, in the necessary means to his more ultimate goals, whatever the latter may be, or later come to be. In this category are the interests in the continuance for a foreseeable interval of one's life, and the interests in one's own physical health and vigor, the integrity and normal functioning of one's body, the absence of absorbing pain and suffering or grotesque disfigurement, minimal intellectual

---

[14] *Ibid.*   [15] *Ibid.*, pp. 152–153.   [16] Feinberg, *Harm to Others*, p. 33.
[17] *Ibid.*, pp. 33–34.   [18] *Ibid.*, p. 34.
[19] *Ibid.*, p. 35 (emphasis in original).
[20] Feinberg's main concern is the harm principle as articulated by John Stuart Mill and its applicability to the criminal law. He therefore concludes that 'only setbacks of interests that are wrongs, and wrongs that are setbacks to interests, are to count as harms in the appropriate sense'. *Ibid.*, p. 36. Our concerns are more varied, as we will end on focusing on the idea of whether actions which are consented to (in particular, actions leading to the death of a patient) can be considered harms. It is therefore not necessarily appropriate for us to follow Feinberg completely, at least at this point.
[21] *Ibid.*, p. 37.

acuity, emotional stability, the absence of groundless anxieties and resentments, the capacity to engage normally in social intercourse and to enjoy and maintain friendships, at least minimal income and financial security, a tolerable social and physical environment and a certain amount of freedom from interference and coercion.[22]

Feinberg refers to these interests as welfare interests.[23] These welfare interests are especially important because they provide the things necessary for us to achieve our more ultimate aims. Additionally, welfare interests 'make a chain that is no stronger than its weakest link'.[24] Infringements of welfare interests, then, would constitute serious harm. Even so, Feinberg does not argue that only infringements of welfare interests count as harm.[25] Infringements of mere wants, however, are not sufficient to truly be considered harm. This is because wants are not significant enough to give us a direct interest in the events or actions concerned.[26] What, then, of the pleasant sensation we get from the satisfaction of our wants? Is this sufficient to ground an interest? Feinberg says no. He indicates that interests and desires are aimed at external things as opposed to internal states.[27] Thus, the satisfactory states that occur when our wants are satisfied are insufficient, in and of themselves, to provide us with sufficient interests so that interference with them would be considered harm.[28] Nor do all instances of situations which we would wish to avoid count as harmful. There are things which may cause discomfort, irritation or offence without any necessary setback to our interests.[29] These would not be considered significant enough to constitute harm.

In addition to a conception of interest, we also need a conception of setback for our description of harm to be meaningful. If we consider our interests to be capable of placement on a graph, we might consider anything which positively affects our interests to be beneficial and those which negatively affect our interests to be harmful.[30] A setback, then, is something which makes the achievement (or maintenance) of that interest less likely. However, it is worth mentioning the idea of a baseline or zero mark to our graph. It may be that a small change upward on the graph is beneficial to someone at the lowest end, but it may still be insufficient to be truly beneficial in the sense of truly addressing

[22] *Ibid.*   [23] *Ibid.*
[24] *Ibid.*, citing the arguments of Nicholas Rescher in *Welfare: The Social Issue in Philosophical Perspective* (University of Pittsburgh Press, 1972), p. 6.
[25] Feinberg, *Harm to Others*, pp. 37–38.   [26] *Ibid.*, p. 42.
[27] *Ibid.*, p. 43.   [28] *Ibid.*   [29] *Ibid.*, p. 45.
[30] Neither Feinberg nor I are suggesting that our interests can be placed on a graph as easily as a bank balance may. It is merely to provide a crude analogy which may make visualisation of the question of setbacks of interests more clear. *Ibid.*, p. 53.

the interest in question.[31] A minuscule lessening of pain suffered by a patient may be beneficial but, if it does not put the patient's pain in a manageable state, it is not likely to be seen as being a substantial or meaningful benefit.[32] Consequently, it is worth keeping in mind a baseline measure for the interests we will be considering.

To summarise, something is a harm if it sets back an interest we have in something. The two types of interest which are particularly important are ultimate interests (our life goals, etc.) and welfare interests (those things we need to achieve our ultimate interests). Not all interferences with interests, however, are necessarily harms. It may be that there is an excuse or justification for the interference with the interest or it may be that the interest is not one worthy of protection. There may also be wants which should be considered separate from interests. Interference with wants is unlikely to be considered harm. A setback to an interest occurs when the achievement or maintenance of that interest is to be considered more unlikely as a result of the interference with that interest. This, then, provides our conception of harm.

Now that we have a conception of harm, it will be much easier to explore the nebulous principles of non-maleficence. As stated in Beauchamp and Childress, the principle of non-maleficence is the principle of avoiding or minimising harm. According to them, the principle should be articulated as 'One ought not to inflict evil or harm'.[33] The principle of non-maleficence, then, is a negative moral obligation.[34] It does not require us to do something positive but to avoid doing something.[35] We should avoid as much as possible setting back the ultimate and welfare interests of others when there is no excuse or justification which would allow it. We should also, as Beauchamp and Childress state, avoid unnecessary risks of harm to others.[36] This concern about the risk of harm is most often linked with medical negligence issues. There is, however, some impact upon issues at the end of life. One of the issues which has to be addressed in end-of-life decisions is the harm that certain interventions (or failures of intervention) will cause for a particular patient. Consequently, it is necessary to explore what the risk of future harm to the patient will be in those particular circumstances. So, doctors will need to evaluate whether the drugs given to a patient to control pain but which may depress respiration are worth providing despite the risk of harm that may be present. These are not easy to answer in all circumstances and our ability to recognise and

---

[31] *Ibid.*, p. 54.   [32] *Ibid.*
[33] Beauchamp and Childress, *Principles of Biomedical Ethics*, p. 151.
[34] *Ibid.*   [35] *Ibid.*   [36] *Ibid.*, p. 153.

appropriately account for risk may not be perfect, but we will need to make sure these issues are within our consideration.

3   The principle of beneficence

With an understanding of harm, it becomes much easier to explore the concept of benefit. Benefits, unlike harms, are actions which are designed to promote or improve the interests of an individual. So, if we return to the idea of plotting interests on a graph, a benefit is any action which improves or raises the value of that interest on the graph. A beneficent act is one that is done to benefit others. The principle of beneficence, as Beauchamp and Childress explain, is the moral obligation to act in a way that benefits others.[37] On its face, then, the principle of beneficence is easy enough to understand.

There is a complex issue that requires further examination. That question is whether there ought to be a moral obligation to act for the benefit of others. The principle of non-maleficence is a negative one. In other words, it only requires that we refrain from doing certain things. The principle of beneficence, on the other hand, appears to be a positive one. It requires that we do certain things instead of merely not doing them. As this is usually a more considerable ethical burden,[38] it is worth exploring in detail the extent to which we may need to engage in these positive actions. Otherwise, we may end up expecting individuals to act benevolently towards such a wide variety of people and in such a wide variety of cases that it becomes impossible to abide by the ethical principle.

Beauchamp and Childress argue that there is no duty of general benevolence to others.[39] Instead, they cite with approval the following statement from Slone: 'One has an obligation to prevent serious evil or harm when one can do so without seriously interfering with one's life plans or style and without doing any wrongs of commission.'[40] Anything more, they suggest, would lead to too significant an ethical burden to expect individuals to perform.[41] If we have no ethical duty of general benevolence, though, we do have specific duties. These are duties in relation to specific discernible individuals and include those to whom we have special relationships (family, friends, contractual duties, etc.).[42] Outside those contexts, Beauchamp and Childress argue that a specific individual (X) has a duty of benevolence to another (Y) in cases where the following conditions are met (and X is aware of the relevant facts):

---

[37] *Ibid.*, p. 197.   [38] *Ibid.*, pp. 197–198.   [39] *Ibid.*, pp. 199–201.
[40] *Ibid.*, p. 202.   [41] *Ibid.*, p. 199–201.   [42] *Ibid.*, p. 202.

1. Y is at risk of significant loss of or damage to life or health or some other major interest.
2. X's action is needed (singly or in concert with others) to prevent this loss or damage.
3. X's action (singly or in concert with others) has a high probability of preventing it.
4. X's action would not present significant risks, costs or burdens to X.
5. The benefit that Y can be expected to gain outweighs any harms, costs or burdens that X is likely to incur.[43]

They make specific note of the critical nature of the fourth condition. That condition means that even if Y is to lose his or her life as a result of X's inaction, if the burden on X is too great then there is no obligation to act on X's part.[44] It is therefore only in situations where all of the conditions are met that X is required to act.

We can better explore this conception of benevolence if we look at some test cases which are seen as being particularly troubling. Peter Unger explores the issue of whether we ought to be contributing more towards charitable causes and provides us with a number of possible scenarios where we might be called upon to help others. One such scenario is as follows:

The Vintage Sedan. Not truly rich, your one luxury in life is a vintage Mercedes sedan that, with much time, attention and money, you've restored to mint condition. In particular, you're pleased by the auto's fine leather seating. One day, you stop at the intersection of two small country roads, both lightly travelled. Hearing a voice screaming for help, you get out and see a man who's wounded and covered with a lot of his blood. Assuring you that the wound is confined to one of his legs, the man also informs you that he was a medical student for a full two years. And, despite his expulsion for cheating on his second year final exams, which explains his indigent status since, he's knowledgably tied his shirt near the wound to stop the flow. So, there's no urgent danger of losing his life, you're informed, but there's great danger of him losing his limb. This can be prevented, however, if you drive him to a rural hospital fifty miles away … Now, if you aid this [individual] you must lay him across your fine back seat. But, then, your fine upholstery will be soaked through with blood, and restoring the car will cost over five thousand dollars.[45]

[43] *Ibid.* It is worth noting that Beauchamp and Childress cite others specifically at this point including E. D'Arcy, *Human Acts: An Essay in Their Moral Evaluation* (Oxford: Clarendon Press, 1963), pp. 56–57; and Feinberg, *Harm to Others*, ch. 4.
[44] Beauchamp and Childress, *Principles of Biomedical Ethics*, p. 202.
[45] Unger, *Living High and Letting Die*, p. 25.

Do you, under our analysis of benevolence, have a duty to assist? Part 1 is clearly satisfied as the individual is at risk of significant loss to life if he is not taken to the hospital. The same goes for parts 2 and 3. You are the only one around for many miles so it is up to you to act and the action of bringing the individual to the hospital will have a high probability of helping the individual. The difficult bit is likely to be part 4. The actions you will have to do in this case involve driving someone to the hospital which is a reasonable distance away, costing you time and inconvenience. It will also adversely affect your expensive vehicle as the costs of repairing or replacing the upholstery may be beyond your means. The question then becomes whether these count as significant costs and burdens to you. Beauchamp and Childress do not give us a real test for 'significant' unless, in fact, part 5 actually presents us with that test. There may be some appeal to this sort of explanation. The burdens to you in this particular case may be substantial. However, the benefit to the dying individual is even more significant. So, we may rightly determine that you have a moral duty of beneficence in this situation.[46]

This may become more difficult, though, if we think of another situation. Suppose we have another of Unger's cases:

The Envelope. In your mailbox, there's something from the U.S. Committee for UNICEF. After reading it through, you correctly believe that, unless you soon send in a check for $100, then, instead of living many more years, over thirty more children will die soon.[47]

Do you have a duty in this case to send the money to the charity? Again, if we look at our five-part test, there may be some considerable questions. Part 1 of the test again is clearly satisfied. In this case, parts 4 and 5 are also clearly satisfied. Part 2, however, seems to be at issue. Sending in your money to a charity may save 30 lives but it is not clear which lives that may be. It might, therefore, seem open to question whether your action is needed (singly or in concert with others) to prevent this loss or damage to the individuals (whomever that might be). As discussed above, we do not have duties to the world at large to be benevolent; we only have those duties in regard to specific cases. But, if the duty of benevolence is being addressed to an indeterminate group, then it is likely that the real duty seems to be general. Part 2 of this test may be as crucial as part 4 because it explains why we feel we have a

---

[46] You may or may not have a legal obligation, of course, depending on your jurisdiction. Here, though, we are only concerned with the moral duties you might have.

[47] Unger, *Living High and Letting Die*, p. 9.

moral duty in the first case but not in the second, even though the cost to us in the first might be substantially greater.[48]

Duties of beneficence, therefore, are determined by a complex set of issues including the potential harm to the person helped, whether that person is determinate, the costs and burdens put on the person doing the helping and the relationship between the benefit and the costs put on the helper. Additionally, certain roles or relationships that we have may alter what beneficent duties we possess. All of us may have some duty to stop and help someone injured in an accident. A doctor's duties in that situation would likely be more extensive than the duties that non-doctors possess in a similar situation. Moreover, my duties in relation to my friends, family or Sherman may be significantly greater than someone else's who does not have any relationship with those individuals. The five-part test provided, then, will not necessarily give us the entire picture but it does give a general idea about how we can best analyse the duties of beneficence that we have.

4   Death as a harm or a benefit

This leaves us with one final question for this chapter and it is the most difficult for our purposes. That question is whether death can be a benefit. It is worth starting with the obvious point that there is no question that death is a harm in a number of cases. The question before us, then, is not whether death is never a harm. It is a harm in perhaps almost all cases. This, then, necessitates the subsequent point that death is rarely likely to be a benefit as it is difficult to see how something could be a harm and a benefit at the same time under our definitions. The limited question before us is whether death can ever be a benefit or whether it is always some sort of harm.

To answer this question, it is worth returning to our idea of what counts as a benefit and what counts as a harm. These were based upon the interests of the individual and whether the action in question positively affected that interest or negatively affected it. Anything which positively affected the interests of the individual was considered to be a benefit (provided that it was above a certain baseline); anything which negatively affected it was considered to be a harm. So, in order for death to be a benefit, it would have to positively affect some interest that the individual has. On the face of it, it seems absurd that death would

---

[48] It is worth noting that Unger is not convinced that you have no duty to send the money to UNICEF or, indeed that there is any real difference between the cases involving the vintage sedan and the envelope. *Ibid.*, pp. 24–61.

somehow positively affect someone's interests. Indeed, if we consider the welfare interests set forth by Feinberg, they include the interest in the 'continuance for a foreseeable interval of one's life'.[49] Since welfare interests are not cumulative and the interference with one welfare interest cannot be replaced by greater respect for other welfare interests,[50] we might argue as a consequence that death can never be a benefit as it always interferes negatively with at least one of the welfare interests of the individual.

Cases at the end of life are more complex, however. In many ways, we might argue, the welfare interest in the continuance of a foreseeable interval of one's life ceases to be a particular interest as it cannot be satisfied. Instead, this is a case where the patient has only the other welfare interests which can be affected. Some of these include the absence of absorbing pain, minimal intellectual acuity, emotional stability and a tolerable social and physical environment.[51] All of these could be adversely impacted by continuance of life in a situation where the patient is in significant unremitting pain, suffering from a loss of control over their surroundings, or afflicted with a medical condition which adversely affects their mind (such as dementia). These are very specific cases which are outside our normal considerations about life as a benefit. Moreover, as noted above, the interests of the individual are specific to that individual. These are thus personal choices about those things which matter to that individual. Our interests cannot be universalised.

In these cases, it may be that the only way to relieve the pain, suffering and other concerns that the patient has is to end that patient's life sooner rather than later. Such a decision may best allow the individual to promote the majority of the interests that matter to that individual. It may be that, in such a case, the interest in continuation of living takes a back seat to other interests about the lack of pain or loss of faculties. However, and it is important to stress this fact, because these interests are unique to the individual, it is the individual who can provide the best description of his particular set of interests (what Feinberg calls an interest network[52]). So, if death is a benefit, it is only because the specific individual sees their collection of interests in a particular way.

5   Conclusion

In conclusion, we have considered the concepts of harm and benefit in this chapter. Taking the work of Feinberg and Beauchamp and

---

[49] Feinberg, *Harm to Others*, p. 37.   [50] *Ibid.*
[51] *Ibid.*   [52] *Ibid.*, pp. 55–61.

Childress as our guides, we have explored how harm and benefits are concepts which rely on individual interests and the effect that actions and events may have upon those interests. Actions or events which positively affect the interests of an individual are a benefit and those which negatively affect the interests of an individual are a harm. From these concepts of harm and benefit, we can construct the twinned principles of non-maleficence and beneficence. Non-maleficence is a negative moral principle which means that it requires that we refrain from doing certain actions. It is therefore the more wide-ranging of the two principles we have considered in this chapter. Beneficence, on the other hand, creates positive obligations which require us to act in certain ways. It is therefore more limited in scope due to the fact that a general requirement of beneficence would be too burdensome. Instead, beneficence only applies in a limited set of circumstances, either when we have specific relationships with individuals or in very specific cases.

The bigger question for our purposes, though, was the question of whether death can ever be considered a benefit and continuation of life a harm. As we have seen in the final section, the answer to these questions relies on the specific interests of an individual. While it may be that, in general, death is harmful, there may be a limited set of circumstances at the end of life where death better promotes the interests of the individual. In such a case, death would, in fact, be beneficial. However, the interests that are involved in these sorts of determinations are ones which are determined by the individual in question. They are not universalised and we cannot therefore use our own conception of what might be in an individual's interest to override their perception of whether death is beneficial or not.

7 Dignity

1 Introduction

The concept of dignity has been integral to end-of-life decision-making for a significant period of time. Arguments about 'death with dignity' have been instrumental in this. We don't, for example, argue about 'death with autonomy' or 'death with beneficence'. Additionally, the concept of human dignity within broader notions about human rights (either moral or legal) is an important one, with human dignity being a foundational concept for many human rights documents and national constitutions.[1] Even so, the concept of dignity within bioethics is notoriously under-defined. It is probably the least defined of the concepts we have been considering. There appears to be no definitive discussion about what it is supposed to entail, let alone how it should be applied. It is used by both sides in various debates (including end-of-life ones) about possible treatments.[2] Sometimes, it appears to be a sword; other times it is used as a shield. Its slippery and undefined nature has led some to suggest that it is not really a self-contained idea at all.[3] Instead, the argument is that dignity is just synonymous with other concepts such as autonomy or respect for persons.[4]

I think, though, that this is too easy a way out. The repeated references to and citations of dignity mean that individuals in the moral community place some force behind the idea. What is necessary is an attempt to determine the place of dignity within the larger confines of bioethics and the role it is to play in end-of-life decisions. That means

[1] D. Feldman, 'Human Dignity as a Legal Value: Part One' (1999) *Public Law* 682–702.
[2] For example, the group Dignity in Dying is an organisation which supports the legalisation of assisted suicide. See www.dignityindying.org.uk (accessed 21 June 2011). On the other hand, a number of proponents suggest that death with dignity cannot include assisted dying. See L. R. Kass, 'Defending Human Dignity', in E. D. Pellegrino, A. Schulman and T. W. Merrill (eds.), *Human Dignity and Bioethics* (University of Notre Dame Press, 2009), pp. 297–331, 311.
[3] R. Macklin, 'Dignity Is a Useless Concept' (2003) 327 *BMJ* 1419–1420.
[4] *Ibid.*

creating clarity about the concept itself and the philosophical under-pinnings of dignity. To that end, we have several tasks in front of us. First, it will be important to explore the different notions of dignity which are sometimes used and may create misunderstandings. From those various ideas of dignity, we shall choose to examine the most important – human dignity – in further detail. This will require that we look at the foundational justifications for human dignity. All of these will be found, however, to have insufficient support either because they will not form convincing arguments for sceptics of human dignity or because they lack a factual basis. It will then be necessary to develop a more convincing argument in favour of human dignity based upon social justification of the concept. Problems with a social justification for the ethical concept of human dignity will then be considered in our final section.

2   Category/definitional issues

The problem with the concept of dignity starts with definitional problems. By this, I do not mean there is a lack of a definition for dignity. Instead, the problem with dignity is that it appears to be used to encompass a number of possibilities.[5] As a result, it can sometimes be difficult to figure out exactly what is meant by dignity within a particular argument. This may mean that individuals are talking past each other when they are discussing and debating the concept of dignity. It is crucial, then, to get to grips with the various ways in which dignity may be used.

First, it may be used as an aspirational idea. This seems to be the way we use dignity when we use it as a synonym for nobility or when we talk about 'dignified behaviour'.[6] We see dignity in this sense as being something which people ought to aspire to and as an ideal. It is thus not an ordinary quality that individuals have but a superlative designed to emphasise uniqueness or some special quality possessed by the person in question.[7] We can also use this definition of dignity in a negative sense when we complain about people being undignified. We use the

---

[5] H. Spiegelberg, 'Human Dignity: A Challenge to Contemporary Philosophy', in R. Gotesky and E. Laszlo (eds.), *Human Dignity: This Century and the Next* (New York: Gordon & Breach, 1970), pp. 55–56, cited in Beyleveld and Brownsword, *Human Dignity in Bioethics and Biolaw*, p. 50.

[6] Beyleveld and Brownsword, *Human Dignity in Bioethics and Biolaw*, pp. 58–63 (citing the case of Diane Blood as an example of acting in a dignified manner).

[7] *Ibid.* See also N. Bostrom, 'Dignity and Enhancement', in Pellegrino *et al.* (eds.), *Human Dignity and Bioethics*, pp. 173–206, 175.

term dignity in this sense when we complain about people stooping below some appropriate level by, for example, being on reality television or having toilet paper on their shoe at an exclusive party. Dignity in this sense appears then to be action-based; it is based upon what the individual does in certain cases.[8] When used in this way, the superlative definition of dignity may pose particular problems as it may superficially resemble other notions of dignity – in particular, the notion of human dignity we shall consider below. The difference between these cases is that in the first instance of dignity as an aspirational characteristic, we are discussing incidents where someone has fallen below some idealised standard. In the second, where we are articulating a concern about human dignity, the individual in question has done something which seems to violate their human-ness, however defined. As one deals with an idealised standard and one deals with presumably normal human action, it is important to keep these two conceptions of dignity separate, despite how close they may appear in our normal everyday conversation. More importantly, the notion of dignity as an aspirational concept is not one we will consider much further. While it is important, presumably, to have notions of ideal conduct sufficient to make this notion of dignity useful in our everyday language, its use as an ethical concept is fairly limited in the circumstances we are considering. What is needed is a more universal concept of dignity as opposed to one which specifies an idyllic set of characteristics for individuals to aspire to.

Another way of conceiving of dignity is the one used in the phrase 'death with dignity'.[9] While this shares some aspirational qualities with the previous description, there are significant differences between the two. This conception of dignity seems to be external in a way that the other conception is not. It is not dependent on what the individual does, but on the external circumstances surrounding the case.[10] This may, of course, include ideas about what the individual does, but the focus appears to be on the totality of circumstances. So, when we discuss death with dignity, we appear to mean that the circumstances

[8] In particular, Beyleveld and Brownsword suggest dignity in this sense is most easily apparent in cases of adversity. See Beyleveld and Brownsword, *Human Dignity in Bioethics and Biolaw*, p. 59.

[9] Again, for a specific example, see the website of the group Dignity in Dying, www.dignityindying.org.uk.

[10] Hazel Biggs, for example, states that '[f]or a person seeking death with dignity, overriding autonomy by insisting on utilising every available therapy is inherently destructive of human dignity and can compromise her quality of life'. H. Biggs, *Euthanasia: Death with Dignity and the Law* (Oxford: Hart Publishing, 2001), p. 146. It is worth highlighting that Biggs also defines dignity in the three ways outlined here, although not, perhaps, as distinct categories in the way I have done.

surrounding the death are sufficient in some sort of normative way and are likely to include the actions of others (such as health-care staff) in addition to anything that the patient does directly.[11] Additionally, this notion of dignity appears to be something which can be gained or lost. When we talk about this conception of dignity it is always in terms of making sure that patients possess it and that it is not taken away. This seems to indicate that we are at least worried that it can be taken away and are optimistic that it is something that can be gained if it is not already present. However, it is not necessarily an ideal condition. It is not the best of situations we can hope for, but one we find as being sufficient under the circumstances. It is therefore not as much a statement about excellence as the first type of dignity we have considered. This conception of dignity corresponds to one presented by Deryck Beyleveld and Roger Brownsword in their book *Human Dignity in Bioethics and Biolaw*. They present two different ways to categorise dignity claims. The first is called dignity as empowerment.[12] Beyleveld and Brownsword argue that dignity as empowerment can be closely linked to autonomy and autonomous actions. It is about respecting the choices of particular individuals and its function is to 'reinforce claims to self-determination rather than to limit free choice'.[13] It thus corresponds to the way in which we have been conceiving of dignity when we discuss 'death with dignity'.

While this gets us closer to a conception of dignity which could be used as an ethical principle, it also seems like it borrows too much from the concept of autonomy to be a stand-alone ethical principle.[14] When we discuss 'death with dignity', what we often seem to mean is that the individual has some sort of control over the dying process and that their wishes are respected.[15] That seems suspiciously like the notion that the individual's choices ought to be respected because the individual is best suited to determine what helps them achieve what they wish to achieve.[16] If this is the case, it is worth wondering if we need a separate concept of dignity if autonomy will offer the same protection. If we are going to consider dignity to be an important ethical concept, it needs to add something to our moral discussions and the one that features in our claims about death with dignity does not appear necessarily to do so.

---

[11] *Ibid.*
[12] Beyleveld and Brownsword, *Human Dignity in Bioethics and Biolaw*, p. 11.
[13] *Ibid.*, p. 28.
[14] See, e.g., M. Nussbaum, 'Human Dignity and Political Entitlements', in Pellegrino *et al.* (eds.), *Human Dignity and Bioethics*, pp. 351–380, 372.
[15] Beyleveld and Brownsword, *Human Dignity in Bioethics and Biolaw*, p. 238.
[16] Nussbaum, 'Human Dignity and Political Entitlements', pp. 351–380, 372.

A third conception of dignity is what we refer to when we talk about human dignity. Unlike the previous two conceptions of dignity, this one does not appear to be aspirational in any form. On the contrary, it is something which appears to be basic to any human being.[17] In other words, any human has this form of dignity merely by being human. This means it applies to all humans regardless of any disabilities, conditions, illnesses, etc., which might adversely impact them in other ways.[18] Furthermore, while the other two possibilities relate either to actions performed by the individual or to external characteristics, this form of dignity does not appear to be based on either. Instead, the dignity involved in human dignity appears to be an inherent characteristic which cannot be reduced or taken away.[19] Nor does it seem that it can be supplemented. Indeed, it appears not to be a value which varies from person to person but is the same for everyone. This conception, as opposed to the previous two, does provide us with a description of dignity that can be built on. It is not a statement about ideal characteristics like the first, but it is also different from notions of autonomy. It therefore provides us with a unique principle which we can take account of when considering ethical treatment at the end of life. This also has parallels in the approach used by Beyleveld and Brownsword. The second possibility for dignity, according to them, is called dignity as constraint.[20] This is the idea that human dignity forestalls us from making certain decisions. It represents 'an "objective value" or good … such that, if an act violates this value, human dignity is compromised irrespective of whether the party so acting freely agrees to perform the act in question'.[21] It is, under this conception of dignity, not then a synonym for autonomy but an additional value which puts limits on the autonomous abilities of ourselves and others.[22] This seems to fit much better with the idea of human dignity which is proposed as the third possibility above.

In conclusion, there are a number of ways in which we might use the term 'dignity'. We can use it as an aspirational quality which indicates some characteristic of excellence. We may use it as synonym for autonomy. We may use it as a distinct notion which provides some sort of objective value about humanity which is different from autonomy or the other principles we have been considering. Conceiving of dignity as a

---

[17] Spiegelberg, 'Human Dignity', pp. 55–56, cited in Beyleveld and Brownsword, *Human Dignity in Bioethics and Biolaw*, p. 50.
[18] D. P. Sulmasy, OFM, 'Dignity and Bioethics: History, Theory and Selected Applications', in Pellegrino *et al.* (eds.), *Human Dignity and Bioethics*, pp. 469–501, 473.
[19] *Ibid.*, pp. 469–501, 475, 476.
[20] Beyleveld and Brownsword, *Human Dignity in Bioethics and Biolaw*, p. 11.
[21] *Ibid.*, p. 34.   [22] *Ibid.*, p. 27.

distinct value will provide us with the most influential notion of dignity. It will allow us to explore this notion of shared human values and abilities without going over previously trodden ground about autonomous decisions and choice. It also seems to fit more with the claims which are often made in relation to dignity that argue that dignity prevents us from making certain choices. Consequently, we are likely to get the most use out of using dignity in either the human dignity sense above or Beyleveld and Brownsword's notion of dignity as constraint. It will therefore be the notion of human dignity used through the rest of this chapter when considering dignity.

3   Philosophical justifications for dignity

Deciding on which conception of dignity to focus on is only the first step. If human dignity as described exists, then it requires a philosophical justification for its use as an ethical principle. Initially, we may run into a similar problem with dignity as we had with moral status. There, concerns were expressed as to why it was that moral status claims sometimes revolved around species membership. We may make the same claims about human dignity. Why is it only humans which have dignity (or at least the dignity we care about)?[23] Can other entities have dignity? If so, what is the basis for separating out that dignity which humans possess from whatever dignity other entities possess? In order to answer these questions, we need to know what it is that makes humans unique in relation to the concept of dignity.

The first justification we shall consider is a theological one. In particular, this is a viewpoint commonly associated with the Judaeo-Christian worldview. Under this justification, humans are unique among all entities created by God because they alone are created 'in the image of God'.[24] Everything, of course, has been created by God but when he created humans, he created them to be special and that specialness comes from the fact that he made humans in his image.[25] It may not be

---

[23] H. Kuhse, 'Is There a Tension between Autonomy and Dignity?' in P. Kemp, J. Rendtorff and N. M. Johansen (eds.), *Bioethics and Biolaw*, vol. II: *Four Ethical Principles* (Copenhagen: Rhodes International Science and Art Publishers and Centre for Ethics and Law, 2000), pp. 61–74, 69–70, cited in Beyleveld and Brownsword, *Human Dignity in Bioethics and Biolaw*, p. 22.

[24] A. Schulman, 'Bioethics and the Question of Human Dignity', in Pellegrino *et al.* (eds.), *Human Dignity and Bioethics*, pp. 3–18, 8. R. P. Kraynak, 'Human Dignity and the Mystery of the Human Soul', in Pellegrino *et al.* (eds.), *Human Dignity and Bioethics*, pp. 61–82, 79.

[25] The use of the pronoun 'he' to refer to God is standard in these sorts of arguments because the Judaeo-Christian God is generally seen to be male. Of course, God need

especially clear in these circumstances exactly what 'in God's image' means – for example, does it refer to physical characteristics? Mental ones? A soul? – but whatever it means, human dignity is either this image of God in us or provides us with the reason to ascribe dignity to all humans.[26] Whatever the truth or falsity of that description of reality (if it is even simply true or false), that version of events is notoriously difficult to prove. Nor is it likely to prove convincing or even persuasive to those not already predisposed to being persuaded. If one does not accept the initial premise that God exists and that God created humans in his/her/its image, then the rest of the argument simply does not work, irrespective of how strongly it is argued. As such, it does not provide sufficient support to ground a universal claim about human dignity. Those who are not willing to be convinced about the nature of God (or at least the nature of God necessary for the argument to work) will have no reason to accept the rest of the argument or the concept of human dignity.[27] Considering that a significant portion of the world does not accept the Judaeo-Christian God, it would appear to be a rather flimsy basis on which to build a conception of dignity. Non-believers will need something which does not require the theoretical underpinnings of dignity deriving from humans being created in the image of God.[28]

This has led some to argue that human dignity comes instead from rationality. This stems primarily from Kantian notions of treating humans as an end in themselves.[29] Kant argued that humans should be treated as an end in themselves because of their rationality.[30] Human dignity, therefore, arises from the rationality that humans possess. Of course, all humans are not rational and none are probably rational all the time. So, instead of requiring actual rationality, dignity under this justification only requires the radical capacity for rationality.[31] A radical capacity is one which an individual could conceivably use in the right circumstances, but this requires a bit of further explanation. A capacity is something someone has if they have the ability to do something. So, for example, if I can play the saxophone but do not happen to be doing

---

not be male or female or even gendered in any way. Readers should feel free to replace 'he' with 'she' or 'it' if they prefer.

[26] Kraynak, 'Human Dignity and the Mystery of the Human Soul', pp. 61–82, 79.

[27] D. C. Dennett, 'Commentary on Kraynak', in Pellegrino *et al.* (eds.), *Human Dignity and Bioethics*, pp. 83–88.

[28] *Ibid.*, p. 10.

[29] Schulman, 'Bioethics and the Question of Human Dignity', pp. 3–18, 10.

[30] *Ibid.*

[31] For a discussion about radical capacities, albeit in a slightly different context, see Finnis, 'A Philosophical Case against Euthanasia', pp. 30–33; Finnis, 'The Fragile Case for Euthanasia', pp. 47–50.

so at the moment, then I have a capacity to play the saxophone. I have the radical capacity to play the saxophone if I do not currently have the ability to play that musical instrument, but I could develop it. So, if I received instruction, I could learn to play. The same is true of rationality. I have the capacity for rationality if I have the ability to be rational, even if I am not currently using that ability. I have the radical capacity for rationality if I could develop the capacity, even if I currently do not possess it. So, using rationality as the basis for human dignity requires only the radical capacity for it, not the actual ability.[32]

Unfortunately, if we remember the chapter on moral worth, this is not sufficient. Certain individuals who are human do not have the capacity for rationality, whether couched in terms of radical capacities or not. Anthony Bland post-Hillsborough, for example, does not have the capacity for rational thought; nor do anencephalic infants. The reason they do not have the capacity for rational thought is that neither Anthony Bland after the disaster at Hillsborough nor anencephalic infants possess a brain. If they do not (and presuming that what we know about how we think is at all accurate), then it is not possible for them to be rational in any way. Radical capacities require the ability to develop the capacity, but this also does not exist in the case of Anthony Bland or anencephalic infants. If one argues that it is possible that they have the radical capacity because what we know about how we think could be false (and it can be), then there is no reason to presume that Anthony Bland or anencephalic infants possess the characteristic but other entities without brains (such as tables, chairs or this book) do not. Arguing otherwise seems to rely on one of two fallacies. The first is simply circular reasoning. It suggests that all humans have the radical capacity for rationality.[33] Since Anthony Bland and anencephalic infants are human, they too must possess the radical capacity for rationality. Why? Because they are human and all humans must possess this capacity.[34] The real work then does not appear to be done by the concept of rationality at all. Instead, it relies only on the species classification of human. The point of relying on rationality, though, was to avoid reliance on species classifications to determine why humans were special and the only species possessing dignity. If, when the chips are down, we merely rely on that notion anyway, rationality seems to play no real part in the equation. Alternatively, one might argue that humans have the radical capacity because it is somehow necessary for being a human

---

[32] P. Lee and R. P. George, 'The Nature and Basis of Human Dignity', in Pellegrino *et al.* (eds.), *Human Dignity and Bioethics*, pp. 409–433, 410.
[33] *Ibid.*, pp. 409–433, 411.   [34] *Ibid.*

being. In other words, the radical capacity for rationality is required for something to be a human being. It is correct that the only entities which we currently know have knowledge of rationality are humans, but that does not mean that rationality is somehow necessary for humanity. The only thing necessary to be a human being is to be a member of the species *homo sapiens*. To be a member of that species only requires that one have a specific number of chromosomes in a specific genetic pattern. That is all there is to it. Attributing other characteristics as being necessary or central to being a human being is simply false. Human being is a biological classification and therefore requires only a biological distinguishing characteristic. Rationality is not that characteristic and therefore is not necessary for being a human being.

It is important to be clear about this because the alternative seems like it could lead to trouble. If the possession of a radical capacity for rationality is considered necessary to be a human being, then it seems just as possible to argue that individuals who do not possess it are not human beings.[35] Anthony Bland then does not somehow obtain the radical capacity for rationality, but instead ceases to be a human being. The same would go for anencephalic infants. That seems a terrible outcome but is actually more in line with what we know than the alternative. So, if radical capacity for rationality is necessary to be a human being and thus a possessor of human dignity, then it seems more consistent to deny them the status of human being. As I stated above, while logically consistent, this is a terrible result. Whatever else they are, Anthony Bland and anencephalic infants are human beings. They are deserving of human dignity as much as the rest of us and their inability to be rational due to physical limitations is irrelevant. Indeed, due to the vulnerability of individuals such as Anthony Bland and severely disabled newborns, we might suggest that they are most in need of the protection of concepts such as human dignity. The rest of us can rely on autonomy or our own abilities to forestall decisions which we would not prefer. Those who do not have the radical capacity for rationality do not have such philosophical weapons at their disposal. All they may have is the concept of human dignity and we therefore must make sure that it includes them – not as an afterthought, but centrally. The problem then lies with the use of rationality as a distinguishing criterion (much like it does for moral status claims). It cannot support the moral weight it

---

[35] Indeed, to the extent that there is overlap between questions of moral status and questions of human dignity, this is exactly the argument used by authors such as John Harris and Peter Singer (although they are talking about persons and not humans). See Chapter 2.

must for it to provide a convincing justification for human dignity. We must look somewhere else.

Beyleveld and Brownsword have presented a theory of dignity as well. This theory, which has been mentioned in the previous section, argues that there are two types of dignity: dignity as empowerment and dignity as constraint. The theory of dignity they present is based neither on theological values nor or Kantian rationality. It thus provides us with a third option for a philosophical justification for dignity. Beyleveld and Brownsword rely instead on Gewirthian agency to ground their ethical theory.[36] Gewirthian agency does not require rationality as such, but only requires that the individual in question be an agent.[37] However, there is not a considerable difference between agency and rationality. What they do present is a precautionary principle which helps expand the number of possible agents.[38] Due to our inability to be sure about other minds, we should err on the side of caution and treat other entities as agents as far as it is possible to do so (i.e. as long as it does not interfere with our ability to treat other things which are more likely to be agents as agents).[39] While this certainly helps in a number of cases (e.g. newborns and other children under two years old), it probably does not help to the extent we need if we wish to make dignity something possessed by all humans. Again, the problem relates to the Anthony Blands and severely disabled newborns who do not appear, no matter how much we wish to exercise caution, to be capable of the agency necessary for this to work. We can, of course, simply treat them as such but then we could expect sceptics to wonder why we do not extend our claims for dignity to other entities which are not human. So, there does not appear to be any reasonable stopping point at the line of humanity if we use the precautionary principle as Beyleveld and Brownsword argue.[40]

Again, we appear to be in a particular bind. Dignity is an ethical concept we want to have. It seems to protect a number of individuals who might not otherwise have protection. There is, unfortunately, not a convincing philosophical justification for that protection which has been found. Theological ones are unlikely to convince those who are not

---

[36] Beyleveld and Brownsword, *Human Dignity in Bioethics and Biolaw*, p. 69.
[37] *Ibid.*, p. 70–72.
[38] *Ibid.*, pp. 113–134. This is very similar to the precautionary principle outlined in the chapter on moral status. Indeed, my articulation of the precautionary principle there has been based upon the concept of a precautionary principle outlined in *Human Dignity in Bioethics and Biolaw*.
[39] *Ibid.*, pp. 122–123.
[40] As noted, this only applies to our concerns about dignity as such. The precautionary principle can and should be applied at the moral status stage of the inquiry and would apply to all entities whether human or not. See Chapter 3.

within the specific theological tradition. Characteristic-based notions, such as rationality and agency, only protect a number of human beings and that protection cannot be extended to all humans. Where, then, can we look for a justification for human dignity as an ethical value?

4   An alternative justification for dignity

If neither theological arguments nor inherent characteristics seem capable of justifying our belief in human dignity, then we shall have to look elsewhere. To do so, it is worth looking more closely at why we see dignity as being important and what it is supposed to protect. Claims of dignity are used primarily in cases where it is lost or in danger of being lost. It is, of course, mentioned in many human rights documents, but even in those cases it is couched in terms of protecting human dignity as opposed to fostering or developing it.[41] Human dignity, then, seems to act primarily as a sort of ethical brake – something which prevents us from doing certain things instead of allowing us to do something. Furthermore, discussions about dignity are frequently used in situations relating to actions involving others, not just as actors but also those acted upon. In other words, we do not generally make claims about our own human dignity. Instead, those claims are made about others' human dignity. We argue that others have not been treated with sufficient dignity, whether those be people who have been exploited for others' gain; exploited for their own gain (such as in the famous French dwarf-throwing cases);[42] or forced into situations we see as dehumanising (e.g. the use of the Ludovico technique on Alex in *A Clockwork Orange*). Even when used as an argument to prohibit things like genetic engineering, cloning or stem-cell research, the primary argument appears to be that the results of these things will be dehumanising to others (the genetically engineered, the cloned individual or the embryo).[43] At best, it appears to be a claim about humanity at large losing some essential dignity. It is therefore never about us as individuals.

What this seems to indicate is that the driving force behind this ethical principle is not inherent characteristics. Contrariwise, the concept of dignity appears to owe much more to the social community of being

---

[41] For a list of such documents, see Beyleveld and Brownsword, *Human Dignity in Bioethics and Biolaw*, pp. 9–10; Feldman, 'Human Dignity as a Legal Value: Part One'.

[42] Conseil d'Etat (27 October 1995) req. nos. 136–727 (Commune de Morsang-sur-Orge) and 143–578 (Ville d'Aix-en-Provence), cited in Beyleveld and Brownsword, *Human Dignity in Bioethics and Biolaw*, pp. 26–27.

[43] Kass, 'Defending Human Dignity', pp. 297–331, 304–305.

human.[44] We can see this most clearly if we consider the problem of cloning. Assume that cloning could be perfected and that it is now possible to create a clone of someone. Further assume that the general use for cloned humans in this future reality is as receptacles for organs which are then used for transplantation, eliminating the dual problems of organ shortage and rejection. The clones in question would be human beings when they are created (having, presumably, the requisite number of chromosomes and the particular genetic pattern necessary) but they are treated as if they are individualised organ banks. The concern, then, is that these clones are not being treated in the way that they should. They are entitled to be treated as other humans but are instead treated as something less. Alternatively, if we consider the other prediction about cloning (that people will spend large amounts of money acquiring the DNA of a popular celebrity to make clones of that particular individual), we see an instance where either the celebrity is treated as a commodity (since they are only the originator of the DNA) or the clone is seen as merely an attempt to create someone else. It is not an attempt to create a distinct individual.[45] So, in both cases, we have concerns about how those cloned individuals are treated by others and about their place within the social community. Our concern is thus a social one.

If we take this seriously, then a search for inherent characteristics which form a foundation for human dignity is unlikely to succeed. Dignity appears to come from our being part of a particular social group – that of human beings. Since the requirement for participation in this social group is to be a member of the species *homo sapiens*, all who fit within that criteria are capable of joining the group. As such, all human beings are entitled to be treated as part of that group. Human dignity is the expression of that entitlement but it does not depend on the possession of particular characteristics which all humans are expected to have. Human beings are entitled to be treated as if they matter because membership in the social group entitles one to that consideration. Additional characteristics such as rationality are thus not necessary. In practice, this means that even humans such as severely

---

[44] For other arguments which agree that there is at least some social component to a conception of dignity, see H. Rolston III, 'Human Uniqueness and Human Dignity: Persons in Nature and the Nature of Persons', in Pellegrino *et al.* (eds.), *Human Dignity and Bioethics*, pp. 129–153, 130, 133; C. Rubin, 'Human Dignity and the Future of Man', in Pellegrino *et al.* (eds.), *Human Dignity and Bioethics*, pp. 155–172, 169.

[45] This concern also arises in the scenario where, for example, a parent uses the DNA of a deceased child to create a clone of that child.

disabled newborns or those in PVS are entitled to belong to the group and therefore matter in this important way. It is also worth emphasising that one need not be able to participate fully in the social group in order to gain the protection of membership in that group. All that is necessary is that members within that group (and again, the group in question is humankind) see the individual as being capable of membership.

What this conception of dignity means for long-term issues such as genetic engineering and cloning is beyond the scope of this book, but it is worth further exploring what dignity means for someone like Anthony Bland. As he is a human being, he is entitled to membership within the relevant group. He is therefore entitled to dignity. What this means is the following: Anthony Bland is entitled to be treated as someone who matters. Being treated as someone who matters means that interests that the individual has are worthy of consideration, particularly those which primarily impact the individual and only the individual. Those interests should come first from the individual himself (if possible), but may be inferred if the individual is incapable of expressing interests. This is what differentiates dignity from autonomy. Autonomy interests can only exist in situations where the individual is capable of choosing them. Dignity interests, on the other hand, can exist even in situations where the individual is not capable of making a choice. Moreover, dignity entails that Anthony Bland be treated as being worthy of respect apart from his interests. This does not mean that the treatment of the individual need be against his interests, just that we need not rely on them for answers on how to treat him. So, for example, we do not need to know that it is against his interests to treat him as a table for us to know that Anthony Bland should not be treated in that manner.[46] This is particularly important in cases such as Anthony Bland where it may not be clear what interests he has or even if he has any at all.[47] In those cases, then, it is crucial to be able to make ethical claims in regards to our treatment of him without having to rely on his interests to do so.

The possibility of divorcing one's dignity from one's interests, however, may cause concern. If someone's dignity can be infringed without an infringement of their interests per se, does this mean that we can act against their interests in protecting their dignity? An example of this happened in France and has been previously alluded to. In a

---

[46] In other words, human dignity requires that we do not subject others to 'undignified conduct'.

[47] Lord Mustill, for example, states: 'The distressing truth which must not be shirked is that the proposed conduct [removing the nasogastric tube] is not in the best interests of Anthony Bland, for he has no best interests of any kind.' *Airedale NHS Trust* v. *Bland* [1993] 1 All ER 821 at 894.

famous case, French police stopped dwarf-tossing competitions in bars and clubs.[48] These competitions involved larger men seeing who could throw a willing participant as far as they could. These events were stopped by the authorities because they violated the 'human dignity' of the participants, especially those being used as human projectiles.[49] What is particularly relevant for our purposes is that one of the dwarves in question, Manuel Wackenheim, argued against the ban on the basis that it provided him with a job, a sense of self-worth and allowed him to move in professional circles.[50] In other words, he claimed that his dignity was not being infringed because he had chosen to participate in these competitions. Despite his assertions to the contrary, the French courts decided that the French authorities could prohibit dwarf-tossing on grounds of human dignity.[51] This then may provide an instance where autonomy rights and dignity rights are in conflict. It would be easy to argue that in those cases either autonomy or dignity always prevails, but that is not necessarily the best option. It may be that in the case in question, there is little reason to prefer the French authorities' decision about what was best for Mr Wackenheim over his own. It may be in other cases that the dignity of the person should be preferred, such as when a person attempts to sell him or herself into slavery. Presuming such a case violates human dignity (and there is no reason why it would not), there is little reason to accede to the individual's request that it is an autonomous decision and therefore deserving of respect.

On the whole though, it may be that dignity should often be seen as secondary to autonomy concerns. If the individual is worthy of respect (as dignity requires) then that should include respect for those interests that the individual has even if we may disagree with those interests. Consequently, when those interests are expressed as choices by the individual and there is no overwhelming reason to override them (such as in the case of 'voluntary slavery' above), then the autonomy interests of the individual should prevail even if we think that decision may violate their dignity to a degree. It is only in cases where there is an overwhelming and significant dignity violation in play that it seems acceptable to override the individual's autonomy interest. The only other possibility may be in cases where there is direct harm to others which results from the autonomy decision of the individual, although it should be clear in that case that the autonomy interest may be insufficient on its own anyway.[52]

---

[48] Beyleveld and Brownsword, *Human Dignity in Bioethics and Biolaw*, pp. 26–27.
[49] *Ibid.* [50] *Ibid.*, p. 26. [51] *Ibid.*, p. 27. [52] See Chapter 5.

Dignity, then, is a complex system of values which makes it different from some of the other ethical principles we have considered. Concepts such as autonomy or harm may be complex but they only encompass one single idea. Dignity, on the other hand, is a synthesis of a number of other values including aspects of autonomy and moral status. The benefit this has is that dignity can fit better with the other principles we have considered and that there can be a mutual bolstering of the ethical values which underlie these principles. It may also, of course, lead to a sort of 'double-counting' at points, with some values being considered both part of an autonomy interest and based upon dignity. On the whole, though, the ability to mesh with other principles and support those other principles should be seen as a benefit of this approach.

5   Two possible problems

Conceptualising human dignity as a social value as we have creates problems which will need to be addressed. First, some may wonder why speciesism is not fatal to the conception of dignity the way it may be to some of the possible moral status approaches examined in Chapter 2.[53] There is some justification for this way of thinking. Human dignity as described here is certainly speciesist. It relies on only the criteria of being a human being without any other characteristics. As such, any human being qualifies for human dignity while any other entity does not. There are two possible responses to this. First, it should be noted that human dignity is only one principle among many. So, while human dignity may not apply to entities which are not human, this does not mean that no other principles do either. Other principles may provide sufficient support for the interests of other non-human entities. Furthermore, just because human dignity applies only to humans it does not mean that there are no comparable dignity claims which may attach to other species. As the conception of dignity arises from the social group of which the entity is a part, it may be that dignity could vary with species groups. Finally, it is important that moral status not be speciesist because it provides the overall justification for determining whether entities matter at all. This needs to be as broad as possible so that it can include all relevant entities which might be considered. Dignity, on the other hand, can relate only to a smaller group. Thus, while human dignity is speciesist, the effect of that speciesism can be limited.

[53] Kuhse, 'Is There a Tension between Autonomy and Dignity?', pp. 61–74, 69–70, cited in Beyleveld and Brownsword, *Human Dignity in Bioethics and Biolaw*, p. 22.

More important is the counter-argument that socially constructed values can usually be withdrawn by the social group in question. As a result, it might be argued that this puts the conception of dignity on shaky ground, as any human could have the protection of human dignity revoked if others decide to remove it. This might especially be a problem if certain groups (such as racist groups) decided that other groups (such as minorities) were excluded from the classification of human dignity. It is crucial to remember, however, that the relevant social group for dignity is humankind, not groups within that larger classification. As such, it depends on whether humans in general think that others belong within the category containing human dignity. So, while racist groups may wish to exclude minority groups from the benefits of human dignity, other groups are not required to agree to such a determination. Indeed, considering the place that claims to human dignity have in universal human rights statements, it is unlikely that such groups would succeed in denying dignity to minority groups. Moreover, it is worth remembering that we are considering ethics and not law. This distinction is key because while law deals with basic requirements, ethics deals with idealised conduct. In other words, merely because one can do something does not mean one ought to do so. Merely because one could attempt to redefine human dignity to exclude certain groups of humans one wished to exclude (for whatever reason) does not mean that it is considered good ethical practice to do so. Those, then, that wish to remove certain groups or individuals from the protection of human dignity would require justifiable reasons for doing so. Since the only criterion for the possession of human dignity is that one be human, those wishing to remove human dignity from anyone else who is human would not have a justifiable reason for doing so. Our concerns then about the removal of dignity from vulnerable groups should thus be minimised.

6   Conclusion

In conclusion, in this chapter we have considered the ethical concept of dignity. As shown at the beginning of the chapter, dignity may be used frequently as an argument for various positions, but the foundation of the concept has received little attention. It has therefore required that we create a conception more than we might have done for other ethical principles we have considered. Additionally, the concept of dignity is often beset with definitional problems as it may mean many things. We have chosen to focus on the notion of human dignity (what Beyleveld and Brownsword refer to as dignity as constraint) as the applicable one.

Having decided upon a specific conception of dignity, we looked at some of the common justifications for human dignity and found that they are generally lacking. This required that we justify human dignity through socially constructed values. While this may cause some issues, it is the most justifiable basis for human dignity as it protects all of those entities which require protection and does so without attributing to them characteristics which they might not possess.

This ends our separate discussions about ethical principles. We have examined a number in isolation, but that is not, in and of itself, sufficient for our purposes. We now need to understand how these principles interact to form a general ethical framework we can use to discuss end-of-life decisions. That process of integrating our ethical principles into a coherent overall structure is the task of the next chapter.

8   A comprehensive ethical approach

1   Introduction

We now have a set of ethical principles. Unfortunately, having those principles does not, in itself, give us a coherent ethical approach to end-of-life decisions. It is also important to understand how the set of principles interact with each other. It will be crucial to know when these principles will provide mutual support for one another; it is also useful to know when they might clash. When clashes arise – as they inevitably will – it is likewise vital to know how to navigate these difficulties. Our purpose, then, in this chapter is to bring together the ethical principles which have been considered in Chapters 2 to 7 to create an ethical system which can be used to answer the ethical problems created by end-of-life care.

Again, it is worth emphasising that the approach taken here is *an ethical approach* not *the ethical approach*. I do not claim that the way that the principles are synthesised in this chapter is the only way to do so, even if what I have said in previous chapters is accepted. Nor do I claim that other approaches using these principles are necessarily worse than the one presented. I am, of course, presenting what I think is the most justifiable way to combine the principles we have considered into a coherent ethical approach. But the claim to correctness that I am making in regard to that does not necessitate a claim that only those approaches which are entirely consistent with mine are correct. Other approaches may be just as correct; others may claim that other approaches are better. I claim only that, on my understanding of the principles I have outlined in the previous chapters, this is the best method I know for combining them into a coherent ethical approach.

2   Moral status

When considering how these principles combine to form a coherent whole, we should begin with the concept of moral status. Since a multi-criterial system of moral status has been created, entities may become morally relevant for a variety of reasons. It is worth re-stating what those criteria are. The eight principles which form the system for moral status are as follows:

1. **The Respect for Life Principle**
   Living organisms are not to be killed or otherwise harmed, without good reasons that do not violate principles 2–7.
2. **The Anti-Cruelty Principle**
   Sentient beings are not to be killed or subjected to pain or suffering, unless there is no other feasible way of furthering goals that are (1) consistent with principles 3–7; and (2) important to human beings, or other entities that have a stronger moral status than could be based upon sentience alone.
3. **The Agent's Rights Principle**
   Moral agents have full and equal basic moral rights, including the rights to life and liberty.
4. **Developing Agents Principle**
   Within the limits of their own capacities and of principle 3, all developing moral agents who are capable of sentience but not of moral agency should be treated as if they were full moral agents.
5. **The Ecological Principle**
   Living things that are not moral agents, but that are important to the ecosystems of which they are part, have, within the limits of principles 1–4, a stronger moral status than could be based upon their intrinsic properties alone; ecologically important entities that are not themselves alive, such as species and habitats, may legitimately be accorded a stronger moral status than their intrinsic properties would indicate.
6. **The Interspecific Principle**
   Within the limits of their own capacities and consistent with other principles, human members who do not qualify as moral agents or developing moral agents and non-human members of mixed social communities have a stronger moral status than could be based upon their intrinsic properties alone.
7. **The Transitivity of Respect Principle**
   Within the limits of principles 1–6, and to the extent that it is feasible and morally permissible, moral agents should respect one another's attributions of moral status.
8. **The Precautionary Principle**
   Within the limits of principles 1–7, when determining the moral status of a particular entity, the burden of proof should lie with those

seeking to assign the status of the entity instead of the entity itself. If there is reasonable doubt about a particular entity, it should be treated as being within the highest available class of moral status to which it might belong.

With these as a guide, we can then consider the moral status of various possible entities. Doctors and other health-care workers will be entitled to full moral status due to their moral agency. Competent patients will also generally be considered morally relevant because they are moral agents. They are thus entitled to full moral status under principle 3. This would also be the case for those agents who may be currently incompetent but have not suffered a loss in the qualities necessary for moral agency. Thus, a patient who has lost no cognitive abilities but is presently in a coma would still be considered a moral agent and is thus entitled to full moral status. Things become more difficult when we examine the moral status of incompetent patients who have suffered a diminution of mental abilities. They are unlikely to be as clear a case of moral agency as those who are competent. Under principle 8, we are required to consider them to be moral agents provided there is insufficient proof that they are not moral agents. Thus, in many cases, it is appropriate to consider them to be moral agents even if we are not completely sure whether a particular individual is a moral agent or not. When looking at patients which are more clearly not moral agents under the criteria we have discussed, then their moral status is likely to be determined by principles 4 or 6. Principle 4 applies to developing moral agents and would be used to determine the moral status of those patients who are not currently moral agents but have the capacity to develop into them (e.g. newborn children). Other patients, however, would not be classified as developing moral agents but would also not satisfy the criteria for moral agency (e.g. those in PVS or those with advanced dementia). Those patients would be considered members of social communities under principle 6 and would thus be entitled to greater moral status than they might be based merely on the criteria they possess. As such, we are likely to be able to consider them to have advanced moral rights approaching those of moral agents. This would even include having their wishes respected (as far as is possible) when considering treatment options in relation to them. As a result, all of the patients we will be considering are entitled to at least some level of moral status. In other words, when deciding what treatment options might be available for them, it is necessary to consider the interests of these individuals because the individuals matter. We cannot simply decide on treatment which is considered expedient or beneficial only to others with no thought given to its effect upon the patient in question. This does not mean that what is best for the patient will always control. There will be other individuals concerned and it may be that their interests control, such as when a patient's best interests conflict with what might be considered the doctor's ethical responsibilities. They must, however, be considered as part of the decision-making process.

Deciding, however, that these particular individuals have moral status is only a starting point. All it determines is who matters. What it does not do is tell us how they matter or which moral rights attach to particular individuals. That requires bringing in the other ethical principles we have considered and determining how they might apply to specific groups of individuals, particularly in light of the moral status those individuals might have.

3   Autonomy

We shall begin that discussion with the concept of autonomy instead of either the value of life or moral responsibility. The reason why it is important to start with autonomy claims is that those claims play a particular part in concerns about the value of life and about questions relating to harm and benefit. It is therefore crucial to understand how notions of autonomy interact with the claims for moral status before we further explore the impact upon either the value of life or harm claims made by individuals. In order to do that, it is worth summarising what was determined in relation to autonomy in the previous chapter on the subject. As stated there, there are a number of different conceptions of autonomy which might be used. The one which was determined to be most useful for our purposes is that presented by Beauchamp and Childress.[1] Their version of autonomy requires that a decision must be made intentionally, with sufficient understanding and without controlling undue influences. It should also be remembered that autonomy is a process-based concern; in other words, what matters is the decision-making process as opposed to the decision made through that process. Finally, as we have conceived of autonomy, there are certain pre-requirements for an autonomous decision. Our ethical duties in relation to the promotion of autonomy then do not simply relate to allowing people to make autonomous choices. Instead, our ethical

---

[1] Again, it is worth emphasising that, for the most part, while the conceptions are articulated differently, there is probably little practical difference between Beauchamp and Childress's concept of autonomy and the one presented by Gerald Dworkin. In both cases, it is unlikely that something which is conceived of as an autonomous decision under one approach would not be an autonomous decision in the other.

duties relate to the fostering of autonomous decisions and we therefore have duties in relation to creating the conditions necessary for autonomous decisions, in addition to allowing autonomous decisions to have certain respect.

With that summary in mind, we can turn to how we ought to respect autonomous decisions in end-of-life care. The easiest group of individuals in question are competent patients. Competent patients will have full autonomy rights under the conception of autonomy being considered. The decisions of competent patients, provided they are made using the appropriate process, are entitled to respect from others. Just as importantly, we need to make sure that competent patients have the ability to make autonomous decisions by ensuring that the preconditions necessary for autonomous decisions exist. That means that sufficient information about the decisions needs to be presented to the individual in question and in a way that allows the patient to understand the information that they have been given. It also means that we should allow, as far as is practical, patients to have sufficient time and space for reflection. That normally means that discussions with patients about health-care options should happen early enough in the process that patients will have sufficient time to process and understand the information that they are given, along with being able to request any support from friends and family that they might need. In other words, patients should be able to expect health-care professionals to not only respect the decisions they make, but also respect the patient enough to facilitate their decision-making process. It does not mean, however, that health-care practitioners are not entitled to try to persuade patients to make specific health-care decisions, provided that persuasion does not rise to the level of undue influence. Health-care practitioners, like anyone else, are entitled to present their views to the patient for consideration and to try to talk the patient out of a particular decision if they feel it is unwise. However, while they may attempt to persuade the patient, they cannot prevent a patient from making a decision which is ultimately the patient's own. Decisions reached as a result of this process should be entitled to respect as far as possible, even if those decisions lead to the death of the patient. Consequently, even a decision for assistance with dying made by a competent patient should be entitled to respect unless certain caveats discussed below exist.

Those classified as developing moral agents under principle 4 of our moral status criteria should be considered differently. They are unlikely to be able to exercise full autonomy under the criteria. As such, it is unlikely that they should be extended full autonomy rights. Instead, developing moral agents should be entitled to respect for their autonomous decisions to the extent they are able to make them. In addition, considering the emphasis on the development of these individuals as moral agents, we are likely to need to provide them with enhanced support in relation to the development of the pre-conditions necessary for autonomy. Since these individuals may be less able to request sufficient information, for example, more effort may be required in order to make sure that these patients get the information that may be necessary and in a way which will be understandable to them. However, it is important to pay attention to the abilities of the patient. Newborns, for instance, are unlikely to be able to make autonomous decisions no matter how much information and time for reflection is provided to them. So, it may be that we are required in certain cases to act on their behalf. In doing so, it is important to keep in mind that the decision that is being made is one that is, as far as is possible to gauge, the best possible decision for the individual in question. However, this is not an exercise of autonomy as the patient is unable to act in any way as a chooser. Instead, we would need to utilise other values in order to determine what treatment ought to be given to the patient.

The same is likely to be the case for those who were once moral agents but are no longer moral agents. In such cases, our primary aim would be to put into effect the autonomous decisions which the individual might have made while a moral agent. Thus, if any sort of advance directive had been made by the patient, then it should be considered a moral requirement to implement that particular treatment decision, provided it is clear from the directive what the patient actually wanted. Again, we need to understand what the patient was considering at the time, and advance directives should be designed to facilitate that. It is also incumbent upon those involved with the patient in long-term care scenarios to make sure that they understand the extent and limits of any advance directive. Thus, doctors or other health-care professionals involved in long-term treatment should make sure that they understand what a patient might mean if they suggest they wish to 'die with dignity'. In cases where it is not apparent on the face of it what the patient might have wanted under the circumstances, the first task should be to attempt to make the best assessment of what the patient might have actually wanted in such a situation. It is therefore a determination based not upon objective best interests but upon what, in fact and as far as is possible, the patient would have wanted had they been able to prepare in advance for the situation. For someone like Anthony Bland, then, the decision should be based upon what Anthony himself would have wanted, although, again, this would not be an autonomous decision but the use of other values to determine treatment. This may be difficult in cases when the person in question may not have ever considered the idea (as Anthony Bland does not appear to have done), but in those cases, our best efforts should be extended to determining, as best we are able to do, what it is they would have wanted.[2]

A final group of patients we should consider is those who have not ever been competent, nor is there any realistic chance that they will develop the cognitive abilities to ever be autonomous decision-makers. In these cases, it seems a fiction to argue that we ought to treat them according to what we believe they would have wanted if competent. Those who may once have been moral agents but are now not are likely to have a pattern of behaviour or beliefs or other evidence about what they would have wanted in a particular scenario, even if they had not themselves considered it. Those who have never been competent will not have such a history. Instead, we will need to treat these individuals based upon a more objective standard of what is best for them; although, to the extent that they are able to make these decisions, we should allow them to do so. But, in a majority of treatment decisions, there will be no autonomous decision to respect. As a result, decisions will have to be based upon other criteria.

This leaves one final group of individuals who are particularly relevant to these sorts of decisions, and that is doctors or other health-care practitioners. It may sometimes be forgotten in the midst of calls for greater autonomy for patients but doctors and other health-care practitioners are moral agents and their autonomous decisions are also worthy of respect. What that means within the context of the decisions we are considering is that doctors, like patients, should not be forced to do things which are against their autonomous decisions. In other words, patients are generally able to request that doctors do certain things, but doctors need not comply in all cases. It may be the case, of course, that the patient's autonomy interest prevails in certain conflicts. A case where this might happen is one where the patient wants the doctor to remove treatment which the patient has not consented to, but in such

---

[2] A particular problem, though, may exist in cases where a patient has created an advance directive for a condition which is different from being in PVS. In these cases, it may be that the patient such as those with advanced dementia may be still conscious and sentient but not competent. These cases may be more problematic when an individual, when still competent, created an advance directive stating that they would like particular health-care decisions such as the withdrawal of particular treatment or assisted dying if they were to end up in a state of advanced dementia but, having fallen into that condition, the patient appears to be relatively happy. In those cases, should we prefer the decision of the competent past patient over the incompetent present patient? These cases will be considered more fully below in the discussion on the value of life.

cases it may be that the doctor need not actually remove treatment if others are also capable of performing that action. So, if the doctor has a moral objection to the removal, he cannot prevent the removal entirely, although he may not be compelled to perform the relevant actions himself. In general, though, and particularly in cases of assisted dying, doctors and other health-care practitioners should not be denied the ability to exercise their autonomous decisions, provided they are not harming the patient or acting against the wishes of the patient by doing so.

4   Harm and benefit

The way in which we protect the autonomous decisions of patients leads on to a discussion about harm and the twinned ethical principles of beneficence and non-maleficence. Harms as considered in this book follow the definitions put forth by Joel Feinberg. He argues that harms are those times in which we have a setback to our interests, in particular, to our ultimate or welfare interests. We may have setbacks to other things, like wants, but these are not necessarily harms. Anything which promotes our interests is a benefit; anything which sets them back is a harm. We should also remember, though, that considerations of harm and benefit will be at least partially determined by the benefit/harm baseline of the individual. If a person is already in considerable pain, for example, a minuscule lessening of that pain is probably insufficient to constitute a benefit as it has been described in this book.[3] From that definition of benefit, it then becomes more readily apparent how we ought to construe the principles of beneficence and non-maleficence. Non-maleficence, the duty not to harm people, is the duty to avoid causing harms which we need not cause. Beneficence, the principle based upon helping people, is that we ought to provide benefits to people if we are in a position to do so. Since non-maleficence is a negative interest and beneficence is a positive one, non-maleficence is a broader and more wide-ranging principle than beneficence. Again, within the context of the discussion here, this is most likely to involve discussions about treatment decisions.

In cases of competent patients, a setback to welfare or ultimate interests is individually determined. It is the person him or herself who determines which things are against their interests and which things

---

[3] That, of course, does not necessarily mean we should not do it. It merely expresses the view that whatever beneficial effect the lessening of pain has in the circumstance is not likely to rise to the level of something we would consider to be a benefit.

are not. It thus does not matter if the general population would consider a particular result to be beneficial or not within the context of particular medical treatments. What matters is whether the individual in question would consider it to be a setback to their interests or not. If it is a setback to interests, it is harmful, even if the majority of the population would not consider it to be the case; if it is not, it is beneficial despite the fact that the majority may disagree. This may become particularly important when we consider whether death can ever be a benefit or whether it must always be considered a harm. Considering the description of something as harmful or not depends entirely on an individual's assessment of its value, in which case it is possible for death to be considered a benefit. All it takes is for the individual in question to consider it to be beneficial to their interests. It seems likely that cases in which death is seen to be a benefit are rare, but they are also not likely to be non-existent. So, there will be times when even the death of the patient would satisfy the ethical principle of non-maleficence and beneficence.

Again, things will be more difficult in cases where we cannot rely on the patient's own determination of harm and benefit. In these cases, which would cover all cases of patients lacking competence where we do not have an advance directive, we are normally bound by a decision based upon what we believe is likely to be the case under the circumstances. In cases of patients who were once moral agents but have now ceased to be, we may be able to rely either on statements they have made in the past or on general information which would allow us to infer how they see a specific treatment. However, in other cases, we are likely bound by a more objective determination of what counts as a benefit or a harm. While the individual determination should be considered the preferred option, sometimes that is not possible either because there is insufficient information to determine the patient's views or because the patient is one for whom it is impossible to determine their autonomous wishes under the circumstances (primarily those who have never been moral agents). For those who are developing moral agents, our concern should be in allowing those agents to develop if that is possible, and, as such, our determination of what counts as objectively harmful or beneficial might be different from those who are not capable of developing into moral agents. That does not mean, however, that those who are not going to develop into moral agents can be treated less extensively than those who are. It merely means that we need to consider their development when considering the treatment options which are available to us.

5   The value of life

A further ethical concept which builds upon the nature of autonomy is how we conceive of the value of life. As indicated in Chapter 3, the conception of the value of life which is to be preferred is not one which relies exclusively on either of the two standard positions which are generally referred to as either the Sanctity of Life (SOL) or Quality of Life (QOL) positions. Instead, we should conceive of the value of life as a complex value which includes not only the inherent value one places on life but also the biographical features which add or detract from that inherent value. As such, the value we place on life is based, at least in part, upon the notions of autonomy which allow us to construct those lives which we value.

Again, for those patients who are competent, this means that determining the value of life should be relatively easy. In these cases, the value of the life of an individual patient is determined by the individual him or herself. If the life is one which the individual values, then that valuation of the life is controlling. That does not mean, of course, that the value of life must determine how we treat the individual. Simply because an individual does not value his or her own life does not mean, necessarily, that others are required to help the individual end it. But, in determining how best to treat that individual, we cannot rely on a valuation of life for that individual which is different from the one that the individual places upon it. Thus, we may be able to create a sufficient argument for an alternative treatment under the circumstances using other principles (harm and dignity, perhaps), but we cannot rely on the fact that we might value the life of the patient differently.

One problem which requires further examination are those cases where an individual may have created an advance directive indicating how they value their life in certain conditions (such as advanced dementia). It may be that although the patient, while still competent, indicated that they would not value such a life, once in that condition the patient is relatively happy but incompetent. It thus becomes a question of whether to give precedent to the valuation of life from the past competent patient or the present incompetent one. In these cases, I find it difficult to prioritise the past valuation over the present one, even if the patient is incompetent. In most cases, we determine the value of our lives at present, not in the past. So, if I am determining the value of my life now, it does not matter very much if the teenage version of myself would not value my current life. All that matters is that I currently value it. I see no reason why this would be different for those patients who are in states such as advanced dementia. While patients in such a condition may not have full autonomy rights, they can still have preferences about their treatment and those should be respected to the extent that it is possible. Thus, in cases of conflict between present and past selves, our present selves should be given priority.

For those who have not yet developed sufficiently to be able to determine the value of their own lives or for those who will never be able to do so, we must again determine their lives based upon the value, considering all of the evidence available to us, that we think that it possesses for the individual. This may be especially difficult when there is little evidence to indicate the answer either way and so our determination may be more objective than otherwise, but we should endeavour to incorporate those things we know about the individual patient.

6 Dignity

This triad of important ethical values – autonomy, harm and benefit and the value of life – work together to provide a very individualised patient-centred view of treatment decisions at the end of life. Their focus on individual choice and the things needed to determine that choice sufficiently ground our behaviour in those things which the patient wants. But just because a patient wants something does not mean they necessarily must get it. Instead, we must also consider those things which might limit those individualised interests. Foremost among those values is the principle which we have referred to as human dignity.

As stated in Chapter 7, the conception of dignity considered within this book is one we might term either 'human dignity' or 'dignity as constraint'. It is a socially constructed value in the sense that it does not rely on inherent characteristics of the individual entity in question but instead relies on the social group of which the individual is a member. What dignity entails is that individuals who belong to the specific group see the individual in question as possessing those things necessary to be a member of the group. The social group on which we base notions of human dignity is the human community. It therefore applies, at least, to all human beings regardless of characteristics they possess. The application of human dignity is more complex than the application of the other values we have been considering because there is less overlap with those values. Instead of being primarily mutually supportive in the way that we have conceived of autonomy, harm and the value of life, dignity often acts as a type of ethical brake. It is used to stop us doing certain things which might be allowable by the other values because of its effect upon individuals who we value. Dignity is thus about the respect that we show other individuals and that our treatment of them needs to be consistent with that respect. When considering how it applies to cases where autonomy interests may be in conflict with dignity interests, it is important to know that only compelling dignity interests may outweigh the autonomous decisions of an individual. These are likely to be extremely rare and limited to cases where the individual has done something like sell themselves into slavery. The limits of this, though, are tricky and it may be impossible to set definite borders on what counts as a compelling dignity interest. In general, though, respect for the individual should include respect for their wishes and life choices, meaning claims about dignity are often secondary to autonomy claims.

The main beneficiaries, then, of claims of dignity are those who are unable to express autonomous wishes. These include those patients who are no longer moral agents and who have not previously expressed any opinion regarding treatment, those who are not yet capable of moral agency and those who were never moral agents. In cases involving the treatment of these individuals, we must have respect for that individual in deciding between the treatment options which are available. This means that we cannot simply treat these patients in ways we consider expedient or for only our benefit. Instead, we must consider what is best for the patient in these circumstances. In considering what is best for the patient, we should consider what it is that the patient may want. This is unlikely to be something we can know with complete certainty, but efforts should be made to attempt to determine, as far as possible, what the patient's wishes might have been under the circumstances. This will be easier in those cases where the patient had once been a moral agent, but it may be possible even in those cases where someone was not a moral agent. If, for example, we return to an example presented in Chapter 3, we may have a situation where a newborn patient seems to derive pleasure from the presence of her parents, such as in the case of *An NHS Trust* v. *MB*.[4] When determining how best to treat the newborn in that case, we ought to consider that fact in our analysis.

Just because the main beneficiaries are those who are unable to express autonomous wishes does not mean that those with autonomy cannot benefit from dignity claims. However, dignity claims for them are more likely to involve claims about dignified conduct in relation to treatment. In other words, concerns about dignity are less likely to be about claims to treatment than claims about how treatment is given. In these cases, dignity claims may reinforce claims for autonomy as it may include aspects of making sure that patients are able

---

[4] *An NHS Trust* v. *MB* [2006] EWHC 507 (Fam.).

to communicate effectively with doctors and be allowed to visit with relatives and friends, thus increasing the pre-conditions necessary for autonomous decisions.

7   Moral responsibility

Our final concern is to determine when those involved in treatment decisions are morally responsible for the results of those decisions. As stated in Chapter 4, there is no justifiable reason for ascribing moral responsibility only to the actions that a person might do. Individuals are morally responsible for both those things they do and those things they fail to do when they have control over their actions, as previously described. In order for someone to have control over an event, they must have control over their bodily movements in a way described as guidance control. Guidance control exists when a bodily movement is 'regularly receptive to reasons' (there are reasons which determine the bodily movements of the individual that are understandable to others and at least somewhat grounded in reality) and reactive to reasons (there are ways in which the individual could translate reasons into action in a particular case). Additionally, it must be something for which the individual would take responsibility. This requires three things: (1) the agent must be able to understand that his or her actions and choices can cause certain things to happen; (2) the individual must see him or her-self as an appropriate target for the feelings of blame and praise which attach to questions of moral responsibility; and (3) the individual must see that those first two things must be based upon evidence available to the individual. If all of those things are true, then we can claim that an individual is morally responsible for a particular event.

We can see this in action when we consider possible end-of-life decisions for which a doctor might potentially have moral responsibility. For example, we can consider a case where a patient is brought into A&E and the doctor must make a decision whether to provide a certain treatment such as an intubation. Let us further presume that the doctor decides to intubate the patient. The doctor does so because she believes that it is the best treatment for the situation. In such a case, the doctor can be determined to be morally responsible for the decision and resulting intubation. She has made a decision based upon reasons (she believes it is the best treatment in the situation). It is a decision which is understandable to others (even if they may disagree with the doctor's assessment, it is understandable that a doctor would perform what she considered to be the best available treatment at the time) and one which is at least somewhat grounded in reality. It is also a decision that is reactive to those reasons because there would be cases (presumably where it is not clinically indicated) where she would not do so. Furthermore, it is something for which she is likely to take responsibility. She understands that the procedure will cause certain results in relation to the patient. She is also likely to understand that her decision to intubate the patient is one which will subject her to blame or praise depending on whether that was actually the correct thing to do. Finally, she will see that her understanding of the causal results of intubation and the praise or blame she might receive as a result are likely to be based upon the evidence that she had in front of her at the time. She will thus be morally responsible for her action.

Likewise, she will also be morally responsible if she decides not to intubate. Let us presume that in an alternative scenario she decides not to intubate the patient. Again, let us further presume that the reason for doing so is because she does not believe it is the best treatment under the circumstances. Again, the decision would be receptive to reasons and reactive to them (since she does so because it is clinically indicated, but there are cases where she would have intubated). Additionally, it is one for which she would take responsibility. It is based upon her understanding of the causal connection between her action and the results and it is one for which she is likely to accept praise or blame depending on whether it was the right thing to do. Thus, for the purpose of determining moral responsibility, it does not matter whether she actually acts or not in the circumstances. It will matter, of course, when we decide what she ought to have done and thus decide whether she is worthy of praise or blame for the events in question, but she will be morally responsible either way.

She will also be responsible for the consequences of that action using the general method for determining moral responsibility. We must remember that there are two types of consequences. The first type is consequence-particulars, and those are the results of the specific causal chain in question. They are therefore based upon the chain of events which occurred in a particular scenario, and if that scenario changes, then the consequence-particular changes. So, for example, in the first scenario above, the result that the doctor intubates the patient is a consequence-particular. A consequence-universal is a more general result which may occur from a number of different consequence-particulars. A consequence-universal in the first case may be that the patient is intubated because that action may occur from a number of different sources (e.g. other doctors or health-care workers, paramedics, etc.) Moral responsibility for consequence-particulars is determined in the same method as used to determine moral responsibility for actions above. Moral responsibility for consequence-universals is slightly more difficult as we must further decide that the results are suitably sensitive to the doctor's actions. So, provided that her actions (or omissions) had some effect upon the consequence-universal, then she will be responsible for it.

In general, then, most of the events we will be discussing will be ones for which a health-care practitioner is morally responsible. Our general concern is with end-of-life decision-making in cases where the doctor may have several options about what to do. In these cases, the doctor's decision about what should be done is likely to be based upon understandable reasons about the patient's best interests, the applicable ethical grounds for the decision and the consequences of that treatment decision. As such, the doctor should satisfy the requirement that the decision in question be reasons-reactive in a vast majority of cases. It is also very likely that the decision in question is one for which the doctor is likely to take responsibility under the criteria expressed above. There may be cases, of course, where the consequences of what the doctor has done may not subject him or her to moral responsibility. This is most likely in cases where the consequences in question are not suitably sensitive to what the doctor did. It may be, for example, that no matter what the health-care practitioner did, the patient would die. The doctor then would not be responsible for the fact that the patient has died. However, they would still be responsible for their actions which may have contributed to that death. It is worth highlighting again, though, that the fact that a person is morally responsible for something does not mean, necessarily, that what the person did was wrong. We are as morally responsible for our praise-worthy acts as we are those for which we deserve blame. The simple fact, then, that a doctor or other health-care practitioner is morally responsible for something does not mean that it ought not to have happened. All it means is that we ought to hold the person accountable for that event. If the action should have been done, then we can praise the individual for what they did; if it should not have been done, we can blame them for what happened. But, in either case, the individual in question has moral responsibility for those things.

As a result of the fact that most of the things done by doctors and other health-care professions will be ones for which they are morally responsible, it is therefore crucial that we allow them the space to make those decisions. This means that they, like patients, are entitled to their autonomy, and holding them morally responsible for their decisions not only allows praise or blame to be assigned to those decisions but also provides another significant reason why the opinions of doctors and other health-care professionals must be entitled to respect. These will be particularly important in cases where the opinion of the health-care practitioner is different from that of the patient. In those cases, part of the concern we must face is the impact of the decision upon the various parties. In situations where a patient requests the withdrawal or withholding of treatment, there is a direct and immediate impact upon the bodily integrity of the patient. Patient wishes should therefore control, even if the doctor disagrees. If, however, the patient is requesting the doctor or health-care worker to perform something which involves providing treatment that the doctor does not believe is appropriate, then the ramifications for the health-care practitioner are significantly greater. In these cases, while patients should be able to request treatment, it is a much more substantial interference with their moral rights and responsibilities to require that doctors or other health-care practitioners always provide treatment regardless of what they believe. Consequently, doctors need not provide particular treatments just because a patient requests them, but only if they further correspond to the moral, ethical and legal duties the doctor has.

8   Specific practices

Developing a comprehensive ethical approach to end-of-life decision-making also requires that one be able to apply the relevant principles to practical situations. However, it is difficult to envisage all the possible situations and all of the possible patient types that exist. Therefore, I will pick only a few illustrative examples of the application of the principles to discuss in further detail. My hope is that they will be sufficient for others to draw conclusions in specific cases which may not be the same as the particular examples.

Competent patients provide the most clear cases under this particular ethical approach. In most cases – including those related to palliative care, withdrawal of treatment and withholding of treatment – the patient's autonomous wish will prevail. The health-care practitioners involved in the decision will have to make sure that the patient has been sufficiently informed and allowed time for reflection in order to ensure that the decision is as autonomous as possible. It should be made clear, though, that what the patient is entitled to do is to request things, particularly in relation to the provision of treatment. Doctors and other health-care practitioners are entitled to their own autonomous decisions and need not agree with the decisions made by the patient. What that may mean, however, is that if a consensus between the patient and the health-care practitioner cannot be reached, then the patient may need to be switched to another health-care practitioner. This will be especially true in cases where the patient wants treatment withdrawn, which the doctor or other health-care practitioner does not feel capable of doing. In such cases, another doctor or health-care practitioner should be brought in who will satisfy the patient's request. If the patient is requesting treatment which the doctor may not wish to provide, again an alternative doctor or health-care practitioner should be provided, assuming that one can be found who does agree with the patient's request.[5] However, the patient does not have a right to demand a particular treatment as that would interfere with the autonomous decisions of the health-care practitioner.

Two practices may cause specific problems. The first is terminal sedation. As defined in Chapter 1, terminal sedation is when a patient is put into a coma-like state. In and of itself, this probably presents no specific problems as it is merely a more extensive version of palliative care. Issues may arise, though, if the patient seeks to be put in terminal sedation and then asks that treatment such as artificial nutrition and hydration be withdrawn. By itself, the withdrawal of nutrition and hydration also provides no issues in relation to the autonomous decisions of patients. The only issues arise when patients request both and it may be that some dignity concerns are raised by this approach. However, while dignity concerns are raised, they are not sufficient to override the patient's autonomous request in this case. It is worthy of note that this approach is not likely to be used in situations where assisted dying practices are allowed, as many may see it as a way around the prohibition on assisted dying. Assisted dying practices cause the other concerns about end-of-life decisions. Under the approach outlined above, voluntary assisted dying practices (either as physician-assisted suicide or active voluntary euthanasia) should be allowable.[6] Presuming that we can be assured that the request for assisted dying is the patient's own and is made with sufficient understanding of the circumstances (and both would be questions of regulation we will look at more specifically in Part II), then the patient's own decision about what constitutes harm, benefit, the value of their own life and their autonomous wish ought to control. Again, there are some dignity concerns about the ending of another's life, but in

---

[5] It may be that no doctor would actually agree to perform the treatment that the patient has requested. In such a case, doctors are not required to provide treatment which they feel is against their ethical duties. Removal of treatment the patient does not want is a different matter as there is a greater interference with the autonomy rights of a patient when being subjected to treatment he or she does not want as opposed to not being provided treatment he or she does want.

[6] Non-voluntary euthanasia will not technically apply to competent patients. Involuntary euthanasia would not be allowable as it violates the autonomous wishes of the patient.

this case, dignity concerns also point to respecting the choices made by individuals about their own life choices. Consequently, assisted dying in some form should be considered acceptable. However, this also can only be the right to request assisted dying for patients. Doctors, who have autonomy interests of their own, need not comply with the wishes of a patient as it may be against the doctor's notions of harm, the value of life and their own life plan. As such, assisted dying practices would only be acceptable if the patient has requested them and the doctor agrees to perform the actions necessary for assisted dying.

Incompetent patients will present a different set of problems. As they will be unable to express an autonomous decision, decisions will have to be made on their behalf. As a result, concerns about dignity will become more important, as do more objective measures of harm and benefit. When considering the range of factors that might influence decisions about the treatment for these sorts of patients, evidence about what the individual patient may want or may have wanted will be important and should be considered. That will not turn a decision into an autonomous one as it does with competent patients, but better understanding how the patient may see harms and benefits may help us to at least come closer to the decision the patient might have made were it possible for them to make an autonomous choice. As it is with competent patients, the main issue of concern may be the distinction between withdrawing or withholding life-sustaining treatment and non-voluntary euthanasia. Some might suggest, as Lord Browne-Wilkinson alluded to in *Bland*,[7] that if we are prepared to withdraw nutrition and hydration from a patient such as Anthony Bland, then we should be prepared to inject him with a lethal substance and kill him quickly instead of letting him starve to death. It is here, though, that dignity concerns will become especially important. Since we cannot know what the autonomous decision of the patient is, we must show respect for the individual and treat them appropriately. This will most likely mean that the patient should not be killed. While it is undoubtedly a thin line, the active killing of an incompetent patient seems to violate the dignity rights of the individual patient to a greater degree than the withdrawal of treatment which may not be providing any actual benefit. The line become even thinner in cases such as Anthony Bland where the withdrawal of treatment seems specifically designed to bring about his death. It may be possible in these very limited cases to argue that the ethical duties of the doctor do not proscribe killing the patient. However, whatever the ethical duties, it may be hard in such cases to provide legal regulation which

[7] [1993] 1 All ER 821 at 884.

will apply only to the Anthony Blands of the world without encompassing a greater range of potential patients. Those concerns will have to wait, however, until Part II of this book.

9   Conclusions

In conclusion, we have examined a range of ethical principles in this part of the book and brought them together in this chapter into a coherent ethical approach to end-of-life decision-making. We have also considered how this approach might be applied in certain cases. However, merely determining the best ethical approach to end-of-life decisions cannot end our inquiry. Those ethical decisions are not applied in a context which is free from legal regulation. It is therefore crucial to consider how the ethical decisions made in this part may be applied by legal regulation in order to present us with a cohesive legal approach to end-of-life decisions. It is to those issues that we will now turn in Part II.

Part II

9 Introduction to Part II

1 Introduction

In the first part of this book, we examined the important ethical principles necessary to determine whether particular medical treatments at the end of life are acceptable. Considering the role of ethics in the actions of doctors and other health-care professionals, it is a crucial starting point to any discussion about end-of-life treatment. Regardless of general acceptability, actions which are unethical should not be performed by those in the health-care professions. As such, it was first vital to determine whether the actions in question violated or supported the ethical duties of those involved in the provision of health care. To that end, we explored the important philosophical concepts of moral status, autonomy, harm, moral responsibility, dignity and the value of life. We also developed an ethical approach utilising those concepts.

Ethics, while important, cannot end the matter. Ethical approaches in general do not have a useful enforcement mechanism. It is true that certain professions, and most health-care professions are among them, have codes of professional conduct and violations of those codes can lead to punishment. However, the compliance mechanisms of these codes are limited, and usually the harshest penalty which can be brought is the expulsion of the individual from the professional group. This can, of course, be a considerable punishment to the individual member but may be insufficient for the group at large, those affected by the conduct or society in general. Legal enforcement mechanisms are much more substantial and, considering the importance of any decision which might lead to death, legal enforcement can be a more appropriate system for protecting society from abuses. Consequently, the second part of this book will be to determine how best to use the ethical theory developed in the first part to evaluate the legal mechanisms which determine the lawfulness of specific end-of-life decisions.

Unfortunately, it is not as simple as merely deciding to make lawful the conduct which has been adjudged to be ethical in the first part.

Ethics and law, while they can be complementary, do not necessarily have the same sorts of limitations, and thus it cannot be as easy as making any conduct which is ethical legal as well. Instead, we must pay attention to the specific limitations on legal regulation and how this may impact upon how we best decide to regulate the conduct we have considered to be ethical. Consequently, we need to address several preliminary points before discussing the legal regulation of end-of-life decision-making and, specifically, how those might be different from the limitations which might exist when considering the ethical ramifications of conduct.

2   Important differences between law and ethics

To briefly sketch some of the preliminary issues, one of our first concerns should be differences between law and ethics and what effect that may have on regulation of conduct. One of the most important is recognition that discussions of ethics may often occur in an idealised setting which is not conducive to legal regulation. For example, when debating ethics, there are many things which we might take as determinable, true or correct without further discussion. Thus, we have discussed in previous chapters the intention of doctors, health-care professionals and patients as being something which we can know for sure and how those intentions might affect our ethical determinations. This is a critical discussion to have as ethical conduct may often depend (or be thought to depend) on differences between what the individual in question tries to do. This is often also an important determination for legal regulation as well. However, when analysing ethics, we may pay little or no attention to the problem of determining those intentions. Instead, we rely on statements such as 'if the doctor has the intention to kill …' without further consideration as to how we might figure out what the doctor actually intends under particular circumstances. This is because the point under discussion is not the evidentiary one but the implications of that evidence.

The law, however, cannot take such things for granted. It is not sufficient to merely claim what a specific doctor's intention is but to be able to prove that intention to a specified standard. It thus does not matter if doctors generally have an intention to kill so much as whether the particular doctor in question had the intention in question. Proof problems, then, which may be absent from ethical discussions, are often crucial to legal determinations.

Additionally, ethics often can deal with idealised conduct. It is about what we aspire our conduct to be. It is a determination of what is best for us to do under the circumstances. It thus provides us with a ceiling for our actions. Law, on the other hand, does not deal with our aspirational conduct but what we are allowed to do. It often gives us the bare minimum we need to do to be acceptable to a particular society. It consequently provides us with a conduct floor. We can see this most clearly when discussing cases of rescue. As discussed in the chapter on moral responsibility, ethically we may have a duty to rescue people when it provides no adverse effects for us. Ethically, then, I may be required to save a person drowning in a pond when I can do so without significant risk of harm to myself. The law, on the hand, generally makes no such claims on us. Even if it is admirable for me to do so, I am not legally required to help someone at risk of harm, unless there are reasons why I have a specific duty in a particular case (for example, I am a parent and it is my child at risk). In determining our legal obligations, it does not mean that the decision not to impose a general duty to rescue disagrees with the nature of our ethical duties, but merely that they could not be something which was legally required. This difference between aspirational conduct and legal obligation is an important one to keep in mind when considering to what extent the ethical decisions from the first part of the book can be made legal requirements.

Furthermore, ethics may not deal with the questions of generality and specificity in exactly the same way as the law does. Ethics are primarily an individual matter. Obviously, when determining an ethical position, individuals want one which is defensible, and that means that the ethical system should be one which consists of general rules (even consequentialism and virtue ethics, which have less reliance on rules than deontological systems, have at least one overriding rule). However, those rules are still to be applied on an individual basis by individuals. I may hope that the position I take in a specific circumstance is one which others will follow, but the requirement is still that I be able to show why it is acceptable under the ethical rules I agree to follow. The law, conversely, is meant to be applied in a more general way. It is what society determines to be acceptable (through the use of various officers of the law including the police and the courts). It does not matter, then, if I can argue that my conduct fits within a particular legal framework if that position is not accepted by those in charge. As a result, the law may be the result of a more co-operative venture than ethics need be. It is not required that I develop my ethical system on my own, of course, but there is nothing about ethical positions which requires that I do so. I could, then, disregard the viewpoints of everyone else when deciding what conduct should be ethical and what conduct should not, but I simply cannot do so in relation to the law. As a result, the law is often formulated in significantly different ways from ethical positions and this may impact the resulting practices.

3   Issues specific to law

In addition to the differences between law and ethics, there are two additional issues specific to law which are worthy of mention. Both were highlighted in the introduction but are well worth reviewing at this stage. The first thing that is specific to law is to remember that there is almost always a regulatory system already in place. When discussing what the law ought to be (as we are doing here), it is usually a comparative exercise. We are not comparing some regulatory mechanism to nothing, but the regulatory mechanism which is already in existence. There may be occasions when this is not true (such as discussions about the regulation of new technology), but in the case of end-of-life decisions, all legal systems will have a current regulation of some sort. They will all have some method for determining which actions health-care practitioners are allowed to perform and which ones are prohibited. We do not often think of this as a regulatory system but it is crucial to keep in mind that the status quo is a current regulatory system.

The second issue is the large issue of what constitutes a successful regulatory scheme. In the context of end-of-life decisions, the routinely used measure of success (specifically for cases of legalising voluntary euthanasia and assisted suicide) is a regime which results in no violations of the applicable regulation. In other words, the regulation must be completely successful in order for it to be acceptable to society. Such a measure of success is unrealistic. No regulatory scheme ever has a complete success rate, no matter how carefully worded, rigorously enforced or severely punished. As a result, on this metric, no regulatory scheme is ever truly effective, but that seems to conflict with reality. Despite not having a 100 per cent success rate, many regulatory schemes in many areas are by and large effective. We should keep the same idea in mind when considering how best to regulate end-of-life decisions. It will not be possible, no matter what regulatory scheme we devise, to have a complete success rate. It may be laudable to have that as an aspirational goal, but when determining effectiveness, we need to take a more comparative position. What we should be aiming at is the minimisation of unacceptable conduct, not its complete elimination. Thus, we should pay attention to which regulatory schemes are most successful at reducing the number of bad behaviours while increasing the number of good behaviours. A regulatory system may still be, by and large, the best one if it manages to have the highest reduction of bad behaviours, despite the fact that it does not eliminate all conduct we wish to avoid.

As noted in the introduction, one of the clearest cases of this phenomenon is the evidence from the Netherlands in relation to the empirical slippery slope. When considering whether the Netherlands provides sufficient evidence of any slippery slope, it is not sufficient to merely cite the fact that there are upwards of 1,000 cases a year of bad conduct – in this case, involuntary or non-voluntary euthanasia. That, by itself, does not prove that we should not allow assisted dying. In order to show that, what is needed is to show that other regulatory schemes are more effective at reducing this bad conduct than a system which allows either assisted suicide or voluntary euthanasia, or both. It would be foolish to pretend that our own regulatory system does not have instances of similar conduct as bad as or worse than the Netherlands.[1] Using the same metric, we should then conclude that our own system of regulating assisted dying by prohibition does not work either. Whether or not that is true, the Harold Shipman case in the UK is not sufficient evidence of effectiveness to prove it. It is thus vital for us to pay close attention to the metrics used to determine effectiveness and make sure they are applied to all regulatory mechanisms in a comparative way.

4   General evidentiary sources

Properly evaluating the effect of these different regulatory systems requires the use of evidence. While many evidentiary sources will be related to specific issues and will therefore be discussed in the chapters in which they are relevant, there are some general sources which will provide substantial evidence for a number of issues. Consequently, it is best to describe those sources of evidence at the beginning of the section instead of necessarily waiting to discuss them. Those sources include the four national surveys in the Netherlands and related comparison surveys, the annual reports from the Oregon Department of Health and the interview study conducted by Roger Magnusson.

4.1   The Netherlands surveys

To date, there have been four national surveys of end-of-life practice in the Netherlands. The first of the four research studies included data

---

[1] For example, in the UK, one could cite Harold Shipman, a doctor who killed around 250 people over his career. See J. Smith, *Sixth Report – Shipman Inquiry: The Final Report* (Crown Copyright, 2005), paragraph 7.78.

from 1990–1991.[2] The report was commissioned by the Dutch government as part of an overall investigation into the effectiveness of the regulations surrounding end-of-life decisions and, in particular, the acceptance of voluntary euthanasia in that country. The investigation was chaired by the Attorney-General of the Dutch Supreme Court, Professor Remmelink,[3] and has subsequently been referred to as the Remmelink Report. The Committee's brief was specifically to obtain information relating to active voluntary euthanasia, but it decided that it was more effective to take a broader view and look at all end-of-life decisions. Additionally, the committee was asked to report on the practice of doctors that led to the death of a patient, whether by act or omission, and whether or not the patient had requested the doctor's practice. The study aims were:

to produce reliable estimates of the incidence of active voluntary euthanasia and other medical decisions concerning the end of life; to describe the characteristics of patients, doctors and situations involved; to assess how far doctors are acquainted with the criteria for acceptable euthanasia; and to determine under which conditions doctors would be willing to report a death by euthanasia as such.[4]

The study, then, was expected to provide only empirical evidence and not provide any further discussion about the ethical or legal nature of any of the end-of-life practices.

The research study, conducted by a team of researchers at Erasmus University under the authority of Professor van der Maas, consisted of three major arms.[5] One part of the research focused on interviews with 405 doctors about practices they had engaged in.[6] The second arm of the research was a questionnaire which asked the doctors of a sample of 7,000 deceased individuals about the practices which had been used in that specific case.[7] The final arm was a prospective survey sent to the 405 interviewed doctors about deaths that had occurred in their practice in the six months after the interview.[8] The doctors were assured that any answers they gave would remain confidential and the Ministry of Justice further provided immunity for all of the participants of the survey.[9] The benefit of this was that it allowed the doctors in

[2] P. J. van der Maas et al., 'Euthanasia and Other Medical Decisions Concerning the End of Life' (1991) 338 The Lancet 669–674.
[3] Ibid., 669.
[4] Otlowski, Voluntary Euthanasia and the Common Law, p. 425.
[5] Van der Maas et al., 'Euthanasia and Other Medical Decisions Concerning the End of Life'.
[6] Ibid., 669.   [7] Ibid., 669.
[8] Ibid.   [9] Ibid., 670.

question to be more forthcoming about the practices they had engaged in. Additionally, instead of asking the doctors whether they had engaged in a particular category of event, the researchers provided descriptions of various practices and asked the doctors whether they had engaged in practices which fit the descriptions.[10] Doctors were therefore not asked if they had participated in active voluntary euthanasia, but whether they had intentionally provided a lethal dose of medication to a patient at the patient's request. This was considered crucial to a determination of the actual incidence rates of various practices, although there have been concerns raised about how this methodology impacts vital questions about the reporting rate of various practices in the Netherlands.

The first two arms of this research design have been replicated by the Dutch on three subsequent occasions – in 1995,[11] 2001[12] and 2005[13] – with only minor differences in overall study design. According to Griffiths, Weyers and Adams, in the 2001 study, interviews with doctors and others involved in a sample of reported cases were added. In 2005, the interview arm of the study was replaced with a questionnaire sent to over 1,000 doctors.[14] However, the basic structure of the study has remained constant, as have the standard questions which are asked in the study. This allows for an easier comparison between the studies.

Furthermore, the Remmelink study has been replicated not only in the Netherlands, but also other places around the globe. The first replication of the study outside the Netherlands was in Australia in 1997.[15] This study did not replicate the interview arm of the original Dutch study but did send a questionnaire based upon the original Dutch one to a random sample of 3,000 doctors in selected disciplines in Australia.[16] The disciplines chosen were ones which, according to the researchers, were considered to be the most similar to those 'attendant to 87% of hospital deaths and nearly all deaths outside hospitals in the Netherlands'.[17] Doctors were asked to complete the survey in relation to the 'most recent death' they had attended over the previous 12

---

[10] *Ibid.*

[11] P. J. van der Maas *et al.*, 'Euthanasia, Physician-Assisted Suicide, and Other Medical Practices Involving the End of Life in the Netherlands, 1990–1995' (1996) 335 *New England Journal of Medicine* 1699–1705.

[12] B. D. Onwuteaka-Philipsen *et al.*, 'Euthanasia and Other End-of-Life Decisions in the Netherlands in 1990, 1995, and 2001' (2003) 362 *The Lancet* 395–399.

[13] A. van der Heide *et al.*, 'End-of-Life Practices in the Netherlands under the Euthanasia Act' (2007) 356 *New England Journal of Medicine* 1957–1965.

[14] Griffiths *et al.*, *Euthanasia and Law in Europe*, p. 149.

[15] H. Kuhse *et al.*, 'End-of-Life Decisions in Australian Medical Practice' (1997) 166 *Medical Journal of Australia* 191–196.

[16] *Ibid.*, 192.   [17] *Ibid.*

months.[18] Interviews were not conducted because the researchers had specific concerns about anonymity and did not want doctors to be concerned about the possibility of prosecution for illegal acts.[19]

A second replication took place in Belgium in 2000.[20] This study was carried out primarily in Flanders, which is the Dutch-speaking part of Belgium. As with the Australian study, the primary focus was on the death-certificate questionnaire as opposed to interviews. The reason why interviews were not done in the Belgian study is not specified, although the Belgian researchers also mention a concern about anonymity.[21] The selection method of the Belgian study was closer to the original Dutch studies than the Australian one because the methods for recording deaths are more similar than in Australia. Thus, the Belgian researchers also used death certificates to determine who to send the questionnaires to instead of a random sample of doctors.[22]

A third study outside the Netherlands, using a similar research design, was done in New Zealand in 2003.[23] The research design was closest to the one used in Australia, as the questionnaire was sent to 2,602 general practitioners from a commercially supplied address list.[24] The doctors in question were asked to fill out the survey in relation to the last death they had attended in the previous 12 months.[25] Again, interviews were not conducted but the questionnaire was the same as that used in the Australian study and was based upon the original Dutch one.[26] It is not clear from the article published in the *British Medical Journal* what methods were used to ensure the confidentiality and anonymity of responses, an aspect of the study considered vitally important in other jurisdictions.

A fourth replication of the Dutch survey design was done in the UK in 2004 by Clive Seale.[27] Seale, as in the Australian study, sent questionnaires to doctors based upon a random sample, as opposed to doctors who had signed death certificates.[28] The total number of questionnaires sent out was 1,000.[29] As in the Australian study, Seale asked the doctors in question to respond about the most recent death.[30] According to

---

[18] *Ibid.*   [19] *Ibid.*

[20] L. Deliens *et al.*, 'End-of-Life Decisions in Medical Practice in Flanders, Belgium: A Nationwide Survey' (2000) 356 *The Lancet* 1806–1811.

[21] *Ibid.*, 1807.   [22] *Ibid.*, 1806–1807.

[23] K. Mitchell and R. Glynn Owens, 'National Survey of Medical Decisions at End of Life Made by New Zealand General Practitioners' (2003) 327 *BMJ* 202–203.

[24] *Ibid.*, 202.   [25] *Ibid.*   [26] *Ibid.*

[27] C. Seale, 'National Survey of End of Life Decisions Made by U.K. Medical Practitioners' (2006) 20 *Palliative Medicine* 3–10.

[28] *Ibid.*, 4.   [29] *Ibid.*   [30] *Ibid.*, 5.

Seale, this may mean that rates of non-sudden and unexpected deaths were artificially reduced as doctors interpreted the question to refer to the most recent 'interesting' death as opposed to merely the most recent death.[31] As with the other studies done outside the Netherlands, interviews were not conducted so that respondents could be assured that any answers given were anonymous.[32]

The final study which utilised the original Dutch design was a six-country European study.[33] The EURELD study, as it has become known, looked at end-of-life decisions in the Netherlands, Belgium, Italy, Denmark, Sweden and the German-speaking part of Switzerland.[34] The study used the original Dutch surveys, which were then translated into the languages of the other countries in the study.[35] As in the Dutch and Belgian studies, participants were chosen based upon death certificates, as opposed to a random sample of doctors.[36] As a result, doctors were asked about specific cases. Interviews were not conducted for the reasons that have precluded interviews in other jurisdictions replicating the Dutch design.

These nine studies provide a wealth of comparative data about end-of-life practices. As set out by the original Remmelink committee, the purpose of these studies has been to describe practices rather than make any specific claims about the legality or ethical nature of any particular end-of-life decisions. While comparisons between the various studies can be made, there are particular concerns about some of the studies which need to be accounted for. For example, not all of the studies had a robust response rate (e.g. the Belgian study and the Italian portion of the EURELD one); interviews were conducted only in relation to the Dutch national studies; and the Australian study has been criticised for a mistranslated question. There is the additional concern raised by Seale about the difference in selecting participants between the English-language studies (Australia, New Zealand and the UK) and those based elsewhere. However, in general, these studies are reasonably comparable and provide us with some useful comparative data for evaluating the question of regulation.

---

[31] C. Seale, 'Investigating End-of-Life Decision Making in U.K. Medical Practice', Address at Institute of Medical Law, University of Birmingham, 22 March 2006.
[32] C. Seale, 'National Survey of End of Life Decisions Made by U.K. Medical Practitioners', 6.
[33] A. van der Heide et al., 'End-of-Life Decision-making in Six European Countries: Descriptive Study' (2003) 361 The Lancet 345–350.
[34] Ibid., 346. [35] Ibid. [36] Ibid.

4.2   Annual governmental reports

There are two categories of annual governmental reports which are of substantial benefit when considering end-of-life decisions. The first are the annual reports by the Oregon Health Department (OHD).[37] These reports are mandated by the Oregon Death with Dignity Act (DWDA). The Act requires the OHD to 'monitor compliance with the law, collect information about the patients and physicians who participate in legal physician-assisted suicide, and publish an annual statistical report'.[38] According to the first report, as required by statute, the OHD has developed a monitoring system for deaths under the Act.[39] This monitoring system has two main components. The first is that physicians are required to inform the OHD any time they prescribe lethal medication for a patient.[40] These reports are reviewed by the OHD and doctors who do not comply with the reporting requirements by not providing sufficient information or by providing 'discrepant' information are contacted.[41] The second aspect of the reporting procedure is a death-certificate review. Death certificates in Oregon are scrutinised by the OHD Vital Records staff.[42] Death certificates related to a death under the DWDA are sent to the OHD State Registrar so that they can be matched with the prescription record.[43] Additionally, the Vital Records staff does occasional audits of death certificates that correspond to physician records to make sure that no cases have been missed.[44] The OHD also conducts in-person or telephone interviews after the submission of the death certificate with all prescribing physicians who had prescribed lethal medication.[45] The interviews were used to gather data which would not have been available from the death

---

[37] The reports can be found on the Oregon Department of Human Services website: http://public.health.oregon.gov/ProviderPartnerResources/EvaluationResearch/DeathwithDignityAct/Pages/index.aspx (accessed 21 June 2011).

[38] Oregon Death with Dignity Act, Oregon Revised Statute 127.800–127.897.

[39] A. E. Chin *et al.*, 'Oregon's Death with Dignity Act: The First Year's Experience' (1999), Department of Human Resources, Oregon Health Division, Center for Disease Prevention and Epidemiology.

[40] *Ibid.*, 2.   [41] *Ibid.*   [42] *Ibid.*

[43] *Ibid.* The description of this practice only appears in the first annual report. Subsequent reports (up until Year 9) indicate that a periodic review of death certificates occurs, but do not specifically mention the role of the State Registrar in making sure that death certificates are matched with prescription records.

[44] *Ibid.*

[45] *Ibid.*, 3. Doctors, instead of participating in an interview, may fill out a survey instead. The survey must be filled out within ten calendar days of the patient's death. The survey can be found at http://public.health.oregon.gov/ProviderPartnerResources/EvaluationResearch/DeathwithDignityAct/Documents/at2form.pdf (accessed 21 June 2011).

certificate or prescription records. This includes data on how long the medication took to cause death and any unexpected side effects of the medication.[46] Patients were not contacted, nor were family members.[47] These reports have been produced for every year the DWDA has been in force. While the reports now provide less explanatory information than they used to (e.g. about the reporting system), they do provide the same statistical information, and important comparisons are made with previous years.

These reports provide data about a number of factors related to the DWDA. They provide biographical data about the patients involved as well as more specific information about the reasons for requesting PAS, the time between request and the actual taking of lethal medication, the length of time between ingestion of the lethal medication and death, any complicating factors and whether any of the doctors have been referred to the Oregon Medical Board. Unfortunately, the reports only cover cases which have been indicated to them as being under the DWDA.[48] Thus, if a prescribing physician did not file the required report, nor was there any indication on the death certificate that the patient had requested PAS under the DWDA, then it would not show up in the annual reports.

A second governmental source of information is the Annual Reports of the Regional Review Committees from the Netherlands. These reports have been prepared and published since 2002, although they have been available in English only since 2007.[49] These reports provide specific information about cases which have been brought to the attention of the Regional Review Committee (RRC). They provide a detailed analysis of the case along with a determination by the RRC as to whether the doctor had acted with due care as required by Dutch law. Additionally, it provides some statistical information about the number of cases which are sent to the RRCs, the doctors involved in these cases and the conditions suffered by the patient.[50] The Annual Review also mentions the number of cases where it was determined that the doctor had not acted in accordance with the due care criteria.[51]

[46] Chin *et al.*, 'Oregon's Death with Dignity Act: The First Year's Experience', 3.
[47] *Ibid.*
[48] Chin *et al.*, 'Oregon's Death with Dignity Act: The First Year's Experience', 9.
[49] Griffiths *et al.* indicate that the reports have been available in English, French and German since 2005. *Euthanasia and Law in Europe*, p. 565. However, the website for the Review Committees only provides English reports from 2007 to 2009. See www.euthanasiecommissie.nl/en/review–committees/annualreport/default.asp (accessed 23 October 2010). The English reports from the website no longer appear to be available (as of 21 June 2011).
[50] Griffiths *et al.*, *Euthanasia and Law in Europe*.   [51] *Ibid.*

While these cases do provide some important information for analysis, their primary purpose appears to be more akin to an aid to doctors working in the Netherlands. As such, cases are used as examples of good practice or of cases which are thought to provide examples of particular issues of which the doctor may need to be aware. As a result, they are more analytical than the simple statistical records provided in the Oregon reports. However, like the Oregon reports, they are only cases which have been reported to the RRCs and will not contain cases where the doctor has failed to inform the proper authorities about his or her action.

4.3   *The* Angels of Death *study*

While both the annual governmental reports and the Dutch national studies (along with those from other jurisdictions which use the same methodology) are primarily quantitative data, there is some qualitative data about end-of-life decisions as well. The primary data comes from a study done by Roger Magnusson, documented in his book *Angels of Death*.[52] The study consisted of 49 interviews with those in the health care and related professions.[53] The interviewees were mostly located in Australia and the US, more specifically in Sydney, Melbourne and San Francisco.[54] They were also primarily but not exclusively involved in the care or treatment of those with HIV/AIDS.[55] Interviewees were self-selected by a snowball method. Essentially, Magnusson recruited volunteers using a variety of methods including flyers, letters to community groups and general invitations given at seminars and conferences where he provided his contact details and asked for volunteers for the study.[56] Once interviewees had given interviews, he asked them to pass along his contact details to other individuals who might be interested in being interviewed.[57] This allowed him to gain access to various networks of individuals to which he would not otherwise have had the chance to meet. It also means that it is not possible to generalise the results of the study, particularly in relation to the incidence rates. Additionally, Magnusson granted his participants both anonymity and confidentiality.[58] Thus, participants chose pseudonyms which are used in the book.[59] While this means that it is not possible to verify the information that Magnusson provides, it also allowed him to provide the interviewees with a guarantee which allowed them to be more honest about their practices.

---

[52] Magnusson, *Angels of Death.*   [53] *Ibid.*, p. 2.   [54] *Ibid.*
[55] *Ibid.*   [56] *Ibid.*, pp. 282–282.   [57] *Ibid.*, p. 283.
[58] *Ibid.*, p. 284.   [59] *Ibid.*

Interviewees primarily related a number of anecdotes to Magnusson about end-of-life practices. During the 49 interviews, the researchers were able to document 203 anecdotes.[60] Of those anecdotes, 105 dealt with PAS or voluntary euthanasia while another 34 related to suicide.[61] The rest related to patient care or other topics. These anecdotes were distinguishable from mere rumour or speculation even when they did not relate to the interviewee directly.[62] However, the vast majority of the anecdotes were related to the interviewee. For example, of the 105 anecdotes which related to PAS or voluntary euthanasia, 88 directly involved the interviewee.[63] These anecdotes could be further broken down into the type of participation by the interviewee, whether in a 'hands-on' role (56.8 per cent of the interviewees in the 88 anecdotes), 'active at the scene' (meaning the interviewee was present and had some role, but was not as active as those in a hands-on role (6.8 per cent)), indirectly involved in facilitating death (21.6 per cent), referral (4.6 per cent), discussion (4.6 per cent) or 'failed to comply with doctor's direction' (1.1 per cent).[64] Looked at differently, of the 49 interviewees, 26, or 53 per cent, had been involved in a hands-on role at least once.[65] Another 4 (8.2 per cent) had been active at the scene and a further 7 (14.3 per cent) were involved in indirect facilitation.[66] Only 11 (22.5 per cent) had no involvement.[67] Additionally, Magnusson was able to provide data about the number of times particular individuals had participated in end-of-life decisions, with some being involved in so many cases that they were unable to give a specific figure and instead referred to the frequency as 'immemorable' or 'too many to count'.[68] As Magnusson states:

Even if one assumes that these numbers are inflated, it is significant that a cohort of less than 50 interviewees, recruited in a variety of ways, should have resulted in so many interviewees who estimated that they had participated in assisted death on a dozen occasions or more. General practitioners ... who gave six separate accounts of involvement in interview, don't even make it into the table [of the dozen top participants]![69]

It is further worthy of note that Magnusson's study did not include only doctors. Other interviewees included community nurses, hospice nurses, therapists and even a funeral director, in addition to general practitioners and hospital doctors.[70]

---

[60] *Ibid.*, p. 131, table 7–2.   [61] *Ibid.*   [62] *Ibid.*, p. 132.
[63] *Ibid.*   [64] *Ibid.*, table 7–3.   [65] *Ibid.*, p. 136, table 7–4.
[66] *Ibid.*   [67] *Ibid.*   [68] *Ibid.*, p. 136.
[69] *Ibid.*, p. 138.   [70] *Ibid.*, p. 128.

Magnusson's study thus provides us with a rich, nuanced view of the types of practices which occur, even in jurisdictions which do not allow PAS or voluntary euthanasia. While, as with most qualitative data, it may be difficult to draw more general statements about practices in a community, it does show the extent of practices which occur as well as a detailed description of how these practices develop, are kept from the public eye and the reasons and rationales behind them. It can thus provide an important source of data to evaluate some of the regulatory mechanisms which exist as well as some of the more common beliefs about the ability to regulate end-of-life decisions.

5   The types of regulatory mechanisms

One final issue should be addressed prior to looking at the specific issues covered in the rest of the book. That issue is what is meant by the term regulatory mechanism or regulatory system. To many, it may seem a deliberately vague phrase and it may not be entirely clear what is covered by those terms. It would therefore be helpful to provide readers with a description of at least the things covered by the terms. Technically, we could consider there to be a difference between a regulatory system and a regulatory mechanism. We could argue that a regulatory system is the broad overarching approach to end-of-life decision-making and that the regulatory mechanism is a specific aspect of that approach. I am not sure, however, that this distinction is particularly vital for our purposes. I do think that it is important that our regulatory scheme for end-of-life decision-making should be consistent across the board and we should consider it as a range of options, but I do not see how there is any necessary reason to focus on the semantic difference between a mechanism and a system. Specific instances of a general policy and the general policy itself will both be vital to our determinations of what is appropriate.

What we should make sure about distinguishing, though, is the many different ways we might implement a particular regulatory approach. Within the legal sphere, we may create laws by legislation, administrative processes, referendums and judicial approaches. It is worth emphasising that these different approaches will have different costs and benefits associated with them. Legislation, for example, may allow for the ability to craft statutes based upon expert information and deliberation, but it may also be hijacked by the political whims of certain groups. Judicial decisions are less likely to dependent on the whims of particular pressure groups (although not always), but cannot often craft detailed rules to implement particular choices.[71] We must be aware of those sorts of issues when determining the best way to implement our ethical decisions as legal ones. This does not apply only to regulatory schemes, but also to specific mechanisms. As an example, one way we may regulate end-of-life decision-making is through the creation of particular rights for either patients or health-care professionals. We should be aware that the creation of rights may have particular costs (through the required creation of reciprocal duties on others) which may not be beneficial overall. Thus, we should also keep in mind whether the specific method used to regulate conduct is the most effective.

6   Conclusion

Having considered in Part I the ethical framework necessary for deciding about the correctness of conduct at the end of life, we now need to explore how best to regulate that conduct through the law. The subsequent chapters will therefore shift the focus from the philosophical discussion of ethics to the practical implications of those ethical decisions. It is only after that discussion that we should be able to make conclusions about the types of end-of-life decision-making we wish to allow.

---

[71] For example, *Brown* v. *Board of Education*, 347 U.S. 483 (1954), the famous racial desegregation case in the US, merely determined that schools should be desegregated. It was up to local authorities to determine the most effective way of doing so.

10   Protection of patients

1   Introduction

We begin our discussion of regulatory issues with two concerns which relate specifically to the protection of patients. Most of the issues which will be raised in this part of the book will likely have some effect upon the patient, whether directly or indirectly. The issues raised in this chapter are specifically related, however, to the protection of individual patients. Of course, as with many of these issues, they can also be framed as larger societal concerns. Even so, the primary focus is on the protection of individual patients who may be seen as being especially at risk. The issues we will be considering are the prevention of suicide and the protection of vulnerable members of society.

2   The prevention of suicide

The first issue we shall consider is the prevention of suicide. The state has often been considered to have a substantial interest in preventing the suicides of its citizens. In fact, one of the compelling state interests which was accepted by the US Supreme Court in its assisted suicide decisions, *Washington* v. *Glucksberg* and *Vacco* v. *Quill*, was the prevention of suicide. For example, Chief Justice Rehnquist's majority opinion in *Glucksberg* states that 'Indeed, opposition to and condemnation of suicide – and, therefore, of assisting suicide – are consistent and enduring themes of our philosophical, legal, and cultural heritages'.[1] Most jurisdictions in history, particularly in the West, have prohibited suicide until relatively recently[2] and most prohibit the assistance of suicide. It

---

[1] *Washington* v. *Glucksberg*, 521 U.S. 702 at 711. The opinion cites the following as support for that statement: T. J. Marzen, M. K. O'Dowd, D. Crone and T. J. Balch, 'Suicide: A Constitutional Right?' (1985) 24(1) *Duquesne L. Rev.* 1, 17–56; see also New York State Task Force on Life and the Law, *When Death Is Sought: Assisted Suicide and Euthanasia in the Medical Context* (New York, 1994), pp. 77–82.
[2] See, e.g., the Suicide Act 1961 in the UK.

seems clear, then, that societies place a tremendous value on the prevention of suicide, either through criminal prohibition or other means.

It might be argued in response to the long tradition of prohibiting suicide that many jurisdictions have now decriminalised suicide. Again, we can point to statutes such as the Suicide Act 1961, which eliminated suicide as a felony. Some may be tempted to argue that such a move indicates that the state interest in preventing suicide is no longer important. Such a claim, however, would likely be false. In general, the decriminalisation of suicide was not due to any particular acceptance of any right to commit suicide or that suicide had somehow become acceptable. Instead, it was a realisation that the criminal law was not the best mechanism for preventing suicide. A decision to commit suicide was considered to be evidence of a mental health issue and, therefore, was seen to be more properly suited to treatment as opposed to punishment for cases of attempted suicide. In cases where the suicide had been successful, it would be, rather obviously, impossible to punish the person committing suicide. As such, most of the usual punishments (e.g. inability to be buried on consecrated ground and loss of all property to the state) fell on the family of the one committing suicide. As those individuals were often not responsible for the crime of suicide, it was not considered to be appropriate for them to be punished.[3] However, the decriminalisation of suicide does not mean that society has accepted suicide.[4]

One particular piece of evidence which is used to bolster this argument is that assistance with suicide is still often criminal. What this does, though, is highlight the uniqueness of statutes which criminalise assistance with suicide. Usually, actions which primarily are used for assistance are only deemed to be criminal if they assist actions which are themselves criminal. So, the criminality of the assistance is dependent on the criminality of the assisted action. This is not the case with assistance with suicide as the assisted action (the suicide itself) is not criminal at all. Consequently, assisting a suicide is often the only time when one can be charged with a criminal offence even though the person doing the main action in question is not subject to any criminal penalty.

Having said that, there is still considerable evidence that the prevention of suicide is a major concern in the regulation of end-of-life decisions. This affects not only the regulation of assisted suicide but also

[3] *Glucksberg* at 713–714, citing Z. Swift, *A System of the Laws of the State of Connecticut* (Windham: John Byrne, 1796), p. 304.
[4] *Glucksberg* at 714–716.

euthanasia and the withdrawal and withholding of treatment, particularly life-sustaining treatment. This chapter, then, will consider how the regulation of end-of-life decisions is impacted by an attempt by the state to minimise or prevent suicide. We will first examine the concept of rational suicide as it is that idea which is most important to end-of-life decisions. The chapter will then consider how the state interest in the prevention of suicide works in practice. In particular, we will examine a claim made by Richard Posner that the allowing of assistance in suicide can actually reduce the number of suicides within a jurisdiction. We shall also consider how the prevention of suicide impacts upon claims for the withdrawal and withholding of treatment, concerns which are frequently overlooked. Finally, we will be able to make conclusions as to the best way that regulation of end-of-life decisions can incorporate an attempt to minimise the number of suicides.

2.1   Rational suicide

When discussing the acceptance of suicide, very few would argue for the acceptance of all possible suicides. There are many suicides which the majority of people feel should be uncontestedly prohibited. This includes the standard cases of unrequited teenage love or other reasons which are considered to be transient. Those kinds of suicides are not really the ones at issue here. Instead, the major issue in relation to end-of-life decisions is the question of rational suicides – i.e. those suicides which are seen to be based upon a deliberate, reasoned decision which others might see as reasonable. The first issue, then, is whether such suicides really exist. Can there ever be rational suicides?

Any discussion about rational suicide should begin with a discussion about Ancient Greek and Roman philosophers. Socrates willingly drank hemlock, although it can certainly be argued that he did so because of reasons unrelated to a wish to die.[5] A more definitive statement in support of rational suicide comes from the Stoics, in particular, from Seneca. He stated that:

---

[5] He, of course, took hemlock because he had been sentenced to death for corrupting the youth of Athens. It is worth noting, however, *The Apology* by Xenophon. In that text, which asserts itself to be a contemporary account of Socrates' trial and death, Socrates does indicate that death is preferable to 'if my years are prolonged, I know that the frailties of old age will inevitably be realized, – that my vision must be less perfect and my hearing less keen, that I shall be slower to learn and more forgetful of what I have learned. If I perceive my decay and take to complaining, how ... could I any longer take pleasure in life?' An online version of *The Apology* can be found at: www.perseus.tufts.edu/hopper/text?doc=Perseus:text:1999.01.0212 (accessed 15 June 2011). The relevant sections are 6–9.

Living is not the good, but living well. The wise man therefore lives as long as he should, not as long as he can. He will observe where he is to live, with whom, how and what he is to do. He will always think of life in terms of quality, not quantity ... Dying early or late is of no relevance, dying well or ill is. To die well is to escape the danger of living ill ...

Just as I choose a ship to sail in or a house to live in, so I choose a death for my passage from life. Moreover, whereas a prolonged life is not necessarily better, a prolonged death is necessarily worse.[6]

Margaret Battin argues that this quotation indicates that the real question about one's life is not sufficiently determined by how long it is. Our lives may be good but short or bad but long. It is not the length which determines the quality of our lives. Nor, indeed, should we consider these deaths to have come too early. As she states:

A self-embraced death, a suicide, Seneca argues, is not a premature end to a complete life. It isn't like a journey cut short, which is incomplete because you don't get there; rather, Seneca maintains, a life cut short can still be complete if it has been lived well – you do get there, so to speak; you've actually lived your whole life.[7]

Merely because Seneca and Socrates have stated something does not necessarily make it true,[8] but it is important to realise that notions of rational suicide are not simply modern constructs. There is thus some evidence to suggest that there can be such a thing as a rational suicide. How, though, could the wilful destruction of one's own existence qualify as a rational decision? Any rational suicide would have to involve a decision backed up by sufficient reasons which can be explained to others. This would presumably mean that an individual can give a set of reasons why, in their own life, that death might be preferable to life. It is likely that the list of reasons which others would find reasonable (let alone convincing) in such a situation are probably fairly small. However, one could consider a life where this is true. It will often

---

[6] Quoted in Battin, *Ending Life*, p. 4.

[7] *Ibid.*, p. 4. It is again worth noting that Socrates appears to make a similar claim. According to *The Apology*, when seeing some of his supporters in tears after the trail, he said 'What is this? ... Are you just now beginning to weep? Have you not known all along that from the moment of my birth nature had condemned me to death? Verily, if I am being destroyed before my time while blessings are still pouring in upon me, clearly that should bring grief to me and to my well-wishers; but if I am ending my life when only troubles are in view, my own opinion is that you ought all to feel cheered, in the assurance that my state is happy' *The Apology*, section 27.

[8] Chief Justice Rehnquist, for example, cites Blackstone who does not speak kindly of individuals like Seneca, referring to 'the pretended heroism, but real cowardice, of the Stoic philosophers, who destroyed themselves to avoid those ills which they had not the fortitude to endure'. W. Blackstone, *Commentaries on the Laws of England*, 4 vols. (Oxford: Clarendon Press 1765–1769), vol. IV, p. 189, cited in *Glucksberg* at 712.

depend upon individual notions of what is acceptable, so, in truth, then, what we have returned to is the discussion about the value of life and there were discussions in that chapter about instances where an individual might determine rationally that death would be preferable to life. In saying that, I do not want to belittle the claim that many (probably most) people who are considering suicide have a treatable mental health issue such as depression. Just because there are some possible scenarios when suicide may be rational does not mean that all possible suicides are rational. A large proportion of them will not be. There will be any number of cases of treatable depression, for example, which would not be considered rational suicides.

The issue then becomes whether it is possible to differentiate between rational suicides and irrational ones. In general, there are some which we could probably give as categorical examples of irrational suicides – the cases of broken-hearted teenagers – but there are probably no categorical examples of rational ones. Instead, determinations of a rational suicide seem much more effective if done at an individual level. Thus, if we were deciding on an acceptable mechanism for regulating rational suicides, it would need to have some method for making an individual determination – either by public officials or, more likely, by people such as health-care professionals. When considering the role of health-care professionals, however, some might argue that health-care professionals may not have sufficient training or expertise to judge the rationality of particular suicide requests. That will, of course, depend on the health-care professional concerned. Psychologists and psychiatrists (and presumably related health-care professionals like psychiatric nurses) would be skilled at determining at least certain types of interferences with rationality such as depression. Even those health-care professionals who are not in a mental health field, though, are likely to have some experience in these sorts of matters. Doctors, for example, may often be required to determine if a patient is competent to make a decision. There is little reason to believe, if they can make that sort of decision, that they could not make the decisions necessary to determine whether a specific decision is rational or not. Again, one might argue that it would not be possible to be completely certain about the decision made by the doctor in these cases. Doctors may sometimes get competency determinations wrong and there is little reason to believe that some mistakes might not be made in these cases as well. While this may be true, this is an instance of applying the wrong metric to our regulatory mechanism. We cannot be 100 per cent sure about these decisions, but we can make sure they are reasonably accurate. We could, for example, limit such decisions to those in mental health fields; we could also provide specific training for doctors. Thus, there seems to be little reason why we could not create a procedure for distinguishing between a rational and an irrational suicide.

2.2   Preventing suicide in practice

The other important question is whether the prohibition on certain types of end-of-life decisions actually reduces the number of suicides. When discussing this we are most likely limiting ourselves to questions about the reduction in suicides for those with health-care concerns. It is difficult to construct a case that the legalisation of particular end-of-life decisions would have any effect upon those committing suicide for financial reasons, for example.[9] We shall therefore limit our discussion to those related to health-care issues when considering the reduction of suicides. Initially, it might seem like any regulation which limits assisted dying will necessarily reduce instances of suicide. Both assisted suicide and voluntary euthanasia could conceivably count as suicides and the elimination of them as a possible acceptable practice would seem to eliminate all of those instances of suicide, resulting in a lower rate overall. However, we will look at three possible ways in which the prohibition of assisted dying may not help reduce the rate of suicide overall. We shall also consider the issue of suicidal intent in relation to withdrawal and withholding of treatment.

The first way that allowing assisted dying in some form might reduce suicide rates was posited by Richard Posner.[10] Posner presented the hypothesis that allowing assisted dying would lower the suicide rate for those populations for which it might be an issue.[11] As this sounds more than a bit counter-intuitive, it is worth describing Posner's argument. The argument is that if people are acting rationally, they will only choose suicide when the costs of continued existence outweigh its benefits.[12] In other words, one would only consider suicide to be

---

[9] We could have an argument that allowing suicide in any context lets society become more accepting of suicide or assisted death generally, and thus we have an overall lack of respect for life. There are a number of possible answers to that particular argument but they are more properly discussed in relation to slippery slope arguments. We shall consider these arguments then in Chapter 13.

[10] R. Posner, *Aging and Old Age* (University of Chicago Press, 1995).

[11] *Ibid.*, pp. 243–250.

[12] *Ibid.*, pp. 245–246. Posner actually states that 'our hypothetical individual will commit suicide … if the expected utility of death now, which is to say the disutility averted by death now, exceeds the expected utility of life plus the cost of suicide'. For our purposes, I am considering the 'costs of suicide' to be part of the benefits of continued existence.

a rational decision when the burdens of life outweighed the costs of committing suicide where costs and burdens were not simply legal or financial but included things like additional lifespan, pain, time with family, etc.[13] So, as long as I think the benefits of continuing to live outweigh its costs, I will not choose suicide. If, on the other hand, I do not consider the benefits to outweigh the costs, then, presuming I am acting rationally, I might consider some form of suicide. In and of itself, this particular hypothesis does not tell us much about assisted dying. However, Posner's argument builds on this economic model of suicide and suggests the following. When considering this in practice, most decisions can be considered in a slightly binary way. I either do something or I refrain from doing something based upon a particular stimulus. If I am thirsty, I will either get a drink or not depending on the cost/benefit analysis of doing so (availability of beverage, how thirsty I am, the trouble of getting the drink, etc.). Variables within that calculation will change the cost/benefit analysis and thereby affect the decision that I reach. Thus, if I am thirsty but it would be a hassle to walk downstairs, put the kettle on and make a cup of tea, then I may decide not to have a drink despite my thirst because of the additional costs of doing so. If, on the other hand, it would be remarkably easy to procure a drink, then I might decide the benefits outweigh the costs even if my objective level of thirst (however we might go about determining that) is not any greater. According to Posner, the benefit of allowing assisted dying is that it may change that cost/benefit analysis and do so in a way that reduces the risk of people committing suicide early.[14] The possible effect that Posner proposes is in the cost of waiting to commit suicide at a further date. He presents an example of going to the doctor.[15] He says that if someone becomes sick on a Friday, they may face the decision of whether to go to the doctor or not. If the doctor's office is only open on Friday and does not reopen until Monday, then the costs of not going to see the doctor are increased difficulties in receiving treatment over the weekend should it become necessary.[16] As a result, even if the individual does not feel all that bad, that person may decide to go to the doctor on Friday just in case. If the doctor is also open on Saturday, though, the person may be less likely to go to the doctor on Friday because they can always go on Saturday instead if their condition deteriorates or does not improve. Since many people will have got better by the following Saturday, they may not need the doctor at all and there is a reduction in doctor's visits despite the additional opening hours.[17]

---

[13] *Ibid.*   [14] *Ibid.*, p. 247.   [15] *Ibid.*, p. 248.
[16] *Ibid.*   [17] *Ibid.*

Posner posits that this might work in a similar way in relation to assisted dying practices. If I am a terminally ill patient, after considering the costs or benefits of continued existence, I may decide that, at the moment, I am capable of coping with my disease and the associated costs of that disease (pain, lack of control, etc.).[18] However, I can envisage a time when that calculation will not be the same and the burdens of my illness will be more significant (especially if it is a disease with a fairly predictable progression). If I know that when the time comes when death is preferable, I will not be able to take my own life (due to physical disability, for example), I may decide to take my life now in order to avoid that future pain.[19] If, on the other hand, it is possible for me to have assistance, and therefore be capable of committing suicide when the burdens actually do outweigh the benefits, I am more likely to delay that suicide. Once that time arrives, I may have changed my mind and determine that life in the particular condition I thought would be unbearable has turned out to be not as bad and I will delay the suicide further. Indeed, I may even decide not to commit suicide at all. Thus, the ability to delay a decision may reduce the incidence of suicide because it reduces the costs of continued living which otherwise might have a greater effect on that decision.[20]

When he proposed this hypothesis, Posner did not have any sufficient data to determine whether his idea was supported by evidence or not.[21] He did compare the rates of suicide among European countries to see if the Netherlands had a greater rate, but did not reach any firm conclusions based upon the limited data available to him.[22] Data which has become available subsequently may shed light on the issue, however, and is worth considering. The first data comes from the book *Seduced by Death*, Herbert Hendin's argument against the Dutch practice of voluntary euthanasia. Within that book, Hendin references the fact that most suicides in terminal illness cases happen shortly after a diagnosis of a terminal condition. These cases are not, then, cases where the individual has determined life to be bad currently but is including the future burden of life in any calculation about suicide. This might lend some support to Posner's argument, although it is just as easy to claim that this evidence shows merely that people committing suicide often do so for irrational reasons.[23] So, any real evidentiary support for that data is probably quite minimal.

---

[18] *Ibid.*, p. 247.   [19] *Ibid.*   [20] *Ibid.*
[21] *Ibid.*, pp. 250–253.   [22] *Ibid.*
[23] Hendin, for example, points out that many of these are cases where a person commits suicide despite the fact that the diagnosis is actually incorrect.

There is other evidence which would be stronger and comes from the Oregon Department of Health Reports. As noted in Chapter 9, these reports are a statutory requirement under the Death with Dignity Act (DWDA) and are created each year. There are a number of cases each year in the reports where patients have requested and been provided with lethal medication under the DWDA. However, the patient has not taken the medication.[24] In some cases, this may be because the patient died before it was possible to take the medication. In other cases, it may be a result of the reporting period (e.g. a patient is supplied with the lethal medication at the end of one reporting period, but has not taken that medication until the start of the next reporting period). In some cases, though, neither of these is at issue.[25] Instead, the patient has requested lethal medication but has not decided to take it. One reason for this may be a change of mind – the patient has decided not to take the lethal medication at all. In other cases, and this is the important group for our purposes, the patient appears to be stockpiling lethal medication for when they might need it. Again, while not conclusive, we do have people who are acting consistently with Posner's hypothesis.[26]

What may be happening in these sorts of situations is what is referred to in other research as 'shifting goalposts'.[27] This is a phenomenon where individuals wish to have a lethal dose of medication, not to take it but to have it available in case it is needed.[28] The medication merely provides a reason for the patient to evaluate his or her life and determine that they do not need the medication.[29] In other words, the presence of lethal medication performs a *life-affirming* function by allowing the individual in question to focus on the reasons not to take the medication instead of focusing on the bad things which result from their disease. It provides them with some aspect of control over their lives which these patients deem to be particularly important. That is not to suggest, obviously, that all patients would require lethal medication for the same effect.

---

[24] Even in cases where the patient may take the medication, there can often be a significant time lag. For example, in 1999, the time between the first request and death ranged from 15 to 289 days. In 2000, it ranged from 15 to 377 days. Oregon Report, Year 3, p. 20. In the sixth report, three patients are noted to have received the prescription in 2002 or 2001 but did not take the medication until 2003. Oregon Report, Year 6, p. 11.

[25] For example, one patient was prescribed a lethal dose of drugs under the DWDA in 2003 but was still alive as of 31 December 2004. Oregon Report, Year 7, p. 12.

[26] An example of this sort of action can be found in the case of Debbie Purdy, who, while not currently considering travelling to Switzerland, still wanted clarification about a time when she may wish to do so. *R (on the application of Purdy)* v. *Director of Public Prosecutions*, [2010] 1 A.C. 345.

[27] Magnusson, *Angels of Death*, pp. 82–83.

[28] *Ibid.*, p. 82.   [29] *Ibid.*, pp. 82–83.

2 The prevention of suicide

Many patients would not require the actual presence of lethal drugs in order to focus on the benefits of their lives instead of the burdens. For some, though, it seems a valuable way to actually prevent depressive thoughts from being put into action. Furthermore, it may allow patients to determine that previously 'unliveable' situations are not as bad as expected. So, there may be cases where there is anecdotal support that the legalisation of assisted dying practices may actually work to reduce the number of patients who go through with suicide attempts.

A final way in which the acceptance of assisted dying might lead to fewer overall suicides relates to the issue of communication. It is possible that allowing patients to request assisted dying practices will open lines of communication which did not previously exist. The interview study by Roger Magnusson provides some anecdotal evidence for this proposition. One interesting fact which arose more than once in the interviews was the belief of the interviewees that, in some contexts, being able to discuss assisted dying with patients allowed them to have a more honest and open communication. What they argued was that by not closing off options for the patient, it allowed the patient to express their fears and concerns more openly. As one interviewee put it, patients really wanted to speak about maintaining control over their lives and once they were able to have that discussion with the health-care staff, 'not infrequently' they decided against pursuing the option of suicide.[30] In other cases, interviewees told stories about patients who refused to continue to discuss things with them once the interviewee had refused to discuss assisted dying practices.[31] As a result of these interviews, Magnusson concluded that 'by not ruling out euthanasia as an option, [interviewees] were better able to explore and alleviate the issues of fear and control that were frequent motivations for euthanasia'.[32] Of course, merely because the interviewees in question saw this as an acceptable method of increasing communication does not mean that it will work in all cases. In some cases, patients may see a health-care professional's willingness to discuss assisted dying as being a sign that the professional in question has either given up hope or sees the patient as one who would be better off dead. In other cases, the health-care professional may not deal well with the discussion, which may cause any number of problems. It is not then something where we can say that the availability of assisted suicide will lead automatically

---

[30] *Ibid.*, p. 80.
[31] For example, one interviewee named Amanda told a story about a patient who 'dismissed' her after she indicated she would not be able to help him commit suicide. The patient later committed suicide by jumping off a building. *Ibid.*, p. 113.
[32] *Ibid.*, p. 250.

to better communication between health-care staff and patients. What it does indicate is that more research is needed to determine the links between this sort of open discussion between patients and carers so that we can better understand how to maximise good communication in these cases.

It also highlights that the issue of communication is not simply limited to cases of assisted dying. Almost all types of end-of-life decisions will involve communication between the patient (or the patient's friends and family) and the health-care staff. Some of these may involve suicidal ideations. For example, while not all cases of a patient requesting that life-sustaining treatment be withdrawn or withheld are the result of a wish to commit suicide, some are likely to be because of this reason.[33] However, it is not required in these cases for doctors or other health-care professionals to ensure that the patient is not making the decision to have treatment withdrawn or withheld because of any desire for suicide. Indeed, some commentators even argue that patient refusals which appear to be based upon suicidal ideations should not be overruled. Luke Gormally argues that 'it is not always easy to distinguish a suicidal refusal of treatment from one reasonably motivated by considerations of the burden of treatment'.[34] I would not dispute the difficulty of trying to determine the motivation of patients in refusal of treatment, but one relatively easy method of determining a person's motivation is to ask him or her why they are doing something. Gormally's suggestion, taken to its logical conclusion, does not require doctors or health-care staff to even initiate a discussion (since it doesn't make any difference to the ultimate decision, why bother having a difficult discussion in the first place?). Again, presuming that patients in the Magnusson study might be acting in somewhat generalisable ways, patients may be bringing up the issue of withdrawal and withholding of treatment for the express purpose of starting such a discussion.

Those from a legal background may fall back on the argument that treatment refusals are required to be honoured by law whereas suicidal ideations in other contexts are not. As long as they are competent and not subject to undue influence, legally patients are generally able to refuse treatment for 'rational reasons, irrational reasons or no reason at all'.[35] For an example of this in practice, we can consider the *Ms B* case from the UK. In the case, a woman who was tetraplegic wished

---

[33] For an example, see *Re B (adult: refusal of treatment)* sub nom *Ms B v. NHS Hospital Trust* [2002] 2 All ER 449. It is worth highlighting that Ms B may or may not have had suicidal ideations. For a fuller explanation, see n. 36 below.
[34] Gormally, 'Walton, Davies, Boyd and the Legalization of Euthanasia', p. 124.
[35] *Re T (adult: refusal of treatment)* [1992] 4 All ER 649 at 653.

to have a ventilator withdrawn. The hospital where she was a patient then had her declared incompetent and continued to treat her. After another mental health professional determined Ms B to be competent, she immediately asked again for the ventilator to be withdrawn because she found 'the idea of living like this intolerable'.[36] Butler Sloss J determined that she was competent and the hospital was therefore required by law to either remove the ventilator or transfer her to a hospital that would, despite the fact that the judge clearly does not agree with the decision.[37] The hospital was even made to pay nominal damages to Ms B for the violation of her bodily integrity.[38]

The concern here is not with the rightness or wrongness of the decision but with the fact that the reality of the situation is not always as clear as the general statement of law. Ms B, at least initially, was determined to be incompetent, largely, it seems, due to her stated wish to have the ventilator withdrawn. In other contexts we may still force-feed patients who are anorexic because they are determined to be 'incompetent'.[39] If, as is generally claimed (and I do not dispute), most people who commit suicide are clinically depressed, then why are these patients not likewise determined to be incompetent and treatment given on their behalf? Why, in fact, wasn't Ms B? To answer that it is merely a question of bodily integrity is only to scratch the surface. If bodily integrity is important, it must be important for a reason, and it is that reason we need to consider. Bodily integrity is important because, if I possess anything, it is my own body and others should not be allowed to do what they want with it unless I agree. There are exceptions to this, but that only begs the question of why those things which are exceptions are considered as such. We could fall back on notions of personal autonomy (and thus perhaps avoid certain troubling cases due to the notion of a lack of an autonomous will), but that will merely lead us back to the question of why an autonomous decision to withdraw treatment made because of a suicidal ideation is different from a decision to request assistance with

---

[36] *Ms B* at 461, paragraph 47. It is worth being clear that Ms B also stated that her wish was not to die, but instead 'not to remain alive in her present condition'. *Ibid.*

[37] Butler Sloss's decision is instructive on this and surprisingly emotional for judicial language. She states that 'I would like to add how impressed I am with her as a person, with the great courage, strength of will and determination she has shown in the last year, with her sense of humour, and her understanding of the dilemma she has posed to the hospital. She is clearly a splendid person and it is tragic that someone of her ability has been struck down so cruelly. I hope she will forgive me for saying, diffidently, that if she did reconsider her decision, she would have a lot to offer the community at large.' *Ibid.* at 473, paragraph 95.

[38] *Ibid.* at 474, paragraph 99.

[39] *Re W (a minor) (medical treatment)* [1992] 4 All ER 627.

suicide for the same reason. If it is acceptable in one case, what differentiates the other case? Why does preventing suicide matter in the one case but not the other? Why aren't we being more explicit about our discussions with Ms B to determine how much difference there really is between 'wishing to be dead' and 'wishing not to remain alive'?

I want to stress that I am not suggesting that we should start checking those who have refused treatment to make sure this is not an attempt to commit suicide. It is merely to argue that if preventing suicide is a major concern, then it ought to apply across the board instead of only in specific cases. It is, in other words, an argument for acting consistently. If we wish to prevent suicide, we need to be clear as to the ways that can be done. If there are ways to distinguish between assisted dying practices and refusing treatment, then these need to be made explicit. It may be that empirically, assisting a suicide affects suicide rates in a way that refusing treatment does not. At the moment, evidence for that conclusion does not exist but it is a theoretical possibility. Alternatively, it may be that there are other factors at play which impact upon the decisions that we make. Again, though, those should be made explicit. If autonomy, through the lens of bodily integrity, is less important than other values we cherish, we should make sure those values are applied in all cases in which they might apply, including cases of refusing treatment.

2.3   Conclusions about the prevention of suicide

To conclude, even though preventing suicide is often cited as an important concern in end-of-life decision-making, its influence is far from certain. It only seems to apply in certain contexts (assisted dying) while being absent in others (treatment refusals), despite the fact that both types of decisions may be influenced by suicidal ideations. Nor is it particularly clear that prohibiting assisted dying will actually prevent suicide. We have looked at three possible reasons why allowing assisted dying may actually serve to reduce the suicide rate. The evidence available to support those reasons is largely anecdotal but it is worth emphasising that there is very little evidence to show that prohibiting assisted dying reduces suicide rates either.

What we should aim at is consistency. If we believe that rational suicide is possible and that there are sufficient procedures which could be implemented to determine whether a particular decision is rational, then there may be limited reasons for prohibiting rational suicides by whatever method. At best though, this will only get us a regulatory procedure for suicide, not for assistance with it. It might then justify the difference, at this point, between withdrawal and withholding of treatment and assisted dying. This is true only if we consider the difference between acting and non-acting to be particularly important, a conclusion put in doubt by the chapter on moral responsibility. Even so, we need to look at additional regulatory issues. Our next consideration is the protection of vulnerable groups.

3   The protection of vulnerable groups

The second major regulatory issue we will consider in this chapter is the protection of vulnerable groups. This is also often considered to be a particularly important interest of the state. It seems incontrovertible that protecting those who might not otherwise be able to protect themselves should be a crucial part of any justifiable system of government. This section, then, will not examine whether the protection of vulnerable groups is an important aspect of regulating end-of-life decision-making. Instead, it will consider which ways are the most effective for protecting those groups.

One initial part of any claim, though, is the determination of what counts as a vulnerable group. Two categories of person are generally considered as vulnerable. The first is minority groups. There are any number of possible minority groups, including women, those of an ethnic or racial minority, those of lower social-economic status, the elderly and members of particular religions. The status of any of these groups as minorities is also unlikely to be contentious (although in terms of proportion of the population, women do not generally constitute a minority). The other category of persons that needs to be considered is those who are disabled. This is also unlikely to be considered a controversial group, at least in general. Some consideration, however, is necessary of who is within that group. For our purposes, we might consider the larger group of disabled persons to be capable of being subdivided into two smaller groups. The first group is individuals who are previously disabled who then require treatment at the end of life. For example, we might have an individual who was paralysed as result of a diving accident many years ago who has now developed cancer which is unrelated to the initial injuries. Alternatively, we might consider those who could be considered disabled as a result of the illness, injury or condition which results in the end-of-life decision. Thus, we might consider someone with motor neurone disease who is wheelchair-bound as a result. By differentiating between these two groups, I do not mean to suggest that either group is more or less disabled than the other. However, it is worth considering them separately because there are differences between the effects of disability in cases where it is related to the underlying end-of-life decision and where it is not. For example, it may be that all medical cases in which there is an end-of-life decision will involve at least some disability of the second type. If this is the case, it may be difficult to evaluate the effect of particular regulatory practices on end-of-life decisions because all of them will have a detrimental impact upon individuals with disabilities. It therefore behooves us to distinguish between these two categories of disability within the chapter.

3.1   How end-of-life decisions may adversely impact vulnerable groups

The argument that end-of-life decisions may adversely affect vulnerable groups is not similar to the one relating to preventing suicide. In the case of preventing suicide, the argument is that regulation is needed to prevent particular conduct. In other words, the argument relies on the assumption that particular events will happen unless there is regulation which prohibits it. In the case of protection for vulnerable groups, the argument is generally that it is not the prevention of particular conduct which is necessary, but that the creation of particular regulations will create conduct which is unacceptable. So, it is not about conduct which is likely to happen if things remain as they are, but that adverse changes will happen in cases where the regulation is changed in a particular manner.

In this case, the argument is that if regulation is changed which allows doctors or other health-care professionals to directly kill patients, then those in vulnerable groups are more likely to be pressured into being participants in such practices. The coercion which happens may be overt in that we have individuals being deliberately and openly pushed to accept an option which would lead to their death. It may also be more subtle with patients being pressured indirectly (or unknowingly) by discussions about the cost of the patient's health care or by other indications that the doctors, other health-care workers or the patient's family and friends, leading the patient to believe that the life of that patient is less worthy of continuing. Finally, arguments may further stress that these factors may exist even if those 'exerting' the undue pressure on the patient are not actually doing so. It may be that patients believe that their family or health-care staff believe their life to be less worthy of continuing despite the fact that neither the family nor the health-care staff actually believe this. Instead, it may merely be the way the patient perceives things. Just because that perception is inaccurate, however, does not mean that it cannot have an effect upon the patient, and we should guard against these results as much as we guard against actual coercion.

This argument is not based merely upon predictions about behaviour but also upon a number of factors which currently exist in our health-care systems. First, in systems such as those in US, there may be financial implications about long-term care which impact upon the family and friends of a patient. If a patient requires expensive long-term care then it may be that treatment consumes much of either the patient's financial resources or those of individuals with financial responsibility for the patient (usually, the parents, children or spouse of the patient). In addition to monetary costs, there may be additional costs such as time and stress which have further adverse effects upon the family and friends of the patient. Doctors and other health-care workers, in addition to family and friends, may not be particularly adept at dealing with terminal situations in patients and may not deal sufficiently well with the patient. For example, doctors may withdraw from patients who they see as terminal and not provide the kind of emotional support needed by the patient. To this we can add the general societal view about at least certain vulnerable groups (perhaps particularly those with disabilities or the elderly) which may put additional pressure on patients. Finally, we have the arguments presented by bioethicists which may be interpreted to mean that those with particular conditions are seen as being less worthy of survival.[40]

What exists, then, is a combination of factors which, some argue, will lead to a situation where those in vulnerable groups will feel pressure to accept a practice of assisted dying even if they did not want to do so. Furthermore, even if individual patients do not always feel pressure, we may increase the feeling (either for those individuals in vulnerable groups or society at large) that those in these groups have lives which are worth less than those of other people. Since we should neither pressure people into taking their own lives nor increase the possibility that

---

[40] As I have done in previous chapters (e.g. Chapter 2), I want to stress that the views of the bioethicists in question, such as John Harris or Peter Singer, do not necessarily reach the conclusions which are often attributed to them. Harris's position, for example, holds that the primary concern is a person's ability to value their own life. As such, it would not be suitable to treat a disabled person against their wishes. In other words, merely because one subscribes to the argument that full moral status is dependent upon personhood does not mean that those who are disabled are not persons or are not entitled to protection of their interests. That does not hold across the board (there may be some who count themselves within the personhood camp who do not grant that status to disabled persons) and even if it did, it does not necessarily change the perception that those with disabilities are more at risk under these theories. It is that perception which may ultimately be the most relevant for our discussion here.

individuals will feel their lives have less worth than others, we should also not accept things which increase the possibility of that sort of pressure occurring. As a result, we should not allow practices such as assisted dying. For example, the New York State Task Force on Life and the Law stated the following:

> No matter how carefully any guidelines are framed, assisted suicide and euthanasia will be practiced through the prism of social inequality and bias that characterized the delivery of services to all segments of our society, including health care. The practices will pose the greatest risks to those who are poor, elderly, members of a minority group, or without access to good medical care.[41]

3.2   Available evidence

As with the claims about preventing suicide, the vital information in the argument is the evidence to support it. The claims which form the basis of the argument are certainly possible and, if they are likely to occur, they provide significant reasons not to allow practices which increase the harm to those in vulnerable groups. The main question, though, is whether these concerns are likely to occur or occur at a greater rate than would have happened if these practices were not acceptable. Merely because something is conceivable does not mean that it must occur.

We could start our search for evidence with the data which shows that doctors in particular often have a lesser value for the lives lived by those in vulnerable groups (particularly the disabled) than those in the vulnerable groups themselves. There is consistent empirical evidence which shows that doctors routinely give a lower quality of life score to patients with disabilities than the patient would give. That certainly provides some evidence that doctors, left to their own devices and allowed to terminate the lives of patients, might choose to end the lives of patients who do not want them to end. We might also find further proof in the number of cases where doctors have sought permission from courts either to not provide or to remove life-sustaining treatment from patients who have exceeded the predictions of doctors as to their life-span. Thus, we have cases of children where the doctors or health-care professionals appear to have decided that the child's life was not worth continuing despite the beliefs of the parents, and the child has gone on to survive.[42] All of this would provide some support

---

[41] New York State Task Force, *When Death Is Sought*, p. xii.
[42] One of the most infamous UK decisions is *Glass* v. *United Kingdom* [2004] 1 FCR 553. In this case, the family of a young patient was involved in a dispute with the health-care staff about his treatment. A Do Not Resuscitate order was put on the chart of the child without the family's knowledge or consent (it does not appear to have been

for the belief that allowing certain end-of-life practices such as assisted suicide or voluntary euthanasia might increase the possibility of harm to vulnerable groups.

Additional evidence, however, does not bear this out.[43] Some is available from the Oregon Death with Dignity reports. These reports, in addition to other information, contain demographic information about the patients who have died under the Death with Dignity Act (DWDA). It seems likely that if those in vulnerable groups were more likely to be subject to undue pressure, we would be able to determine that from the information contained in the reports. However, the reports do not bear that out. The rate at which men and women choose assisted suicide in Oregon is roughly equivalent. Patients who choose assisted suicide are primarily white, are younger than those who do not request PAS, have a university degree or at least some college education and primarily live west of the Cascade Mountains.[44] There is, unfortunately, no specific information about those with disabilities in the official reports but it does not seem particularly likely that those with disabilities would be different.[45]

---

discussed with the family at any point). Additionally, the family objected to the use of diamorphine for the patient, apparently believing it to be a covert attempt by the doctors to kill the child. An attempted mediation between the parties (which may or may not have included a hospital administrator, but did include a police officer as mediator and a lack of any representation by any patient advice service for the patient or his family) was unsuccessful and the case reached a breaking point when the child had respiratory problems: the mother gave the child CPR while other members of the family blocked the room, preventing medical staff from intervening. One member of the medical staff was injured as a result. The European Court of Human Rights held that the child's and mother's rights had been infringed by the hospital and doctors involved.

[43] It is worth paying particular attention in these cases to source material for any evidence. For example, I have read in a number of places (particularly websites) of up to 10,000 individuals in the Netherlands carrying 'Do not Kill me' cards. See, e.g., 'Head to Head: Assisted Suicide', http://news.bbc.co.uk/1/hi/uk/1518583.stm (accessed 21 June 2011); B. Pollard, 'Current Euthanasia Law in the Netherlands', www.catholic-ducation.org/articles/euthanasia/eu0021.html (accessed 21 June 2011); 'Dutch Carry Cards That Say: "Don't Kill Me, Doctor"', www.lifeadvocate.org/1_99/n_notes.htm (accessed 21 June 2011). These are apparently similar to the cards carried by Jehovah's Witnesses which indicate that they do not want a blood transfusion. These cards indicate that the patient is not interested in receiving assisted dying. What is important to realise, however, is that there is no indication where that figure comes from. No source, research study or even telephone poll is cited nor is there any indication of how this figure might have been arrived at. As a result, I think we can, unless more substantial source material is provided to substantiate the point, consider that information to be very suspect.

[44] Oregon Annual Reports, Year 12, table 1.

[45] Unless, of course, we consider everyone with a terminal illness to also be disabled. In that case, 100 per cent of patients who chose PAS are disabled but then that does not seem to be a particularly relevant benchmark. 100 per cent of people with a terminal illness in Oregon who have not chosen PAS will eventually die as well.

Further evidence can be found in an article published in the *Journal of Medical Ethics* by Battin *et al.*[46] This article examined data from the Netherlands and Oregon related to a number of vulnerable groups. These included the elderly, women, the uninsured, people with low educational status, the poor, the physically disabled or chronically ill, minors, racial and ethnic minorities and those with psychiatric illness including depression.[47] The incidence rate of PAS or voluntary euthanasia in these groups was compared to background populations to see whether a disproportionate number of individuals from these groups had used assisted dying practices.[48] The specific data considered by the authors included the DWDA official reports, three additional surveys of Oregon physicians and hospice professionals, the four nationwide studies in the Netherlands and several 'smaller, focused Dutch studies'.[49] The researchers found no evidence that most of the groups of potential vulnerable patients were more likely to have chosen PAS or voluntary euthanasia.[50] The only group where there was a 'heightened risk' of abuse was patients with AIDS.[51] All other patient groups did not show a heightened risk. The researchers concluded that 'the joint picture yielded by the available data in the two jurisdictions shows that people who died with a physician's assistance were more likely to be members of groups enjoying comparative social, economic, educational, professional and other privileges'.[52]

We might, furthermore, raise the additional query that it is difficult to see why assisted dying practices would result in any different behaviour on the behalf of medical and health-care staff than other end-of-life decisions. In other words, if we are going to see a problem, it is as likely to occur in cases of withdrawing or withholding treatment or the provision of palliative care as it is for cases of assisted dying. If doctors and other health-care professionals are likely to push patients into assisted dying because the patient is part of a vulnerable group, they would also seem likely to push patients to refuse treatment or engage in other practices which might lead to the death of the patient. Again, we could point to case law which indicates that sometimes doctors do believe patients to have a lower quality of life than the patient thinks they have, but these issues are not seen as insurmountable in cases of withdrawing or withholding treatment. It would seem unlikely, considering the evidence we have available, that assisted dying practices could

---

[46] M. P. Battin *et al.*, 'Legal Physician-Assisted Dying in Oregon and the Netherlands: Evidence Concerning the Impact of Patients in "Vulnerable" Groups' (2007) 33 *Journal of Medical Ethics* 591–597.
[47] *Ibid.*, 591.   [48] *Ibid.*, 592.   [49] *Ibid.*
[50] *Ibid.*, 594–596.   [51] *Ibid.*, 594.   [52] *Ibid.*, 597.

also not be regulated in such a way as to allow those practices without facing considerable problems related to the abuse of patients in vulnerable groups.

Thus, we have no sufficient evidence to show that there would be any specific issues with vulnerable groups if assisted dying practices were legalised. That conclusion can only be tentative as the evidence available to evaluate the argument is sparse. More research is certainly needed to explore how end-of-life practices impact upon those in vulnerable groups and it is crucial that such research not be limited only to assisted dying practices but should include all end-of-life decisions. Until such research is done, however, we can only rely on the information that we have available. That data indicates that vulnerable groups are not any more likely to be pressured into using assisted dying practices than patients not in vulnerable groups.

3.3   Argument in favour of assisted dying practices

Indeed, we might be able to make an argument that providing assisted dying practices might enhance the protection for patients in these vulnerable groups. The reason for this is that assisted dying practices rely to a considerable extent on the patient's autonomous decisions. Respect for autonomous decisions does not mean acceding only to decisions which we agree with, but also those we might disagree with provided that the patient has exercised the proper processes when doing so. It is easy to agree with a patient's autonomous decisions when they are decisions we would have reached in the same situation; it is much more difficult when they are not. However, it is those we would not have agreed with which are often the ones requiring the greatest respect. Thus, provided we can be reasonably convinced that the decision was reached autonomously, those decisions should be given deference. Allowing a patient to satisfy his or her request, even if we disagree, can be a crucial way in which we respect the autonomy of other patients.

Alternatively, requiring patients to accede to the decisions of others, even if those decisions are made in the best interest of the patient, shows the patient that we do not respect them as an autonomous entity. This may be particularly true for those in vulnerable groups who have often had to fight to have others respect the choices they wish to make. Individuals in these groups have often struggled to be allowed to, for example, participate in the political process. Furthermore, the reasons which were often given for excluding these individuals from decision-making was that they were too easily influenced or could not be relied upon to make rational decisions. In fact, the inability to make

appropriate decisions formed a central part of the argument that decisions should be taken away from these individuals for their own protection. It is a bit troubling that those arguments are returning, again in a
protectionist guise. It is not clear, for example, why those in vulnerable
groups would be more likely to succumb to coercion by health-care
staff than those who are not in vulnerable groups.

None of this should be taken to minimise the very real concerns
which can be brought up in relation to those in vulnerable groups in
relation to access to health care and other resources. It does not matter
if a patient is less susceptible to coercion if the circumstances for the
patient do not easily allow an autonomous choice. So, if a patient has
not been provided with sufficient access to pain relief, it may not matter
how resistant to coercion that patient is; the pain itself may be seen as
coercive. The same may be said for access to medical treatment generally, specialist care for particular illnesses, or any of the number of ways
in which medical care may not be sufficient under the circumstances.
The solution to these problems, however, is to work for greater access
to treatment for vulnerable groups and to make sure that the options
available to those in these groups are the same as those for individuals
not in those groups. That leaves only the question about whether it is
better to wait until the access questions are resolved before agreeing to
end-of-life decisions such as assisted dying. As the evidence available
does not indicate that the acceptance of assisted dying leads to greater
problems, there does not appear to be any particular reason why we
cannot regulate end-of-life decision-making in general as opposed to
waiting. As before, future data may change this conclusion, but, currently, there does not appear to be any evidence to support an argument
for heightened risk.

3.4   Conclusions about the protection of vulnerable groups

In conclusion, the protection of vulnerable groups is an important state
interest and we ought to be particularly cognisant of this interest when
considering how best to regulate end-of-life decisions. However, we
must also pay close attention to the empirical evidence we have. The
evidence which is available does not indicate that those in vulnerable
groups are subject to a heightened risk for end-of-life cases. While more
research is necessary for a firm conclusion, the preliminary data shows
that the primary patients who engage in assisted dying are likely to
be white, middle-class, college-educated individuals. They are likely to
be younger than the background population and reasonably affluent.
This does not mean we ought to avoid considering the effect that the

regulation of assisted dying will have on vulnerable groups, but that we also make sure that decisions are made on the best available evidence.

4   Conclusions about the protection of patients

In this chapter we have considered both the issue of the prevention of suicide and the protection of vulnerable groups. Both are often presented as viable reasons why particular end-of-life practices should not be acceptable, particularly those which fall within the broad category of assisted dying practices. It is argued that the state has a compelling interest in the prevention of suicide and the protection of those who are suicidal. Furthermore, the protection of those in vulnerable groups who are unable to protect themselves, or are unable to do so as effectively as those not in vulnerable groups, is also considered to be an important and compelling state interest.

However, as has been explained in this chapter, even if one accepts both as compelling interests, it does not mean that the conclusion to exclude assisted dying practices is assured. While the prohibition on assisted dying may seem like it will obviously prevent suicides, the reality is that there is insufficient evidence to reach this conclusion. Instead, there are reasons why it can be asserted that the acceptance of assisted dying practices is just as likely to lower the overall suicide rate as raise it. Moreover, if the prevention of suicide is really an overpowering state interest then it needs to be applied across the board. We should therefore consider the prospect that the prevention of suicide should also make other practices at the end of life, such as the withdrawal of treatment, much more difficult. If, on the other hand, we consider some interests to be able to override the state's interest in preventing suicide, then we need to look closer at whether those same interests can be applied in cases of assisted dying as well. Consequently, the prevention of suicide may be seen as important, but the result of that importance is far from certain.

The same could be said for the protection of vulnerable groups. Again, while the protection of individuals who might not be capable of protecting themselves is a primary aim of governments, we ought to make sure that the state is doing so effectively. In other words, we should not allow governments to say that they are protecting vulnerable groups if they are not actually doing so. In order to properly evaluate those claims, we need to consider the available evidence. That evidence, while not extensive, does not show that jurisdictions which allow assisted dying are less effective at protecting vulnerable groups. Indeed, the primary patient who 'uses' assisted dying practices appears to be part of the majority more often then they are in the minority or are particularly vulnerable. While, as with many of the issues we will be considering, more evidence is needed, the preliminary data indicates that the protection of vulnerable groups is not a compelling reason to avoid the acceptance of assisted dying practices.

More generally, two of the most important lessons which can be drawn from this chapter are the importance of consistency across practices and the use of empirical evidence. If we are truly concerned with an effective regulatory scheme for end-of-life decisions, then we need to more properly explore how important issues apply to a multitude of possible actions, not just ones such as assisted suicide or voluntary euthanasia. Additionally, when considering how particular issues should be best regulated, it is important to keep a close eye on the evidence which can be used to examine whether particular regulatory schemes provide the desired effect. It is not then a question of considering whether a particular argument is theoretically possible, but which of the various possible choices we have most effectively achieves the important regulatory aims that exist. The patient, however, is only one of the individuals involved in end-of-life decisions. There are others who need to be considered. Foremost among them are the medical practitioners. It is to the consideration of some of the issues related to them that we shall now turn.

11   The impact on health-care practitioners

1   Introduction

After the patient, the most important individual involved in end-of-life care is the health-care practitioner. It is the health-care practitioner who must provide information and advice to the patient as well as being the one most likely to implement any treatment regime which has been agreed. This is often a doctor but it need not be. Instead, health-care practitioners who are involved in end-of-life care may be other specialists such as nurses, community health workers, psychiatrists or others. While a majority of discussion centres on the doctor, other health-care workers are often subject to many of the same ethical and legal limitations on conduct that bind doctors. It is thus worthwhile considering the effect on all health-care practitioners instead of focusing entirely on doctors. Doing so, however, does not change the focus from the ethical and legal issues, nor does it change the essential questions which must be answered. For example, while doctors may be the ones most associated with the problem of 'playing God', nurses or other health-care professionals also can have sufficient chances to engage in this sort of conduct as they may have access to lethal medication and be in charge of vulnerable patients.[1] It is therefore prudent to make sure that any regulatory system designed to prevent certain practices from being carried out by doctors also limits the ability of others to engage in the same sort of actions. Alternatively, even if a decision is legal and ethical, the emotional and psychological ramifications of particular treatment options which lead to a patient's death may be greater on staff such as nurses who may have a more significant relationship with patients than a consultant doctor whose interaction with the patient is limited. It is thus fundamental that we cast a wide net when considering the effect of

[1] 'Nurse Guilty of Killing Patients', http://news.bbc.co.uk/1/hi/england/west_yorkshire/7267409.stm (accessed 21 June 2011); H. Carter, 'Nurse Gets Five Years for Seeking to Kill Two Patients', www.guardian.co.uk/society/2004/jun/19/health.uknews (accessed 21 June 2011).

end-of-life decisions on those involved in the provision of health care. The issues which can be considered of paramount importance when exploring the impact upon health-care professionals include a number of things which will have personal and direct repercussions on the individual health-care professional. The aforementioned issue about health-care professionals 'playing God' is one such direct result. Others include the distrust of health-care professionals as a result of participation in particular end-of-life practices as well as the psychological effects of participation. More general issues which will be examined in this chapter include the codes of professional conduct which are binding on health-care professionals (and the changes which may be necessitated by regulation of end-of-life decisions) and the challenges to the overall professionalism of those working in the care of the dying.

2   Direct impact upon health-care practitioners

In this section, our attention will be focused on issues which are directly related to the health-care professional. They are thus issues which are based upon direct actions by the individual in question, have direct effects upon them or relate to perceptions about that individual. There are three which are particularly relevant. The first is that allowing certain practices may permit health-care professionals to 'play God'. The second is that, whether or not health-care professionals do 'play God', patients and other members of society will have an increased distrust of health-care professionals (especially doctors) if such practices are allowed. Finally, we shall explore the psychological effects upon health-care professionals about providing certain treatments at the end of life.

2.1   'Playing God'

One of the prime effects of allowing doctors and other health-care practitioners to engage in activities which bring about the death of the patient is that it provides even greater power to an individual who already has a considerable amount within the relationship.[2] Health-care practitioners generally have greater knowledge than the patient or family and friends. They are also the ones who provide care and thus control the types of treatment which a patient may or may not be able to have. Furthermore, they are less likely to be compromised (or at least we hope they are) by pain, disease, illness, discomfort, fear and

---

[2] See, e.g., L. R. Kass, 'Neither for Love nor Money: Why Doctors Must Not Kill' (1989, Winter) 94 *Public Interest* 25, 35–37.

stress which further skews the balance of power between the health-care practitioner and the patient. All of these factors are a large enough concern to things like patient autonomy in the best of circumstances. However, the argument goes, if we further allow doctors to provide specific treatments at the end of life such as assisted dying, we provide them with the ability to 'play God' by allowing them to decide who lives and who dies.[3] We would be giving ultimate power to those who already have too much, and this means patients cannot be protected from abuse.

It is crucial at the start to be aware of what is being argued to avoid conflating two separate problems. The first is that health-care practitioners involved in end-of-life care might get a specific diagnosis, prognosis or evaluation wrong. Patients may be misdiagnosed or the prognosis may be incorrect.[4] Doctors and other health-care workers making an evaluation about the quality of life of a patient, for example, may underestimate important factors relevant to that patient. All of those, if done honestly, do not count as the issue of playing God, which would seem to involve *intentional* conduct. Playing God, then, is about doctors or other health-care workers making conscious decisions about whether they think the patient should live or die irrespective of other factors and focusing not on the patient's best interests but on their own interest in power. While mistakes are obviously worrying and should be limited, that is a much different concern than health-care practitioners deciding that the ability to play God means they will treat patients in a different manner than they have previously. The issue under discussion here, then, is about whether doctors will engage in conduct where they intentionally bring about the death of a patient for motives which are less than pure.

Support for this argument is often found in the actions of a limited number of doctors and other health-care professionals who have been subject to criminal sanction. For example, in the UK, those making this sort of argument are likely to point to either Dr Harold Shipman or Dr John Bodkin Adams. Dr Shipman was the notorious serial killer responsible for about 250 deaths, according to the Sixth Report of the Shipman Inquiry.[5] His reasons for the killing are unknown, although the Sixth Report theorises that part of his reason for killing patients had to do with an interest in drugs and their effects.[6] A possible forerunner

---

[3] See, e.g., *ibid.*, 35.
[4] See, e.g., *Glass v. United Kingdom* [2004] 1 FCR 553.
[5] J. Smith, *Sixth Report – Shipman Inquiry: The Final Report*, paragraph 7.78.
[6] *Ibid.*, paragraph 7.73. It also states that his 'most likely' early victims were ones who were terminally ill. *Ibid.*, paragraph 7.72.

and 'role model' to Shipman was Dr John Bodkin Adams.[7] Adams is the doctor tried in the famous *R* v. *Adams* case which sets out the doctrine of double effect.[8] Adams admitted at the trial that he had 'eased the passing' of some of his patients who had died in his care, primarily those who were old ladies.[9] It was later determined that this may have been up to 400 patients, 132 of them cases where he was named in the will (as he was in the Morrell case which led to the trial).[10] Those outside the UK might point to Dr Arnfinn Nesset, a Norwegian doctor, who may have killed 138 of his patients in the late 1970s, or to any number of other doctors, nurses or other health-care professionals who have killed multiple numbers of patients.[11] Indeed, Herbert Kinnell has suggested that 'medicine has thrown up more serial killers than all the other professions put together with nursing a close second'.[12] He further states that 'there are enough recorded instances of multiple murders by doctors (real or bogus) to make a prima facie case that the profession attracts some people with a pathological interest in the power of life and death'.[13] Consequently, it is not possible to dismiss out of hand the idea that at least some health-care professionals may not have the best interests of patients in mind when engaging in practices at the end of life. Doctors and other health-care professionals are not, unfortunately, immune from the problem of members of their profession being less than ideal ethical examples of that practice. Some, like Shipman and Nesset, are so far below that standard that they can reasonably be described as simply being evil.

The question, however, is not whether such people exist who hold a medical degree or work as a health-care practitioner. The crucial question is whether more individuals will go down this route if certain practices are legalised. In other words, it is worth remembering two important points. First, most of the individuals used in this argument acted contrary to the existing law. Shipman and Nesset (and possibly Adams) were serial killers who were already acting outside the law and it is therefore not likely that a change in the law would have had an effect upon their practices. A change in law, thus, does not seem to make those predisposed to be serial killers any more or less likely to be serial killers. Second, and more importantly, while Shipman and Nesset and

---

[7] H. G. Kinnell, 'Serial Homicide by Doctors: Shipman in Perspective' (2000) 321 *BMJ* 1594–1597, 1596.
[8] *R* v. *Adams* [1957] Crim LR 365.
[9] Kinnell, 'Serial Homicide by Doctors', 1596.
[10] Ibid.; *R* v. *Adams* [1957] Crim LR 365.
[11] Kinnell, 'Serial Homicide by Doctors', 1596.
[12] *Ibid.*, 1594.   [13] *Ibid.*

others may have held a professional title and may have been purporting to act as doctor when engaged in their crimes, they should not tarnish the reputation of the profession as a whole as a result of those crimes. In other words, Shipman and Nesset are examples of serial killers, not doctors. Whether they are or are not typical examples of serial killers, they are certainly not typical examples of health-care professionals, a vast majority of whom would never contemplate similar actions. That is worth keeping a focus on because the concerns raised by this issue are about whether ordinary doctors and health-care professionals are more likely to engage in serial-killer behaviour if the legal landscape looks a particular way than if it looks a different way. That, though, seems to rely on some rather dubious claims about both health-care practitioners and those who commit multiple murders. For example, it seems to presume that many health-care practitioners are merely a change in the law away from being serial killers. That claim does not appear to be particularly plausible and evidence would need to be presented that it is the case.

It may be objected that the issue does not relate to serial killers. Instead, the concern is that doctors, even if they would not engage in multiple killings, might engage in certain killings more frequently than they otherwise would. We might look for support for this claim from at least one anecdote told to Magnusson in *Angels of Death* by Liz, a hospital nurse.[14] The unit where Liz worked appears to have accepted patients for the primary purpose of giving them a lethal injection, and she even stated in the book that there was a specific protocol for these injections.[15] She further seems not to have any specific problems with assisted dying practices as a general rule.[16] Despite this, she was involved in one case she believed was quite different and what she relayed to Magnusson seems to be a clear case of involuntary euthanasia. This case involved a patient on a specialist AIDS ward. He was, according to Liz, 'not close to the end of his life'.[17] He had, however, been slowly losing control over his bodily functions, required a catheter, could not move his arms and had neurological problems.[18] Even with these problems, though, Liz stated that he had been 'determined to live' and enjoyed spending time with his mother and his pet dog.[19] Liz further indicated that he had, on the day in question, even asked her when he was going to go home.[20] While Liz was convinced that the

[14] Magnusson, *Angels of Death*, pp. 234–238.
[15] *Ibid.*, p. 196.   [16] *Ibid.*, pp. 236–237.
[17] *Ibid.*, p. 234.   [18] *Ibid.*
[19] *Ibid.*, p. 237.   [20] *Ibid.*, p. 235.

patient was neither terminal nor unhappy, the doctor for the patient told the nursing staff to send his mother home and then charted an infusion of drugs she said was 'designed to kill' the patient.[21] The doctor stated to the nursing staff that they should 'get it up and get him out of here by sundown'.[22] The process involved 'at least a couple of nurses, a couple of registrars and a senior physician'.[23] Liz considered the doctor involved to have murdered the patient and specifically stated that the drugs were not therapeutic.[24] She further considered this to be a case where the doctor was intending to play God, stating that 'the doctor played God, *he thought he was God ... he'd decided this was the time for this patient*'.[25]

Such a story might seem to be strong evidence about health-care practitioners playing God. Indeed, Liz even uses that phrase when telling the tale. Furthermore, it does also appear to include a number of people including nurses and doctors. It is worth pointing out, however, that this was one of only two anecdotes of its type in *Angels of Death* out of the 203 anecdotes.[26] Considering the nature of the study, we cannot consider it to be statistically generalisable, as the actual figures are possibly greater or less than that. More importantly, though, the incident in the *Angels of Death* anecdote happened in a jurisdiction where assisted dying was illegal. It was therefore not a situation where doctors had been engaged in open, legal practices and then changed to an illegal practice in this situation. All of the practices involved were illegal. We might then question whether the operative factor in 'playing God' was assisted dying or some other factor. Moreover, in order for this issue to dictate policies, we would need to be sure that doctors would routinely engage in this behaviour. At the moment, despite the story told by Liz, there is insufficient evidence to show this. We are instead presuming that doctors are likely to be corrupted by the ability to end life without providing any significant proof that they would do so or even specifying why they would act in this way. This does not mean that some doctors

---

[21] *Ibid.*   [22] *Ibid.*   [23] *Ibid.*, p. 236.
[24] *Ibid.*   [25] *Ibid.*, p. 237 (emphasis in original).
[26] The second involved an interviewee named Harry who was a GP. Harry was not directly involved in the case but provides an account of a possible homicide involving the boyfriend of a wealthy patient with AIDS. The boyfriend, who happened to be a nurse, was the sole beneficiary of the patient's will. Harry visited the patient at his home after the patient had been discharged from the hospital and Harry became aware 'that [the patient] was receiving an "extremely high dose" of morphine (several hundred milligrams) through a syringe driver'. The patient had died by 1 p.m. the next day. Harry, however, told police he had 'no evidence whatsoever' to confirm the allegation of murder and also said to Magnusson that '[the dose] wasn't outrageous ... it wasn't ... a lethal dose'. *Ibid.*, p. 234.

or health-care providers might decide, as the physician did in the case Liz presents, that the power over life and death has particular appeal and overuse that power. But, we would need to have a sufficient number of health-care professionals engaging in this practice, and we do not have any evidence of that.

Finally, we might question why this issue cannot be handled reasonably well by regulation. One way, for example, to limit the possibility of health-care practitioners 'playing God' is to only provide them with more limited abilities. For instance, if a doctor is only able to engage in a practice like assisted dying after the patient has requested it, then it is hard to see that the circumstances exist for a doctor to believe they have unfettered power to play God in end-of-life cases. If they were further subject to reporting requirements with the possibility of investigation for abuse, these 'unfettered' powers become even more limited. Consequently, even if there were evidence that 'playing God' was a significant problem, it appears to be one which could be readily handled by regulation.

2.2   The distrust of health-care professionals

It may be that while the concerns about health-care professionals actually playing God are unsubstantiated, the real problem is with the perception of members of the community about them. So, even if health-care practitioners are not, in fact, more likely to engage in troubling conduct as a result of the legalisation of particular end-of-life decisions, the public may believe that they are, which may cause problems for patients in that they now become worried that the individual coming into their hospital room is going to kill them instead of taking care of them.[27] There are several important questions that need to be answered when considering this particular claim. First, we would need to find proof that patients will be worried about this, but evidence again is quite scarce. For example, there are claims that people in the Netherlands are carrying 'Do not euthanise' cards, but there is little actual evidence of such a practice.[28] There does not appear to be any more substantial evidence from either the Netherlands or Oregon which indicates this is a particular problem. Even Leon Kass merely presents this as a speculative claim and not one for which he provides hard evidence.[29] It is certainly plausible, of course, that individual patients may have concerns

---

[27] See, e.g., Kass, 'Neither for Love nor Money', 35.
[28] See n. 43, Chapter 10.
[29] See, e.g., Kass, 'Neither for Love nor Money', 35.

about specific doctors or even in general, but it is hard to find evidence of a global distrust of health-care professionals which would result.

Even if we assumed *arguendo* that there was sufficient proof that enough individuals would be worried about this to make it worthy of further discussion, it again seems to be a problem which could be specifically handled by close regulation and then the provision of information to patients. If end-of-life decisions required, for example, patient consent – as almost all suggested regulations require – this could be explained to patients. Those who had not consented, then, need not fear that a doctor is entering the hospital room to kill them, as those actions would be no more legal than if all practices were criminalised. Furthermore, assuming that reporting and investigation are made standard practice, patients should be even more convinced that their doctors are not coming to kill them as any actions would be subject to scrutiny. As long as regulations are clear as to what is required and that these can be adequately relayed to the public, there seems to be no greater reason why a patient in a society which allowed forms of assisted dying need fear their doctor or health-care practitioner any more than one in a society which outlawed such practices.

Additionally, if public opinion surveys are to be believed, a majority of people in a number of jurisdictions would actually support greater powers for medical staff at the end of life, including the possibility of assisted dying practices. We might then question whether the knowledge that a doctor or other health-care professional could engage in certain practices might provide patients with a reason to feel better about the people caring for them. This might occur in at least a couple of different ways. First, those who are not in discussions with their doctors about particular end-of-life practices may feel that the doctor has reaffirmed the belief that the patient will continue to live in tolerable circumstances. Alternatively, those who have had discussions may feel relieved that they and the health-care practitioners have consulted on the relevant options and everyone is clear as to what the patient desires. This may provide the patient (and perhaps the family) with confidence that their wishes are being respected even if it becomes necessary to act in more emergency situations where consultation with the patient or the family is not possible. Finally, those with whom doctors have been in discussions about ending the patient's life may feel relief that their suffering is coming to an end and that the doctors, nurses and others involved in their care have been sympathetic to their concerns. These possibilities are not guaranteed, obviously, but they appear no more unrealistic than those of patients becoming fearful about doctors coming into their rooms to kill them.

2.3   Psychological effects

A third factor related to the health-care practitioner which should be taken into account is the psychological effects on him or her. Those who are engaged in end-of-life practices may experience a number of psychological effects, whether or not the practices in question are legal. This includes health-care professionals being affected by participation in decisions which end life, the pressure to take part, again whether the practice is legal or not and problems associated with participating in practices when they are illegal. We shall begin with an exploration of the effect of taking part.

2.3.1   The psychological effect of taking part   Whether done for a good motive or bad, whether done for justifiable reasons or ones which are not, or even whether the actions involved are legal or not, participating in events which lead to the death of the patient are likely to be difficult for health-care professionals. The prime purpose of a doctor or other medical staff is to bring the patient, as far as possible, back to a state of health. When health-care professionals are unable to do this, it is liable to have detrimental effects on their psyche. When they not only are unable to bring the patient back to health but also are unable to stop losses of patient dignity, comfort and control along with considerable pain or other problems, any effects on those providing treatment are potentially exacerbated. Even if a doctor, nurse or other health-care worker feels they could not have done anything differently than they did, this may not provide any solace if the results of treatment are unsatisfactory. If the end result is the death of the patient, and most importantly if that death is the direct result of an end-of-life decision, the effect of those decisions may weigh heavily on medical staff. Those may not be reduced despite the fact that the patient in question has requested the end-of-life treatment or the health-care professional feels justified in what they have done. In reality, for a vast majority of the population – even for those who argue for the legalisation of assisted dying – death is not a preferable state of affairs. Death is not a good outcome even if it may be seen as the best outcome under the circumstances. If we allow health-care workers to engage in practices which bring about death, we need to be cognisant of the effect those decisions will have on those engaged in performing those actions. Doctors or other health-care professionals may feel like they have done something wrong or they may feel 'like a killer' irrespective of whether such actions are sanctioned by law or ethics.

In some ways, of course, this is a good thing. We want health-care professionals to be cautious about these practices. We want them to exercise restraint and see any action which brings about death – whether that be assisted dying, the removal of treatment or any other medical practice – as something which should be undertaken only if other choices are not available. We want them to be clear about what the patient wishes as well as being as certain as they can be about the medical condition of the patient. We want them to be sure what the result of that action is as well as the costs associated with it to the patient, the patient's family and friends and the health-care practitioner. These provide important safeguards whether or not they are enshrined in law. However, we must also be aware that these come at a cost to the health-care practitioner. Any regulation must therefore take account of these normal reactions in health-care staff. That is not to suggest that things such as post-decision counselling needs to be made mandatory but that space should be made available, both before and after any decision is implemented, which would allow medical staff to come to grips with any decision that is made. Regulation, then, may be most effective if it provides time and opportunities for health-care staff who may make difficult decisions in end-of-life cases.

We must also consider the effect of the current prohibition of certain practices on the psychological well-being of those engaged in the provision of health care. On the surface, it would seem like this would be a benefit of currently prohibiting the practice. Medical staff can inform patients or family members who request aid in dying that such practices are neither legally nor ethically permissible, and this would provide a ready-made excuse which allows individuals to avoid difficult cases. Anecdotally, though, this appears to not always be the case. Again, we can explore some of the findings from the *Angels of Death* study. That study indicated that a number of doctors, particularly those involved with HIV/AIDS patients, had been under considerable strain and stress for providing assisted dying. For example, a GP named Harvey stated: 'I find it very stressful dealing with it. Having assisted people before … there is only a finite [number] of times you can do it.'[30] He further referred to it as 'ugly' and 'very draining'.[31] Other interviewees admitted to being burned out, either in general or in regard to specific cases.[32] Those who participated in HIV/AIDS cases were hit especially hard as that disease had significant social stigma attached to it.[33] Health-care practitioners often came from the same at-risk communities and,

---

[30] Magnusson, *Angels of Death*, p. 106.
[31] *Ibid.*   [32] *Ibid.*, pp. 241–244.   [33] *Ibid.*, p. 241.

as such, often associated with patients.[34] Furthermore, they formed relationships with patients which were closer than normal and would take on roles which were more appropriate to friendships than to the professional relationship between health-care worker and patient. Consequently, if a dying process was particularly difficult or painful, this would tend to impact upon the health-care practitioner in question quite heavily.[35] Moreover, and unsurprisingly, silence is an integral part of the way unauthorised assisted dying practices are planned. Those involved as health-care professionals – either by prescribing medication, assisting in the death or covering up the actions of others – are thus incapable of discussing either their actions or the results of those actions with others, even those to whom they are otherwise close.[36] This inability to talk through issues or problems provides further difficulties to the existing stresses of participation.

Of course, an easy answer to the stress and strain that occurs for those engaged in unauthorised end-of-life practices is to simply refrain from engaging in those actions. If the individual is not participating in illegal actions, then they would not have to hide it from others nor would they have the stress and strain associated with actually engaging in conduct which is illegal. We certainly do not spend much, if any, time considering the stress and strain that other criminals are put under in regard to their conduct. We might argue that doctors and other health-care professionals likewise cannot consider themselves to be above the law and must accept the consequences of their actions, even if those consequences are internal and not criminal sanctions. It may not be that easy for health-care practitioners to refuse to participate, however. There are repeated references in *Angels of Death* to feeling like they are required to participate because others will not.[37] This is particularly true of those in roles other than that of doctor who may feel pressure to participate because the patient's doctor will not. This seems especially true, at least as far as the evidence from Magnusson's study is generalisable, for those in the counselling professions such as psychologists or psychiatrists.[38]

The conclusion should not be that merely because it makes dealing with the after-effects of participation easier means that all assisted dying practices should be made legal. The psychological effects on health-care practitioners are important to consider but cannot be used as a decisive factor. What it does remind us, though, is that while the patient is the most important person involved in these cases, it does not

[34] *Ibid.*, pp. 241, 243–244.   [35] *Ibid.*, p. 241.
[36] *Ibid.*, pp. 124–125.   [37] *Ibid.*, pp. 19, 106.   [38] *Ibid.*, p. 19.

mean that all others become secondary figures and that their needs and concerns should not also be addressed.

2.3.2   The pressure to take part   The pressure to take part in illicit assisted dying practices does not merely have to come from the situation. As noted above, some participate because they believe that no one else will do so if they do not. While this might be only a justification on the part of the individual participating, doctors and other health-care professionals do indicate that patients and family members ask them to engage in those practices even though assisted dying remains illegal in almost all jurisdictions. Most surveys of doctors and other medical staff in a range of countries bear this point out.[39] It is never a majority but there is a clear minority of individuals who have requested those providing care for them to end their lives.[40] Furthermore, we have interviewees from *Angels of Death* who have stated they were pressured into providing assisted dying for patients, sometimes in situations which were quite troubling. Three interviewees, Tim, Gary and Gordon, all related instances where they felt that family members were trying to get them to euthanise a patient in situations where it was not necessarily clear that it was what the patient would have wanted, whether the patient was competent or whether the doctor in question knew enough about the situation to be able to make a reasonable determination of important factors. Tim, for example, provided two lethal injections to a patient he had never met prior to the evening in question and who was unable, due to a brain infection, to participate in the discussion.[41] Instead, Tim based his decision upon what the family insisted the patient would have wanted.[42] Gary helped to euthanise a patient when 'it was difficult to get an appreciation of whether he was depressed or demented'.[43] Gordon, perhaps the most troubling case, felt 'absolutely cajoled into' helping complete a botched suicide, at least partially because 'it was 4 o'clock in the morning, I had a cold and I felt dreadful and I just wanted to get out of there'.[44] All three of these cases happened in jurisdictions where euthanasia was illegal.

The current prohibition does not seem, therefore, to preclude patients (or those close to the patient) from requesting aid in dying, nor does it

[39] E. J. Emanuel, 'Euthanasia and Physician-Assisted Suicide: A Review of the Empirical Data from the United States' (2002) 162 *Archives of Internal Medicine* 142–152, 147.

[40] *Ibid.* See also D. Meier *et al.*, 'A National Survey of Physician-Assisted Suicide and Euthanasia in the United States' (1998) 338 *The New England Journal of Medicine* 1193–1201.

[41] Magnusson, *Angels of Death*, p. 164   [42] *Ibid.*, pp. 164–165.

[43] *Ibid.*, p. 211.   [44] *Ibid.*, pp. 206–208.

even seem to prevent doctors or other medical staff from being 'cajoled' or pressured into participating in these actions. There may be additional issues when considering the types of doctors who may be pressured into these actions. Tim was a new doctor at the time of the events he relayed and Gordon appears to have been sick (and perhaps compromised in his judgement?). In such cases, it appears that patients are assisted not by the best doctor who may be available to deal with their particular case, but the one most easily convinced to help. Considering the other problems involved (such as the 'cowboy phenomenon' and the problem with drugs outlined below), this could cause serious problems for all concerned. Patients may not receive the option they wished as limitations on care may be exposed, doctors may have insufficient know-how or expertise to deal either with the medical condition or with the proposed actions, or doctors may be concerned about other things which adversely impact upon treatment (such as avoiding criminal sanction). A system which is supposed to be robust turns out to be less than we hoped and, more importantly, focuses power and control on people who are not necessarily well-suited to that task.

We may accept these problems if the alternatives are even worse. Thus, we might posit that requests of this sort might increase in cases where the action in question is legal. If patients, family and friends are willing to request these practices in situations where it is illegal, are they not more likely to ask in cases where the threat of criminal prosecution is absent? Theoretically, this seems plausible, although I am unaware of any research which examines this point and provides solid data to confirm it. Assuming, therefore, that the number of requests would increase, it is worth considering what the ramifications of an increased number of requests would be. Increased requests for particular end-of-life decisions does not inevitably mean that more requests will be granted. It may be the case, for instance, that while requests go up, these additional requests are all denied by health-care professionals (for whichever reason they decide to do so) and there is therefore no actual increase in specific practices. Alternatively, while some of those requests are granted, it may be that other requests, which under a different system would be made and granted, are refused under a new regulatory regime. In both cases, then, while the number of requests for action goes up, the actual incidence level of action does not. This is obviously speculative, though, and incidence rates from jurisdictions which allow assisted dying, for example, have seen a rise between the rate of uptake at the start of legalisation and the rate of uptake later on (although the Netherlands appears to have levelled off at this point).

If there are no benefits to the incidence rate, though, there may still be reasons why bringing such practices out into the open is useful. First, one of the benefits of an open practice may be that the *right* individuals are asked to participate. This does not just mean qualified medical personnel (although they would probably be necessary) but also health-care practitioners in the right specialisms. It would mean that medical doctors, for example, may be more prevalent than community health workers and psychologists who may not have a sufficient understanding about the drugs involved in lethal doses. Conversely, it may mean that those with concerns about depression, dementia or other mental health issues are seen by professionals with expertise instead of those without because of a fear of bringing outsiders into a criminal action. Moreover, it may also mean that those who become involved also have sufficient experience and are not compromised themselves by illness or other incapacitating factors. In other words, it may be that bringing these actions out into the open helps avoid the problems of finding someone willing to act as opposed to someone qualified to act.

3   Professionalism of the euthanasia underground

These lead to one of the biggest issues about underground euthanasia practices – the question about professionalism. Contained within this set of problems associated with the so-called 'euthanasia underground' are a number of factors which call into question the professionalism of those engaged in practices which are currently illegal. One of the important factors of this claim of non-professionalism is the secrecy issue which has already been touched upon. However, this will need greater investigation, along with issues of the 'cowboy phenomenon', the trial-and-error nature of the practice and the lack of oversight which is routine within these underground practices.

Since it has already been discussed a bit, issues surrounding secrecy are a useful starting point. As noted above, due to the illicit nature of assisted dying practices in most jurisdictions, those who participate are required to keep the nature of their involvement a closely guarded secret. This may mean that even those close to the health-care practitioner (e.g. a partner) can remain unaware of their actions.[45] While this can have significant ramifications for the psyche of the health-care practitioner, it is not the only consequence of the increased need for secrecy. Other issues which are likely to have a considerably greater effect upon the patient are also possibilities. For example, one of the

---

[45] *Ibid.*, pp. 124–125.

primary ways that doctors maintain secrecy is by avoiding being present at the actual death. They may prescribe the lethal dose of medication and instruct those present about the best method of administering those drugs, but avoid the appearance of illegality by being absent at the actual time of death.[46] If the death goes ahead as predicted, this may not present difficulties for any of the parties concerned, but things often do not go as planned. Patients may have unexpected reactions to drugs and those participating do not necessarily know how to deal with them. Additionally, patients may have other complications which would be easier to address with the presence of the doctor. This might help prevent, for example, the prospect that those at the patient's bedside may have to kill the patient more directly, usually through smothering the patient with a pillow.[47] Those with medical expertise being absent from the scene may be beneficial to them but it can have dire effects for the patient.

Furthermore, one of the vital 'rules' in illegal assisted dying is to make sure that any evidence which is available is inconclusive. There are two ways this can be accomplished. The first is through the use of drugs which are chosen primarily for their ability to either mask what has actually happened or which are already in use (and therefore will be expected to be in the patient's system). Drugs may be chosen, then, not for how effective they are in providing the required outcome, but for their inability to provide crucial evidence.[48] The second is that the body is cremated as quickly as possible.[49] If the body is cremated, then it is generally not possible for a coroner or other authorities to be able to determine the exact cause of death.[50] Without this information, there will be little reason to look further into a specific case. This may affect the ability of others to grieve or cause additional detrimental effects to the family of the patient.[51] More importantly, in all of these cases, it is not possible for those concerned primarily about the patient to be sure that what was best for that individual was the option taken in the case.

---

[46] *Ibid.*, pp. 224–225.
[47] This appears to be the one of the two most used methods if the drugs do not work as expected. The other is strangulation. *Ibid.*, pp. 166–167, 242–243.
[48] *Ibid.*, pp. 226–227.   [49] *Ibid.*, p. 227.
[50] *Ibid.* This is also why Dr Cox was prosecuted on charges of attempted murder instead of murder directly. Lillian Boyes had been cremated prior to the investigation and it could not therefore be proven that the potassium chloride he had injected her with was the actual cause of death. *R* v. *Cox* (1992) 12 BMLR 38.
[51] It may not seem like a big example but one account of an assisted suicide in *Angels of Death* indicated that the patient had to have a 'much smaller [funeral] than the deceased had originally planned' and the funeral was brought forward. Magnusson, *Angels of Death*, pp. 227–228.

Furthermore, the level of secrecy necessary may sometimes impact upon the ability of even those participating to converse about particular treatments. An illustration of this is found in a story told by Erin, a hospital nurse interviewed by Magnusson. He discussed a conversation between himself and a physician at the hospital where he worked:

> 'Use as much morphine as you need,' said the physician. 'I'll sign for it.'
> Erin was taken by surprise.
> 'Do you know what I mean?' said the physician.
> 'I'm not sure,' said Erin. 'Do you want me to make him comfortable or do you want me to make him *ultimately* comfortable?'
> 'Yes', responded the physician.[52]

Erin appears to have understood this conversation to mean that the doctor wanted the patient to be killed and the patient did die later that night.[53] The conversation, however, is fraught with ambiguity. Not only does the physician in question not make it clear whether or not the patient was supposed to be made 'ultimately comfortable' as opposed to 'comfortable', but it is also not necessarily clear what 'ultimately comfortable' was to mean. The implication appears clear but it does presumably allow the doctor, if either Erin or the physician is caught, to claim that death was not the intention of the conversation. While that is understandable under the circumstances, it also means that it is not entirely clear what any of the parties involved actually wanted.

Connected to the issue of secrecy is the trial-and-error nature of the euthanasia underground. Since doctors and other health-care practitioners may be loath to talk to colleagues about their actions, there is little opportunity to exchange information about effective drug combinations.[54] Essentially, then, every individual starts from scratch instead of building on the experiences of others in the field.[55] This can cause substantial problems for patient care as those involved may have little idea about how to actually go about killing a patient effectively and with as little pain, discomfort and loss of dignity as possible. To provide one example, it is not as easy to kill someone by stuffing them full of pills as

---

[52] *Ibid.*, p. 192 (emphasis in original).
[53] *Ibid.*   [54] *Ibid.*, pp. 145–150.
[55] One way to show this is through the sheer number of different drugs used by members of the euthanasia underground interviewed by Roger Magnusson. According to *Angels of Death*, interviewees had used one or more of the following: analgesics such as morphine, sedatives, anti-depressants, insulin, anti-psychotic drugs, potassium chloride, anti-nausea drugs, barbiturates, betablockers and lethabarb, a drug used primarily to euthanise animals. *Ibid.*, pp. 145–149. This can be overstated, though, as not all those participating wanted the drugs to have the same effect. In particular, some of those involved preferred to have a patient die quickly while others wanted patients to die more slowly. *Ibid.*, p. 149.

might generally be believed. The body has a number of natural defences which must be overcome for that to happen. One of those defences is the expulsion of poisonous material by vomiting. As a result, any drug cocktail which is designed to kill a patient probably must contain anti-nausea medication. It is, however, not always included as part of a drug cocktail. This has led to some patients dying in much less preferable situations than they had imagined. Indeed, in one case, a patient had to ingest his own vomit in order to kill himself.[56] In cases where this does not happen, those present may have to resort to 'some manual work' – which is the killing of a patient through strangulation or smothering – or by 'emptying the doctor's bag' into the patient.[57] Patients who are not afforded either of these options – either the ability to retake medication refused by the body or friends who are willing and able to directly kill them – may be made even worse off by the attempted suicide than they had been previously. None of the options available, then, provide a compelling reason to keep the situation as it is.

Both the issue of secrecy and the trial-and-error aspect of the euthanasia underground appear to be problems of circumstance. They are created by the essential aspects of performing illegal activities and need not be fundamental characteristics of practice or of the individuals involved. More troubling issues arise, however, when looking more closely at some of those involved in underground euthanasia practices. Magnusson refers to these individuals as 'cowboys'. A reasonable number of the individuals interviewed by him fit into this category.[58] Those who fit into this group tended to see themselves as rebels against the medical establishment. They would refuse to abide by guidelines in addition to doing what they could to buck trends, subvert drug studies, paid little attention to guidelines in relation to professional distance and refused to abide by either legal or ethical rules.[59] What may be most worrying about the conduct of these individuals is that they often refused to abide by their own guidelines, even when they asserted that these set out the criteria for their own actions.[60] Others, while not rising to the level of 'cowboys' were noteworthy because they participated in assisted dying but did not want to see it legalised.[61] One of the main reasons for this apparent disconnect was that these individuals were concerned that legalisation would result in too much bureaucracy and legal oversight. Some expressed reservations about legalisation because

---

[56] *Ibid.*, p. 205.   [57] *Ibid.*   [58] *Ibid.*, pp. 239–241.
[59] *Ibid.*, pp. 104–110.   [60] *Ibid.*, p. 106.
[61] Magnusson indicated that 11 interviewees did not want to see the practice regulated despite the fact they had been involved in the practice. *Ibid.*, pp. 108–109.

they felt that, if assisted dying were legalised, this would mean that only doctors would be able to participate and they would lose input into clinical decision-making.[62] One nurse asked 'why should doctors be the only ones who can make these decisions?'[63] These opinions become even more troubling when one realises how little concern most of the interviewees had about being investigated, prosecuted or convicted of a criminal offence.[64] Many asserted in interviews that there was a minimal chance of being caught and even if they were caught, there was only a small chance they would be prosecuted.[65] These individuals did not fear investigation or prosecution because they believed that there was only a small chance that authority figures such as police or prosecutors would care about someone who was likely to die within a short period anyway and that evidence and testimony would be hard to obtain.[66]

This unsettling pattern may be even worse when we explore the lack of oversight and professionalism which follows at least some of those engaged in the euthanasia underground. To explore that, we can return to the story presented to Magnusson by Liz, which is discussed in the 'playing God' section above. In that case, we appear to have a doctor engaging in deliberate and intentional involuntary euthanasia within a hospital setting.[67] These actions include not only directing the nursing staff to put up a drug cocktail 'designed to kill' the patient, but also to make sure that members of the patient's family were not around to see it.[68] Even when health-care practitioners involved in underground euthanasia practices do not act as the doctor did in that case, they have attempted to exercise control over a number of functions associated with the dying process, including the timing. For instance, one GP, Paula, agreed to participate in the suicide of a patient but it had been originally scheduled for a time when she was on holiday.[69] The patient therefore brought forward the time of his death to coincide with her vacation plans.[70] The time involved appears to have been only a little more than a week, but the timing was purely for the convenience of the doctor.[71] We are told no more details about the event but it is worth speculating whether the patient might have felt it necessary to move the date of his suicide even if the additional week had been important. Especially if Paula's contribution was critical, it might have been that the patient in question lost time they should have had for reasons which have nothing to do with the patient. This is, of course, not as serious an issue as the one relayed by Liz who, if the account she provides is

---

[62] *Ibid.*, p. 107.   [63] *Ibid.*, p. 108.   [64] *Ibid.*, pp. 110, 228.
[65] *Ibid.*, p. 228.   [66] *Ibid.*   [67] *Ibid.*, pp. 234–237.
[68] *Ibid.*, p. 235.   [69] *Ibid.*, p. 225.   [70] *Ibid.*   [71] *Ibid.*

accurate, has described something which was an organised murder of a patient. These smaller aspects of controlling the process, though, may be equally important within the context of a specific case and the lack of oversight calls into question the idea that we can merely leave the regulation of assisted dying practices as they are.

Consequently, we have a very worrying situation. Magnusson, for example, argues that 'deception permeates every aspect of illicit euthanasia practice.'[72] He further states that:

> Illegal euthanasia illustrates dramatically what we might call 'medical anti-professionalism'; that is, an absence of appropriate training, an absence of oversight, an absence of accountability, and an absence of principles guiding involvement. Unlike therapeutic medical procedures ... euthanasia is largely carried out informally, in an idiosyncratic environment largely lacking in norms and control.[73]

4   Professional codes of conduct

Another substantial concern about the legalisation of certain end-of-life practices is the effect that this will have upon medical ethics. Kass has been a particular critic on this point.[74] He has argued that it is fundamentally against the role and position of doctor for someone to be involved in the death of patients.[75] He draws attention to the adage that doctors are there to care for their patients but not to kill them.[76] He concludes that, if doctors were to be allowed to aid the dying of patients, then this will turn them into something else as it is so far removed from their expertise and job description.[77]

One possible, and often used, response to this argument is to point out that merely because doctors or other health-care professionals may engage in some practices which appear to be at odds with their primary purpose does not mean they lose their role. Even if the doctor's primary aim is to cure the patient,[78] once that possibility no longer exists, other options must become available. The analogy is provided of an automobile mechanic. A mechanic's primary purpose may be to bring a vehicle back to working order. If that is not possible for whatever reason, a mechanic does not cease to be a mechanic because he or she then fulfils the alternative purpose of scrapping the vehicle. There is nothing inconsistent with those two aspects of a mechanic's job so there should not be, so the argument goes, anything wrong with doctors performing

---

72 *Ibid.*, p. 229.   73 *Ibid.*
74 See, e.g., Kass, 'Neither for Love nor Money'.
75 See, e.g., *ibid.*, 44–46.   76 See, e.g., *ibid.*, 36–37.
77 See, e.g., *ibid.*, 44–46.   78 See, e.g., *ibid.*, 30, 34.

two similarly superficially inconsistent roles. As long as we remain clear as to the priorities of the role – i.e. curing when that is possible – then having disparate roles does not create any problems on its own. Some may argue in response, though, that this analogy minimises the problem as doctors are not sufficiently similar to mechanics nor is the average patient similar to a car. The analogy, therefore, is seen as glib and the argument as a whole as unsatisfactorily connected with the real issues which doctors would have to address. Scrapping a car, it should be noted, hardly involves significant ethical issues,[79] whereas killing a person certainly does.

The essential point worth examination is whether Kass's central dichotomy actually works. Is killing a patient inconsistent with caring for them? This was discussed generally in the previous chapter on harm during the discussion of whether death is always a harm, but it is worth repeating. Things were harmful if they set back an interest of the individual. Thus, whether or not death counted as a harm was based upon whether or not it set back an interest. In a majority of cases, this will obviously be a setback to the interests of the individual and thus death would be a harm. However, it is possible to envisage cases (and quite a few of them will involve the sorts of cases we have been discussing) where death did not set back an interest of the individual and thus was not a harm. The difference between caring and killing works in a similar way. Caring would seem to be about supporting and fostering the interests that an individual has. In most cases, this would seem to prevent killing from being caring. For a very small minority, though, death might be part of the interests that an individual has. In such cases, we might, despite the general rule, consider killing as part of caring. If this is correct, then Kass's central distinction is not valid and we need not accept that doctors should only care and never kill because, at times, that could be impossible.

Some support for this argument can be found in the statements made by interviewees in *Angels of Death*. In that study, a number of health-care professionals indicated that they believed that assisted dying practices were not unethical.[80] Mark, a clinical psychologist, indicated that 'killing someone who is suffering ... is in the service of decency and respect'.[81] Others indicated that it was part of the spectrum of care that should be provided to patients and was not different from other types of end-of-life treatment. A hospital nurse named Chris went so

[79] Although the method of doing so might. For example, the environmental impact of particular schemes for scrapping vehicles may have ethical implications.
[80] Magnusson, *Angels of Death*, pp. 16, 104.   [81] *Ibid.*, p. 18.

far as to state 'you don't [give] euthanasia instead of offering palliative care, you offer euthanasia as an option, as part of that whole package'.[82] When explaining why, many referenced the pain, suffering and loss of dignity which results in end-of-life care as reasons why death can be preferable to living.[83] More importantly, while many of these individuals seem to have little time for medical ethics in general, they did have an ethical framework that they followed. What was crucial was that the ethical framework they employed fitted with the practical realities of the situations they were facing. Erin, for example, argues that medical ethics was 'very nice in theory' but was '*not the stuff that's dealing with the folks in bed, you know*'.[84] However, he further stated that 'I was doing harm, you know. And for the first time, I took those [ethics] principles back out and really looked at them, as a care giver ... but also trying to understand what the patient was going through'.[85] For him at least, this seemed to include the idea that assisted dying was ethical and was not actually harm.

We need not accept, of course, Erin or Mark's theories on ethics any more than they need accept ours. What is worth exploring, though, is the ramifications of their theories. If professional codes of ethics changed to allow assisted dying, would other changes be necessary and what impact would those changes have? As has been shown in Part I, most of the ethical codes which currently exist would face little or no real revision if one accepted that causing death can sometimes be in the best interests of patients. Concepts of harm, beneficence, non-maleficence and autonomy already encompass the foundational claims necessary to accept the idea that death is sometimes an acceptable response. Nor are other concepts such as dignity or even the value of life necessarily inconsistent with this view. So, the acceptance of assisted dying or other practices which cause death need not be incompatible with professional codes of ethics.

Being consistent with professional codes of ethics does not mean it is being suggested that it is something that health-care practitioners should always do, nor is it being suggested that doctors have a duty to cause death in certain situations. Codes of ethics should be changed so that assisting a patient's dying is permissible but not that it be compulsory. Conscience clauses, for those who have fundamental problems with killing, should remain within any system of ethics. These conscience clauses must remain because notions such as autonomy require that the opinions, aims, purposes and goals of the health-care

---

[82] *Ibid.*, p. 69.   [83] *Ibid.*, p. 78.
[84] *Ibid.*, p. 16 (emphasis in original).   [85] *Ibid.*

practitioner must be included in any discussion and not simply dismissed. Accepting that does require a discussion about two important caveats – emergency situations and the duty to refer. If one accepts that doctors may avoid participating in certain end-of-life practices in general, that does not mean they can relinquish this ability in all cases. It may be determined that doctors or other health-care workers must proceed despite their reservations in cases of emergency. It may be argued, as it sometimes is with other medical options such as abortion, that the autonomy of the health-care worker can be limited in cases where there is a compelling emergency.[86] Whatever the benefits of such a system in instances such as abortion, I do not think assisted dying cases should follow the same method. First, considering the procedural safeguards that will be discussed in Chapter 14, there should not be emergency cases of assisted dying. Practically, then, the issue should not arise. If it did, though, forcing doctors to cause the death of a patient in ways they think inappropriate or wrong is likely to do greater overall harm than otherwise. Consequently, conscience clauses should still remain in effect even in emergency situations. The duty to refer in cases where a patient requests assisted dying but a health-care worker refuses is a much closer call. Again, conscience clauses could require medical personnel unwilling to perform certain actions to refer patients to those who will. While there can be debate on the point, this seems more acceptable than requiring health-care professionals to act in emergency situations. The mere act of referral is not sufficiently causative that those who see assisted death as wrong can be immune from the requirement of referral. It does provide some limitations on the ethical conduct but this would be outweighed by the limitations placed upon others.[87] As a result, health-care workers, while not required to agree with or perform any particular practice at the end of life, should be required to refer if necessary.

5   Conclusion

In conclusion, we have looked at several issues in this chapter which directly affect the doctor or health-care professional. We have considered whether the acceptance of certain practices means that doctors will begin to play God or that others will think that they will. Neither,

---

[86] Abortion Act 1967, Section 4.
[87] The courts, for example, have taken this view. For example, in the *Ms B* case, if the original hospital was unable to remove her ventilator, they were required to transfer her to a hospital which would be willing to do so. *Re B (adult: refusal of medical treatment)* [2002] 2 All ER 449 at 475, paragraph 100.

however, was seen as being highly plausible or incapable of regulation. Furthermore, we considered the psychological effects of certain practices on the health-care worker, especially as they relate to underground or illegal practices. We further considered the issues which arise when practices such as assisted dying go underground and what legalisation means for the professionalism of these types of conduct. Finally, we considered the effect of legalising assisted dying on professional codes of conduct. While all of these were issues worthy of discussion, most could be handled effectively by regulation. Having considered both the patient who receives end-of-life care and the health-care practitioner who performs it, it is now time to widen our focus and consider the viewpoints of others who might be associated with end-of-life decisions.

12   Greater societal issues

1   Introduction

There is an argument that Part II of this book is all about societal issues. All of the concerns discussed in the previous two chapters can be characterised in the terms of their wider societal impact. For example, we can consider both the prevention of suicide and the protection of vulnerable groups not as claims about individual patients but as expressions of wider societal decisions about groups of individuals. Seen in that way, everything is a greater societal issue. However, while it is possible to see the issues expressed in previous chapters in those terms, the focus is on individuals in specific circumstances writ large. The emphasis in this chapter, on the other hand, is not about individual responses but about issues which are less likely to be seen as claims about collections of individual actions, but as issues which are best addressed or considered at a macro level. Thus, the primary aim of this chapter will not be to discuss issues which can be related necessarily to individuals in question, but to more diffuse societal groups. First, we shall consider the question of the impact of end-of-life decision-making on the wider community. This means we shall scrutinise the question of what effect the specific end-of-life decision may have on family, friends or others who might have a connection with the patient or the doctor involved. After consideration of this issue, we shall explore methods to investigate and prevent abuses of societal regulation in end-of-life decisions. Specifically, we shall examine the ways we might go about attempting to prevent instances of illegal conduct and how to effectively address those practices when they happen.

2   The wider community

2.1   Introduction

One issue which arises when discussing any end-of-life treatment involves neither the doctor nor the patient but is primarily concerned with wider societal claims: the effect that any end-of-life decision (or the ability to make a particular end-of-life decision) may have on the wider community. Those looking for an example of this in practice need look no further than the case of Terri Schiavo in the US. The case was a fairly straightforward family matter. Terri Schiavo was a woman in Florida who had spent a number of years in a vegetative state after having suffered cardiac arrest.[1] Her husband, as Terri's guardian, petitioned the court to remove the feeding tube which was keeping her alive. Terri Schiavo's parents objected to the removal of the tube, insisting that she was conscious and would not have wanted the feeding tube removed. A protracted legal battle between the parties resulted which brought in any number of outside influences.[2] This included pro-life and disability rights groups on the side of the parents, in addition to several courts (including the US and Florida Supreme Courts) and the Florida Governor, Jeb Bush, the US Congress and the President of the United States.[3] Her case became a cause célèbre for many in the US and the removal of the feeding tube was met by a variety of legal actions, legislative actions and protests. Despite this, the feeding tube was withdrawn and Terri Schiavo died on 31 March 2005.[4]

For some, the public outcry in the case might have seemed a bit strange. Legal guardians had been legally entitled to have treatment withdrawn from patients in a vegetative state as far back as the 1970s with the New Jersey case of *Quinlan*.[5] This ability to withdrawn treatment had been further accepted by the US Supreme Court in the case of *Cruzan*.[6] Other than the potential factual question involved about whether Terri Schiavo was or was not in a vegetative state, the case did not appear to differ greatly from any number of cases across the US (and the rest of the world). To others, though, the case brought up profound questions about life and society's involvement with treatment decisions which are seen as dubious, ill-informed or morally questionable.[7] They thus protested against not only the ability of Terri Schiavo's husband to remove the feeding tube in her particular case, but the

---

[1] 'Terri Schiavo Dies' www.guardian.co.uk/world/2005/mar/31/usa?INTCMP=SRCH (accessed 16 June 2011).
[2] *Ibid.*   [3] *Ibid.*   [4] *Ibid.*
[5] *In re Quinlan*, 355 A 2nd 664 (NJ, 1976).
[6] *Cruzan* v. *Director, Missouri Department of Health*, 497 U.S. 261 (1990).
[7] 'Terri Schiavo Dies' www.guardian.co.uk/world/2005/mar/31/usa?INTCMP=SRCH; N. Hentoff, '"Judicial murder" and Terri Schiavo' www.washingtontimes.com/news/2005/jul/10/20050710-100558-1213r (accessed 16 June 2011); M. Johnson, 'Who Speaks for Terri Schiavo?' www.sfgate.com/cgi-bin/article.cgi?f=/c/a/2005/03/22/EDGEPBSQDM1.DTL (accessed 16 June 2011).

ability of guardians to remove feeding tubes in general.[8] The case of Terri Schiavo then became not only one about a particular individual but a referendum on how the US treated patients of her sort. It was thus a question about the societal impact of decisions like the one the court was asked to ratify in her case.

As a result, it is imperative to consider not only how end-of-life decisions might affect the health-care professionals and patients involved, but also the effects upon the wider community. When doing so, we should be careful not to duplicate concerns which are really disguised arguments addressed elsewhere, such as the slippery slope. It is also crucial to remain cognisant of the fact that the wider community is not a homogeneous group. It is not even something which can probably be considered as a single entity. Any society is made up of a number of different groups, on a number of different levels. We might have immediate groups of families and friends, larger groups of acquaintances, regional groups which are broader and often might have very little interaction with the specific patients and doctors involved and national groups which are significantly unlikely to have any intimate connections with the local parties involved in a case. These groups are unlikely to always have similar interests or goals and thus the interests of the wider community may be difficult to definitively discern. Additionally, we will need to consider how best to deal with the complex interactions between different societal groups.

This section will therefore analyse the effects of end-of-life decisions upon the wider community. It will explore the interests of those in immediate groups to the patient such as friends and family. It will also take into account the effects upon more tangential groups such as regional or national societal groups. This will include considerations about the impact of end-of-life decisions upon members of a community who would not ever use such practices in their own cases. It will also judge how best to balance the interests of these disparate groups when making decisions about end-of-life treatment and the treatment options which are available to patients and doctors at the end of life.

2.2   *Immediate groups*

We will begin our discussion with immediate groups of family and friends. These are individuals who have close personal relationships to the patient and are therefore likely to be directly impacted by any

[8] M. Johnson, 'Who Speaks for Terri Schiavo?' www.sfgate.com/cgi-bin/article.cgi?f=/c/a/2005/03/22/EDGEPBSQDM1.DTL.

end-of-life decision for the patient. Obviously, the limits of such a group are impossible to completely define. For some patients, this may be a large group including many extended family members or other individuals who others would see as mere acquaintances. Others may consider this group only to be a close-knit group of immediate family and a few close friends. It may even be that certain individuals may not be in overlapping groups (i.e. one person may believe another to be part of his or her immediate group while the other may not reciprocate the feeling). Whatever its limits, though, the group of immediate family and friends is most likely to have a direct effect on the patient and be directly affected by the decision of the patient and medical staff.

As this group is the one most likely to be intimately involved in any end-of-life decision, consideration of their interests is likely to be the most difficult. Individuals themselves may be torn about their feelings towards different options available to the patient. For example, a close friend or relative of someone dying of a painful terminal illness may not want that person to suffer but may also have philosophical, emotional or religious objections to the ending of the patient's life. Alternatively, others may be accepting of the ending of life in theory but object to it in a particular case for personal reasons. What is important for the purposes of regulation, however, is not the actual instantiation of those feelings but to what extent those feelings or interests of others should help determine what is or is not acceptable for the patient. To what extent, for example, should the feelings of others prohibit a patient from requesting or a doctor from complying with certain practices?

To determine the extent of influence that immediate groups of families and friends might have, though, it is worth having some understanding about the possible ways they might interact with patients and health-care professionals. Generally, they are not believed to have much impact when considering different types of end-of-life care. This is particularly true in cases of assisted dying but is also worthy of investigation in other cases of end-of-life treatment which might lead to death. Due to the stated pre-eminence of autonomy concerns, immediate family and friends are often not included in any discussion about treatment options. Instead, patients are seen as being atomistic deciders, with doctors either agreeing to implement a particular decision or refusing, but the essential relationship is that between a doctor and patient. Even in cases where the patient is incompetent and a guardian has been appointed to make decisions on behalf of the patient, the guardian is seen as merely a surrogate for the patient and is addressed primarily in that light.

Immediate family and friends, however, often play an important role in end-of-life cases. They are likely to provide crucial emotional, personal and financial support to the patient and may be instrumental in decision-making, either through the provision of advice or through help in the decision-making process (friends or family members may, for instance, be more adept at asking for information from health-care staff). Just because a family member or friend is more vocal does not mean, of course, that they would necessarily provide any benefit to the decision-making process. Friends or family may be no better suited than the patient to deal with the stress and complicated information in order to make a decision. They may be no better equipped to understand or retain the information than the patient, nor are they necessarily more likely to be able to evaluate the recommendations of health-care staff. In addition to providing these needed roles for the patient, friends and family will often have their own needs. Those involved in helping to care for the patient may require space and time to deal with the stress involved in caring for those with terminal illnesses. It may take some time for those close to the patient to come to terms with the terminal illness of the patient, sometimes even more time than it may take the patient him or herself. None of these, though, are readily capable of regulation within an end-of-life context. There are areas where regulation might be useful, but these are generally within the confines of broader reform about health care or about employment. For example, a particular state may decide to require employers to give time off to those caring for terminally ill patients in a similar way to maternity-leave regulations. Alternatively, governments may provide state-sponsored carers or health care to provide for those who are terminally ill (even if they do not provide universal health care).

A more serious problem is the detrimental effect that immediate family and friends might have, whether unintentional or not. This may include outright coercion of a patient, indirect pressure or undue influence which falls short of coercion, or other attempts to influence the patient or doctor in ways which are not beneficial to the patient. An illustration of this can be found in the famous UK case on consent, *In re T (an adult)*.[9] In this case, a pregnant young woman was brought into hospital after a car accident. After being admitted, the young woman, T, had three conversations with her Jehovah's Witness mother. Despite not being a Jevovah's Witness herself, T asked health-care staff after each occasion whether she would be able to refuse a blood transfusion.[10]

⁹ [1992] 4 All ER 649.   ¹⁰ *Ibid.* at 655.

The questions, according to the staff, came 'out of the blue'.[11] They informed her that she was able to do so and T did refuse. After T lapsed into a coma, her boyfriend and father, neither of whom was a Jehovah's Witness, petitioned the court to allow the doctors to give T a blood transfusion.[12] The trial court agreed, as did the Court of Appeal. One of the three reasons given by the Court of Appeal was that T had suffered undue influence as a result of her mother.[13] Unfortunately, we do not know the content of the conversations between T and her mother as they were in private and neither testified during the case (T was unable because she was in a coma; the mother was called to testify but never attended the hearings).[14] However, the facts of the case indicated to the court that T had been pressured into refusing a blood transfusion by her mother and this invalidated her consent.[15] To any who have read the case, it can be debated whether the interpretation of the facts of the case by the court is correct. If the facts as the court understands them, though, are true, then it is clear why 'consent' in such cases should not be valid. This may be important in situations at the end of life where subtle indications of influence over the patient may indicate a serious problem which vitiates consent.

Furthermore, we might consider the court's decision to be correct even if we cannot prove that the events happened in the way the court seems to think. It may be enough for us to accept that the facts in question are in dispute. Again, then, we may consider this to be a question about the burden of proof and what ought to happen when we cannot prove something to a sufficient level. The court's decision is at least a plausible interpretation of the surrounding circumstances and what happened in the case. The daughter did have a history of doing at least some things merely to please her mother (such as going to church every once in a while).[16] The daughter's requests to refuse blood transfusions

---

[11] *Ibid.*   [12] *Ibid.* at 656.
[13] The first other ground was that T was not competent to make a decision due to the medication, stress and her medical condition. *Ibid.* at 660. This seems a bit dubious as all patients brought into emergency settings are likely to be suffering from similar problems. Consequently, no one undergoing emergency procedures, according to this rationale, would be competent to make decisions. The second additional ground was that T was given incorrect information. She was told at the time of her refusals that blood transfusions would not be necessary and that alternative treatments were available. It later developed that the transfusions were required and no alternatives would have been successful. Due to the surrounding facts of the case (which indicated that T had a tendency to try to please her mother at least occasionally but only when it seemed to involve minimal effort on her part), it is unclear whether the refusal would have been made had T known a blood transfusion was crucial to her survival. *Ibid.* at 657–658.
[14] *Ibid.* at 655.   [15] *Ibid.* at 652.   [16] *Ibid.* at 658.

did occur after conversations where only she and her mother were present.[17] Both the boyfriend and father testified that T was definitively not a Jehovah's Witness, while there is no dispute that the mother was a devout one.[18] In light of those facts, the court's opinion that T's mother had exercised influence over her to get her to refuse a blood transfusion is at least plausible. It might be objected that we are imputing improper motives to the mother but this need not be the case. Again, presuming she is a devout Jehovah's Witness, getting her daughter to refuse a blood transfusion is vital for spiritual reasons (as T would go to hell for receiving blood products under that faith) and there is no particular reason why T's mother would have had greater information about the necessity of the transfusions than T did. So, there is no requirement that T's mother exercised her influence, if she did, for anything other than what she saw as the best decision for T. Alternatively, of course, T's mother might not have exercised influence over T at all. We could, consistently with the facts as described in the case, presume that T had a religious conversion as a result of the accident and the impending birth of her child. She may have then asked her mother for advice on how to be a Jehovah's Witness and what that entailed. If she had, one thing we might presume T's mother to have told her was that she was required to refuse blood transfusions, which T then did. This scenario may be as plausible under the facts as the one where the mother improperly influences T. Even if it is, however, all it does is highlight the question about doubt and what response we ought to have in questions of doubt. In a case like this, it seems reasonable that when we have doubt, we ought to either (a) act to preserve the status quo until such time as we can resolve the doubt, or (b) go with the action which seems most consistent with the patient's beliefs under the circumstances. Both options in the *Re T* case would have pointed to overriding the refusal of treatment and providing the blood transfusion. Other cases, of course, are unlikely to be so clear-cut. We may have cases where the preservation of the status quo would require that we keep the patient alive but that the action which seems most consistent with the views of the patient indicate we should let them die. States will need some way to resolve this sort of dispute. My own preference is for (b) over (a) provided that is possible, but it need not be that way. What does appear crucial, however, is that whichever method is used to determine these proof problems should be clear, easily accessible and consistently applied across the jurisdiction. This means that had the case been reversed (i.e. the daughter having been a devout Jehovah's Witness and the mother apparently trying to

---

[17] *Ibid.* at 655.   [18] *Ibid.* at 658.

talk her out of refusing a blood transfusion), we ought to apply the same rule that the undue influence of the mother should vitiate consent.

Not all issues which involve close friends and families are necessarily contrary to the issues related to the patient. One particular concern is the opportunity to say good-bye to a patient. There are two different scenarios we might consider important. The first is a patient who is dying in a place like a hospital or nursing home which may restrict access to the patient by non-health-care staff. In particular, in these types of cases, young children may be prohibited, as may pets, which some will consider to be 'part of the family'.[19] There may, of course, be any number of policy reasons why these decisions have been made. They may also place added stress on the patient and cause significant harm to those close to the patient. Allowing the patient to see a young child or pet may improve the mood of the patient and permit the normally excluded family, friend or pet to spend needed time with the individual in care. This is not, most likely, something which could be dealt with by national or state legislation. Instead, this is most likely dealt with most appropriately at a local level in the hospital or nursing home. Institutions could, for example, allow specific hours for young children and pets to visit the patient or they may seek to provide a specific location (away from potential liability issues or breakable materials) which allows those close to the patient to visit who might normally be refused an opportunity. As stated, this may provide important psychological benefits for the patient as well as providing family with a needed opportunity for closure prior to death.

There may also be difficulties in an assisted dying context in jurisdictions where such practices are illegal. The normal impression of cases of assisted dying is of a lone patient and a single doctor. This is likely due to how reports of assisted dying by those acting outside the law, such as Dr Jack Kevorkian in the US, are presented. In reality, a number of people might participate in a case of assisted dying even if it is illegal. Participation, though, is likely to be limited to those who the patient, doctor or those assisting can be sure will agree and not disclose what has happened.[20] While this may be prudent under the circumstances, it may also prohibit certain individuals, either who would wish to be present or whom the patient would be wish to be present, from being told about the events. This may include any number of 'death rituals', such as getting rid of particular things of sentimental value, but also

---

[19] M. Krant, *Dying and Dignity: The Meaning and Control of a Personal Death* (Springfield, IL: Charles C. Thomas, 1974), p. 98.

[20] Magnusson, *Angels of Death*, pp. 223–224.

'pre-death wakes', parties, dinners or other events which are designed to celebrate the life of the patient.[21] In some sense, these are an attempt to defy the power of the patient's death but also to give those who will be left an opportunity to say good-bye.[22] In addition, certain individuals may be present at the death itself, even if they have no part to play in the actual dying process. Unfortunately, under the current prohibition of assisted dying practices in many jurisdictions, some may miss out because they are not included. Sometimes, this is merely because either the patient or those assisting in the dying process may feel that those excluded individuals will bring unneeded attention to the death. For example, Magnusson conducted an interview with a person named Margaret.[23] She had assisted in the death of her brother but did not feel that she could include her parents in those events because of their religious beliefs.[24] However, she later overheard them making 'pro-euthanasia' statements.[25] This, obviously, does not mean necessarily that her parents would have agreed with her actions in the case. They may have, and they may have additionally wanted the opportunity to be present at the death of their son. Legalising assisted dying, then, may provide benefits for those who are connected to the patient. They may provide an opportunity to participate in death rituals which may provide closure or catharthis for the family or friends. This may thus provide another reason to consider the legalisation of assisted dying. By itself, increasing the involvement of immediate family and friends is unlikely to be a convincing reason for legalising assisted dying. Within the context of other, more compelling reasons, though, it may add additional weight. At the very least, it may provide us with some reason to think that the effect upon the wider community might not be as bad as is sometimes feared.

2.3   Regional or national societal groups

More regional, national or international groups may, in some ways, be easier to accommodate. Those groups are less likely to have significant interaction with the specific patient and therefore issues are more likely to be phrased in general terms.[26] That is not to discount the feelings that individuals within these groups might have, but merely to indicate that the complexities of an individual case may not be as crucial to decision-making as it may be for more immediate groups of family

---

[21] *Ibid.*, pp. 141–143.   [22] *Ibid.*, p. 224.
[23] *Ibid.*, pp. 223–224.   [24] *Ibid.*, p. 224.   [25] *Ibid.*
[26] Although as the *Schiavo* case shows, that is not always the case.

and friends. It is also worth remembering the information presented in previous chapters about opinions of particular populations in regard to assisted dying practices and the information provided about vulnerable groups. Both of these factors have been discussed individually, but are part of the collective concern about the effect of end-of-life decision-making on a specific community, region or state.

The data on opinion polls will be discussed in greater detail in the following chapter, but as a precursor, the opinion poll data showed that the UK and the US both had a majority in favour of assisted dying practices, at least to some extent. The US had a rate of around 66 per cent of people who favoured assisted dying in some circumstances, although only about 33 per cent would have supported it in all circumstances.[27] In the UK, the rate is higher, with around 75 per cent being in support of assisted dying practices.[28] We should also remember that the data in relation to vulnerable groups, while not extensive, did not show that members of those groups were more likely to be pushed into taking an assisted dying option than those who were not.[29] Indeed, the most extensive evidence we have from the Netherlands and Oregon shows that the general patient who uses assisted dying tends to be white, middle-class, college-educated and with an average age younger than that of those who die of the underlying diseases. We therefore have little reason to uphold objections based either on majority opinions or questions about vulnerable groups, even if put in terms of a societal interest. Nor do we have any evidence that changes in the regulation to allow assisted dying have any long-term costs to the community at large in terms of a general loss of the 'respect for life'. There is no evidence to support this claim either from the Netherlands, Oregon or anywhere else where assisted dying is practised.

If those are not a viable issue, the remaining issue for larger groups may be whether or not the effect of things happening within a jurisdiction which others object to constitutes a sufficient basis for concern. In other words, even if members of these larger groups are not directly affected by a particular practice, are they entitled to object to the fact that a practice is happening within their jurisdiction? This has long been part of the discussion about liberal democracies and the limits of government. At the forefront in this discussion is the Hart–Devlin debate between H. L. A. Hart and Lord Devlin. While their debate

---

[27] Emanuel, 'Euthanasia and Physician-Assisted Suicide', 142.
[28] These include MORI polls and British Social Attitudes polls as well as those done by NOP. House of Lords Select Committee on the Assisted Dying for the Terminally Ill Bill. *Report [HL Paper 86-I]* (London: Stationery Office, 2005), paragraph 217.
[29] Battin *et al.*, 'Legal Physician-Assisted Dying in Oregon and the Netherlands'.

focused on the Wolfenden Report in the UK, the essential claims of the debate are relevant in a multitude of scenarios. The focus of the debate is two books. The first was *The Enforcement of Morals*, written by Lord Devlin.[30] Devlin argues in that book that society ought to be allowed to make criminal conduct which happens in private between consenting adults, even if there is no larger harm created by that conduct.[31] He does not allege that any and all private conduct can be regulated in this manner, though. He argues that it is only the type of conduct which is seen as being contrary to society's values which can be prohibited by the criminal law.[32] In order to offset the problem that this will make citizens possibly subject to the tyranny of the majority, Devlin asserts that a simple majority of society is not sufficient. Instead, he proposes what is essentially a reasonable person standard. If the actions in question are something the 'reasonable person' would see as being against society's morals, then it can be prohibited.[33] If it cannot, then it cannot be prohibited, even if a majority are opposed to the action in question.[34]

Hart's response is published in *Law, Liberty and Morality*.[35] In his response, Hart essentially relies on the 'one simple statement' from J. S. Mill which was discussed in the chapter on autonomy and paternalism.[36] Hart argued that liberal democracies should not prohibit conduct done by consenting adults which does not fall foul of the harm principle. Thus, exposing oneself in private to others is perfectly fine as long as everyone has consented to it. Exposing oneself in public is not, as it is likely to harm others (e.g. children). He thus carves out two separate spheres of morality. There is a public sphere where actions can be prohibited. There is also a private sphere where actions cannot be prohibited no matter how much others might see them as foolish or wrong, provided there is no harm to others. He also specifically addresses the point about whether any psychological distress caused by the fact that others are engaging in conduct which one finds offensive is sufficient to constitute harm.[37] Hart argues that it is not. He states that considering this harm misconceives the role of government in a liberal democracy. Governments should not interfere with the free consenting choices of members of society merely because others might be offended at things happening within their jurisdiction. As one of society's aims is to allow individuals to pursue their own vision of a

---

[30] P. Devlin, *The Enforcement of Morals* (Oxford University Press, 1965).
[31] *Ibid.*, pp. 24–25.   [32] *Ibid.*, p. 15.
[33] *Ibid.*   [34] *Ibid.*, p. 17.
[35] H. L. A. Hart, *Law, Liberty and Morality* (Stanford University Press, 1963).
[36] *Ibid.*, p. 5.   [37] *Ibid.*, pp. 45–47.

good life, it would be counter-productive to allow those who object, even without any harm to them, to prohibit conduct merely because it is happening within their society.[38] Consequently, governments cannot prohibit conduct if others are merely offended about a particular action or practice.

Hart's argument is the more convincing of the two. First, it is difficult to see how one could reasonably utilise the 'reasonable person' standard that Devlin articulates. He likens it to a jury decision but it would seem to be particularly difficult to subject these types of decisions to a jury or jury-type system. If we do not use that system, though, there does not appear to be any other alternative which does not end up being a simple opinion poll, either of the general public or of those in power (who may or may not be representative of the general public). Moreover, Hart does appear to have a firmer grasp on the notion of a liberal democracy. Many people in a society may do things which offend us. They may even do so to the point of physical illness. That does not mean, however, that we are entitled to a veto over these practices. I may, for example, be particularly offended by the prevalence of literature I find to be substandard. It may even make me physically sick to have to read writing which I conceive of as being below acceptable standards. That does not seem to give me any reason to override those who do like the literature I think is bad. Indeed, as I can simply avoid reading it or paying any attention to it, it seems like the easiest way out of the problem is for me to do that instead. Even if a number of people agree with me, it does not mean that our opinions on literature should necessarily override those who do like the literature in question. In other words, the question is whether my interests should override the interests of others, and unless I can point to some actual harm to ground my claim, there is no reason to prefer my preferences to theirs.

Even if one argues that Devlin's argument is correct, though, it is worth emphasising that it does not provide sufficient reason to prohibit assisted dying in this context. As noted above, opinion polls actually show that a majority of people are in favour of at least limited access to assisted dying. While, as Devlin argues, a simple majority is insufficient to trigger the criminal prohibition of conduct, it is difficult to see how a particular practice can offend a society's morals if a majority of them are actually in favour of it. So, Devlin's reasonable person standard would not provide a sufficient reason to prohibit assisted dying practices.

---

[38] *Ibid.*, p. 47.

2.4   Conclusions about the wider community

In conclusion, there are a number of issues which need to be taken account of when considering the impact of end-of-life decisions on the wider community. In particular, we should be more cognisant of the effects that these decisions may have on immediate family and friends. In some instances, such as where the presence of young children or pets is concerned, this can be done at the local level in the particular institution. At other times, it provides additional reasons which should be considered in general policy decisions by governments of particular jurisdictions. This includes questions about death rituals and ways to combat the stress and strain that affects those close to a terminally ill patient.

The same cannot really be said for broader groups which have less interaction with particular patients. Opinion polls and evidence available about vulnerable groups does not show that these are especially strong concerns. Nor, as our examination of the Hart–Devlin debate shows, should we consider the possibility of offence as being a particularly strong interest which should override more compelling interests of the individual. As such, while we need to consider the effect upon immediate groups of friends and family, we need not consider the effects on the wider community as an interest in itself.

3   Investigation and prevention of illegal conduct

Our second broad societal concern is the interest in the investigation and prevention of illegal conduct. As with most regulations, a crucial issue is how a jurisdiction may best ensure that the law is being followed. This is only more vital in a situation such as end-of-life decision-making which involves the possibility of harm and death to individuals. Governments, then, need to be able to effectively police these kinds of practices to make sure that laws are not being ignored, power – especially the power possessed by doctors in a clinical setting – is not being abused and that the system in general works as effectively as it can. Unfortunately, for end-of-life decision-making, there is the constant problem of doctor–patient confidentiality. This presents several different issues for end-of-life decision-making and the investigation and prevention of illegal conduct. First, the fact that doctors are able to claim any information is subject to confidentiality may make it significantly more difficult for police to make an initial determination of wrongful conduct. It may thus be difficult for police or other investigatory agencies to be able to decide which cases require further investigation as the preliminary information is likely to provide insufficient reason, on its own, to justify looking any further. As a result, many of the things that doctors or other health-care workers who engage in illegal practices do are to ensure that an investigation is not started. For example, in the *Angels of Death* study, doctors who engaged in underground euthanasia practices often made sure that a sympathetic funeral director was contacted as soon as possible to collect the body.[39] It was also considered to be standard practice to make sure the body was cremated, again as early as possible under the circumstances.[40] The stated reason for this practice was that a cremated body was incapable of being subject to an autopsy to determine the drugs in the patient's system.[41] Without this evidence, it would be very difficult for police or other investigators to be able to show that the patient had died by other than natural causes, especially when the cause of death listed on death certificates indicated the underlying disease.[42]

It does not get any easier once the first hurdle is overcome, however. Even if police or investigators are able to decide which cases are worthy of further investigation, it may be very difficult for them to get the additional information necessary to properly investigate suspected instances of illegal conduct. If they investigate a particular death that they think is suspicious, all they are likely to find is a cremated body and a death certificate which was unlikely to seem suspicious. Indeed, even if a particular death did raise questions, the cremation of the body often required prosecutors to switch a charge of murder to one of attempted murder.[43] Furthermore, much of the information which is necessary for the investigation and possible prosecution is likely to be within the exclusive control of the investigated party. Unless a doctor has indicated specifically on medical charts, for example, which drugs have been injected into the patient, there is not likely to be any way to trace the substances which have been administered. Some may note that most hospitals have systems in place for tracing particular drugs, making it easier to determine which patient has received which drugs. Many of these, however, involve self-reporting among medical staff and, even if they do not, there are ways around these particular systems. For example, we can look at Erin's story in *Angels of Death*.[44] Erin was a male nurse working in a hospital.[45] A female colleague approached him carrying two vials of

---

[39] Magnusson, *Angels of Death*, pp. 183–186.
[40] *Ibid.*, pp. 226–227. [41] *Ibid.*, pp. 226–229.
[42] *Ibid.*, pp. 228–229. [43] See, e.g., *R* v. *Cox* (1992) 12 BLMR 38.
[44] Magnusson, *Angels of Death*, p. 193.
[45] Erin apparently highlighted to Magnusson that the hospital in question was a Catholic one. *Ibid.*, p. 193. That not only makes the anecdote more surprising but

morphine. The female nurse indicated to Erin that the drugs had been removed in her name and that, while she did not want to put Erin in an uncomfortable situation, she believed that 'he could do what needs to be done'.[46] What this means was that the female nurse, who had signed out the drugs, was not the one giving them to the patient. Erin, who was being asked to inject the patient, would not show up on the record as having been issued the drugs. Without any way to link the female nurse and Erin to the particular case, there is likely to be little reason to know what happened.[47] This may be even more true if the investigation requires information from conversations or other sources which are less likely to be written down. All that the person being investigated needs to do is to lie, and since there is no evidence to the contrary, it may be difficult for police to insist the contrary is true.

What this all means is that the regulation of end-of-life decisions needs to include various mechanisms which can be used to investigate and prevent illegal conduct. This often includes reporting systems where doctors and patients are required to submit reports or other evidence about the practices which are occurring. A reporting system can take several forms, however, and it will be worth exploring some of the current systems in some depth. It will also be worth exploring additional ways to deal with the investigation and prosecution of illegal conduct.

3.1   Reporting systems

No jurisdiction of which I am aware mandates that all cases of withdrawing and withholding life-sustaining treatment be reported to any specific body. All deaths, obviously, have to be recorded and most if not all death certificates will indicate a cause of death, but there is no specific requirement that deaths resulting from the withdrawal or withholding of treatment be labelled as such. The same is true for deaths which result from palliative care. Certain deaths may be brought to the attention of legal authorities, either because of specific factual circumstances[48] or because medical or legal officials wish to seek clarification about aspects of the law. However, there is usually no requirement that

---

also indicates that one of the supposed important safeguards – the moral stance of hospitals and those working in hospitals – may be less successful than it is perceived to be.

[46] *Ibid.*, p. 193.   [47] *Ibid.*

[48] For example, the *Bland* decision resulted from the fact that Anthony Bland had been injured as a result of the Hillsborough disaster and it was still considered an open investigation by the coroner.

all deaths resulting from these methods should be reported to government.[49] The only jurisdictions which do have a reporting procedure for deaths related to end-of-life decisions are those which allow some form of assisted dying. The Netherlands and Belgium have similar reporting mechanisms and Oregon, while it differs from the Netherlands, also requires that deaths be reported. It is worth considering, as a result, the differences between those two reporting systems and the possible problems which have been created by those systems.

3.1.1   Description of current reporting systems in the Netherlands and Oregon   The Netherlands reporting system has been subject to a number of changes over the years. These changes have been largely based upon perceived deficiencies in previous reporting systems, most notably the concern about the reporting rate – a concern discussed more fully below. While a study of the historical development of the Dutch reporting system may be illuminating, our focus will be on the current system. At present, once a doctor has assisted a patient to die either through physician-assisted suicide or euthanasia, they are required to submit a report to the Regional Review Committees (RRCs). The RRCs were created in 1998 and consist of a doctor, a lawyer (who chairs the committee) and an ethicist. The RRCs are independent of the prosecutorial authorities. They review all of the cases, including cases which have been referred to them by parties other than the treating doctor. They have the power to investigate a particular report, including the ability to ask for further information from the doctors or to ask the doctors to give testimony either by phone or in person. They are also entitled to seek additional information from others including a required independent consultant.[50] These committees are able to make definitive judgments about whether a doctor in a particular case has been careful or not. If the RRC determines that the doctor has been careful, then the case is closed. If they have determined that a doctor has been 'not careful' they can then refer the case to prosecutors.[51] These decisions must be made within six weeks and must be in writing. A formal written decision is

---

[49] It was recommended in the *Bland* case that subsequent cases of withdrawal of treatment from incompetent patients should go to the courts. However, this only applied to those patients who were determined to be incompetent and the specified reason for the suggestion was so that a sufficient body of case could be developed to guide the practice of medical professionals. Thus, it was never supposed to be a long-standing policy but merely one which existed until medical professionals became confident in their ability to judge which sorts of treatments the courts would allow to be withdrawn and in what circumstances.
[50] Griffiths *et al.*, *Euthanasia and Law in Europe*, p. 205.
[51] *Ibid.*

therefore given in every case. The RRCs also produce annual reports. We therefore have a considerable amount of data relating to the working of these committees.

What these reports indicate is that a majority of cases reported to the RRCs do not go any further. For example, in 2005, the RRCs asked for additional information from the reporting doctor in 6 per cent of cases.[52] They asked for additional information from the consultant in 2.5 per cent of all cases and someone other than the reporting doctor or consultant in 0.3 per cent of cases.[53] Most often the requested additional information related to the consultation, the patient's suffering, the carrying out of euthanasia (e.g. the drugs used) or the voluntariness of the request.[54] Out of the 15,832 cases reported by the doctor during the period 1999–2006, the doctor was considered to be careful in 15,804 cases.[55] Of the remaining cases, 32 were cases where the committee was not considered competent to decide, 21 were cases where the doctor was considered careful but the case was referred to the Medical Inspector and 25 were considered 'not careful' and referred to the prosecutorial officials.[56] The two primary reasons that cases were determined to be not careful were questions about whether the consultation was adequate and whether the patient's suffering was unbearable.[57]

The Oregon reporting system is also mandatory. Any doctor who assists a patient to die under the Death with Dignity Act is required to report such deaths to the Oregon Health Department (OHD). Unlike the RRCs, however, the OHD is not an independent review agency which makes determinations about the legality of the doctor's actions.[58] The OHD's only statutory duty is to compile the data contained within the material they receive and prepare an annual report on the working of the Act.[59] As a result, while there are annual reports which are prepared, there are no individual judgments like in the Netherlands nor is there an independent investigation.[60]

---

[52] The majority of that 6 per cent came from requests for further written information (3.8 per cent). Less frequently, the RRCs asked for additional information by telephone (1.6 per cent) and in only 0.5 per cent was the doctor required to give evidence in person. *Ibid.*
[53] *Ibid.*   [54] *Ibid.*   [55] *Ibid.*
[56] *Ibid.*   [57] *Ibid.*, p. 206.
[58] Oregon Death with Dignity Act, 127.865 § 3.11.
[59] *Ibid.* The data from the annual reports are described in Chapter 9.
[60] The reports have also become much more limited in scope. The reports from the early years contained significantly more detail about the process of assisted dying in Oregon compared to the present ones. Compare, for example, the report for Year 1 to the report for the current year.

3.1.2   Evaluation of reporting systems   The creation of a reporting system, whether for assisted dying or for any other reason, does not, by itself, mean that the investigation and enforcement of legal rules is possible. The reporting system must also be effective. Doctors must use the reporting system and be truthful when they are reporting cases. Investigators must be able to verify information which is capable of corroboration, request further information if necessary and be confident in their ability to discern when doctors are not being truthful. Society in general must be able to have confidence in the decisions made as a result of the reporting of doctors and investigation by authorities, as well as being sure that reports are used properly and that both patients and medical professionals are properly protected. Both the Netherlands reporting system and the Oregon one have come under fire for not being as effective as supporters have claimed, although the precise reasons are not the same. For the Dutch, the primary problem has been the rate of reporting. For Oregon, the main concern has been the possibility of untruthful responses. Both issues will now be explored in greater detail.

3.2   The Dutch reporting rate

Concerns about the rate of reporting under the Netherlands system have plagued the Dutch since they began the national studies in 1990. The reporting rate in 1990 was 18 per cent. This had climbed to 41 per cent in 1995 but had reached only 54 per cent in 2001. By 2005, the rate had increased to 80 per cent. This has led Griffiths, Weyers and Adams to suggest the following:

> Regarded as the results of an experiment in legal control, such data are little short of spectacular. A new policy concerning behaviour that the state cannot observe directly, that requires expenditure of time and energy and involves some unpleasantness, and that requires the people concerned to run the risk of external criticism or even legal sanctions, started with an effectiveness of about zero, as one would expect. Within a decade and a half, this policy was producing the desired effects in four-fifths of all cases ...[61]

Others, however, will note that that still leaves 20 per cent of all cases being unreported. It is also probable that the cases which are not reported are those which are the greatest concern. As such, many will not share the opinion of Griffiths, Weyers and Adams and suggest instead that the policy has been a failure. If doctors will not report cases, then they

---

[61] Griffiths *et al.*, *Euthanasia and Law in Europe*, p. 199.

cannot be properly investigated. If they cannot be investigated, then conduct which is outside the bounds of law is unlikely to be caught and punished. More importantly, patients may be being killed when they do not want to be killed or in cases where it is not considered to be appropriate (when a patient is incompetent, for instance). For the Dutch, this rate has been a continual embarrassment and they have engaged in any number of methods designed to correct the low reporting rate. The general consensus has been that the problem with the reporting rate is that doctors, who know that they should report any assisted dying death as a 'non-natural' one, have instead been indicating on official records and reports that the deaths were natural.[62] In other words, the main concern was that the Dutch doctors were lying about what they had done. Methods, then, were taken to increase the rate of truthfulness among doctors.[63] This included changes to the reporting procedure to make it easier and more efficient as well as assurances to doctors that they would not be prosecuted provided they had acted appropriately. This has culminated in the Regional Review Committees described above and it is worth highlighting the considerable improvement between 2001 and 2005. Again, though, while the increase is substantial, it is still not close to 100 per cent, which is the obvious hope.[64]

A newer hypothesis has been proposed which might explain the problem. The new hypothesis does not focus on the lying of doctors, but examines the four national surveys in greater detail. As explained in Chapter 9, the surveys do not actually ask doctors if they have engaged in 'euthanasia' or 'physician-assisted suicide'. Instead, the surveys ask doctors about descriptions of practices. Thus, instead of asking a doctor if he or she has committed euthanasia, the survey asks a doctor if he or she injected the patient with medication which may have shortened or ended the patient's life. If the answer to that is yes, then the doctor is asked a number of other questions about intention and related issues. It is the researchers who then attach a particular label to those practices depending upon the answers given by the doctor. While this has some significant benefits for the research, it also means that the researchers

---

[62] *Ibid.*, p. 200.   [63] *Ibid.*

[64] It is unlikely that the response rate would ever be 100 per cent. Even if the other problems were dealt with, there are still some doctors who simply refuse to submit reports at all. *Ibid.*, p. 197. This is, of course, an issue that needs to be minimised, although it is unlikely to ever be completed eliminated. Some doctors, for what they perceive to be good reasons or not, will not report and it may not be possible to change their minds, either through changes in the process, prosecution or other methods. Keeping the number of doctors who take this view to the minimum number possible should be seen as an aim of any reporting system, although the methods used to reduce this number are similar to the ones used to increase the response rate in general.

may be attaching a particular label to a practice which is different from the one the doctor would have given to the events in question. In other words, while a researcher might have considered a particular case to be an instance of euthanasia, the doctor might not have done so. Doctors on the whole, then, might not be engaged in the practice of lying and are, in fact, reporting all the cases they believe should be reported.[65] It is simply that doctors and the researchers disagree over whether a specific case is actually an example of 'euthanasia' or not.[66]

This hypothesis was studied by two researchers in the Netherlands. Den Hartogh recalculated the response rate based upon the assumption that doctors did not classify a case as euthanasia based upon their intention but by the drug used by the doctor.[67] Using what is referred to as a 'rough and ready' way of calculating the rate, he came to the conclusion that the reporting rate in 2001 was about 90 per cent instead of the 54 per cent that is indicated by the national surveys.[68] A second researcher, Van Tol, further investigated the hypothesis and concluded that doctors 'report almost all cases' that they believe are considered euthanasia.[69] Further support for this hypothesis is in the fourth national survey. In the 2005 survey, doctors were asked in the death-certificate survey to indicate how they would classify the particular death. In about 25 per cent of the cases the researchers had determined were euthanasia, the doctors classified them as something different.[70] Most of the time, the doctors indicated that they considered the death to be the result of palliative care or terminal sedation. Apparently, this is due in large part to the fact that doctors seem to classify their cases based upon, as suggested by Den Hartogh, the drug used as opposed to the intention of the doctors.[71] In cases where a muscle relaxant is used, doctors tend to see the case as euthanasia.[72] On the other hand, if morphine or other opioids are used, doctors were much more likely to classify the case as palliative care or terminal sedation.[73] What this means for the reporting rate is striking. If cases involving opioids are excluded from the reporting, the rate in 2005 was 99 per cent; the rate was 73 per cent in both 1995 and 2001.[74] If this is correct, then the Dutch do not have the problem with the reporting rate which has always been suggested. This has led Griffiths, Weyers and Adams to suggest that:

The new approach to the reporting rate first suggested by Den Hartogh, given a solid empirical and theoretical foundation by Van Tol, and overwhelmingly confirmed in the 2005 national research, entirely changes the policy problem.

[65] *Ibid.*, p. 202.   [66] *Ibid.*   [67] *Ibid.*, p. 203.
[68] *Ibid.*   [69] *Ibid.*   [70] *Ibid.*   [71] *Ibid.*
[72] *Ibid.*   [73] *Ibid.*, pp. 203–204.   [74] *Ibid.*, p. 204.

It is no longer principally one of inducing doctors to be honest about what they are doing, but rather one of accomplishing a higher degree of what Van Tol calls 'cognitive solidarity' between, on the one hand, doctors whose reporting is the foundation of the entire system of control, and on the other hand those who seek to measure or control what doctors do.[75]

That, of course, does not mean that there is not still a problem. It merely means that doctors are willing to report cases that they believe fit within the category of euthanasia and a significant number of them do not lie as has always been thought. There is, however, a substantial disconnect between the way the researchers see the practice of euthanasia and the way doctors do. Prosecutors, as well, do not see euthanasia in the same way as doctors do.[76] This is still a significant problem and needs to be corrected. Those within the Netherlands need to come to firm conclusions about what they wish to see doctors report and make sure that doctors understand those regulations. Currently, this does not appear to be happening. It is worth highlighting again, though, that the essential problem may not be the one which has always been feared – that doctors performing euthanasia will always be, irrespective of the importance of reporting, reluctant to tell authorities what they have done in cases of assisted dying.

3.3   The usefulness of the Oregon reports

Oregon, as far as it is possible to tell, does not have the same response-rate problem that has plagued the Dutch. It may be, of course, that doctors in Oregon are no better or worse than their Dutch counterparts in reporting incidences of illegal behaviour. However, there is no empirical evidence which indicates a refusal to report as a problem with the Oregon Death with Dignity Act. This does not mean, though, that the Oregon reporting system is free from criticism. In Oregon, the problem is not perceived to be a failure to report at all, but a failure to report the truth.

This problem has also arisen because of government-sponsored research, in this case, the OHD annual reports. There were admissions made in the reports of early years that the researchers could not vouch for the veracity of the reports they had been given and that the reports may be a 'cock and bull' story.[77] Much has been made about this admission from commentators. Additionally, some have argued that there is important information which the reports should contain and do not.

[75] Ibid.   [76] Ibid., p. 203.
[77] Keown, Euthanasia, Ethics and Public Policy, p. 180.

For example, some have argued that the reports should also include an indication of whether a prospective patient was refused aid in dying under the Act and how many times a refusal was given prior to the reporting doctor agreeing to provide assistance.[78] This particular claim arises from the first reported case in Oregon where a patient had seen two previous doctors before being given assistance under the Act by a doctor associated with Compassion in Dying, a group which has long supported the legalisation of assisted dying practices.[79] It further came to light that one of the refusals was from the family doctor of the patient and they had known each other quite well.[80]

Since these are two separate issues, it is worth considering them independently. The first is the question as to whether Oregon doctors are really lying. It is worth being clear when examining this as to what was actually stated by the Oregon annual reports. While a considerable amount of fuss was made about the admission by the researchers, it should be highlighted that the researchers were not stating that they had any reason to believe that doctors were, in fact, lying on the official reports.[81] The researchers did not point towards any evidence which showed or even suggested that the reports they had received were false.[82] So, the Oregon researchers were not indicating in the annual reports that they believed they had been lied to by doctors filing reports under the Death with Dignity Act. Nor am I aware of any subsequent information which has come out indicating that doctors in Oregon are prone to lying on the reports. All that the Oregon researchers indicated was that they could not provide independent verification of the material contained within the reports.[83] They could provide the statistical data and could confirm that data was consistent with the reports they had received. Due to the statutory role played by the OHD, however, they did not have the investigatory power to be able to verify the content of that data as being true. We should therefore be clear as to the actual problem with the Oregon reports. The issue should not be whether the doctors involved are lying. It may be that they are, or it may be that they are not. We are simply incapable of knowing at the present time. The real issue with the Oregon reporting system is that the OHD does not

---

[78] *Ibid.*, p. 173. See also K. Foley and H. Hendin, 'The Oregon Experiment', in K. Foley and H. Hendin (eds.), *The Case against Assisted Suicide* (Baltimore: Johns Hopkins University Press, 2002), pp. 144–174.

[79] H. Hendin, K. Foley and M. White, 'Physician-Assisted Suicide: Reflections on Oregon's First Case' (1998–1999) 14 *Issues in Law and Medicine* 243–270, 244.

[80] *Ibid.*

[81] A. E. Chin *et al.* 'Legalized Physician-Assisted Suicide in Oregon: The First Year's Experience' (1999) 340 *New England Journal of Medicine* 577–583, 583.

[82] *Ibid.*   [83] *Ibid.*

have any investigatory powers and neither, really, does anyone else.[84] Consequently, it is not possible for Oregon to determine which doctors have been untruthful and to what extent they were untruthful. That is, obviously, a considerable problem. If governments are unable to investigate potential wrongdoing, it will be difficult to curtail it. It is therefore an argument in support of a system for investigating the reports as opposed to merely creating a system which has reporting. There can be any number of ways that an investigatory process is created in addition to supplement the mandatory reporting system. Probably the easiest to implement would be to simply require that all reports go to the police as well as the OHD, and to charge the police with investigating any suspect reports. Alternatively, one could require, as draft legislation sometimes does, a pre-death panel.[85] This would be a panel – usually of legal, medical or ethical experts – whose role it is to explore these things prior to the death of the patient. If the panel agrees, then the patient may be assisted to die. If not, then the patient is not able to do so. A third possibility is the use of post-death panels such as the Regional Review Committees used in the Netherlands. These panels do not investigate the case prior to the death of the patient but do investigate after the report has been filed. These investigatory panels have the ability to explore in greater depth the material contained within the report and refer any cases which are problematic to the proper authorities. A final suggestion, again from the Netherlands, involves the use of specifically trained medical professionals (called SCEN doctors by the Dutch) who act as consultants in assisted dying cases.[86] They provide a pre-death screening and advice to medical professionals. While their role does not supersede the role played by the RRCs, the involvement of the SCEN doctors is considered to be best practice and is looked upon favourably by the committees. Whichever method is chosen, however, it is clear that the Oregon system requires a more robust investigatory mechanism.

The second problem concerns the material which is relayed to the OHD in the official reports. It is crucial that the right sort of information be contained within the reports which are submitted by doctors. Doctors should be required to make sure that the information which is provided is sufficient for investigators to be able to discern which cases are suspicious and which are not, as well as providing greater

---

[84] The reporting procedure is explained more thoroughly in Chapter 9.
[85] See, e.g., Terry Pratchett's suggestion at www.guardian.co.uk/commentisfree/2010/ feb/01/terry-pratchett-alzheimer-assisted-suicide (accessed 21 June 2011).
[86] Griffiths *et al.*, *Euthanasia and Law in Europe*, p. 195.

information about the workings of the process in general. Agencies should also have the ability to modify the official reports to make sure that evidence which may not have initially been seen as crucial can be added and information which is not but was thought to be can be removed. States, however, should also be aware that too much or irrelevant data is not to be preferred merely in order to have it. More relevant data, not simply increasing the overall amount of data, needs to be the paramount justification for what is contained in the report. The suggestion noted above about refused requests provides a good analysis of this. Knowing the number of previous refused requests for a patient may lead to pertinent information but is not necessarily relevant on its own terms. Simply knowing that a patient has had a previous request for assistance denied does not mean, in and of itself, that anything was wrong in the particular case. Even if, like the first recorded case, there were multiple refused requests or that previous refusals came from doctors with longer-standing relationships does not mean that the subsequently accepted request was problematic. Charged circumstances may account for the different decisions, as may a host of other factors which have nothing to do with the inherent correctness or incorrectness of a particular decision.[87] The number of refused requests, without further context, probably tells us very little. This does not mean that the number of previous refused requests cannot be part of a package which does tell us useful information. If, for example, doctors within a particular practice or aligned with a particular group tend to take patients who have been refused elsewhere even by doctors who do not have conscientious objections, this might provide us with a sufficient reason to look further. It may be that there is nothing untoward in such cases but it may be that there are factors which need to be considered. Thus, if this was to be considered part of the report, the purpose for which it is being used as well as why the information may be relevant need to be clear. If there are significant reasons for its inclusion, those can be stated in relevant documentation. If it is merely being collected for the sake of collecting data, then it may be problematic to do so. It should also be stressed that the information must be the type of information which is readily available to the doctor, especially if the reporting individual is subject to sanction for providing misleading or incorrect information. So, it may be important to consider whether doctors would have sufficient information about, for example, previous refused requests and

---

[87] For example, the previous doctors may have had conscientious objections to the practice of assisted suicide. If this is the case, those doctors should not be required to perform assisted suicide and could rightly refuse the request without it making any fundamental statement about the 'appropriateness' of the request.

in such a manner as to be able to verify its truthfulness. If a doctor is unlikely to know the information or is not likely to be able to confirm its veracity, it may be unfair to require a doctor to provide it and suffer penalties if it later turns out to be wrong. Thus, when considering what kind of information needs to be provided in official reports, we need to consider the usefulness of that data as well as the available means for collecting it.

3.4   Other problems with reporting systems

In addition to the main problems listed with the Dutch and Oregon reporting systems, there may be other problems which occur with any reporting system for end-of-life decisions. While these may not be considered to be significant, they are worthy of a brief discussion. The first of these concerns is perceived adverse effects for doctors. Even if doctors know that they have complied with the relevant guidelines (and thus do not fear prosecution as such), there may be reasons why doctors are reluctant to report cases under a reporting system. They may believe that the reporting system created needless inconvenience by requiring the filling out of lengthy forms about their practices.[88] Doctors may also fear that reports, if they became public, might subject them to needless public scrutiny irrespective of whether that scrutiny included any authorised investigatory agency. Doctors may feel that, for example, if the names of doctors participating in certain practices were disclosed in the media it would have an adverse affect upon their ability to help patients. Doctors may also fear the process of investigation, even if they believe they have done nothing wrong.[89] They may fear that the investigation will take a considerable amount of time, that those investigating may see things differently from the doctor or that other factors may make the investigation process itself particularly worrisome.[90] Finally, doctors may be concerned about the effect that reporting has on the rights of patients or the wishes of a family.[91] They may believe that the filing of reports about end-of-life decisions interferes with the grief that families suffer and that patients will be concerned about the amount of information which might be submitted with the report.

These concerns can be best addressed by the processes which are part of any reporting system. For example, the question of inconvenience can be best handled by the forms themselves and what information is considered necessary to input as part of them. Questions about

[88] Griffiths *et al.*, *Euthanasia and Law in Europe*, p. 197.
[89] *Ibid.*   [90] *Ibid.*   [91] *Ibid.*

subjecting doctors to public scrutiny or the effect upon the family can be tackled best by considerations about the confidentiality of the submitted forms. The period of investigation can be expressly stated by rules setting out time limits, as happens in the Netherlands. All of these, then, are issues which can be readily addressed by the rules for the reporting process.

The same can be said for an additional problem related to insurance claims. One possible issue which may arise from any end-of-life decision which causes death is that it may adversely affect either health insurance or life insurance claims that the patient may have. For example, many life insurance policies will have suicide clauses which invalidate the policy if the patient died as a result of suicide. Doctors may have concerns about whether a patient who dies by making a particular end-of-life decision (for example, for physician-assisted suicide) is invalidating a life insurance policy. Most jurisdictions, however, specify in any legislation that death by certain medical decisions at the end of life are not cause for invalidating insurance policies.[92]

3.5   Prosecution and conviction of illegal activity

The reporting and investigation of potential abuses is only the first step to any effective enforcement of regulations. Once conduct which is illegal has been found, it needs to be prosecuted. This may seem an obvious truism but it is well worth emphasising as any number of current prohibitions on end-of-life decision-making often do not prosecute offenders. Prosecutions, either within the bounds of law or through professional regulations, rarely occur in instances where a doctor has not complied with the appropriate rules for end-of-life decisions. Even if they do, convictions seldom result. Sometimes, of course, this results from problems related to the provision of evidence by prosecution officials who may be hampered by the doctor–patient confidentiality questions we have been exploring. At other times, however, even when it is clear from the evidence what has occurred, it does not mean that a conviction has resulted.[93] Finally, even if a prosecution had ended in a conviction for the doctor, there may be only a minimal punishment applied to the defendant.[94] All of these present significant problems

---

[92] See, e.g., Oregon Death with Dignity Act, 127.875 § 3.13.
[93] Timothy Quill was not indicted by a grand jury nor was he sanctioned by the New York Board of Medicine. However, his actions are quite clear as they are outlined in the article he published in the *New England Journal of Medicine*. Quill, 'Death and Dignity'.
[94] *R* v. *Cox* (1992) 12 BLMR 38.

for any system of regulating end-of-life decisions. If practices which
have been made illegal have been made so for a reason, our reticence to
apply the appropriate punishments – by prosecutors, judges, juries and
professional bodies – seems inappropriate. On the other hand, if our
responses to investigations of conduct which is considered illegal are
more indicative of our views, it is worth investigating why we continue
to hold onto the illegality of certain practices.

Prosecutorial policies are rarely discussed openly to allow those
charged with prosecuting cases to have needed discretion. At best, there
are usually statements about how prosecutors should take into account
the evidence, the possibility of conviction and the public interest in
bringing the case but all of those are vague and unspecific. Moreover,
prosecutors are not often subject to review for failing to bring cases,
especially when the public is unaware that a case existed.[95] As a result,
it is often difficult to get precise facts about the actions of prosecutors
in cases involving end-of-life decisions. In addition to any problems
this causes for those seeking to evaluate prosecutorial policy, it will also
have adverse effects on doctors and patients. The recent *Purdy* case
in the UK is an indication of this.[96] In the case, Debbie Purdy was a
woman suffering from progressive multiple sclerosis.[97] She was considering travelling from her home in the UK to Switzerland for the purposes of assisted dying.[98] In order to do so when she was ready to die,
she would most likely have needed the help of her husband to travel.[99]
She was concerned, though, that if he did help her, he would be subject
to criminal prosecution under the Suicide Act, which makes it illegal
in the UK to assist a suicide. She petitioned the courts to require the
Director of Public Prosecutions (DPP) to issue guidance as to when
prosecutions would be brought in cases similar to hers so that she could
properly determine whether to involve her husband. In the last decision
of the House of Lords, her appeal was upheld and the DPP was directed
to promulgate guidance about assisted suicide and when a prosecution
would be brought.[100] The DPP complied by promulgating an interim
policy on 23 September 2009 and beginning a consultation process

[95] There are, obviously, notable exceptions such as the *Jepson* case in the UK. *Jepson* v.
The Chief Constable of West Mercia Police Constabulary [2003] EWHC 3318 (Admin).
This case involved the judicial review of a decision not to investigate and then prosecute a doctor who had, allegedly, failed to comply with the Abortion Act in the
UK by terminating a foetus with a cleft lip and palate. Even in that case, the police
were merely directed to reinvestigate and put the case forward for prosecution if it
merited it.
[96] *R (on the application of Purdy)* v. *Director of Public Prosecutions*, [2010] 1 A.C. 345.
[97] *Ibid.* at 381–382.   [98] *Ibid.*
[99] *Ibid.*   [100] *Ibid.* at 395–396.

about the policy. This concluded with the publication of a final policy in February 2010.[101]

The policy of the DPP, then, gives some guidance about when prosecutors should bring cases for assisting a suicide, although the policy itself makes it clear that it does not change the underlying legal status of assisted suicide within the UK.[102] It thus does not change the law to make assisted suicide legal. All it does is to provide some indication of when prosecutors are likely to bring a prosecution against those who have broken the law. The guidance does not provide detailed statements which can be read as definitive judgments in advance, however. It provides general statements about the types of things that prosecutors should consider when deciding whether a prosecution is in the public interest. So, while there are no certain answers contained in the policy, it does provide a general scheme which can be used by prosecutors and the public. Most importantly for our purposes, the DPP's guidance does not prioritise the help of a doctor or other health-care practitioner. Doctors and other health-care workers are, on the contrary, excluded from assisting a patient to die.[103] In fact, the 'assister' which seems most likely to avoid prosecution according to the guidance is someone without professional ties to the patient, who assists wholly for the reason of compassion and who provides minimal assistance.[104] The policy is thus unlike the assisted dying policies of a number of other jurisdictions such as the Netherlands, Belgium and Oregon, where the stated preference has always included a health-care professional. This may be in part because the case in question before the House of Lords involved a patient wanting her husband to help her travel to a jurisdiction where assisted suicide was legal and therefore would have been at the forefront of the DPP's consideration when setting out the guidance. It may also be partially because the guidance primarily deals with (although not exclusively so) cases where patients travel to another jurisdiction for assisted dying. It is not primarily seen as involving cases of assisted dying within the UK.

It may also be difficult to determine the actual effect of the policy. Prosecutions for assisting a suicide or euthanasia were exceedingly rare prior to the publication of the policy and usually occurred only in cases where the defendant had made it very obvious that something had happened. Even publicised cases of people helping someone to travel to

---

[101] Director of Public Prosecutions, *Policy for Prosecutors in Respect of Cases of Encouraging or Assisting Suicide* (London: Stationery Office, 2010). Available at: http://tiny.cc/8y8li (accessed 21 June 2011).

[102] *Ibid.*, paragraphs 5, 6.   [103] *Ibid.*, paragraphs 43, 14.

[104] *Ibid.*, paragraph 45.

Switzerland for assisted dying had not brought a prosecution previously.[105] The policy, therefore, may bring some public clarity to what prosecutors were doing anyway. Unfortunately, the policy is too new for anyone to have done any comprehensive research about the policy, so its impact is uncertain at the moment. What it does do for us is to highlight the inherent problems in bringing a prosecution in these sorts of cases.

Once a prosecution has been brought, we must still deal with the significant problem of conviction and sentencing for violations of any regulation on end-of-life decisions. We can consider this through the lens of three cases which have been brought before the courts in the US and UK. The first is the US case of Dr Timothy Quill. Dr Quill is a well-known figure in the US with regard to end-of-life decision-making. This comes primarily from a case involving a patient he had named Diane. She was suffering from cancer and asked Dr Quill to provide her with a sufficient amount of drugs to kill herself.[106] After a period of reflection which included contacting an anonymous medical ethics hotline, he agreed to the request and gave Diane the drugs. She went to a cabin she owned by a lake, asked her husband and son to take a walk and died after ingesting the drugs she had been given by Dr Quill.[107] The reason we have this information is that Dr Quill wrote an article for the *New England Journal of Medicine* where he detailed the events in question.[108] In other words, we have Dr Quill's own statements as a matter of public record. There are no concerns about identity as he writes in the first person in the article, attaches his name to it and at no point indicates anything other than it is a true account of one of his cases.[109] We thus appear to have a clear case of illegal conduct on the part of Dr Quill as well as a wealth of evidence on which to convict him. Despite

---

[105] One such case is that of Daniel James. He was a 23-year-old man who had been injured in a rugby match and had become paralysed as a result. Seeking to end his life, Daniel travelled to Switzerland with his parents to a Dignitas clinic, where he eventually committed suicide with assistance. The West Mercia police investigated Daniel's suicide to determine whether or not his parents and a family friend should be prosecuted for murder. The DPP refused to prosecute and published a report explaining why on 9 December 2008. That report can be found at: www.cps.gov.uk/news/articles/death_by_suicide_of_daniel_james (accessed 21 June 2011).

[106] Quill, 'Death and Dignity', 693.

[107] *Ibid.*   [108] *Ibid.*

[109] A previous short article in the *Journal of American Medicine* (*JAMA*) entitled 'It's Over, Debbie' also purported to be a first-person account by a doctor who had engaged in euthanasia somewhere within the US. Anonymous, 'A Piece of My Mind' (8 January 1988) 259(2) *JAMA* 272. It was published anonymously and the editors refused to disclose who had submitted the article. Therefore it was incapable of being traced back to the original author. It was also unclear whether the story was a true account of something which had happened to the author or was merely fictional.

that, when the case was brought before a grand jury in New York, they refused to indict.[110] Dr Quill was also brought before the New York Medical Board, but they also refused to sanction him, claiming that he could not have been sure of the purpose for which Diane was going to use the drugs, even though the article clearly indicates that he knew she was intending to use the drugs to kill herself. Dr Quill even wrote a further article where he again confirmed that he knew the reasons she had requested the drugs and what she was going to do with them.[111]

There are further problems that prosecutors might face at trial due to the (infamous) doctrine of double effect. This is a specific legal doctrine which holds that doctors may prescribe medication to patients which shortens life provided that the intention of the doctor in doing so was for pain relief. The doctrine of double effect has been used throughout history in a variety of different contexts but appears to have first been formulated by Christian theologians.[112] It has four important components.[113] First, the action under discussion must be something which is not morally wrong. It must be at least neutral on moral terms. Second, the agent must intend to bring about the good effect but not the bad one. The bad effect must be merely foreseen but not the purpose of the action in question. Third, one cannot achieve the good end by the bad means. In other words, the bad effect cannot be used to achieve what is considered the good end.[114] Finally, the bad effect must be proportionate to the good effect. In other words, the bad effect cannot clearly outweigh the good one.[115]

In legal terms, this has generally been limited to cases where a doctor prescribes pain medication to patients in sufficient doses that it may have an effect upon respiration.[116] The seminal case in the UK

---

[110] It is worth stating, for those unfamiliar with the US grand jury system, the oft-quoted statement that 'a good prosecutor could get a grand jury to indict a ham sandwich'. Sol Wachtler, the former New York State chief judge appears to be the author of the statement which also appears in the novel *Bonfire of the Vanities*.

[111] Quill, 'The Ambiguity of Clinical Intentions'.

[112] James Rachels, *The End of Life* (Oxford University Press, 1996), p. 16.

[113] *Ibid*.

[114] Sometimes people will argue that the doctrine of double effect can be used to justify things like terrorism. They argue that the terrorists could claim that their intention is not to destroy buildings or kill people but to achieve their stated political or religious aims. Thus, they do not intend the killings but merely foresee them. This is an incorrect attempt at using the doctrine of double effect because it fails this third requirement. Even if we assume the stated political and/or religious aims were good, they are accomplished by the bad effect. Therefore, the doctrine of double effect is inapplicable in such cases.

[115] Huxtable, *Euthanasia, Ethics and the Law*, pp. 11–12.

[116] Medical research has indicated that pain medication, even if taken in large doses, does not actually lead to patients dying any quicker. N. Sykes and A. Thorns,

about this was the previously discussed *R* v. *Adams*, where a doctor had injected a patient named Mrs Morrell with a combination of morphine, heroin and a sleeping agent. She received four injections, two after she had fallen into a coma, and she died shortly thereafter. At trial, Dr Adams argued that he had not intended the death of Mrs Morrell but had merely intended to deal with her pain. There were several concerns raised by Dr Adams's conduct, including the fact that he, despite claiming otherwise on the death certificate, was entitled under the will of Mrs Morrell to a Rolls Royce car and a chest of silver. Even with these concerns, Devlin J instructed the jury that they could find Dr Adams not guilty if they thought the primary purpose of the injections had been pain relief. The jury acquitted Dr Adams and the defence has been part of English Common Law ever since.[117] What this has meant is that doctors often have a ready-made defence to the death of a patient and can claim the doctrine of double effect provided that the drugs they use are capable of a therapeutic effect.

This brings us to the final problem which is in the sentencing of doctors even if a conviction is possible. The main UK case of euthanasia is a Crown Court decision in *R* v. *Cox*.[118] Dr Cox injected his patient, Lillian Boyes, with two ampoules of potassium chloride after she had repeatedly requested that he kill her.[119] Ms Boyes, who was suffering from rheumatoid arthritis, had been in considerable pain and was terminally ill. After injecting her, Dr Cox noted the drugs he had administered on Ms Boyes' medical chart.[120] This came to the attention of a nurse who realised that potassium chloride does not have any therapeutic effect in that dosage and informed the authorities. An attempted murder charge was brought against Dr Cox,[121] who was unable to use the doctrine of double effect because of the drug he had used and its non-therapeutic effect. Dr Cox was convicted by the jury but he received only a

---

'Sedative Use in the Last Week of Life and the Implications for End-of-Life Decision Making' (2003) 163 *Archives of Internal Medicine* 341; N. Sykes and A. Thorns, 'The Use of Opioids and Sedatives at the End of Life' (2003) 4 *The Lancet Oncology* 312; A. Thorns and N. Sykes, 'Opioid Use in the Last Week of Life and Implications for End-of-Life Decision-Making' (2000) 356 *The Lancet* 398. Consequently, the doctrine of double effect, at least in terms of defences to criminal charges by medical professionals, may not ever be factually true. Either the doctor intended the patient to die or the pain medication was not the cause of death. Despite this, the doctrine of double effect still is considered a valid legal defence for doctors.

[117] Those interested in the details of the Adams case would be well served to read Huxtable's *Euthanasia, Ethics and the Law*, which details some of the more disturbing elements of the case, at least according to the Detective Chief Superintendent who investigated Dr Adams. *Euthanasia, Ethics and the Law*, p. 98. These were also discussed previously in Chapter 11.

[118] *R* v. *Cox* (1992) 12 BLMR 38.

[119] *Ibid.*   [120] *Ibid.*   [121] *Ibid.*

12-month suspended sentence as a result.[122] He was also, like Dr Quill, not struck off the medical register, although he did have to undergo a period of retraining and was required to be supervised for a period of time. This is consistent with the general practice that those who commit illegal acts involving end-of-life decisions such as assisting a patient to die often receive very minimal sentences.

As a result, the criminal justice system may seem an unsatisfactory vehicle for regulating end-of-life decisions. Prosecutions for violations of the law regarding end-of-life decisions are rare, even where there is sufficient evidence to bring a case to trial. Even if a prosecution is brought, there is no guarantee that judges and juries will convict a doctor for engaging in assisted dying practices. Finally, even if a conviction is possible, sentences are likely to be minimal. It is hard to claim that the process is best suited to creating a deterrent to engaging in criminal behaviour.

Alternatively, one might consider a quasi-criminal body such as the Dutch Regional Review Committees, which were described previously. These bodies take the responsibility of investigating and deciding out of the hands of the criminal justice system for a majority of end-of-life cases. Only the cases considered to be egregious are handled within the criminal justice system. Instead, the standard cases are handled by the RRCs which can build up expertise about these kinds of cases and the relevant information about them (such as the drugs used), which can be vital to determining what happened in a specific set of facts. However, the RRCs are unlikely to be effective in jurisdictions where the practices in question are illegal per se and very unlikely to be useful without an efficient reporting system. As part of a comprehensive solution to end-of-life decisions, they have an important part to play, but would not be useful on their own to curb the problem inherent in many jurisdictions about end-of-life decision-making.

4   Conclusion

In conclusion, we have considered two issues in this chapter which primarily affect the larger community as opposed to the individual patient–health-care professional relationship. This includes concerns about the effect of end-of-life decisions on the larger community. We considered that the effect is likely to be different as there may be any number of different communities which are impacted by a particular case. This may include immediate family and friends, local communities and

---

[122] Otlowski, *Voluntary Euthanasia and the Common Law*, p. 144.

more regional and national ones. The impact upon these communities is varied and we need to consider carefully how much influence each community ought to have in relation to end-of-life decisions. The emphasis in this chapter was on more immediate groups as this group is often the least considered by the literature but is also the most affected. However, some consideration was given to the larger communities and, in particular, the question about whether the fact that something is happening in a society which someone disapproves of is sufficient reason to claim that person is harmed.

We also considered the problems inherent in investigating and preventing instances of illegal activity. We looked at the current reporting systems in the Netherlands and Oregon and problems which exist under those systems as well as additional problems suggested by commentators. We have also looked at the questions surrounding the prosecution and conviction of doctors who might have engaged in conduct which is considered illegal. As has been shown, there are significant problems with the way these are currently handled in most jurisdictions, with instances of illegal conduct being rarely prosecuted and even more rarely punished. If we take the issues raised about end-of-life decision-making seriously, this should be of fundamental concern.

13   Slippery slope arguments

1   Introduction

One of the most fundamental issues involved in any discussion about end-of-life care is the infamous slippery slope argument. These arguments are used fairly regularly across the spectrum of issues, whether specifically in bioethical issues or in public policy more broadly. Their frequent use, however, does not mean that they are readily understood. In fact, there are many confusions about slippery slope arguments, how they operate, and how best to evaluate them. As a result, it will first be necessary to describe slippery slope arguments in some detail and explain the two main types of slippery slope argument. It will also be vital to explain the mechanisms of how a slippery slope operates and why it is not, in all cases, an example of bad reasoning. After we have set that groundwork, it will be possible to explore the specific slippery slope arguments which are used in the end-of-life context.

2   Slippery slope arguments

We shall start our discussion with a description of slippery slope arguments. Slippery slope arguments often go by different names such as 'thin edge of the wedge' arguments or 'camel's nose' arguments, but they are all essentially the same thing.[1] These form a subset of what philosophers call, more broadly, arguments from consequences. A slippery slope argument argues that something should not be done for reasons other than intrinsic qualities of the event in question. Instead, the focus is on the consequences of that event. It proposes that since the consequences of an action are undesirable, we should prevent things from coming into existence which allow those consequences to exist. In other words, to prevent something bad from happening, we should

[1] E. Volokh, 'The Mechanisms of the Slippery Slope' (2003) 116 *Harvard Law Review* 1026–1137, 1032.

refuse to do some other thing, even if that other thing is not actually bad in itself.

The structure of a slippery slope argument takes the following general form. We could consider some event (A) which is under our control. Usually, in the context in which we are discussing slippery slope arguments, this involves state regulation of something, but that need not always be the case. Our initial event A is not bad in itself. Usually, it is either something generally conceived of as being good, is considered good by the intended audience[2] or is something we generally consider to be neither good nor bad. However, there is also another event we can call B. B is an event which is believed will result from A and is definitively something we don't want to happen. Since B follows from A, we should avoid allowing A to occur, even if the only bad result is that it leads to B.[3]

Consequently, we need two elements to make a slippery slope argument. The first element we can call the slope aspect. We need there to be at least two distinct practices, and the second needs to be considered worse than the first. In other words, we need to have a downward slope from a morally and/or legally acceptable first practice to a morally and/or legally unacceptable second practice.[4] There may be intervening steps between the two practices but there only needs to actually be two distinct practices.[5] The second and usually more controversial element is the slippery aspect. This is the likelihood of sliding from A to B. There are two important factors which should be resolved when considering the slipperiness of any particular slope. First, it is important to consider the likelihood of slippage. It will make a difference if the slide from A to B is merely possible or whether it is probable.[6] The more likely it is that a slide from A to B will happen, the greater force the slippery slope argument will have.[7] If, conversely, there is only a theoretical

---

[2] The intended audience may be especially crucial depending upon the slippery slope argument employed. The argument is only effective as a persuasive tool if those hearing the argument consider A and B (the bad effect) in the same light as the speaker. If the audience, however, sees B as being preferable to A, then there is likely to be little persuasive appeal. See S. W. Smith, 'Evidence for the Practical Slippery Slope in the Debate on Physician-Assisted Suicide and Euthanasia' (2005) 13 *Medical Law Review* 17–44, 20.

[3] D. Enoch, 'Once You Start Using Slippery Slope Arguments, You're on a Very Slippery Slope' (2001) 211 *Oxford Journal of Legal Studies* 629–647, 631.

[4] Volokh, 'The Mechanisms of the Slippery Slope', 1030.

[5] Enoch, 'Once You Start Using Slippery Slope Arguments, You're on a Very Slippery Slope', 631.

[6] R. G. Frey, 'The Fear of a Slippery Slope', in G. Dworkin, R. G. Frey and S. Bok (eds.), *Euthanasia and Physician-Assisted Suicide: For and Against* (Cambridge University Press, 1998) pp. 43–63, 44, 46.

[7] *Ibid.*

possibility of a slide from A to B, the particular argument in question is unlikely to have much force. The second factor which may impact upon the slipperiness of any specific argument is the steepness of that slide. Essentially, this is a claim about how bad B actually is. If B is very bad, we may be more loath than normal to accept the possibility of slide, even if that possibility is not very large.[8] On the other hand, if B is not particularly bad at all, then a greater likelihood of a slide may seem less important. Thus, when considering the slipperiness of any potential slide, we need to consider the likelihood of its occurrence as well as the detrimental effect of B. When we add those two issues to the additional requirement of a downward slope, we have the essential requirements of a slippery slope.

What is vital to any slippery slope argument, though, is a special type of link between A and B. It is not merely that one needs to be concerned with cases where a jurisdiction has allowed A and B has then happened. For a slippery slope argument to work, B must be a result of A's implementation. A must, in some way, cause B to happen.[9] If it does not, then we do not have a sufficient connection between A and B to justify a slippery slope argument. Instead, we have some other connection between the two practices and this should be evaluated accordingly.[10] Requiring some sort of causal connection means there are two general forms that a slippery slope argument can take. These are commonly referred to as an empirical (or sometimes practical) slippery slope and a logical slippery slope argument. The empirical slippery slope argument is based upon the available evidence. It argues that a slide from A to B will occur if A is implemented not because of any logical necessity between A and B, but due to other factors which can be empirically evaluated.[11] Thus, it is a claim about what will, in fact, happen if A is allowed.

A logical slippery slope, on the other hand, requires merely a logical connection between A and B. Instead of proof of an empirical connection, it requires a logical argument to show that acceptance of A somehow leads logically to the acceptance of B. For a logical slippery slope argument to work, then, one is required to show that the acceptance of A leads necessarily to the acceptance of B.[12] Most arguments which are considered to be logical slippery slope arguments, however, are not really best classified as such. Instead of being slippery slope arguments (which posit the existence of two different events and a causal

---

[8] Enoch, 'Once You Start Using Slippery Slope Arguments, You're on a Very Slippery Slope', 636.
[9] S. W. Smith, 'Fallacies of the Logical Slippery Slope in the Debate on Physician-Assisted Suicide and Euthanasia' (2005) 13 *Medical Law Review* 224–243, 229.
[10] *Ibid.*   [11] *Ibid.*, 224.   [12] *Ibid.*

link between them), most of these arguments are really disguised arguments from consistency. An argument from consistency does not hold that there is a causal connection between two different events; it posits that two seemingly different things are similar on relevant grounds.[13] Since they are similar on relevant grounds, they should be treated similarly and thus if we treat A in X way because of some relevant criteria Y, then we should treat all things with relevant criteria Y in X way as well, including B. This classification distinction is important because the way in which the two arguments are evaluated are not the same.[14] As stated above, slippery slope arguments are evaluated based upon three criteria: (1) is there a downward slope between A and B? (2) Is there a likelihood of moving from A to B? And (3) what is the seriousness of B as a bad event? Arguments from consistency, however, are not evaluated in a similar manner. Instead, arguments from consistency are evaluated on whether or not A and B are similar on relevant grounds. This is likely to involve the related questions of whether both A and B have the same relevant grounds, whether those grounds are really relevant and whether there are any additional relevant criteria which change how we deal with A and B. Most of the arguments presented in relation to end-of-life decision-making are the second sort of argument. They are arguments from consistency as opposed to really being slippery slope arguments at all. Some commentators have even questioned whether there can ever be a purely logical slippery slope argument. That particular question is beyond the scope of this book, but it is worth emphasising that most of the arguments which call themselves logical slippery slope arguments are not, in fact, slippery slope arguments.[15]

Before moving on to the specifics of end-of-life decision-making, it is worth considering the possible mechanisms for a slippery slope. Slippery slopes are often considered to be fallacious arguments. The general response to a slippery slope argument is to contend that if we can make a relevant distinction between two things now, there is no reason to suppose we cannot make a relevant distinction later. That need not be the case, however, for a slippery slope argument to work.

---

[13] *Ibid.*, 230.   [14] *Ibid.*

[15] Slippery slope arguments may also be confused with the sorites paradox. Enoch, 'Once You Start Using Slippery Slope Arguments, You're on a Very Slippery Slope', 646. A sorites paradox is one which relies upon the vagueness of language in particular cases. The two most famous examples of a sorites paradox are those relating to determining when a collection of grain becomes a 'heap' and when a bald man ceases to be 'bald'. Sorites paradoxes do not rely on the same causal grounds as slippery slope arguments, but on the vagueness of the boundaries of particular words and concepts. For further information about sorites paradoxes, see D. Hyde, 'Sorites Paradox', http://plato.stanford.edu/entries/sorites-paradox (accessed 17 June 2011).

Arguments based upon real causal connections where there is a considerable likelihood of some bad effect (or a likelihood of a particularly bad effect) are not necessarily invalid. They merely require sufficient proof of the causal connection and the risk of a slide. One way we can better consider the ways in which this may occur are the various mechanisms by which a slide may be implemented. For example, it may be that different groups have different priorities. Eugene Volokh describes a voting pattern called multi-peaked preferences which may provide a scenario where a slippery slope can result.[16] We can imagine a situation where there are three distinct voting groups on a particular issue. Group 1 prefers option A to the pre-regulation state and the pre-regulation state to option B. Group 2 prefers option B most of all but further prefers option A to the pre-regulation state. Group 3 prefers the pre-regulation state and also prefers option B to option A. Presuming that no single group has sufficient voting power to overrule the other two, Groups 1 and 2 may vote to implement option A (as they prefer it to the pre-regulation state). Groups 2 and 3 may then act to implement option B as they prefer that to A. All parties were acting rationally, but it is important to realise that Group 1 had an instrumental part in the implementation of B, its least favoured option. If Group 1 does not help to implement option A, then it is not possible for Group 3 to implement B because Group 2 would not vote for it (as they prefer the pre-regulation state to option B). It might then be best for those in Group 1 to not vote for A if they believe that the other two groups will try to then implement option B. Those in Group 1 will not get what they most want (option A) but they will also avoid what they want least (option B). Other ways in which slippery slopes may result from rational decision-making include cases where the regulation of A leads to lower costs when it comes to regulating B, the regulation of A changes attitudes towards B, people may become desensitised to decisions made previously, or momentum to implement B may occur after the enactment of A.[17] In none of these cases may individuals be acting irrationally, nor do they necessarily result from a failure to make relevant distinctions between A and B.

3   The logical 'slippery slope' argument

With these preliminaries in mind, we can now turn to consideration of the first of the two general types of slippery slope arguments used in end-of-life decision-making. We shall begin with the so-called logical

[16] Volokh, 'The Mechanisms of the Slippery Slope', 1048–1049.
[17] *Ibid.*

slippery slope, although as stated previously, these are more generally arguments from consistency as opposed to true slippery slope arguments. In any case, it is useful to start by determining what exactly counts as A and B in these arguments. Unfortunately, there is no standard slippery slope argument which is generally used and therefore many will have different starting points. Generally, however, the starting point, or A, of the slippery slope argument is the legalisation or decriminalisation of assisted dying, either as assisted suicide, (active) voluntary euthanasia or both. The bad effect, or B, is often less consistent. For example, the most extreme slippery slope argument presented in the literature about end-of-life decisions is that proposed by Leo Alexander.[18] Alexander argued that the 'B' in the slippery slope is the atrocities committed by the Nazi Party in the Second World War, particularly the concentration camps, the unethical scientific experiments that happened in those camps and the resulting genocide. He argued that one of the decisive factors which led to those practices was the earlier euthanasia policy within Nazi Germany and, specifically, the determination that not all lives were worthy of being lived.[19] He argued that that policy paved the way for the mindset of the doctors and scientists involved which allowed them to see the victims of their decisions as being something less than human. While everything should be done to avoid any repeat of the atrocities committed under the Nazi regime, the argument as a whole is unpersuasive. First, it does not adequately explain the Nazi policy which possibly led to the complicity of doctors and scientists. The first reported instance of 'euthanasia' within Nazi Germany was a case where the parents of a disabled newborn child petitioned Hitler to allow them to terminate the child because it would not be a useful part of the German 'volk'. It was not, therefore, a case of assisted suicide or voluntary euthanasia. It was, instead, a case of non-voluntary euthanasia. Even if one ignores that important difference between the Nazi euthanasia policy and the arguments for assisted dying, there is still little reason to believe that Nazi extermination policies would be a likely result of any liberalisation of assisted dying practices. It presumes, without providing anything in the way of empirical support, that the euthanasia policy was the determinative factor in the subsequent Nazi atrocities. However, one could claim instead that they all form part of the racist Nazi ethos, which was in place well before the euthanasia policy.[20] In other words, it may be difficult to find a causal connection between the euthanasia policy and the resulting genocide because both

---

[18] Rachels, *The End of Life*, pp. 176–177.
[19] *Ibid.*   [20] *Ibid.*

were likely caused by a more fundamental factor – the philosophical underpinnings of the Nazi regime. One could reasonably contend that without those philosophical underpinnings about racial purity, Nazi death camps are an unlikely result of a policy of assisted dying. As further support for this, we could consider all of the additional cases of genocide or mass killings by governments. This would include the mass exterminations in Stalin's USSR, the executions and starvation under Pol Pot's Khmer Rouge regime, the current situation in Darfur in the Sudan and any number of other instances of genocide or mass killing. None of these also had a background euthanasia policy. Alexander's argument, therefore, not only fails to address all of the relevant factors which were in play in Nazi Germany, but also comparing those factors with similar cases in other places.

A more moderate logical argument has been presented by John Keown, and is more representative of the arguments utilised in the literature.[21] Keown does not argue that the legalisation or decriminalisation of assisted dying practices will lead to Nazi death camps. Instead, he argues that the resulting slide will end up in cases of non-voluntary and involuntary euthanasia.[22] As he argues, the problem with legalising assisted suicide or voluntary euthanasia is that these will necessarily require us to accept the legalisation of involuntary and non-voluntary euthanasia in the future. The reason for this is that the legalisation of assisted dying, presuming a doctor is involved, relies upon the doctor making a decision that the patient's life has no value.[23] Keown argues that the decision that the patient's life has no value is doing the 'real work' in the argument in favour of assisted dying and does not require that the patient be competent. As a result, it should apply equally in cases where the patient is incapable of expressing an opinion. As an alternative, Keown suggests that if the concerns about patient autonomy are doing the real work in assisted dying arguments, then there is little reason to limit those autonomous decisions to only those patients who are terminally ill.[24] Instead, any individual, including despondent teenagers, should be entitled to make the autonomous decision to end their lives. In either case, though, the legalisation of assisted dying will result in unintended consequences which we generally would wish to avoid. Keown thus presents his argument as a dilemma with either option being unsatisfactory. The only reasonable decision, he decides, is to refuse to legalise assisted dying.[25]

[21] Keown, *Euthanasia, Ethics and Public Policy*, pp. 70–80.
[22] *Ibid.*   [23] *Ibid.*, pp. 76–78.   [24] *Ibid.*, pp. 78–79.
[25] *Ibid.*, p. 80.

Were the dilemma sound, it would certainly present a strong case against the legalisation or decriminalisation of assisted dying. However, the argument is not as sound as it first appears. Keown presumes that there are only two interests at play (autonomy and the mercy interest) and that only one of them is doing the real work while the other is basically superfluous. As discussed in Part I of this book, that is not the case. There are a multitude of interests at work when discussing end-of-life issues, and all of them have an important part to play in any ultimate decision. It is not simply a case, then, of finding the one which is doing the real work and ignoring all of the other important aspects. Even if we did consider only the two possibilities put forward by Keown, there is no particular reason why both together are not necessary for the required justification to work.[26] The essential problem is a difference between necessary and sufficient conditions. A necessary condition is one which is required for a particular state of affairs to result. A sufficient condition, on the other hand, is one which creates a particular state of affairs. The two are not synonymous and a condition may be necessary but not sufficient or sufficient but not necessary. A condition is necessary but not sufficient if it is only one of a set of conditions which must be satisfied before a particular state of affairs results. Thus, a sperm cell is necessary for conception, but it is not sufficient as you also need an egg cell, the right environment and a number of other factors for successful conception. A condition can be sufficient but not necessary if there is more than one way to get to a particular state of affairs. Thus, an aeroplane is a sufficient condition to travel from the US to the UK, but there are other ways in which it might be accomplished (e.g. by boat). In response to Keown's argument, then, we can simply avoid the dilemma as he has posed it.[27] Both requirements are necessary for a complete justification of assisted dying but neither is sufficient on its own. As a result, this sort of logical argument fails.

It is worth considering whether it is then possible to save this particular type of argument from the fallacy outlined above. In other words, is there any way we can construct this sort of argument while accepting that the interests involved are only necessary but not sufficient? Unfortunately for those who wish to argue against the legalisation of assisted suicide and voluntary euthanasia, this does not appear to be the case.[28] Keown's argument requires that we be forced to choose between

---

[26] H. Lillehammer, 'Voluntary Euthanasia and the Logical Slippery Slope Argument' (2002) 61 *Cambridge Law Journal* 545–550; Smith, 'Fallacies of the Logical Slippery Slope in the Debate on Physician-Assisted Suicide and Euthanasia', 231–233.

[27] *Ibid.*

[28] Smith, 'Fallacies of the Logical Slippery Slope in the Debate on Physician-Assisted Suicide and Euthanasia', 234–236.

relevant interests. Otherwise, those interests naturally limit each other. Thus, the autonomy interest involved prevents a doctor from making a decision only on the grounds of whether the patient's life is 'worth' living because without the autonomous request, the doctor has no cause to make such a decision. Conversely, the use of a beneficence interest allows a limitation to those who are terminally ill because it is also a decision which must be in general agreement with values consistent with general medical ethics. As a result, it is not one where doctors are likely to agree to provide assisted dying for despondent teenagers.

There is one final possibility. We could consider this argument as not presenting a logical point, but an empirical one.[29] Thus, the argument might be not that these interests are incompatible with each other, but that they end up being considered incompatible in real life. When that happens, one or the other interest takes priority and thus, empirically, one of the interests explained will subsume itself under the other. This is a possibility which will be considered in the next section, although it is worth highlighting that at least some of the individuals in question do not consider it to be an empirical argument and instead rely on it as a logical one.[30] More importantly, if changed into an empirical argument, it loses the vital benefit of a logical argument. A logical argument, slippery slope or not, is a global argument. If we must necessarily logically hold one thing if we agree to another, then that relationship applies in all similar situations. Thus, if the logical argument was true, it would apply to all jurisdictions considering whether to legalise assisted dying. An empirical one, on the other hand, is not necessarily global. It may be that there are jurisdiction-specific requirements which either make the slippery slope argument more likely or less able to be regulated effectively. So, an empirical argument is more dependent on the individualised facts of a particular jurisdiction. That does not mean, obviously, that it is an unimportant argument but merely that it might lack the universal characteristic of the logical argument. However, as the logical argument is ultimately unsuccessful, we need to consider more fully the empirical slippery slope argument.

4   The empirical slippery slope argument

Simply because the logical argument fails does not mean that the empirical slippery slope argument will do likewise. First, it is more properly characterised as a slippery slope argument as opposed to a logical one. More importantly, the empirical argument is not based upon logical

---

[29] *Ibid.*, 236–238.   [30] *Ibid.*, 237.

necessity. Instead, the force of an empirical slippery slope is based upon whether the move from A to B will happen irrespective of whether it is logically required. It will encompass cases of mistake or other changes which would not necessarily be logically required but still likely to happen. As a result, we need to consider the empirical slippery slope further.

The empirical slippery slope, however, is more difficult to evaluate. Most slippery slope arguments are speculative since they happen prior to the legalisation of A. Consequently, empirical evidence may be difficult to find. Additionally, any empirical evidence is likely to be inconclusive. It can indicate trends and probable results, but any evidence is unlikely to ever be robust enough to determine conclusively whether a move from A to B will happen.[31] We must also keep in mind some important considerations regarding the evidence. First, we must be aware that what is necessary is a particular type of evidence. We cannot simply rely on evidence that a jurisdiction which has allowed A now has B and claim that this proves the slippery slope as a result. Nor is it sufficient to show that B has followed A in a particular jurisdiction. The mere fact that a second regulatory event follows a first chronologically does not show that there is a causal link between the two, and it is that link which is necessary for the slippery slope argument.[32] For example, we may have a case where a particular B happened after A but did so later than it would have without A. We may also have cases where A and B are relatively unrelated or related only in conjunction with a more fundamental basis (such as with the Nazi euthanasia policy and the mass genocide that occurred later). What needs to be shown instead is that B occurred as a result of A. This can often be difficult in cases where a number of causal factors may be involved and it may be unclear as to which of the various factors was causative or how much those factors might have been part of any overall group of causative factors. We therefore need to consider whether there is sufficient empirical evidence to show that B becomes *more likely* after the enactment of A.[33]

To determine whether this causal connection exists, it is often useful to have a clear idea of the supposed mechanism of any potential slippery slope. This is not always easy to determine in the case of end-of-life decisions. However, there appear to be two main possibilities. First, it is often claimed that allowing certain forms of assisted dying will lead to a change in attitudes, particularly among medical staff.[34]

---

[31] *Ibid.*, 22.   [32] *Ibid.*
[33] *Ibid.*; Enoch, 'Once You Start Using Slippery Slope Arguments, You're on a Very Slippery Slope', 631.
[34] Keown, *Euthanasia, Ethics and Public Policy*, p. 277.

More specifically, it is often claimed that allowing assisted dying will lead to doctors and other health-care professionals having a lesser respect for life, which could allow them to move from assisted dying to non-voluntary or involuntary euthanasia. Alternatively, a slide might occur as a result of difficulties in holding to particular distinctions.[35] This is not a claim that these distinctions are illusory, but that distinctions which are clear in theory may be difficult to adhere to in practice. Claims about doctors being unable to comply with regulations due to time constraints, financial implications, difficulty in making determinations about particular things (such as depression or how long a patient has to live), vague language or the inability to enforce regulations all fall within this broad category.

The first possibility seems easier to evaluate. If the allowing of assisted dying practices leads to a change in attitudes, we ought to be able to see the results of those changes in opinion surveys, focus groups and other measures of social attitudes. Specifically, we should see changes in opinion surveys in one of two ways. The first is a simple before and after picture. If we consider evidence of societal attitudes before and after a change in our initial regulation, we should be able to discern whether that change in regulation resulted in a change in attitude. Moreover, unless and until that opinion reaches a plateau, we should see a continued increase after regulation as people become more aware and more comfortable with that regulation. If we do not see these, then we have at least some proof that a slippery slope based upon a change in attitudes is not likely. As with all arguments based upon empirical data, it will be important to consider how those data were collected and any possible problems which may impact upon the reliability of the data. This includes known biases which may result from the selection of participants in opinion surveys, in addition to general concerns about all such survey methods. Sample populations may not be representative of the general population being surveyed or there may be insufficient numbers to make any robust decisions. We should also keep in mind that many results may change depending on the question. Surveys may not ask questions in a sufficiently precise manner, for example, which may lead to individuals answering questions in a way different than they would have had more precise questions been asked. Survey questions may also be vague or otherwise difficult to understand. They may also fail to be consistent across different surveys, leading to problems with comparisons. Even considering those caveats, opinion polls at least

---

[35] *Ibid.*, pp. 73, 75.

provide us with some reliable data regarding the views of a population and it is worth considering them.

The second possibility is to contrast attitudes from jurisdictions which regulate end-of-life decisions differently. Thus, even if there does not appear to be much of an increase within a jurisdiction, there may still be differences between the attitudes of the general population within that country towards particular end-of-life regulations and those of other places which do not regulate end-of-life decisions in a similar manner. This may provide us with additional information about the impact of the regulation upon attitudes. As with the before and after pictures, though, there may be any number of issues when interpreting the data. There is often a greater chance that questions in different jurisdictions are not worded in a similar manner and comparisons may be difficult as a result. There may also be any number of culturally specific factors which may make any comparisons difficult. Consequently, contrasting attitudes from difficult jurisdictions may often be problematic unless the research study is designed to address these concerns. There is one such study which is relevant for our purposes as it was specifically designed to compare two different jurisdictions. Willems et al. carried out a comparison study of the attitudes of physicians in the Netherlands and the US state of Oregon about end-of-life decisions.[36] The study used the same questions in both the Netherlands and Oregon and asked about physicians' attitudes towards increasing morphine even if premature death was a likely consequence (what we have termed the double effect doctrine), physician-assisted suicide and euthanasia.[37] In the Netherlands, 67 doctors participated in face-to-face interviews and 132 physicians in Oregon participated in shorter telephone ones. Each of the participants was given four identical vignettes about practices at the end of life. The first was based upon a patient in extreme pain (Vignette 1). Others involved a patient who was debilitated but not in pain (Vignette 2), one where the patient has well controlled pain and is not debilitated, but feels that he or she will be a burden to others (Vignette 3), and one where the patient has well controlled pain, is not debilitated but feels that life is meaningless and worthless (Vignette 4).[38] The results of the survey are presented in Table 1.

---

[36] D. Willems et al., 'Attitudes and Practices Concerning the End of Life' (2000) 160 Archives of Internal Medicine 63–68. At the time of the study, the residents of Oregon had voted to legalise physician-assisted suicide but it had not come into effect due to legal challenges. According to the researchers, this might mean that generalising the results of this study to all physicians in the US might not be possible. It is worth noting, however, that there is no empirical evidence that doctors within Oregon have any different views than doctors in other US states. Ibid., 63.

[37] Ibid., 64.   [38] Ibid., 65.

Table 1. *Willems* et al. *study (* indicates statistically significant results)*

Vignette	Endorsed increasing morphine (The Netherlands)	Endorsed PAS (The Netherlands)	Endorsed euthanasia (The Netherlands)	Endorsed increasing morphine (Oregon)	Endorsed PAS (Oregon)	Endorsed euthanasia (Oregon)
Vignette 1	96	56	59*	97	53	24*
Vignette 2	43	52	49*	36	37	14*
Vignette 3	6	9	4	24	24	7
Vignette 4	15	18	14	20	22	7

As can be seen from the evidence, many of the attitudes of doctors in Oregon and the Netherlands are reasonably similar. Only the results from the first two vignettes are statistically significant and only then on the question of endorsing euthanasia.[39] The third vignette also shows some marked differences between doctors in the Netherlands and Oregon, although those results were not considered to be statistically significant.[40] Considering the lack of statistically significant results, it is difficult to determine whether this study provides any evidence in support of an empirical slippery slope based upon changes in attitudes. There are statistically significant rates on endorsing euthanasia between the two jurisdictions, although that may be merely a difference in the legal setting as there is no significant difference on any other end-of-life decision (and one would expect that were it a more global attitude change).

One study, of course, is insufficient to make any determinations about any slippery slope argument. Unfortunately, it is the only direct comparison data which actually seems to exist. The researchers indicated at the time that it was the first comparison study which involved asking physicians the same questions in different countries and there have not been any subsequent surveys which I have found which have looked at attitudes.

There is a European study which compares the views of members of the public in 33 countries about their views on euthanasia.[41] The study relies on data from the European Values Study in 1999–2000. The questionnaire asked individuals to 'Please tell me whether you think "euthanasia (terminating the life of the incurably sick)" can always be

[39] *Ibid.*   [40] *Ibid.*
[41] J. Cohen, 'European Public Acceptance of Euthanasia: Socio-demographic and Cultural Factors Associated with the Acceptance of Euthanasia in 33 European Countries' (2006) 63 *Social Science and Medicine* 743–756.

justified, never be justified or something in between'.[42] Respondents
were asked to give a rating on a ten-point Likert scale. A response of 1
indicated that the respondent thought that euthanasia was never justified; 10 indicated that it was always justified. Respondents were also
able to answer 'I don't know' to the question. Mean responses to the
question ranged from a 6.68 in the Netherlands to a 2.23 in Malta. The
mean score for the overall acceptance of euthanasia across Europe was
'just below 5'.[43] Countries which were above the mean score included the
Netherlands (6.68), Denmark (6.61), France (6.16), Sweden (6.07) and
Belgium (5.97).[44] Countries below the mean included Germany (4.34),
Italy (3.86), Portugal (3.50), Ireland (3.31) and Malta (2.23).[45] Great
Britain (meaning England, Wales and Scotland) was right in the middle at 4.99; Northern Ireland (3.93) was below the mean.[46] Switzerland
and Liechtenstein were not part of the survey. In and of itself, though,
this probably does not tell us very much. The Netherlands is top but it is
unclear from the study itself whether that is due to the euthanasia regulations within the country or whether the Netherlands has suited its law
to the views of its citizens. As a result, then, the best we can probably
say about the information is that it indicates places in Europe where,
if further liberalisation of euthanasia laws were to happen, it might be
more likely.[47]

What we can do is look at certain countries in more detail if they
have a reasonable amount of research about the change in attitudes
over time. As is generally the case, we can start with evidence from the
Netherlands, the country which is generally considered to have allowed
voluntary euthanasia for the longest period of time. Within that country, the Social and Cultural Planning Bureau (SCP) has been polling
attitudes towards euthanasia and assisted dying. The question used by
the SCP between 1966 and 2004 was 'Should a doctor give a lethal
injection at the request of a patient to put an end to his suffering?'[48]
In 1966, the first year the question was asked, 40 per cent of people
answered yes, while 12 per cent thought it depends and 49 per cent
said no.[49] In 1975, those numbers had changed to 53 per cent saying
yes, 24 per cent that it depended and 24 per cent answering no. Ten
years later in 1985 (roughly the time when assisted dying practices

---

[42] *Ibid.*, 746.   [43] *Ibid.*, 747.
[44] *Ibid.*, 748.   [45] *Ibid.*   [46] *Ibid.*
[47] There is additional information in the study which breaks down the responses by
numerical value. That provides a more detailed picture than the one given above but
still is unlikely to provide much in the way of evidence regarding the possibility of a
slippery slope.
[48] Griffiths *et al.*, *Euthanasia and Law in Europe*, p. 24.
[49] *Ibid.*

were decriminalised following the *Schoonheim* case), 55 per cent said yes, 33 per cent said it depends and only 12 per cent said no.[50] In the last survey using this question, 51 per cent said yes, 39 per cent said it depends and 9 per cent said no.[51] If one looked only at the numbers from 1966 and 2004, it would appear that the survey data supports an argument relating to a slippery slope based upon a change in attitudes. The percentage of people who answered yes rose from only 40 per cent in 1966 to 51 per cent in 2004. More importantly, at least according to some commentators,[52] the number answering no dropped from 49 per cent in 1966 to 9 per cent in 2004. This is quite a substantial difference. However, closer inspection shows that the marked increase in yes responses and decrease in no responses happened *prior* to the changes in the law. Looking at the no responses, that rate is halved by 1975 to 24 per cent and then further halved again to 12 per cent by the time of the *Schoonheim* case. The decrease after that is only 3 per cent. It thus seems like the major attitudinal change in the Netherlands happened before the change in the law.

A jurisdiction which can be compared to the Netherlands is the US, where there is also considerable evidence. In 2002, Ezekiel Emanuel published an article which surveyed a number of different studies.[53] As might be expected, he discovered that public support for assisted dying practices depends on the questions which are asked as well as the types of responses which are possible to a given question.[54] As a consequence, support for assisted dying in the various surveys ranged from 34 per cent to 65 per cent in favour of PAS or voluntary euthanasia. Emanuel therefore posits that the best way to understand the evidence is by a 'Rule of Thirds'.[55] In essence, about one-third of the American general public supports assisted dying (either as PAS, voluntary euthanasia or both) under any circumstances. One-third of the population is against assisted dying under any circumstances. The final third of the population supports assisted dying (again, either PAS, voluntary euthanasia or both) in some contexts but not in others. Perhaps surprisingly, this spread of opinions has been largely unchanged since the mid 1970s. In a survey from 1950, only 34 per cent of those surveyed supported assisted dying practices.[56] In 1973, using the same question, support for assisted dying had risen to 53 per cent. Four years later, again using the same

[50] *Ibid.*   [51] *Ibid.*   [52] *Ibid.*
[53] Emanuel, 'Euthanasia and Physician-Assisted Suicide'.
[54] *Ibid.* For example, surveys which allow respondents a range of choices (like the Likert scale used in the European Values Study) often produce a more nuanced picture of opinions than ones which rely on a simple yes or no.
[55] *Ibid.*, 142.   [56] *Ibid.*, 143.

question, support had risen further to 60 per cent, where it has been reasonably steady ever since.[57] Furthermore, members of the public do not appear to differentiate between PAS and euthanasia, supporting them at roughly similar levels.[58] However, they do support withdrawal and withholding of life-sustaining treatment at a much higher rate of about 90 per cent. Finally, neither those with terminal illnesses nor carers of those with terminal illnesses (including those who are recently bereaved carers) have different attitudes from the general public on rates of assisted dying.

Doctors and other health-care workers have also been subject to a number of opinion surveys in the US. As with the research on the general population, there can often be concerns about the way questions are worded or the answers which are allowed to a particular question. However, based upon a number of studies, it appears that doctors are less likely to support assisted dying practices than the general public.[59] It appears that roughly half of non-physician medical staff support assisted dying in some circumstances.[60] Health-care staff can, however, better distinguish between PAS and voluntary euthanasia than the general public, and those who support assisted dying practices tend to prefer PAS to euthanasia. It is also worthy of mention that those in medical specialities which have less to do with end-of-life care (e.g. psychiatrists, obstetricians, surgeons) are more supportive of assisted dying than oncologists.[61]

We can also bring in available evidence from the UK. In the 2004 Select Committee Report on the Assisted Dying for the Terminally Ill (ADTI) Bill looked at all of the available public opinion polls from the UK.[62] The Committee found that 'virtually all' of the opinion research conducted was opinion polls as opposed to focus groups, which meant that the results might be 'one dimensional'.[63] According to the report, the '[s]imple, direct questions placed without a proper explanatory context and with limited options for reply can sometimes produce results which in fact may be misleading'.[64] There were four basic attitudinal surveys referenced by the Select Committee.[65] They were a MORI poll in 1987 which showed that 72 per cent of the population supported the legalisation of euthanasia;[66] NOP polls conducted in 1976, 1985,

---

[57] *Ibid.*   [58] *Ibid.*   [59] *Ibid.*, 144–146.
[60] *Ibid.*, 149.   [61] *Ibid.*, 146.
[62] House of Lords Select Committee, *Report*, paragraph 215. The actual analysis was done by an organisation called Market Research Services (MRS).
[63] *Ibid.*, paragraph 217.   [64] *Ibid.*   [65] *Ibid.*, paragraph 218.
[66] The MORI poll was commissioned by 'two organisations active within the Pro-Life movement'.

1989 and 1993 which showed a 'similar pattern of support' for the proposition that adults should be allowed 'to receive medical help to an immediate peaceful death if they suffer from an incurable physical illness that is intolerable to them';[67] NOP polls in 2002 and 2004 which showed over 80 per cent support for the proposition that 'a person who is suffering unbearably from a terminal illness should be allowed by law to receive medical help to die, if that is what they want'; and British Social Attitudes surveys done in 1984, 1989 and 1994 which showed a majority rising from 75 per cent to 82 per cent in favour of doctors being allowed to end the life of a patient suffering from 'a painful incurable disease'.[68] MRS explored these figures in greater detail and found 'little or no correlation' between views on assisted dying and the age, gender, social class or political party allegiance of the respondent.[69] It did find some correlation between views on assisted dying and regular church attendance, race, UK nationality, education, other moral issues such as abortion and capital punishment and whether the respondent was able-bodied.[70] More opponents of legalisation were regular church attenders and/or Scottish (as opposed to other UK nationalities). They were also opponents of abortion and, 'to some extent', capital punishment, and, somewhat surprisingly, the able-bodied were more likely to oppose legalising assisted dying.[71] The attitudes of those with disabilities were considered to be more mixed. A poll by the Disability Rights Commission in 2003 indicated that disabled people were concerned about the possibility they may be threatened by any euthanasia legislation, although this result was based upon a small sample.[72] A YouGov poll survey carried out in 2004 on behalf of the Voluntary Euthanasia Society, however, showed that disabled people supported the ADTI Bill to the same extent as able-bodied people.[73]

The Select Committee also considered the opinion surveys carried out in respect to health-care practitioners. The MRS report indicated that the opinions of doctors and other health-care workers were likely to be more informed than those of the general public and therefore those surveys 'generally enjoy a higher level of credibility'.[74] The MRS report also indicated that health-care professionals were more likely to see the issue as 'less straightforward' than the rest of the population and that those who had more to do with end-of-life decisions were 'less sure' about changing the law in favour of euthanasia.[75] More specifically, the

---

[67] *Ibid.* All of the NOP polls (in 1976, 1985, 1989, 1993, 2002 and 2004) were commissioned by the Voluntary Euthanasia Society.
[68] *Ibid.*   [69] *Ibid.*, paragraph 220.   [70] *Ibid.*
[71] *Ibid.*   [72] *Ibid.*, paragraph 221.   [73] *Ibid.*
[74] *Ibid.*, paragraph 227.   [75] *Ibid.*, paragraph 228.

Select Committee noted a number of surveys.[76] There was a 1987 NOP poll of 301 GPs. The results of that survey indicated that if the law was changed to allow assisted dying practices on the lines of the ADTI Bill, 53 per cent would not carry out assisted dying, 35 per cent would consider carrying out assisted dying and 10 per cent might do so. A further study in 1993 of 312 GPs and consultants found that 46 per cent of those surveyed would be prepared to consider practising euthanasia if they were asked by a competent patient and 32 per cent would not.[77] A 1995 omnibus study of 2,150 doctors by *Doctor* magazine found that 44 per cent of those surveyed supported a reform of the law while 53 per cent did not. Furthermore, 43 per cent would consider practising euthanasia if it were legalised. An BMA News Review survey of 750 GPs in 1996 found that 46 per cent of GPs supported legal reform and 44 per cent rejected it. A second survey carried out in 1996 by Sheila McLean found that 43 per cent of the 1,000 doctors surveyed supported assisted suicide while only 19 per cent supported euthanasia. A postal survey of 322 UK psychiatrists in 1998 indicated that 38 per cent believed that euthanasia should be legalised and that 35 per cent would be willing to assess patients for potential suitability. In a 1999 survey of 333 geriatricians, 80 per cent felt that euthanasia could never be justified but 23 per cent felt that it should be legal in some circumstances.[78] A 2003 Opinion Research Business survey conducted on behalf of Right to Life found that 22 per cent of the 986 respondents would favour a change in the law while 61 per cent would be opposed. Two surveys were conducted on behalf of the Voluntary Euthanasia Society in 2003 and 2004 which indicated that one-third of doctors might favour a change in the law to allow assisted dying, although there was 'some indication of waning support for euthanasia between the two years'.[79] Surveys of the readership of *Nursing Times* in 1988 and 2003 found that 44 per cent of those surveyed in 1988 would have been willing to participate in the administration of lethal drugs to terminally ill patients who were suffering, while two-thirds of readers in 2003 believed that euthanasia should be legalised. Finally, qualitative research carried out in 2004 by Help the Hospice found that 'the introduction of euthanasia legislation was seen within the hospice movement as capable of changing the ethos

[76] *Ibid.*, paragraph 229.
[77] *Ibid.* There were also a significant number of undecided responses.
[78] *Ibid.* The report does not explain how those figures are arrived at as it would seem to indicate that either we can have 103 per cent of doctors in the survey or at least 3 per cent of them thought that euthanasia could never be justified but still should be made legal in some circumstances.
[79] *Ibid.*

of hospice care for the worse and of eroding the relationship of trust between physicians, carers and patients'.[80]

The evidence from the UK, then, seems roughly similar to that of the US. Doctors and other health-care workers are less likely to support assisted dying practices than the regular population. Additionally, those who work more closely with end-of-life decisions or terminally ill patients tend to be less in favour of a change in the law than those who do not work in those specialities. If the polls are accurate, the support in the UK appears to be a bit greater than that in the US, with the US having only two-thirds of the population supporting assisted dying in at least some circumstances while the proportion in the UK appears to be closer to three-quarters. In any case, those results are lower than the Netherlands, although they do not appear to be dramatically so. Instead, it may simply be an indication of cultural differences between these jurisdictions. More importantly, all of the increases in these countries appear to happen at roughly the same time, that being the mid 1970s through to the mid 1980s. As a result, we do not appear to have any evidence to support an empirical slippery slope argument based upon a change in attitudes.

If there is no evidence for a slippery slope based upon attitudes, there may still be a slippery slope if practices change irrespective of whether attitudes do. We would have evidence of that connection if we can show that cases of B – non-voluntary and involuntary euthanasia – rise as a result of the presence of A – PAS or voluntary euthanasia. In and of itself, of course, this cannot prove the causal connection necessary for the slippery slope to work. However, it can at least provide us with the beginnings of the required evidence. To truly be effective, it would be best to evaluate evidence of non-voluntary and involuntary euthanasia in a jurisdiction prior to the legalisation of PAS or voluntary euthanasia and compare it to rates after legalisation. Unfortunately, the jurisdiction for which we have the most evidence, the Netherlands, does not have any evidence from prior to the decriminalisation of euthanasia in 1985. What we do have is four national studies about end-of-life practices. The first study was the government-sponsored Remmelink Report, which compiled data from 1990. This study had two major components.[81] The first was a death-certificate study, where the researchers sent a survey questionnaire to the responsible doctor for a sample of all deaths in the Netherlands. The second part of the Remmelink study

---

[80] *Ibid.*
[81] A third component, a prospective study, was not replicated in any subsequent national research in the Netherlands.

Table 2. *The Netherlands surveys (%)*

	1990	1995	2001	2005
PAS	0.2	0.2	0.2	0.1
Voluntary euthanasia	1.7	2.4	2.6	1.7
Total assisted dying	1.9	2.6	2.8	1.8
Pain-relief with life-shortening effect	18.8	19.1	20.1	25
Non-treatment decisions	17.9	20.2	20.2	16
Termination of life without explicit request	0.8	0.7	0.7	0.4

consisted of physician interviews which explored some of the questions in greater detail. Subsequent surveys have mainly followed this methodology, although there have been some changes.[82]

The four Dutch surveys cover a range of end-of-life practices. While there are slightly different rates from the two different arms of the research, the death-certificate ones are generally considered to be the more reliable.[83] Therefore, we will consider that data throughout the rest of the chapter. The information from the four surveys is replicated in Table 2.

Looking initially at the data from the Netherlands, it does not appear that there is evidence of a slippery slope from the Netherlands. As suggested, if there were, we would expect to see a rise in the level of our bad effect, in this case the category called 'termination of life without explicit request', especially if the amount of PAS and voluntary euthanasia is also rising. While the rate of assisted dying practices rose from 1990 to 2001, the rates of terminations of life without explicit request did not. In fact, they declined from 0.8 to 0.7 per cent of all deaths (although that difference was not considered to be statistically significant). The rate, then, of terminations of life without explicit request can best be considered to be stable up until 2001 and have declined further since then. There is thus not the increase which might have been expected for the slippery slope argument to be successful.

However, it is also worth noting that some of those figures are in dispute. While not contesting the figures overall, Keown has argued that the figures have been interpreted incorrectly.[84] The issue relates to some of the data for the categories of pain relief with life-shortening effect and non-treatment decisions. When collecting this data, the

[82] See discussion of the Dutch surveys in Chapter 9.
[83] Griffiths *et al.*, *Euthanasia and Law in Europe*, p. 149.
[84] Keown, *Euthanasia, Ethics and Public Policy*, pp. 95–101.

Dutch surveys included questions about the intention of the doctors when engaging in these practices. Doctors were given three possible options when discussing their intentions. The first was with the explicit intention of shortening life. The second was with the partial intention of shortening life. The final category was that the doctor did not intend to shorten life but did 'take into account the probability' that the practice in question would have that effect. The Dutch researchers did not include any of this data in the voluntary euthanasia category nor did they include it when considering the termination of life without request. Keown, on the other hand, argues that both those practices which included the explicit intention of shortening life and the partial intention of shortening life should be considered within the category of either euthanasia or termination of life without request, depending on the rest of the circumstances.[85]

There are certainly arguments in favour of the position that Keown adopts. If intention is particularly relevant to a discussion about euthanasia (and our definition, like Keown's, depends upon intention to a certain extent), then we should consider those practices which intend to kill as euthanasia even if they superficially look like cases of something else. Even so, there are a number of reasons why it is important to keep the evidence of these practices separate. First, for comparative reasons, keeping voluntary euthanasia and pain relief distinct allows us to make distinctions which are necessary for the evaluation of evidence.[86] The studies which can be compared with the Dutch studies all use similar definitions and therefore also do not count pain relief with life-shortening effect or non-treatment decisions as euthanasia or termination of life without request. Nor do they necessarily provide the evidence necessary to make those determinations. If we consider the Dutch data in such a way but not the data from other comparative countries, then the results of that comparison will be skewed. We will consequently have an inaccurate picture as to the rates of euthanasia and terminations of life without request. Secondly, the creation of a distinct category is useful because it allows us to explore a distinct category of behaviour which is often not acceptable in other jurisdictions.[87] PAS and voluntary euthanasia as the Dutch researchers have defined it are legally permissible only in countries like the Netherlands. Providing pain relief, whether or not performed intentionally to shorten

---

[85] *Ibid.*
[86] Smith, 'Evidence for the Practical Slippery Slope in the Debate on Physician-Assisted Suicide and Euthanasia', 34–35.
[87] *Ibid.*

life, is not. Doctors are allowed in most jurisdictions to provide pain relief with life-shortening effect under the doctrine of double effect. While strict adherence to the doctrine would likely require a detailed exploration of the intentions of the doctors in question, in reality this rarely happens. Instead, police officers and prosecutors will consider any instance of pain relief which fits the outward signs of the doctrine of double effect as being simple pain relief without euthanasia.[88] Moreover, cases of non-treatment decisions are rarely considered to be euthanasia, voluntary or not, even if there is a statement that the doctor intends the death of the patient. For example, the doctors in *Bland* seem to have clearly intended that Anthony Bland should die as a result of the non-treatment decision and the judges accept that particular intention. The same is true in US cases such as *Cruzan*. Even those who oppose the legalisation of euthanasia do not suggest that we look closely at the intention of doctors in similar cases.[89] If we included this information, then, there would be little basis for an actual comparison as all jurisdictions would allow voluntary euthanasia and PAS in some circumstances. It is only if these practices are conceptually distinct will we be able to have a useful comparison of various practices. Finally, it is not at all clear that providing pain relief with life-shortening effect is, in fact, clinically accurate. Studies have shown that, despite the generally accepted knowledge about pain relief, providing opioids in large doses does not actually increase the likelihood of the patient dying. If this is correct, then it would not be possible for those providing pain relief to actually kill a patient, even if that was their intention. As such, they could not engage in the practice of euthanasia. For all of these reasons, the definitions used by the Dutch researchers will be the ones used for this chapter.

If the data from the Netherlands compared to itself does not provide any necessary proof for a slippery slope argument, that does not end our inquiry. Just because the data from the Netherlands do not show a rising rate of termination of life without request, it does not mean that the rate is not significantly higher than other countries. In other words, the mere fact that the rates in the Netherlands appear to be relatively stable does not mean that there is sufficient evidence to conclude that the slippery slope has not happened if those rates are unnaturally high compared to other jurisdictions. We will therefore need to compare the rates of end-of-life practices in other jurisdictions in order to get a more complete picture. Luckily, there are studies from other countries

---

[88] Huxtable, *Euthanasia, Ethics and the Law*, p. 102.
[89] Gormally, 'Walton, Davies, Boyd and the Legalization of Euthanasia'.

which explore end-of-life decisions that use the Dutch methodology. This should make it easier to compare those studies to the Dutch ones we already have. On the down side, there are not a considerable number of studies. In fact, there are only studies available from Australia, Belgium (prior to the change in the law) and the UK as well as a pan-European study, so results based upon this evidence will be merely tentative.[90] Even so, they give us a good starting point for comparison. We can begin by considering the figures from these various studies. The results of these studies and the Dutch studies discussed previously are summarised in Table 3.

As can be seen from the table, there is additional information which puts the slippery slope argument in doubt as the Netherlands does not appear to have a substantially greater rate than other countries. Both Australia and Belgium had higher rates of termination of life without explicit request than the Netherlands, even though they did not have greater rates of PAS or voluntary euthanasia. The UK did not have higher rates of assisted dying or termination of life without explicit request than the Netherlands, but that just seems to underline the point that the acceptance of PAS and voluntary euthanasia does not create any causal connection with the rates of termination of life without explicit request. There are concerns, however, about both the Australian and Belgian studies. Both were criticised for failing to have interviews like their Dutch counterparts. Both studies had decided against interview components based upon the idea that doctors would be unwilling to discuss conduct which was illegal within the jurisdiction in which they were practising. This is, as it turns out, possibly an incorrect assumption about doctors' willingness to participate in interviews,[91] but there was no reason not to believe it was a significant problem at the time. In addition, the Belgian study was criticised for a low response rate and the Australian study was criticised for mistranslating a particular question on the surveys. In respect to the problem with the Australian study, the surveys were based upon the original Dutch ones and translated into English for use in the Australian survey. Unfortunately, a mistranslation in one of the questions was said to increase the likelihood of answers which would lead to a greater rate of practice than might have normally been the case had the question

---

[90] The studies are detailed in Chapter 9. The New Zealand study mentioned in Chapter 9, while based upon the original Dutch surveys, does not indicate results in a similar manner. For example, the New Zealand survey does not indicate how many cases, if any, of 'termination of life without explicit request' there were. It is therefore not of particular use in determining the slippery slope concerns we have been exploring.

[91] We could consider the interview study done by Magnusson as an example.

Table 3. *Comparison of surveys from the Netherlands (NL), Australia (AU), Belgium (BE) and United Kingdom (UK) (%)*

	NL 1990	NL 1995	NL 2001	NL 2005	AU 1997	BE 2000	UK 2004
PAS and voluntary euthanasia	1.9	2.6	2.8	1.8	1.8	1.3	0.16
Pain-relief with life-shortening effect	18.8	19.1	20.1	25	30.9	18.5	32.8
Non-treatment decisions	17.9	20.2	20.2	16	28.6	16.4	30.3
Termination of life without explicit request	0.8	0.7	0.7	0.4	3.5	3.2	0.33

been translated correctly. While the criticism is correct that one of the questions was mistranslated, it appears that the mistranslation did not relate to a question involving PAS, voluntary euthanasia or termination of life without explicit request. Instead, the question related to non-treatment decisions. Thus, while the question was mistranslated, it does not appear that the problem would affect the rates of termination of life without explicit request which are at the heart of any slippery slope claim.[92]

The final survey which is comparable to the original Dutch studies is the pan-European EURELD study. This study looked at end-of-life decisions in six countries – the Netherlands, Belgium, Italy, Denmark, Sweden and the German-speaking part of Switzerland. The study used the original Dutch surveys, which were translated into the languages of the other countries in the study. Response rates for the surveys varied from a low of 44 per cent in Italy to 75 per cent in the Netherlands.[93] The results of the study are listed in Table 4 below.

Again, then, the evidence does not bear out claims of a slippery slope from PAS and voluntary euthanasia to termination of life without explicit request. While the Netherlands does have a higher rate of termination of life without request than Italy, Sweden and Switzerland, it has a lower rate than Belgium (again the survey was carried out prior to the change in regulation) and Denmark. It is also worth remembering that Switzerland also allows assisted suicide. We thus have no evidence to show that the Netherlands is sliding down a slippery slope towards non-voluntary and involuntary euthanasia. Their own rates of

---

[92] Smith, 'Some Realism about End of Life', 72, citing Seale, 'Investigating End-of-Life Decision-Making in U.K. Medical Practice'.
[93] Further details about the EURELD study can be found in Chapter 9.

Table 4. *EURELD study in Belgium (BEL), Denmark (DNK), Italy (ITA), the Netherlands (NLD), Sweden (SWE) and Switzerland (SWI) (%)*

	BEL	DNK	ITA	NLD	SWE	SWI
Response rate	59	62	44	75	61	67
Rate of PAS	0.01	0.06	0.00	0.21	0	0.36
Rate of voluntary euthanasia	0.30	0.06	0.04	2.59	0	0.27
Pain relief with life-shortening effect	22	26	19	20	21	22
Non-treatment decisions	15	14	4	20	14	28
Termination of life without explicit request[a]	1.50	0.67	0.06	0.60	0.23	0.42

a In the EURELD study, this category was referred to as 'Ending of Life without the Patient's Explicit Request'. In order to make comparisons easier, I have used the terminology from the original Dutch studies. Nothing turns on the semantic difference between the two.

termination of life without request have reached a plateau and began to decline, if the 2005 survey is accurate. There is thus little evidence of increased practice among Dutch doctors. Furthermore, the Dutch rate of non-voluntary and involuntary euthanasia is not higher than countries which do not (or did not) allow assisted dying practices. Of course, it may be that additional research would show the data we have to be anomalies but until that point, there is little reason to believe that a slippery slope would result from the legalisation of assisted dying practices.

Two final possibilities remain for a slippery slope. The first relates to the other possibility presented by Keown. His first argument is that the acceptance of PAS and voluntary euthanasia will lead to non-voluntary and involuntary euthanasia. This has been shown to lack evidentiary support. The second argument presented by Keown is that PAS and voluntary euthanasia will become more accepted and thus will cease to be a last resort. Again, we have some data on this. First, we can return to the evidence from the Netherlands which did show an increase in voluntary euthanasia between 1991 when it accounted for 1.7 per cent of all deaths and 2005 where it accounted for 2.6 per cent of all deaths. That might provide some evidence in support, even if it is belied by the results of the 2005 survey, which saw a decrease to the initial level of 1.7 per cent. A second source of information is the Federal Control and Evaluation Committee (FCEC) reports in Belgium. The number of cases which have been reported has risen from 24 in the second quarter of 2002 to 110 in the fourth quarter of 2005.[94] That is a considerable increase in the number of cases. It is true that the increase has not been steady and some quarters have shown a decrease from previous ones, but, in general, there is a trend towards a greater number of cases in Belgium. This then might provide some support for the idea that the acceptance of assisted dying practices will mean that they become increasingly more utilised. However, the same increase is not shown when considering the data from Oregon. Oregon only allows PAS and not voluntary euthanasia. According to the official reports of the Oregon Department of Health, 59 people ingested lethal medication in 2009.[95] This accounts for a total of 19.3 deaths as a result of PAS per 10,000 deaths in Oregon. This is an increase over the first year of the Death with Dignity Act when only 15 people died (5 out of every 10,000 deaths), but the increase is much less marked than that in Belgium. It is also significantly lower in real terms as, while only 460 patients have died under the Death with Dignity Act since it was passed in 1997,[96] 1,430 patients died in Belgium between 2002 and 2006, according to the FCEC reports.[97] These figures do not necessarily show that Keown's second argument is valid as the increase in Oregon is sufficiently less than the one in Belgium. What it may show is that the acceptance of PAS results in lower rates of uptake than the acceptance of voluntary euthanasia. However, as there are many cultural differences which may be in play it is hard to reach anything resembling a firm conclusion. It is doubtful we can even reach a tentative one. At best, we have an issue which requires substantial further research but it may indicate a practical consideration when considering the types of regulation for end-of-life decisions.

Secondly, a number of concerns have been raised about the specific regulations used by the Dutch to regulate PAS and voluntary euthanasia. All of the guidelines originally promulgated by the KPMG (Dutch Medical Association) have been breached at one time or another.[98] The most telling example of this is the reporting rate which was discussed previously in Chapter 12. Additional concerns are raised about other guidelines. For example, one of the concerns raised about the Dutch guidelines is what constitutes a failure to have other treatment options as required under the regulations. More specifically, questions arose in the Netherlands over whether treatment options which had been refused

---

[94] House of Lords Select Committee, *Report*, paragraph 212.
[95] Oregon Reports, Year 12.   [96] *Ibid.*
[97] Griffiths *et al.*, *Euthanasia and Law in Europe*, p. 342.
[98] Keown, *Euthanasia, Ethics and Public Policy*, p. 136.

by the patient still counted as 'available' options. Under the Dutch guidelines, euthanasia should not be used if there are other treatment options available and thus it became a question about the definition of 'available'. Originally, many, including the Dutch Supreme Court, the KPMG and the Ministers of Justice and Health in the Netherlands, had concluded that treatment options which were refused by the patient were still 'available'. This was changed in the 2002 law which makes it clear that treatment options which have been refused should not be a bar to euthanasia. This may be less evidence of a slide but instead is evidence that regulations should be consistent with other principles. In this particular case, continuing to use treatment options rejected by the patient is likely inconsistent with concerns about autonomy and consent as, at least for adults, there is always the ability to refuse treatment. Furthermore, there is less evidence about these particular concerns if we examine the regulations in Oregon. The official reports from Oregon do not indicate that there are significant regulation problems in that state. As an example, only one doctor in the 2009 report was referred to the Oregon Medical Board. The doctor in question was referred for failing to submit a written request form.[99] So, even if one had concerns about the Dutch regulations, it does not mean that PAS and voluntary euthanasia cannot be effectively controlled.

The fact that there does not appear to be any conclusive evidence of a slide towards non-voluntary and involuntary euthanasia does not mean, though, that there are not concerns raised by the Dutch experience which should be considered in any regulation of assisted dying. The first is the liberalisation of the possible grounds for assisted dying. Two cases from the Netherlands are worthy of mention. The first is the *Chabot* case.[100] In this case, a psychiatrist named Chabot helped a patient to die who was not terminally ill. Instead, she had been suffering from grief as a result of losing both of her children. Dr Chabot diagnosed the patient with 'an adjustment disorder consisting of a depressed mood, without psychotic signs, in the context of a complicated bereavement process'.[101] The patient, Hilly Boscher, refused all anti-depressants and bereavement counselling. After examining the patient and having seven other psychiatrists examine her medical records (the majority of whom agreed with his diagnosis), Dr Chabot agreed to assist her death.[102] Charges

---

[99] As discussed previously in Chapter 12, there have been concerns raised about the veracity of the reports submitted in Oregon. However, there is no evidence to indicate that there are actual cases where doctors have not reported accurately.

[100] Otlowski, *Voluntary Euthanasia and the Common Law*, pp. 404–409.

[101] *Ibid.*, p. 405.   [102] *Ibid.*

were brought against Dr Chabot. The Dutch Supreme Court held that there was no requirement that suffering is terminal or physical and Dr Chabot, therefore, was not convicted on this ground.[103] The second is the *Sutorius* case.[104] In this case, a doctor helped a patient to die who was not suffering from any disease at all but was simply 'tired of life'.[105] While the doctor was acquitted in the lower courts, the Dutch Supreme Court convicted him on the grounds that this was an insufficient reason for providing assisted dying.[106] Both of these cases, while insufficient to show a slippery slope, still provide warnings which should be considered during any attempt to regulate assisted dying.

Finally, there may be some concerns raised with the 2002 legislation which, for the first time in the Netherlands, allows assisted dying for two categories of patients – children and those who are incompetent but have written a living will.[107] Neither of these groups would have been eligible to request assisted dying prior to the new legislation. Children between the ages of 12 and 15 may request assisted dying (and the doctor may comply) provided that the parents of the children agree. Children aged 16 to 17 may request assisted dying (and the doctor may comply) even if parents have not agreed, although the legislation states that they should be consulted. Doctors may provide euthanasia for those over 16 who are not competent provided they had made a living will indicating their desire for euthanasia while they were still capable of making a decision. Again, to some, this will appear to be an expansion of Dutch practices towards non-voluntary euthanasia (as children and those who are incompetent are usually considered to fall under the category of non-voluntary euthanasia); to others, this will simply be bringing the regulations more in line with patient autonomy (as all decisions must be made by a patient). Whatever position is adopted, it does raise issues which should be addressed at the regulation stage. Either one can permit or prohibit those particular actions without changing the position over assisted dying generally. In other words, it is certainly possible to allow PAS and/or voluntary euthanasia while still prohibiting children or those who are incompetent from being participants. We do this in other situations (marriage and contracts, for instance) so there is no regulatory reason why it needs to happen.[108]

[103] He was convicted, however, because he had failed to consult with a doctor who actually examined the patient. *Ibid.*, p. 407.
[104] Griffiths *et al.*, *Euthanasia and Law in Europe*, pp. 35–39.
[105] *Ibid.*, p. 36.   [106] *Ibid.*, p. 37.
[107] J. de Haan, 'The New Dutch Law on Euthanasia' (2002) 10 *Medical Law Review* 57–75.
[108] Again, we might look to Oregon, which does not allow children or those who are incompetent (whether or not they have signed a living will) to participate.

5 Conclusion

In this chapter we have considered the slippery slope arguments which are often used to argue against the allowing of assisted dying practices. As has been shown, the logical slippery slope does not provide any convincing reason for prohibiting assisted dying practices. Nor is there any convincing empirical evidence which indicates that an empirical or practical slippery slope is possible. There are, however, concerns that need to be kept in mind when considering how best to regulate assisted dying practices. These include concerns about putting specific regulations into practice (such as the availability of other options) and conceptual distinctions about the kind of suffering which might be sufficient. Those are not sufficient to suggest that we should prohibit these practices but do indicate that we should make sure we are careful when we consider how best to regulate them.

With this chapter, we have concluded our discussion of the three major issues which are supposed to ban assisted dying practices *in toto*. None have been found to be compelling enough to require an outright banning of either PAS or voluntary euthanasia, although they have brought issues which will need to be considered when designing regulation. Our next task is to consider a number of issues in relation to the way in which we regulate these practices which falls short of an outright ban.

14   Necessary procedural protections

1   Introduction

Having examined all of the major issues involved in the regulation of end-of-life decisions, our final task before concluding is to explore ways to provide protection for the various parties and to avoid some of the more pressing concerns raised in Part II. A significant amount of time in previous chapters has been spent assuring readers that particular possible problems can be handled by a sufficient regulatory scheme but little effort has been expended in exploring the ways in which regulation can do that. This chapter's primary focus will be on the methods available to regulate end-of-life decisions so that potential issues do not become actual ones.

As with previous chapters, though, there are two important caveats that need to be kept in mind throughout this chapter. The first has been discussed previously but is worth repeating at this stage. That is the question about what constitutes an effective regulation. There are a number of assertions that any and all regulations relating to decisions or treatments at the end of life need to be completely effective in order to be ones which are acceptable for implementation. Regulations which do not meet this exacting standard should not be used. It has been argued several times already in this book that this standard is impossible to meet. No regulation is ever completely effective, even criminal ones. For any number of reasons, individuals within a regulatory system may break rules, misunderstand them or otherwise engage in conduct which is contrary to the specified regulatory system. A system of regulation which is 100 per cent effective is therefore not possible to obtain. That does not mean, obviously, that we should avoid trying to minimise instances where people act outside the specified regulations. What it means, though, is the simple fact that a regulation not being followed in all cases does not mean it cannot be effective. Instead, a regulation is effective if it is, by and large, one which is complied with by a majority of people. In other words, our question is not whether any regulation is completely effective but whether it is more effective than other regulatory schemes. The second caveat we will need to pay attention to is the difference between theoretically justified and practical efficiency. Previous chapters have highlighted whether distinctions which are possible are in fact justified on principles of consistency. In other words, we have tended to focus on whether conceptual ideas were consistent with other ideas. If they were, then the standard argument has been that these ought to be treated in a similar manner. While that is a valid starting point, there may be times when practices which are conceptually similar and thus ought to be treated in similar ways should not be treated consistently because of additional effects. So, for example, transaction costs or investigative costs may be prohibitive even if two practices in an ideal world would be subject to the same regulations. Unfortunately, we do not live in an ideal world and must therefore take account of practical problems which limit our abilities to regulate conduct efficiently.

With these two caveats in mind, we shall consider three important broad areas of regulation. The first is regulation in relation to requests by patients for specific treatment options. As this area of regulation is primarily patient-centred, we will be focusing on ways in which we can ensure (as far as possible) that those decisions are well considered, voluntary and based upon sufficient and accurate information. The second area we shall be exploring is the procedure after the request. This process is much more centred on the health-care professional. We will need to make sure (again as far as possible) that the health-care practitioner has ensured that the request is valid, that safety measures such as psychological screening and second opinions are utilised and that the method of causing death, if this is what is desired, is the best method for doing so. Finally, we shall consider the reporting and investigation of end-of-life decisions. This will include discussion of issues surrounding the most effective and efficient way to have healthcare workers identify and record their practices, as well as ways to investigate those practices. This will include further discussion about ways to provide approval for actions which are consistent with regulation as well as punishment for those which are not. Once we have explored all of these possibilities, we will have a checklist to be able to determine whether effective and efficient regulation of end-of-life practices is possible.

2   The request

Determining whether the regulations necessary for a request for a particular end-of-life decision are valid requires first an understanding about what is essential for that request. What, then, are the essential characteristics of a viable request? Generally, we consider a request by a patient to be a valid one if it is based upon a reasonable understanding of available information, it is voluntary and the patient has sufficient capacity to make the decision.[1] Thus, if a patient wishes to decide upon a particular treatment, we rely on the doctors or other health-care practitioners to ensure that the patient has sufficient information to be able to make a decision and that the patient has understood that information. We would also expect the health-care workers to investigate further if there are concerns about whether a particular decision is actually a voluntary one or if there are concerns about the patient's capacity. We may not always agree with the ways that doctors or other health-care providers go about satisfying these duties in all cases,[2] but we rarely see it expressed that the doctors or health-care workers do not have these particular responsibilities. Presuming that is a relevant starting point, we would expect the same to be the baseline requirements in cases of end-of-life decisions. In other words, when expressing a decision about end-of-life treatment, patients would have to meet the minimum standards for deciding which we use in general medical cases.

There are therefore some preliminary checks which would need to be made in any request. First, it would be necessary to ensure that the patient has sufficient information in order to make a decision. That means, at a minimum, that they would have information which is as accurate as possible, answers the relevant questions as well as can be expected under the circumstances and is presented to the patient in an understandable way. Second, the patient must have actually understood the information. This means that not only must things be presented in a particular way to patients, but the patients must have actually had sufficient time to process material so that they truly understand it. Both of these are not issues which can have hard and fast rules attached to them as individuals process information in different ways. Some people may require a longer period to understand material or may need the material presented to them in different ways than other people. Regulations,

---

[1] Mental Capacity Act 2005, s 3. Beauchamp and Childress suggest the following five elements as being important to the notion of informed consent: competence, disclosure, understanding, voluntariness and consent. *Principles of Biomedical Ethics*, p. 120.

[2] Two areas which have always caused controversy are decisions made by pregnant women, especially if those decisions are likely to hurt the foetus, or those by children under the age of majority within a jurisdiction. For cases involving pregnant women, see, e.g., *Re MB (adult medical treatment)* [1997] FCR 541; *St George's Healthcare NHS Trust v. S* [1998] 3 All ER 673. For cases involving children, see, e.g., *Gillick v. West Norfolk and Wisbech Area Health Authority* [1986] AC 112, [1985] 3 All ER 402; *Re R* [1992] Fam 11; *Re W (a minor) (medical treatment)* [1992] 4 All ER 627.

then, cannot be prescriptive as to the form, style and time necessary to make a decision but they should require that sufficient time, evidence of understanding and sufficient information have been presented to the patient. None of these matter, however, if the patient is not competent to make decisions or lacks decision-making capacity with that particular decision. Thus, in addition to making sure that the patient has received sufficient information and that they understand what they have been given, doctors and other health-care practitioners must make sure that a patient is competent to make a decision in the specific case. This does not mean that the patient must be competent in all cases, because a patient can be competent to make certain decisions without being competent to make others.[3] Understandably, since we are discussing questions about end-of-life treatment, the level of competence needed is likely to be quite high. Despite this, the focus should be on the ability to make the particular decision in question as opposed to general questions about the patient's competence.

All of these preliminary matters are likely to fall on the doctor or other health-care practitioner to evaluate. Some have argued that this causes problems as doctors are not equipped, or are not any better equipped than anyone else, to be able to make these sorts of determinations.[4] They argue that doctors can get patient competence wrong, in that patients who are not competent may be found to be competent or vice versa. Furthermore, health-care practitioners may be no more adept than anyone else at being able to present information to patients in a way which is clear and understandable, nor are they necessarily experts at making sure the patient has understood. Finally, it can often be argued that the information provided by health-care practitioners may not be accurate, even if this is unintentional. There are some reasonable answers to these issues. First, the argument is again presuming that the applicable standard is the elimination of all errors. As has been stated previously, that should not be the measure used as it is not an achievable one. Instead, the applicable standard should be obtainable by ordinary individuals. Consequently, our standard is not whether we can prevent all instances of incorrect evaluations, but how to best minimise them. So, as long as our process is robust enough to provide confidence in our ability to make decisions in a majority of cases, that is the best that can be expected. Moreover, it is worth highlighting that doctors

---

[3] Mental Capacity Act 2005, § (2)(1); Beauchamp and Childress, *Principles of Biomedical Ethics*, p. 112.
[4] N. L. Cantor, 'On Kamisar, Killing and the Future of Physician-Assisted Death' (2003–2004) 102 *Mich. L. Rev.* 1793–1842, 1809.

and other health-care workers make these sorts of determinations on a regular basis. They are often expected to determine whether a patient is capable of making a particular decision or not, even in cases where the consequences of that decision can be significant. We rarely question, for example, whether a doctor is able to tell whether a patient is competent to undergo chemotherapy unless there are questions which arise in a particular case. Otherwise, we simply tell them that patients must be competent to make decisions and let them get on with it. Finally, the duty to ensure that the patient is competent being the responsibility of the medical staff dealing with a particular issue does not limit their ability to request help if they are unsure about aspects of that treatment, even if it relates to competence or understanding. Doctors and other health-care practitioners have access to any number of resources such as family members, patient support organisations, psychologists, psychiatrists, counsellors and others who can provide answers and advice if they are unsure. We could further specify what health-care practitioners ought to do in cases of uncertainty. For example, we could regulate these decisions so that if doctors or other health-care workers are unsure as to whether a patient is competent or has understood everything they ought not to engage in those practices until they are. This does run counter to the general presumption that people are competent unless determined otherwise, but that does not mean it could not be done. It would just require specific legislation but this could be justified under the circumstances.

In addition to the capacities of the patient, he or she must also be eligible for the types of end-of-life treatment we are considering. In particular, we would need to explore whether types of assisted dying, for example, should be available only to those who are terminally ill or whether it should be extended to others such as those who are chronically ill. The Oregon legislation requires that a patient be terminal (defined as dying within six months). The Dutch legislation, on the other hand, only requires that a patient be subject to 'unbearable suffering' which includes chronic illnesses as well as terminal ones. Some may argue that there should be no distinction made between those who are terminally ill and those who are chronically ill. Both are likely to be in considerable pain and suffering from the indignities of their medical condition. If, so the argument goes, the patient who is terminally ill is allowed to die, then the ethical principles and legal regulations we have been exploring would apply equally to those in chronic situations. Others, however, could point to crucial differences between the two groups. Those with a terminal illness are dying; those with a chronic illness are not. Moreover, allowing assisted dying for chronic illnesses may raise additional issues about particular groups such as the disabled. While not all those who have chronic illnesses would identify themselves as being disabled, many would and those individuals may feel as though regulations which allow them to terminate their lives send uncomfortable signals about the value of their lives. If, then, we wish to allow those with chronic illnesses to be allowed assistance in dying, we would need to provide a test to determine when those illnesses were significant enough. We could not just allow chronic illness itself to count – diabetes is, after all, a chronic illness – we would need to require an additional factor such as 'unbearable suffering'. Any standard chosen would have to be sufficiently clear and narrow as to prevent the problems we have been considering. My own preference is to limit cases of assisted dying to terminal illness because it is only those which can truly be considered to be at the end of life. Consequently, the way that the relevant ethical and legal interests interact is different than it is in cases where life will continue, even if that life does not continue in the manner in which the patient would like.

There are additional issues which would be specific to end-of-life decisions based upon the fact that the decision has such final ramifications for the patient. Considering that finality and to attempt to minimise mistakes, there are three further regulations we might contemplate putting into place. The first is to require that any request be made in writing. Patients wishing to make at least some end-of-life decisions would thus be required not only to request the particular practice or treatment but to do so in writing. This could require a specific form, such as the one provided in the Oregon legislation,[5] or merely a written request of any sort. It is, however, imperative that the request be written instead of oral. The benefit of a written request as opposed to any other form is that it indicates the importance of the request to the patient, provides documentary evidence which is, hopefully, hard to fake and is easy to evaluate for those investigating these sorts of practice. The burdens of a written request may be that it is difficult to use in emergency situations, may prove difficult in certain cases if patients are unable to write a request and may emphasise form over substance. Despite these apparent issues with requiring a written request, the insistence upon some sort of proof of the actual request would appear to be a reasonable standard to adopt. It may be that some sort of visual recording is considered acceptable in cases in which a written request is not possible, but the reasons against requiring a recordable request do not seem overwhelming, whereas the ability to document the request in order to

---

[5] ORS 127.897 § 6.01.

evaluate it later on seems a crucial aspect of the investigation of conduct. As such, there is little reason to argue against a written request.

It must be made clear, however, that it is only part of the process and that the written request by itself is insufficient to prove that the end-of-life practice in question should have been performed. Along with the written request, it is often required that witnesses to the request be present and sign the form.[6] There are usually further limitations on the ability of people to be witnesses since those with particular relationships with the patient (such as those who might benefit under a will) and the treating medical team are often prohibited from acting as witnesses.[7] The purpose of witnesses, like the written request itself, is to provide documentary evidence and further proof that the request made was genuine. It provides further verification that patients have not been put under undue pressure, have understood the information and have made a serious request. However, given the way that regulations requiring witnesses are often written, the verification itself might be at issue. Often legislation is written so that only one of the witnesses need not be a member of the patient's family.[8] In such a case, a patient may be being coerced by a family member and that individual is one witness with the other 'independent' witness being a friend of the family member.[9] While that person might be technically independent according to the statute, it is not someone we would necessarily see as being a reliable source for the information which the witness is to provide. It might then be beneficial for any regulation which stipulates that witnesses must be present to pay close attention to the individuals who could act as a witness. For example, those in professions which are associated with a position of trust (chaplains, those involved with patient advice and support groups or attorneys) might make good choices for witnesses if we are particularly worried about providing evidence of a lack of coercion. Individuals in other groups such as notaries might also be used. Whatever criteria are used for picking witnesses, however, it should be made clear to those acting as witnesses what their duties are. Furthermore, attention may be paid to whether punishments might be acceptable for those who act improperly as witnesses. So, in a case like the one mentioned above, not only would the family member be subject to sanction for coercing the patient, but the witness who provided verification against coercion, assuming they knew or had reason to know about it, would also be

---

[6] ORS 127.810 § 2.02.   [7] *Ibid.*   [8] *Ibid.*
[9] John Keown, for example, presents a hypothetical scenario where the patient's heir and the best friend of that heir would be sufficient to act as witnesses. *Euthanasia, Ethics and Public Policy*, p. 172.

punishable. In doing so, we should remain cognisant of the fact that the witnesses are only one safeguard among many. Doctors, other health-care workers and others are likely to have responsibilities as well which are likely to help militate against the occurrence of witnesses acting in an improper manner.

The third and final question is whether patients should be the only ones capable of initiating a request for certain end-of-life decisions or whether a doctor may be able to recommend such a practice. The argument against allowing doctors to suggest end-of-life decisions is that it sends signals to the patient that he or she is no longer wanted or that the medical team has lost hope. On the other hand, patients may feel more free to discuss the topic if a doctor can initiate the discussion. Moreover, it might be seen as beneficial were certain practices to become legal for doctors to have discussions with patients about what it is that the doctor is willing to do in particular cases. Thus, if a doctor is never willing to participate in assisted dying, it may be seen as beneficial for the doctor to state that up front instead of waiting until the problem arises. Even so, those two can probably be treated separately. It should be considered worthwhile for health-care professionals and patients to have discussions about what is considered acceptable practice and what is not, but that is not the same thing as a health-care worker initiating a discussion about end-of-life practices with a patient in which the patient is then required to make a relatively immediate decision about those practices. Policing a policy where doctors and health-care practitioners are not allowed to initiate a discussion about end-of-life matters would be extremely difficult to do. Unless either the patient or the medical practitioner disclosed what happened during the initial discussion, it is not likely to become known what led to the request as these are usually not documented. What could be done is to have both the health-care team and the patient sign a document specifying who initiated the discussion, which could then be added to the documentary evidence in the case. That should at least provide us with some solace about the fact that both parties would have had to consider the initial discussion when deciding whether to proceed with the request. Others may argue that there should be little theoretical difference between whether a doctor or a patient initiates the discussion. As long as the other requirements of the discussion have been met, there is little reason to believe that the mere fact that the doctor or other health-care worker started the discussion has had an effect upon the ultimate conclusion. This may be accurate but this might also be one of those times where problems can be avoided, even if they are likely to happen only in a very limited number of cases. Consequently, it seems like it would be best practice for regulations to require that the patient is the only one who can initiate particular discussions.

To sum up, then, the primary purpose of regulation surrounding the request is to make sure that the decision made by the patient is fully informed, voluntary and without coercion. In order to accomplish this, it has been suggested that patients be given sufficient information as well as time to make a decision. It has further been suggested that the request ought to be made in recordable form, most likely in a written document. Furthermore, to help reinforce our confidence about the request, witnesses should be required who can be counted on to provide an impartial verification of the competence of the patient and the voluntariness of the decision. Finally, while there may be little theoretical difference between whether a doctor or a patient initiates the discussion, practical difficulties suggest that it is best if the patient is the only individual capable of beginning the request process. Having explored the procedural protections surrounding the request, we now should turn to the processes involved once a request has been made. Unlike the requests, which focus primarily on the patient, the processes after the request are likely to centre on the health-care practitioner.

3   Procedures leading to death

A number of the procedural protections which focus on the period following the request leading to the death are similar to those related to the request itself. This is not surprising due to the connection between the possible issues raised about the death and those which come afterwards. Not all of the duties, however, are connected and additional responsibilities arise once a request has been made. While the requirements after the request is made centre on the medical team involved in care, there are important roles which the patient is still required to fill.

The first three issues which need to be addressed follow on from the request by the patient. The first is whether or not the patient should be made to undergo a psychological screening to rule out the possibility of clinical depression. Those in favour of such a procedure argue that a considerable percentage (sometimes thought to be as high as 95 per cent) of those requesting particular end-of-life decisions are suffering from clinical depression.[10] A compulsory referral for a mental health

---

[10] See, e.g., H. M. Chochinov and L. Schwartz, 'Depression and the Will to Live in the Psychological Landscape of Terminally Ill Patients', in Foley and Hendin (eds.), *The Case against Assisted Suicide*, pp. 261–277, 263; New York State Task Force on Life and the Law, *When Death Is Sought*, p. 11.

evaluation would help to curb this problem as all patients requesting, for example, assistance in dying could be guaranteed to have mental health support. It would also reduce the worry some have about the ability of doctors, nurses or other health-care workers to be able to correctly diagnose when a patient has depression or other mental illnesses. Indeed, legislation in Australia's Northern Territory required that one of the two second opinions required under the Act be from a psychiatrist.[11] There is, thus, some precedent for the requirement of a psychological or psychiatric screening for those wishing to have assisted dying. On the other hand, most current jurisdictions which allow assisted dying in some form do not require mental health screening. Neither the Netherlands nor Oregon[12] require screening as part of their legislation and it is not part of the legal status of assisted dying in Switzerland. In the Netherlands, it is even possible to request aid in dying because of psychological reasons.[13] Oregon and the Netherlands do allow doctors to refer patients to mental health professionals if they feel it is necessary, but it is not a required part of the regulations.[14] When justifying these stances, the general consensus is to argue that mandatory screening is unnecessary. Doctors, nurses and other health-care professionals are capable in most circumstances of referring patients for mental health screenings when they believe they are required and there is little reason to suggest that this situation would be any different. A blanket policy which makes a mental health evaluation compulsory is thus not necessary and would only add needless delay and bureaucracy to the process. It might also stigmatise those who have requested aid in dying. As such, it seems preferable to insist upon the availability of screening only if necessary. The uptake of this will be dependent upon those with the power of referral so it should be considered beneficial if not only the treating doctor but other parties can refer a patient if there are questions. This could include not only other members of the medical team for the patient but also those providing a second opinion.

The second issue is a requirement that the patient has undergone palliative care treatment or exhausted other available treatment options.[15]

---

[11] Rights of the Terminally Ill Act 1995 [Northern Territory of Australia], 7.(1)(c)(ii).
[12] ORS 127.825 § 3.03.
[13] See, e.g., *Chabot*, Nederlandse Jurisprudentie 1994. A description of the essential rulings in the *Chabot* case can be found in Chapter 13.
[14] ORS 127.825 § 3.03.
[15] For example, the Oregon legislation requires that the patient appreciate the relevant facts and be fully informed about 'The feasible alternatives, including, but not limited to, comfort care, hospice care and pain control'. ORS 127.800 § 1.01 (7)(e). The Dutch regulations similarly require that the patient be made aware of 'the situation he was in and about his prospects' and that 'there was no other reasonable solution

These are sometimes treated as two separate issues but they are part of the same concern. The essential claim is that if aid in dying is a last resort, then those wishing to undertake it should be able to show that they have tried all other options. If they cannot prove this, then they ought to be required to take the other possibilities before utilising assistance with dying. The significant problem with this approach is that patients are not normally required to undergo any treatment they do not want.[16] If a patient decides that a particular treatment option is undesirable for any reason, then they may refuse that treatment. We would therefore need a compelling reason to deviate from the general rule about the ability of patients to refuse treatment. It might be suggested that the compelling reason for changing the rule in this case is that the end result is death whereas it is not in other cases. This, though, is simply a misunderstanding of the current state of the law. Patients are allowed to refuse treatment even if it leads to their death. Thus, Ms B was able to request that her ventilator be removed even though it would lead to her death.[17] A patient who is a Jehovah's Witness is allowed to refuse a blood transfusion even if it will lead to the death of that individual.[18] None of the judges deciding *Bland* indicate that Anthony Bland, had he been competent, would not have been able to remove artificial nutrition and hydration, again, even if it led to his death.[19] The same is true in the *Cruzan* decision in the US.[20] The current law thus does not differentiate between those cases where a patient wants to remove or refuse treatment which leads to death and those which do not. The patient's right to refuse in such cases is the same. Considering that, it does not appear that there is a compelling reason to require patients to undertake treatment options they do not want. That does not mean, though, that regulations should not include opportunities for patients to consider options they might have avoided previously. Patients should be made aware of all possible treatment options including those options which are only palliative in nature. Doctors and other members of the health-care team should thus be compelled to make sure that the patient is aware of treatment options which have not yet been tried as

---

for the situation [the patient] was in'. Termination of Life on Request and Assisted Suicide (Review Procedures) Act 2001, Article 2. Lord Joffe's Assisted Dying for the Terminally Ill Bill 2005 also had similar requirements. Assisted Dying for the Terminally Ill Bill [2005] 5 2(2)(e)(iv).

[16] *In re T (an adult)* [1992] 4 All ER 649.
[17] *Re B (adult: refusal of treatment)* sub nom *Ms B v. NHS Hospital Trust* [2002] 2 All ER 449.
[18] *In re T (an adult)* [1992] 4 All ER 649.
[19] *Airedale NHS Trust v. Bland* [1993] 1 All ER 821.
[20] *Cruzan v. Director, Missouri Department of Health*, 497 U.S. 261 (1990).

well as palliative care options which are available. If the patient, however, decides that none of these options is acceptable and is willing to indicate that in whatever manner is considered appropriate (e.g. as part of the request form), then those options should not preclude a patient from making a different treatment choice.

The third issue worthy of discussion is the requirement for second opinions. Again, regulations often mandate that individuals seeking to make particular decisions at the end of life are required to have a second opinion from an independent doctor who has the responsibility of verifying the diagnosis, prognosis, availability of options, need for a mental health referral and other issues.[21] Indeed, this is such a common requirement that there is little dispute as to its necessity. What may be contested is the number, speciality, independence and other characteristics of the doctor providing the second opinion. Thus, some legislation may require more than one second opinion, especially if one of the referrals must be of a particular speciality (such as psychiatry or palliative care).[22] Other regulations might include standards as to the training the second doctor ought to have. For example, while not obligatory under the Dutch law, the Regional Review Committees seem to prefer that doctors providing second opinions be SCEN doctors.[23] This might prove difficult to replicate in jurisdictions without the long-standing practices of the Dutch, but the benefits of such a practice have been discussed elsewhere in this book. What seems integral to any regulation, however, is that a system be put in place which requires at least one second opinion by individuals deemed relevant to the process. This will be partially dependent upon answers to previous questions about palliative care and related specialities so it is not possible to provide hard and fast rules as to how many additional opinions are necessary and who should be entitled to give them. They do provide a valuable method of ensuring that the decisions made are acceptable.

One continuing problem, though, is the extent of independence necessary for the second opinion. It is often suggested that the second opinion will not be truly independent in cases of assisted dying, as the individual providing that opinion must, at the very least, be amenable

[21] ORS 127.820 § 3.02; Rights of the Terminally Ill Act 1995 [Northern Territory of Australia], 5 7; Termination of Life on Request and Assisted Suicide (Review Procedures) Act 2001, Article 2 (1)(e); Griffiths *et al.*, *Euthanasia and Law in Europe*, p. 321 (discussing the Belgian Euthanasia Act).

[22] Rights of the Terminally Ill Act 1995 [Northern Territory of Australia] § 7.(1)(c)(ii),s 7(3).

[23] Griffiths *et al.*, *Euthanasia and Law in Europe*, p. 195.

to the practice.[24] Critics worry that any second opinion will not provide any real assessment of the patient but will instead be a rubber-stamp exercise.[25] True independence should be a necessary requirement, of course, but that does not mean the criticism noted above should be given any substantial weight. It is obvious that the doctor involved in providing a second opinion must not be against the practice being contemplated. Otherwise, the doctor is likely to simply indicate that the patient is ineligible. Accepting a practice, however, does not mean that doctors will accept each and every patient who may seek to participate in that practice.[26] Just because a doctor, for example, believes in chemotherapy does not mean that doctor believes every patient should have it. Doctors, hopefully, only provide treatment options to patients who require them. Thus, a doctor needs to accept the practice in general but that does not mean that doctors who do will be any less rigorous in their decision-making than those who do not.

The first three issues deal with continuing matters that relate to the request itself. The next issue, however, follows from the request but is not specifically related to it. This is the question about waiting periods. While a number of statutes or proposed statutes include waiting periods before a patient may choose a process which leads to death, there are often variations in the length of the period, when it begins to run and other aspects of the procedure.[27] The purpose of a waiting period is to allow the patient time to reflect about the decision and provide them with an opportunity to change their mind if they so desire. Since everyone accepts that patients ought to have the ability to change their mind, even at the last moment, legislation is often designed to include a period which would allow that to happen. While these are frequently part of any legislation, that does not mean there are no potential disadvantages to requiring a waiting period. A patient who is in considerable pain would continue to be in pain during the period required by the regulations. Those who will not change their mind will see that period

[24] Keown, *Euthanasia, Ethics and Public Policy*, p. 75.
[25] *Ibid.*
[26] Smith, 'Fallacies of the Logical Slippery Slope in the Debate on Physician-Assisted Suicide and Euthanasia', 241.
[27] ORS 127.850 § 3.08, which requires that there be 15 days between the first oral request and the writing of the lethal prescription. Additionally, there must also be 48 hours between the written request and the prescription. This can be compared with the Rights of the Terminally Ill Act 1995 [Northern Territory of Australia], § 7(1)(i), which specifies that the patient should not sign the certificate of request until seven days after the initial request. It further specifies in § 7(1)(n) that the doctor should then wait a further 48 hours after the signing of the certificate before assisting the patient.

as needless delay. If the waiting period is concurrent with other post-request procedures, then it may not provide sufficient scope for revisiting the initial decision. A short period may not allow enough space for the patient to think further. Furthermore, patients at the very end of life might die during the waiting period, making that period worthless in the long run. Waiting periods may thus extend the process of dying for little to no actual benefit either in particular cases or more generally. Part of the problem with this concern is that it is based upon an empirical question which has never truly been examined. We do not know, for example, how many patients change their mind during the waiting period required by the Oregon legislation. If we had that information, it would make the claims easier to evaluate. If very few people seem to change their mind during a waiting period, that could indicate that waiting periods are not likely to be effective. Larger numbers might emphasise the importance of waiting periods. The data would not be completely conclusive (e.g. a low number might simply mean the waiting period was too short) but would allow some measure on which to analyse the procedure. Without that evidence, though, an initial decision would need to be made in any legislation. What seems prudent would be to require a waiting period originally but also to require an investigation into the usefulness of that procedure. Changes could be made including the elimination of a waiting period entirely if it was deemed not to be useful. Until that evidence is available, however, it seems most effective to have a waiting period. It would also seem to be effective, I would suggest, if that waiting period required at least some time which did not overlap with other functions. A 15-day waiting period may not be much use if that time is spent on second opinions, mental health screenings and other aspects of the procedure anyway. Since the period is to allow patients time to reflect upon their choice, it ought to include time set aside specifically for that purpose instead of collapsing that period in with other things. As such, while it would not be possible to specify an overall period which would be applicable to all jurisdictions, it should be worthwhile to require that at least some of the time be specific to the waiting period itself.

The final issue is the most important as it is about the method of causing death. Just because a jurisdiction allows aid in dying in some capacity does not mean it allows it in all types of cases. Oregon, for instance, does not allow euthanasia but does allow assisted suicide.[28] Other jurisdictions allow the withdrawal of treatment but not assisted

---

[28] ORS 127.880 § 3.14.

dying in any form.[29] It is therefore worth exploring in depth the benefits and issues surrounding the legalisation of particular methods for causing death. A reasonable starting point for discussion is the current demarcation line between assisted dying and the withdrawal and withholding of treatment. As has been shown throughout this book, there is little difference between the ethical appropriateness of assisted dying in comparison to the withdrawal and withholding of treatment. Most of the issues which are relevant for assisted dying apply equally in cases of withdrawal and withholding of treatment. Considerations such as those related to autonomy, moral responsibility, harm, the value of life and dignity are just as prevalent in cases of the withdrawal and withholding of treatment as they are in cases of assisted dying. Practical issues likewise show little difference between the two. Questions raised about coercion, the possibility of voluntary decisions, discrimination and psychological effects on those participating and others also hold sway in cases where treatment is merely withdrawn or not provided to a patient. As a result, there is little reason to treat assisted dying and the withdrawal and withholding of treatment differently. Even if there is no ethical or practical reason, though, some may argue that there is a procedural difference which mandates that treatment of the two practices be different. However, it is not clear what these procedural differences would be. All of the regulations designed to limit the potential problems do not seem any less likely to work in cases of assisted dying than they do in cases of the withdrawal and withholding of treatment. The only possible difference is that doctors may feel more responsible in cases of assisted dying than they do in cases of the withdrawal of treatment. This, though, is based upon a fundamental misunderstanding about the ways in which we are responsible. As it turns out, we are no less responsible for those things we fail to do as we are for those things we do. Consequently, that does not provide a sufficient basis for differences in treatment but only shows that there needs to be greater attention paid to how we ascribe responsibility.

A more difficult question, perhaps, is whether the acceptance of assisted dying means that all types of assisted dying should be acceptable. If one accepts that one ought to legalise assisted dying, does that mean both assisted suicide and euthanasia should be allowed? If not, where do the differences lie? It may seem obvious that if there are no

[29] *Airedale NHS Trust* v. *Bland* [1993] 1 All ER 821; *Cruzan* v. *Director, Missouri Department of Health*, 497 U.S. 261 (1990); *Washington* v. *Glucksberg*, 521 U.S. 702 (1997); *Vacco* v. *Quill*, 521 U.S. 793 (1997).

practical differences between assisted dying and the withdrawal of treatment, then there should be no differences between different types of assisted dying. However, we can return to the interesting data presented in Chapter 13 relating to the comparative incidence rates in Oregon and Belgium. As noted there, Oregon's rate is significantly lower than that in either Belgium or the Netherlands. No specific research has been done on this point and there are likely to be a number of factors at play. One might be, though, that the difference between the legalisation of all forms of assisted dying and the legalisation of only assisted suicide might be part of the answer. Even in the Netherlands, the uptake of PAS is quite limited, accounting for only 0.2 per cent of all deaths.[30] While that is hardly sufficient to be considered a definitive conclusion, it might (and I would stress might) indicate that the legalisation of only assisted suicide curtails the uptake more than might otherwise be expected. The reasons for that are unclear, although it could be hypothesised that this is because carrying out the final act to cause death makes it more difficult to go through with than euthanasia which is performed by someone else. While specific research would be very useful on this point, if the presumption is that we wish to keep the number of deaths from assisted dying at a minimum and that the preference for euthanasia over assisted suicide indicates at least a tentative wariness on the part of the patient, then legalising only assisted suicide might be the most preferred option. Again, the reasoning is speculative in nature but it does provide some reason for treating PAS differently from active voluntary euthanasia (AVE). However, an argument that could be made in response is that one of the reasons to prefer AVE is that there are fewer overall problems with death through AVE as opposed to PAS. This is because doctors have a greater understanding of the necessary protocols for causing death and can take action in unforeseen circumstances. Patients, on the other hand, have limited possibilities if the initial drug cocktail is unsuccessful and may, as a result, end up in a worse condition than they were before.[31] Allowing a doctor to euthanise a patient therefore provides an important safety net. Even if this is correct, we could institute a regime which prioritised PAS and only allowed AVE in cases where assistance with suicide was unsuccessful. In any case, it seems like it would be a good policy to insist upon PAS if possible and either not allow AVE or only allow it in cases where PAS has failed.

---

[30] A. van der Heide *et al.*, 'End-of-Life Practices in the Netherlands under the Euthanasia Act'.
[31] Magnusson, *Angels of Death*, p. 205.

The only final point that should be mentioned in relation to the manner of causing death is the available drug cocktails. As noted in Chapter 11, doctors currently working in the 'euthanasia underground' had a number of different methods they used to cause death, and not all were effective.[32] One benefit of bringing these practices out into the open is that greater discussion could be had about the ways in which death can be brought about that minimise pain, suffering and discomfort while still being effective. Legislation, however, cannot be an effective method for determining in advance what drug cocktails ought to be used. Advances in pharmacology in addition to individual characteristics of the patient make that impossible. What might be beneficial in legislation is to provide standard effects that drug cocktails should induce (such as minimising pain) while leaving the specifics to medical science.

To summarise, in this section we have considered those regulations which affect what happens after the patient has made a request. We began by discussing the various duties a doctor may have to ensure that a request has been validated. This includes the possibility of mental health screening in cases where it is deemed appropriate as well as making sure that patients have been given the opportunity to consider alternative treatments, even if only palliative in nature. Furthermore, we have considered specifically the procedures involved in getting at least one independent second opinion of the diagnosis and prognosis. In doing so, the SCEN doctors used in the Netherlands were indicated to be evidence of best practice as they allow doctors to have additional advice and support and to minimise mistakes. Next, we explored the issue of waiting periods before a patient is able to die, including the importance that at least part of that period be specifically set aside for the patient to reconsider the decision. Finally, we explored issues around the methods for causing death. It was argued that there is little difference between assisted dying practices such as active voluntary euthanasia and assisted suicide on the one hand and withdrawal and withholding of treatment on the other. Thus, regulations which apply to one can reasonably be expected to apply to the other. Within the context of assisted dying practices, it was argued that while there may be theoretical consistency between active voluntary euthanasia and assisted suicide, the practicalities of implementing both end-of-life decisions meant problems were less likely in cases of assisted suicide than they were for euthanasia. Therefore, cases of euthanasia should be limited to only those cases where assisted suicide could not be effective.

---

[32] *Ibid.*, pp. 145–149, 205.

It was further stressed that, while legislation could not require specific drug cocktails, it could lay down standards which could be used in determining the best methods of causing death in those cases where it was deemed appropriate. Having now considered the procedures relating to the period leading up to and including death, the only group left to consider are those relating to the reporting, investigation and judging of end-of-life decisions. This will be considered in the next section.

4   Reporting, investigation and judgment

The final area of regulation which is worth exploring is the ways in which society can ensure that the best decisions are being made and that they are being made appropriately. This includes methods for ensuring that information is reported to the proper authorities, that information is received by the authorities within a proper period in order to make a decision, that those entrusted with making a decision are able to investigate cases, that those capable of making a decision make the right sorts of decision and are properly constituted to be able to make effective decisions and that those who violate the rules are subject to effective punishments. These, then, are regulations which are most likely to apply, at least in part, after the death of the patient and are designed to ensure the enforcement of general regulations about the end-of-life decisions.

The first crucial question to be addressed is when the evaluation of the end-of-life decision should occur. There are two general possibilities. The first is prior to the death. In this type of regulation, patients and health-care professionals would need to seek prior approval from a specified source before undertaking any practice which brings about death.[33] While none of the jurisdictions which currently allow assisted dying have such a system, draft bills sometimes present it as a way to minimise risks in potential legislation. Moreover, health-care professionals will often present difficult cases to clinical ethics committees for advice and approval. Sometimes, advice is even sought from the judiciary as it was in the *Bland* decision.[34] The benefit of such a system is that it allows for approval by a recognised body in advance which can investigate a specific case to determine whether all of the regulations have been met. If they have, it can allow the practice to continue. If they

---

[33] For example, Terry Pratchett, the noted science fiction author, has suggested that such a panel be a useful way forward. See www.guardian.co.uk/commentisfree/2010/feb/01/terry-pratchett-alzheimer-assisted-suicide.

[34] *Airedale NHS Trust* v. *Bland* [1993] 1 All ER 821.

have not, then bad outcomes can be prevented. This may be seen to be especially relevant in cases of end-of-life decisions as the bad outcome is often death. Even so, there are a number of problems with the approval of practices prior to the fact. First, any approval procedure would take time. Considering the processes involved in assisting death might be quite complicated as they are, adding further delay and stress may not be beneficial to patients in many situations. Furthermore, there is often a difficulty with agreeing to conduct before it happens. If society agrees to accept particular conduct, it must then make sure that the events in question actually correspond to the conduct which was approved. There must therefore be a post-event investigation anyway, if only to make sure that what happened was consistent with what was approved. Approval prior to the end-of-life decision thus seems to be impractical in most situations.

The other standard possibility is to have a post-event investigation. This would require that someone be authorised to investigate after the event what has happened. Usually, this further requires that the health-care professional report the procedures involved to the relevant author-ities along with providing evidence, usually written, that the appropriate standards were complied with in the case. In many, but not all, juris-dictions, the investigating authority has the ability to request further information and even call the health-care practitioner in to provide oral evidence.[35] This is the case in the Netherlands where the Regional Review Committees have this power;[36] however, the Department of Health in Oregon does not have this ability.[37] Sometimes, organisations or agencies may be created for the specific purpose but in other cases, it may be previously existing ones which are given the authority to inves-tigate these particular cases. While jurisdictions which allow assisted dying use post-event investigation as the primary method of enforce-ment and investigation, there are two important issues. The first is that these are dependent upon doctors and other health-care practitioners actually reporting their practices truthfully. This may not always be the case. The second, and potentially greater problem, is that if prob-lems have been found, it is usually too late to rectify any patient issues. In other words, if regulations have not been followed satisfactorily, we

---

[35] Termination of Life on Request and Assisted Suicide (Review Procedures) Act 2001, Article 8(2); Griffiths et al., Euthanasia and Law in Europe, p. 326 (discussing the Belgian Euthanasia Act).

[36] Termination of Life on Request and Assisted Suicide (Review Procedures) Act 2001, Article 8(2).

[37] ORS 127.865 § 3.11.

cannot bring the patient back to life and the other punishments that are available may be limited in nature.

Both of these ways of investigating and enforcing conduct thus have their problems. There may, however, be a compromise position that helps to offset these problems which is being used in the Netherlands. The Netherlands, as mentioned previously in Chapter 12, has begun to encourage the use of specially trained doctors, called SCEN doctors, as the consultant under the Dutch legislation. While SCEN doctors are not licensed to provide authorisation for assisted dying practices in advance, their expertise and training are held in high regard by the Regional Review Committees.[38] As a result, SCEN doctors are, in some way, acting as before-the-fact investigators who can provide advice about proper procedures and help ensure that all practices have been complied with. This does not preclude the Regional Review Committees from doing their mandated investigation and evaluation but it provides greater confidence for doctors who may be unaware of all the nuances of the legislation. This may then provide the best of both types of regulation. Before the end-of-life decision is implemented, specially trained investigators, either on the SCEN basis or some other one, could be used to provide advice and support prior to death. In doing so, if the training is adequate, they may be able to prevent most problems from occurring. After the end-of-life decision has been implemented, a more thorough investigation can be done which includes the reporting of the practice to a designated authority which has the power to inquire further should any issues arise. As with all of these types of procedural regulation, it will not eliminate every possible problem, but with adequate safeguards about reporting and investigation of the actual event as well as proper training for the investigators, many problems are likely to be minimised or eliminated.

In order to accomplish any investigation, whether prior to or after treatment at the end of life, we must have specific safeguards in place to allow for that scrutiny. The first, obviously, is for any regulations to allow an official organisation to have the ability to review cases within that jurisdiction. This is one of the biggest criticisms of the Oregon legislation which does not give the Department of Health this ability.[39] Considering that any investigation will require special mechanisms to account for vital issues such as the problem of doctor–patient confidentiality, the powers of any investigating authority should be clearly set out. This could take the form of granting further abilities to an existing

[38] Griffiths *et al.*, *Euthanasia and Law in Europe*, pp. 138–140.
[39] Keown, *Euthanasia, Ethics and Public Policy*, pp. 172–173.

organisation such as a Department of Health but it could also include the creation of a new body whose primary task is to investigate end-of-life decisions such as the Regional Review Committees used in the Netherlands. Where the review body fits within governmental structures is likely to be less important than how that body is constituted. The Regional Review Committees used by the Dutch provide a possible model for a reviewing body. Those committees consist of a doctor, an ethicist and a lawyer who provide expertise on the panel from medical, ethical and legal perspectives.[40] As end-of-life decisions involve complex matters of a legal, ethical and medical nature, it is prudent to have expertise in those areas available to the reviewing committee. There are other ways this may be accomplished, however. A review committee need not necessarily contain three experts from different disciplines on the panel, provided that expert opinion is available to advise the decision-maker. Thus, each investigation could include a report by an authority on areas outside the fields of expertise of panel members. While the possibility of having such reports might be an acceptable alternative, it is probably less ideal than having the expertise on the panel itself. Those without the requisite expertise may not know what questions to ask authorities within a particular field or may not be able to understand the reports sufficiently to be able to make the best decisions based upon them. Consequently, while there may be other possibilities, the best way forward appears to be a panel made up of expertise within particular fields. This is likely to include legal, ethical and medical expertise, although other jurisdictions have varied the composition of panels. For example, the Belgium version of the Regional Review Committees, the Federal Control and Evaluation Committee (FCEC), does not include anyone with specifically ethical training but instead includes members 'from groups charged with the problem of incurably ill patients'.[41] Whatever its make-up, however, a convincing way forward is through the use of a committee to investigate and evaluate end-of-life decisions.

Having a committee by itself does not mean that any limitations on acceptable conduct will be policed effectively. Those committees must also have evidence from cases available to them. Since an evaluation after the death in question is the most likely mechanism, the most

---

[40] Termination of Life on Request and Assisted Suicide (Review Procedures) Act 2001, Article 3 (2).
[41] Griffiths et al., *Euthanasia and Law in Europe*, p. 324. The FCEC also has 16 members to the Regional Review Committee's three members. Eight of those are doctors, four are lawyers and four are from groups 'charged with the problem of incurably ill patients'.

important aspect of this issue is the reporting procedures. These are the mechanisms which require the doctors to provide certain information to the relevant authorities.[42] This is usually in the form of written records which consist of particular required elements. These include: any written request by the patient, evidence of the patient's medical condition, the patient's prognosis including life expectancy, any required consultations (including second opinions, consultations with palliative care specialists or mental health evaluations), evidence to justify decisions on criteria such as 'unbearable suffering' and the procedure followed by the doctor (or other health-care professional) to bring about death, including drugs used.[43] All of this information is forwarded to the relevant authority which should have, as was indicated earlier, the ability to question the doctor further should there be information which needs to be augmented. There are suggestions for other information which should be reported, such as whether other doctors have refused the request and, if so, the reasons why.[44] The concern with too much additional information, as noted in Chapter 13, is that it may create bureaucratic problems for the authority in question, lead to doctors and health-care professionals being less willing to fill out lengthy reports and require information outside the knowledge of the person submitting the report (who is usually the treating physician). Information, then, should be limited to what is important to make the decision on whether the regulations have been met while allowing for those reviewing the reports to be able to probe further if need be.

Our final concern is the sanctions which should be imposed for failure to abide by the relevant guidelines. As with any criminal punishment, violations of any regulations involving end-of-life care should be clear so that those involved know when they are likely to be breaking the law. Additionally, the punishment should be appropriate for the violation. This may be difficult to discern in cases of end-of-life treatment. Some may argue that this should be based upon the harm committed. If a patient was wrongly killed under the law, this may be

---

[42] ORS 127.855 § 3.09; Termination of Life on Request and Assisted Suicide (Review Procedures) Act 2001, Article 21 [modifying Article 7 of the Burial and Cremation Act (1991)].

[43] ORS 127.855 § 3.09; Termination of Life on Request and Assisted Suicide (Review Procedures) Act 2001, Article 21 [modifying Article 7 of the Burial and Cremation Act (1991)]; Griffiths *et al.*, *Euthanasia and Law in Europe*, pp. 324–326 (discussing the Belgian Euthanasia Act).

[44] Keown, *Euthanasia, Ethics and Public Policy*, p. 173. See also Foley and Hendin, 'The Oregon Experiment', pp. 144–174, which refers more than once to the fact that the Oregon legislation does not require doctors who do not agree to provide assisted dying to be consulted by subsequent doctors.

seen as being tantamount to murder and anyone breaking the law in such a way should be punished in a similar fashion to murderers. This, though, might be too quick a decision. In some cases, the failure to abide by the relevant regulations may be punishable but the harm is not an unwanted death. We might consider, as an example, the *Sutorius* case from the Netherlands discussed in the previous chapter.[45] In this case, a doctor euthanised a patient who was 'tired of life'.[46] This was found to be in violation of the law in the Netherlands, as the patient needed to have an actual medical condition.[47] Despite the fact that the death was then ruled to be in violation of the law, there was no dispute that the patient involved did want to die. If we accept that wish as genuine, then it is not a harm to him (in the way we described harm earlier[48]) to have died. This does not mean that the doctor should not have been subject to sanction; it merely indicates that the harm caused was not death. We might further argue that violations of seemingly technical aspects of any legislation should be punished less harshly than more substantive ones (however defined). Thus, if a patient were to be euthanised when certain aspects of a written request form were not followed correctly but there was no concern about whether this affected the actual consent of the patient, we may wish to punish this less harshly than a case where it was clear that there was coercion of the patient, but the health-care practitioner proceeded anyway. We might, then, not focus upon the harm caused, but on the wrong committed. This is another way in which we might determine the appropriate punishment. This debate between the proper limits of punishment according to either the harm caused or wrong committed is a protracted debate within the theory of criminal law[49] and is beyond the scope of this particular book. What is important to realise, though, is that there are a number of different ways in which proper punishment can be characterised and it is important that legislation pays close attention to the reasons for punishing violations in the ways that it does. If our main aim in punishment is the deterrence of future bad conduct, then we should make sure that we have done so in such a way as to provide the best chance for us to do so.

We thus have a number of issues which need to be thought through when determining the best way to regulate the investigation and evaluation of end-of-life decisions. We must pay particular attention to the

---

[45] Griffiths *et al.*, *Euthanasia and Law in Europe*, pp. 35–39. The *Sutorius* case is also referred to as the *Brongersma* case.
[46] *Ibid.*   [47] *Ibid.*, p. 37.   [48] See Chapter 6.
[49] A. Ashworth, 'Taking the Consequences', in S. Shute, J. Gardner and J. Horder (eds.), *Action and Value in Criminal Law* (Oxford: Clarendon Press, 1993), pp. 107–124.

way in which we evaluate those decisions, when we do so and the evidence we provide to those whose job it is to do the evaluation. We must also pay attention to the ways in which we provide punishment for violations so as to most effectively deter bad conduct and avoid punishing those whose conduct we think is acceptable.

5   Conclusion

In conclusion, we have looked at a variety of practical issues in this chapter. We have explored the manner in which we can best ensure that requests made by patients are not subject to coercion and are being made freely and with proper information. We have further considered ways in which to regulate the process once the request of the patient has been made. While the regulations surrounding the request are most likely focused on the patient, those which come after the request are just as likely to focus on the health-care practitioner who will often have substantial duties once a request has been made. Guidelines, then, should be fashioned so as to provide proper support and advice for those acting once a request has been made in way that is consistent with the values of the jurisdiction. Finally, we have examined the ways in which we can best ensure that any reporting, investigation and evaluation of particular decisions can be done effectively and efficiently. We have paid particular attention to the types of authority which might be called upon to make decisions, as well as the evidence which ought to be available to them. Finally, we have considered the role of punishment and how we can best create a regulatory system which will minimise the risks of harm and conduct which is outside the law.

15   Conclusions

1   Introduction

This book has covered extensive ground since I began with the statement that death and dying are messy. What has hopefully become clear throughout the book is why that is. The issues which have an effect upon our view of end-of-life decisions are fundamental and foundational ones about life, medical treatment, the law and how we treat ourselves and others. Claiming that there are simple answers, claiming that there are irrefutable answers, claiming that there are always answers at all can be a fool's errand. Oftentimes, there are no compelling answers that will please everyone or, indeed, anyone. Death may sometimes be the least worst answer to the questions asked about medical treatment. The least worst answer, though, does not mean it is a good one. Even those arguing for the most permissive regulatory and ethical regimes about end-of-life care do not argue that death is a prize to be won. Nor are those who argue for more restrictive regimes impervious to the pain, agony and dehumanisation which occur in many end-of-life cases. Neither side – irrespective of what might be said on webpages, news reports or newsletters – is inhuman or evil. Everyone is trying simply to find a way through the ethical and legal mazes to find answers about how best to deal with these complicated issues. Civility, understanding and the ability to listen to others sometimes get lost along the way, but there is no reason why that ought to be the case. How we treat the dying says a lot about us as human beings and moral actors. How we treat others when discussing how to treat the dying says at least as much.

What I have tried to do in this book, then, is provide an answer to some of the questions which arise. I do not claim that these are the only possible answers, nor do I claim that they are the only possible correct ones. They are the ones I think are most defensible with the available evidence, but that does not mean others could not have a different, even contradictory, view. This may be because others have different starting points, do not agree with the conclusions reached in the previous chapters or have contrary opinions as to how the various principles and regulatory problems match up. Some may, for example, consider the place of traditional viewpoints to be more important than the value I have placed on them in this book. I take the view that, while we should remain mindful of the views of individuals in the past, those views are often based upon the understanding of the world at that time. In an area such as medical science, where treatments, diseases and our simple understanding of the human body change as quickly as they do, it is not possible to thoroughly ground our views about these things in traditional concepts. That something has always been our understanding does not mean it must continue to be that way.[1] Consequently, a traditional view does not have any added value or weight for being traditional. There will be others who disagree with that understanding. They might argue that while there have been advances in our understanding about various aspects of humanity, the fundamental parts of human beings have not changed. As a result, traditional understandings of things such as moral status or the value of life are crucial because they have undergone scrutiny for generations and we can therefore be more sure about their validity. Recognising that these are important discussions that affect our views does not mean that one must necessarily be correct and the other one incorrect. Both may have validity for particular individuals in particular contexts. These, of course, add to the problems we might face in deciding on the acceptability of particular end-of-life decisions because not everyone will agree with the views of others. All we can ask of individuals is that the views presented be considered, reasonable and as clear as possible.

I can do nothing in this final chapter to add to the considered and reasonable nature of the arguments presented in this book. What has been provided in the previous chapters will have to stand on its own in that regard. I can, however, provide any clarity which might still be lacking by focusing on two important things. First, part of the purpose of this final chapter will be to summarise the main points of the arguments I have presented throughout. If there are any concerns about what has been said or how those arguments fit together, the subsequent summary ought to clear up those doubts. Secondly, there are two lingering questions which I have yet to explicitly answer. I have not put forward a view on whether the end-of-life decisions we have been exploring need to be made by a health-care practitioner. We have discussed the various ways in which end-of-life decisions may impact upon health-care workers but have not explored the larger question of whether they ought to

---

[1] O. W. Holmes, 'The Path of the Law' (1897) 10 *Harvard Law Review* 457–478, 469.

partake or whether, for example, these practices should be left to family members or non-medical members of the community. This may seem an odd question to have avoided but I have done so because I think that in order to answer that one, a firm view needs to be expressed on the other remaining question – after consideration of all of the ethical principles and policy questions, which of the possible practices at the end of life should be acceptable and which ones should not? While I do not doubt that most who have read this book will have a good idea about the views that I would take, I have focused less on the answers to that question than the process of how to reach those answers. That is because the answers are often dependent on the society and legal system which exists. What ought to be done in one system may not be possible or desirable in another. Since my purpose was to provide a roadmap of the questions involved and a way to answer them, it seemed that a focus on the process of making a decision was more important than the decision itself. Of course, I have thought these decisions through, most explicitly in the context of the US and UK legal systems. I can, and will, provide an answer in those contexts which I feel is the most appropriate one. Waiting until now to do so was an attempt to focus previously on the reasons for the decision which will hopefully be of use to people who are either not in the US or UK context or who, even if they are, disagree with those conclusions. Before explaining those decisions, however, I should summarise the arguments which have led us to the conclusions I have reached.

2   Summary of arguments

At the beginning, I made several claims which were at the heart of the arguments presented subsequently. I argued first that any end-of-life decisions were not a series of unconnected practices, but a range of choices which were available to patients, families and medical staff. The potential options thus have an effect upon others and adjustments to the appropriateness of one choice have an impact upon the types of practices that decision-makers have available. Unfortunately, changing a regulatory regime does not affect the underlying medical conditions which afflict us. Those making decisions may be forced, therefore, to accept a practice which is neither best suited for the patient and condition nor one which anyone prefers. We must take care, then, to acknowledge that the regulation of one practice at the end of life affects other practices as well as the one we are regulating, and those need to be accounted for when determining the regulations we wish to have. In other words, we need to accept that end-of-life decisions are a continuum of choices instead of discrete practices. Secondly, I took the position that ethical arguments need to be useful. By that, I meant that ethical principles ought to be ones we can reasonably expect individuals to be able to put into practice and to use to govern their behaviour. If it were not one that those in our moral communities could use, then the principle itself should be subject to change. This was not an attempt to argue that ethics in general should avoid placing any weight on first principles and logical consistency. These are fundamental aspects of any legitimate ethical system. However, first principles and logical consistency can often lead to many different options. When considering the worthiness of those available options, we ought to further consider their practical use. We should not stop merely when finding that a particular decision is logically consistent with a set of first principles. We should then examine those decisions in practice to see if they are actual guides to behaviour. This does not mean, of course, that decisions reached cannot be controversial or must garner majority support to be correct. They do not. Even so, they do need to be decisions which can be exercised by others. Ethics is, first and foremost, a philosophical subject based upon determining the best ways to live. We must, therefore, be able to live with the principles we espouse.

The third claim I made was that decisions ought to be based on available evidence. Decisions about the regulation of treatments at the end of life are complicated, requiring an understanding of the underlying ethical foundations for decisions as well as the practicalities involved in the practices considered for regulation (and those affected by the regulation). Additionally, many of these decisions are based upon claims which are partially based upon events which have not yet happened. Consequently, the evidence available to support a particular conclusion may not be as definite or as strong as we would like. Scepticism about such evidence is therefore warranted. This does not mean, though, that we ought to jettison all attempts to require evidentiary support. Instead, we should focus on the available evidence we have while recognising that there are limits to it. If we are looking to regulate behaviour based upon certain fears, our first step should not simply be to accept those concerns. Contrariwise, we should begin by looking for evidence to support or refute those claims before making further decisions. The evidence will often only be able to give us an idea about the potential pitfalls of regulation instead of firm conclusions, but even an idea as to what is an actual problem and what is not will allow us to focus attention on those issues which are worthy of regulation. The final initial claim I made was in relation to the appropriate standard of evidence which is necessary. In many cases in the debates over end-of-life practices, arguments about regulating particular practices are based upon a standard which is impossible to achieve. Regulations such as those in Oregon or the Netherlands where assisted dying practices are allowed are dismissed because they cannot provide protection from all possible abuses. Since there are cases of abuse within those jurisdictions, it is claimed that other jurisdictions should not follow suit or they will also be subject to the same sorts of abuse. Such an argument, however, forgets two important factors. First, no regulation has ever been completely effective. Even criminal prohibitions on murder and treason (which often attract the harshest penalties) are broken. Claiming that a regulation is ineffective because there are instances where that regulation is broken is thus not a useful measure. The measure of a change in regulation ought to be whether it more effectively *minimises* instances of wrongful conduct. In order to do that, we need a comparison, and this is the second factor that needs to be borne in mind. When making decisions about the regulation of behaviour, we often act as if the current regulation is a given, almost akin to the 'state of nature' used by social contract theorists such as Hobbes and Locke.[2] What we have, though, is a current system of regulation which is no different from any other system of regulation. When exploring the minimisation of wrongful conduct, we ought to examine the effectiveness of the current regulation in addition to determining the impact of potential regulation. In other words, we need to compare both the proposed regulatory changes and the current regulation in order to determine which is more effective. We cannot simply evaluate the proposed regulation in terms of an idealised and largely unhelpful standard if our goal is really to improve our regulatory systems.

With these arguments in mind, Part I of the book focused on the creation of an ethical system which can be used to evaluate end-of-life practices. We started by looking at three foundational ideas which are necessary for any ethical system involving life. These were questions about moral status, the value of life and moral responsibility. These are crucial because before moving onto specific principles we need to know who matters when making moral decisions and when we are responsible for the decisions we make. We must also know the value of life so that we can begin to properly evaluate the choices that have been made. I have argued for what is a broad conception of moral status. While we began the chapter on moral status by looking at different

---

[2] T. Hobbes, *Leviathan* (London: The Fontana Library, 1962 [original publication 1651]); J. Locke, *Two Treatises of Government* (Cambridge University Press, 1960 [original publication 1690]).

versions of uni-criterial methods of determining moral status, all were found to be lacking. This was not surprising as, upon further reflection, we often have varied and complex reasons for deciding that particular entities are morally relevant. Sometimes, this is because the entities in question are human; sometimes this is because the entity has particular characteristics; sometimes it is because of a particular emotional or social connection with the entity. All of these may provide valid reasons to believe that something ought to be considered when making moral decisions. Our conception of moral status, therefore, should likewise be multi-dimensional. The conception of moral responsibility was likewise broad. Following the work of Fischer and Ravizza, I have argued that we are responsible for those things for which we have guidance control. Importantly, this means we are responsible not just for our actions, but also for our omissions as well as consequences, provided that we have the correct relationship to the events in question. We are responsible, then, not just for the things we do, but for those things we avoid doing. Within the context of end-of-life care, this means that doctors and other health-care practitioners can be as responsible for instances where treatment is withdrawn or withheld in the same way that they may be responsible for positive acts. The upshot of these broad conceptions of both moral status and responsibility means we are responsible for far more of the events in our lives and required to take account of more beings than we otherwise might. Indeed, for the purposes of this book, those involved in end-of-life care are likely morally responsible for everything they do or fail to do, and all of the patients we have encountered are morally relevant beings. To some, this may make the conclusions reached irrelevant as nothing appears to particularly turn on our conceptions of moral status and responsibility. However, they are important as a greater understanding of why individuals matter morally and why we are morally responsible provides a firmer foundation for our ethical framework.

Determining the value of life was also a complex rather than a simple method. I have argued that the conceptions generally used – vitalism, the Sanctity of Life and the Quality of Life – provide too simplistic a recognition of the ways in which our lives are valued. Our lives have value not simply because of the fact that we exist or because of the things we can do with that existence. Instead, we value our lives because of a combination of those two elements. Our existence matters in a number of crucial ways but that is not the only way in which our lives have meaning. Additionally, the ways in which we use our lives provide additional value to our mere existence and the biographical aspects of the way our lives have value and meaning can be as important as, and sometimes even more important than, the fact of our existence. Critically, the valuation we put on our lives is a personal decision which cannot be looked at objectively. Merely because someone determines that a specific narrative of their life is valuable, it does not matter if others have a different view. The value we place on life is individual and when we take account of the value of life in our ethical determinations, we need to accept that the value of life is not the one we ourselves place on the choices of others, but the value they place on those decisions.

From these three foundational concepts, we looked further at specific ethical principles which are relevant to end-of-life decisions. These included autonomy, paternalism, beneficence, non-maleficence, harm and dignity. All of these more specific principles need to be applied to the events in question when deciding whether particular actions (or omissions) are acceptable. We first explored notions of autonomy and paternalism. Conceptions of autonomy fall broadly within one of two categories: Kantian versions and Millian versions. Kantian versions, such as those articulated by Onoro O'Neill, were found to have significant flaws. As a result, the chapter focused on Millian notions of autonomy, particularly those put forward by Gerald Dworkin and Beauchamp and Childress. While there are not likely to be many, if any, differences in practice between Dworkin's notions of autonomy and Beauchamp and Childress, it was decided that the latter model was easier to apply. Consequently, autonomy for the purposes of this book was instances where a person made a decision intentionally, with understanding and free from controlling interests. It was further argued that respecting the autonomy of others does not just require avoiding interfering with the decisions themselves, but also provides positive duties to ensure that individuals have the requisite abilities and information to make autonomous decisions. In the context of medical care, this would require, for example, that a doctor or other health-care practitioner does not respect autonomy in a patient by simply failing to object to a decision made by the patient if they have not provided them with the necessary information to make an informed judgement about treatment options. What was further highlighted, however, was that not all autonomous decisions are good. A decision may be a bad one and does not become good simply because it was made autonomously. Therefore, even autonomous decisions may be interfered with by society provided there are sufficient justifications for doing so. This may even include some cases where the interference occurs to protect the individual from his or her own actions. In order to determine when it was appropriate to regulate the autonomous decisions of others, a firm conception of what is meant by the concept of harm was required. The classic definition of harm is the one provided by Joel Feinberg which posits that a harm is something which involves a setback to important interests (what he calls welfare interests) of the individual in question. Something was beneficial if it had a positive effect on those interests. From this understanding of harm, it became much easier to construct a working conception of the ethical principles of beneficence and non-maleficence which guide the behaviour of those in health-care professions. The principle of beneficence requires that we have a positive impact upon at least some of the important interests of an individual. Non-maleficence requires that we avoid having a negative impact on those interests. Essential for our discussions about end-of-life care, death need not always be a harm. If the death of an individual did not set back welfare interests that the individual had, then it was not a harm. Our final principle was dignity. Conceptions of dignity are more difficult, as the concept in general has undergone much less scrutiny than conceptions of harm and autonomy. Indeed, while autonomy and harm often mean roughly the same things to different people, dignity seems to mean many different things to many different people. Our conception of dignity was a socially constructed one which acted as an ethical brake on conduct. It provided us with valid reasons, at least in the case of human beings, to stop and further consider our behaviour. Its primary use was for patients incapable of utilising the protection of other values such as autonomy because there was insufficient reason, in most cases, to allow dignity claims to overrule the autonomous decisions of others. For those to whom such claims are unavailable, however, dignity provided a critically important way to provide support for the interests of those individuals. All of these different principles may pull in different directions and Chapter 8 explored the ways in which we can pull these principles together to form a coherent ethical system. That system would allow us to then determine whether specific practices at the end of life could be ethically justified.

Part II of the book switched focus from the ethical framework for making decisions about the end of life to the practicalities of regulating practices which affect those who are dying. Our first issues related to the patient. Of specific concern were suggested problems surrounding the prevention of suicide and the protection of vulnerable groups. The prevention of suicide is often presented as a valuable societal interest and was thus worthy of attention. However, a number of problems with using the prevention of suicide to regulate practices were presented. First, there is a lack of consistency among practices at the end of life. If the prevention of suicide is really an important governmental interest, it should be applied across the board. Namely, suicide prevention should be a reason to prevent the withdrawal and withholding of treatment in addition to other types of practices such as assisted dying. Yet, even cases which look like reasonably clear examples of patients attempting to die by refusing life-sustaining treatment are not seen as legitimate reasons for state interference with the autonomous decisions of patients. It is thus unclear as to the overarching reason for applying the same interest to justify interventions in other cases. In other words, if the prevention of suicide is a compelling governmental interest, it ought to be one in all end-of-life cases and not just some. Even if one accepts that the prevention of suicide should be sufficient to justify regulation, there is no compelling evidence which shows that the prohibition on particular medical treatments actually prevents cases of suicide. We looked at three explanations which, although there was limited evidence to support them, provided some reason for doubting that the prohibition on assisted dying actually impacted upon the suicide rates in jurisdictions. Questions about the protection of vulnerable groups were likewise very important but there was little evidence to indicate they were actually a substantial problem. Evidence from jurisdictions which allow more types of end-of-life decisions (including assisted dying) did not show that vulnerable groups in those jurisdictions were under increased threat. Instead, those who were likely to choose assisted dying in these jurisdictions were less likely to be part of a minority or vulnerable group than the general population. Thus, while the concerns raised about patients are ones which theoretically need to be accounted for in regulation, it did not appear that the available evidence showed that either provided substantial problems in reality.

After exploring these topics, we turned to those involving the health-care practitioner. The fundamental issues which have an effect upon the health-care practitioner involved questions about their ability to control patients and to 'play God', the perception of those providing care to those receiving it and the general psychological effects of participating in practices which resulted in the patient's death. Again, while this appears at first glance to be subjects which provide substantial reasons to regulate behaviour in a particular way, there was little evidence that doctors involved in end-of-life care will 'play God' more frequently than those who do not have the legal ability to engage in particular practices. Those willing to 'play God' then were unlikely to be affected by regulation because they were already likely to operate outside the legal bounds of medicine. While every effort should be made to prevent people from acting contrary to the law, this does not appear to be a greater problem in those jurisdictions where assisted dying was legal than where it was not. Nor was there any sufficient evidence to show that the general perception of doctors would change. Psychological effects, at least certain kinds, were likely to decrease as both patients and health-care practitioners could receive more effective support if practices were conducted out in the open rather than in secret. After looking at those concerns which would have a direct effect upon health-care workers, we looked at more general concerns related to professional codes of conduct and professionalism in general. While professional codes of conduct would need to undergo a change to accommodate the legalisation of different practices should that change, there was little reason to believe there would be any additional upheaval in codes of conduct. This is not surprising as we saw in the first part that ethical principles could justify a range of practices at the end of life. Professionalism in general was a greater issue but regulation appeared likely to be able to effectively enforce appropriate standards of professionalism.

Beyond the two main participants in end-of-life care, the patient and the health-care professionals, we proceeded to examine the effect of regulation upon the wider community. It was argued that the wider community cannot be considered a homogeneous unit and that we needed to consider different groups within the wider community. In particular, it was stressed that the most direct effects are likely not to happen to the community at large but in more select groups of families and friends. Specifically, it was argued that the effects upon these more select groups are likely to be quite complex and that rules should allow some flexibility in many respects to be able to account for those affected and the ways in which those effects might happen. However, in most cases, the larger and more diffuse the group becomes, the less actual effect there ought to be on individuals. It may be that there are those within a larger community who feel individually impacted by instances of conduct within their community, but the criminal law should not be used to address the problem unless there was a direct effect upon them. A more crucial societal concern is the prevention of illegal conduct. We looked specifically at the reporting systems used by the Dutch and in Oregon to evaluate the ways in which those two jurisdictions attempt to control the behaviour of health-care practitioners and prevent instances of abuse. While the Oregon legislation is worth emulating on particular points, the overall lack of investigative ability poses questions which need to be answered. A more useful system seems to require the ability to evaluate instances within a jurisdiction and present an analysis both in general and of specific cases to prevent the escalation of problem practices. We further explored the problems of investigation in other jurisdictions and the specific problem of a seeming lack of desire to investigate, prosecute and convict those engaged in practices which are illegal. We questioned the social utility of prohibiting practices but not attempting to prevent them, and argued that more honest regulatory schemes were preferable to those which outlawed types of conduct but then did not prosecute that conduct when it happened.

Chapter 13 explored in great detail the significant question regarding slippery slope arguments. We considered both types of slippery slope arguments: the logical and the empirical ones. After a detailed examination of slippery slope arguments in general, we considered the specifics of the two types of argument. The logical slippery slope argument – which is more properly considered an argument from consistency – was not an accurate reflection of the types of philosophical interests contained within the arguments for legalisation of particular practices. In other words, despite claims of a logical slippery slope being compelling, nothing within the argument requires a resulting slide. Nor was there significant evidence to show that an empirical slippery slope argument was likely. When considering specific issues within a broader regime, there were matters which require a closer inspection but nothing which was likely to provide an overwhelming reason to ban particular practices.

Finally, we explored the necessary procedural protections which would be required in any regulatory scheme. We looked at patient-centred protections which focused on the request and on providing greater certainty that it was informed, consensual and voluntary. We then looked at what procedures would be necessary once a request has been made to ensure that the health-care practitioners act most appropriately under the circumstances. This included the necessity of second opinions, both in general and for specific reasons such as the possibility of clinical depression. It also included the issues about waiting periods and the types of lethal medication which could be used. Finally, we looked at specific regimes in order to investigate and prevent abuses. In particular, we explored whether a decision prior to the events in question, one which happened afterwards or a combination of the two was preferable. We also considered who might be best placed to make these decisions, as well as the ways in which they might be able to punish wrongdoing.

What we have learned generally in Part II, then, is that a number of standard arguments raised in the debates on end-of-life decisions do not have any evidentiary support. While we should remain vigilant and continue to do research to make sure that these issues do not become greater problems, if there is insufficient evidence to substantiate the empirical claims on which they are based, we should not use these as reasons to decide on the acceptability of practices at the end of life.

Moreover, since other issues apply equally to types of conduct which we allow as well as ones we do not, we ought to be more critical of attempts to use these issues which arise across the spectrum of end-of-life decisions. This is not to suggest that all concerns raised are either general issues applicable to all end-of-life decisions or lack empirical support. Some do raise problems which regulation would need to address. However, before utilising a complete ban, we ought to consider more limited ways in which we can regulate conduct which allows greater freedom for individual patients and doctors. Close regulation cannot solve all of our problems, of course, but it can minimise a great number and we should be more cognisant of the ability to effectively regulate conduct at the end of life in a manner which safeguards individuals from practices which are questionable while not preventing those which are not.

3   A model for going forward

So where do we go from here? In this section I wish to provide a sketch (and it will be no more than a sketch) of what practices I think should be available for patients at the end of life. I do not suppose that those reading this are likely to be surprised by the suggestions made at this point, but it is worth being explicit as to what I think is acceptable and what is not, and how I would regulate behaviours were I in charge of designing general legislation on end-of-life decisions. As stated previously, my concentration will be on the UK and the US, so it is not necessarily the case that these suggestions would apply in every jurisdiction throughout the world. In fact, they would not. Countries without an advanced health-care system, for example, would require different regulations, as would ones where discriminatory practices are more pronounced (e.g. South Africa under apartheid). Furthermore, countries without strong rights-based legal systems are also likely to be regulated in a different manner. This is not because I think there ought to be a 'right to death'. I don't. The way that the various parties have to interact and the way different ethical principles interrelate makes it impossible to create a right which could be legally enforced. It would simply cause too many problems with the legitimate expectations of others if we granted people a right to die. Rights claims can be important, however, to many of the surrounding issues. Rights claims allow individual citizens to be able to limit governmental excesses in ways which are vital to the ways in which end-of-life decisions should be regulated. As such, I would not argue for the same regulatory scheme in those jurisdictions which did not have ways for citizens to petition the government for redress.[3] A final question, and one which is particularly appropriate considering the focus on the US and the UK, is the effect of a universal health-care system on any regulatory scheme. It could be argued that a jurisdiction without a universal heath-care scheme, such as in the US currently, would create additional problems in end-of-life care due to financial constraints. While I think this is possible, we should also remember that Oregon has had a system of assisted dying for a significant period of time and the states of Washington and Wyoming have also recently allowed assisted suicide (by referendum[4] and judicial decision[5] respectively). So, it is not clear that the simple presence of a managed care system like the US has does dramatically effect the regulation of end-of-life decision-making. Obviously, specific regulations would need to account for differences between systems. For example, it would be prudent to create legislation which eliminates ways in which insurance companies could pressure patients into accepting assisted dying practices for financial reasons but there would be no wholesale differences between jurisdictions with universal health care and those without.

With those caveats in mind, it will come as little surprise that I would support a broad range of end-of-life practices, including voluntary assisted dying. Some cases of end-of-life treatment such as the provision of palliative care are uncontroversial and I will therefore not spend any time discussing them further. Things become more complicated when considering whether to allow palliative care which shortens life. However, since medical science has indicated that the actual impact of ethical concepts like the doctrine of double effect is minimal at best, there is actually not a lot of reason to treat these cases differently than palliative care generally. Treatment which is not clinically indicated, of course, would need to be addressed, but this is better explored through general codes of conduct rather than focusing on end-of-life treatments specifically. Terminal sedation would require specific legislation, but that requires an understanding of the appropriateness of the withdrawal and withholding of treatment as well. Again, at this stage in history, there are few objections to the withdrawal and withholding of treatment, at least for competent patients. In those cases, we generally allow patients to require the withdrawal and withholding of specific treatments irrespective of whether the health-care workers believe it to

---

[3] Different jurisdictions, of course, have different ways of protecting these rights but that is not important for our purposes here.

[4] RCW s. 70.254.020.

[5] *Baxter* v. *State*, 224 P.3d 1211 (Mont. 2009).

be in the best interests of the patient or not. We might wish to ensure that the patient has understood the information presented to them as well as making sure that they are, in fact, competent and are not subject to undue influences, but barring those cases, patients are allowed to refuse any treatment they want to. We could, I suppose, require greater scrutiny of the withdrawal and withholding of treatment generally to allow oversight of the decisions of health-care workers and patients. This might provide benefits both in cases where patients are pressured into withdrawing or withholding treatment by health-care staff or family and friends, or when health-care professionals undeservedly determine that patients are incompetent when they are not. Doing so in a reliable way seems problematic. One possibility is to require reporting similar to the methods I will argue should be used in cases of assisted dying, but this may become an exercise in form-filling as opposed to a reliable method to prevent abuse. Moreover, there does not appear to be any research which indicates that there are a significant number of cases to make it efficient. Additional research, however, should be done in order to gauge whether there are sufficient numbers of problem cases to require further regulation. If there are not, there is little reason to require additional measures which are likely to be only bureaucratic in nature. Since palliative care is acceptable and the withdrawal of treatment is also, then terminal sedation should provide no additional problems. It is difficult to see how the combining of two acceptable practices creates additional concerns provided that the combination does not alter the essential elements of the requisite parts (which it does not).

Assisted dying, whether in the form of assisted suicide or active voluntary euthanasia, is also a practice which I think should be legally acceptable provided that the patient is terminally ill. As has been shown previously, there is little ethical difference between the withdrawal of treatment (in at least some cases) and assisted dying. If the patient and doctor are doing so with the specific purpose that the patient's life ends, then they are making the sorts of ethical claim which are being made in cases of assisted dying. The difference between active and passive ways of accomplishing that goal does not provide an ethical distinction. We are as morally responsible for our omissions as for our actions and if the complex interaction of the various ethical principles provides sufficient justification for allowing a health-care practitioner to remove treatment which is sustaining the life of a patient, then those same principles supply reasons for active measures which end life. However, even though ethically they should be treated in a similar manner, it does not mean that practically we can do so. Because assisted dying means a relatively quick death on average, as opposed to cases of withdrawal and withholding of treatment, it becomes easier to hide abuses in cases of assisted dying. Consequently, we need a regulatory scheme which provides protection for patients. These protections should include:

1. a recorded request (preferably in writing but other methods may be acceptable if patients are unable to write a request);
2. confirmation that the patient has made the request voluntarily, after sufficient information and without undue outside influences;
3. second opinions about the patient's prognosis, diagnosis and available treatment options including palliative care and psychological ones;
4. a waiting period where at least some of the time is merely for reflection;
5. a robust investigation and reporting system; and
6. an effective enforcement regime for abuses which do arise.

In addition, of course, no doctor or other health-care practitioner should be forced to participate in practices if they do not agree with them, meaning that some sort of conscientious objection clause would be included in any legislation. I further think that efforts should be made to prioritise assisted suicide over euthanasia. Oregon has done this by simply outlawing active euthanasia but there may be problems in specific cases if patients have unusual reactions to drug cocktails. In the Netherlands, there is merely the recommendation that assisted suicide is preferred. My preference would be for something which more explicitly made assisted suicide the primary choice except for in a limited number of cases. The benefit of assisted suicide over active voluntary euthanasia is small – the only difference being who does the final act – but it is a meaningful one which ultimately continues to focus control on the patient rather than the health-care practitioner. The required second opinions would need to make sure that patients are aware of treatment options such as palliative care and psychological treatments (e.g. for clinical depression), which raises the question of what sort of doctor should be entitled to give second opinions in these cases. Should, for example, second opinions be required from a palliative care specialist or from a psychiatrist? I think that, while there is some merit to the idea, it is difficult to be prescriptive about these practices without becoming too bureaucratic. It may be clear in some cases that either palliative care or psychiatric therapies may not be appropriate and requiring second opinions to be carried out by doctors in those specialisms would become an exercise in form-filling. However, in the vast majority of cases, either palliative or psychiatric care is clinically indicated and these should be used. What seems most useful, then, is a recommendation in legislation that a second opinion from a palliative care specialist or a psychiatrist be sought in all cases where there is doubt. In other words, if a doctor is unsure as to whether a palliative care referral would be beneficial, then they should send the patient for the referral. It is only in cases where doctors are convinced that such a referral would not be helpful that the second opinion should be from someone else. Additionally, the SCEN programme in the Netherlands appears to be an effective way to provide advice and support to medical staff and protect the interests of the patients. While it is doubtful that the programme could just be transplanted into another jurisdiction, efforts should be made to examine how best to import the ideas of the programme into a jurisdiction allowing assisted dying. The same is true for the Regional Review Committees used by the Dutch. There are substantial benefits to their use as an investigatory and enforcement agency, including the requirement of written reports, consistency of practice and the use of different expertise. Again, it would not be necessary to completely mirror the Dutch agency but a specialist investigatory and enforcement body should be a requirement for any legalised assisted dying practice. What we end up with is a blending of the Oregon and Dutch regulatory practices. Primarily, the regulatory scheme itself has many of the foundational qualities of the Oregon Death with Dignity Act, but provides a stronger investigatory and enforcement mechanism based upon Dutch practices. It would also allow euthanasia in a limited number of cases but would express a strong preference for assisted suicide in most cases.

The final practices, and the ones I find most difficult to reach a conclusion on, are those related to the treatment of patients who are not competent. In other words, what should we do with the Anthony Blands of the world? If the patient has provided an advance directive or approved someone to act as a surrogate decision-maker, then we could merely treat these cases in a similar manner to ones in which the patient was competent. There would be reasons, of course, to provide some additional protection to patients in cases of surrogate decision-makers in order to make sure they are making decisions on an acceptable basis (i.e. for the patient's benefit and not theirs). We might also wish to provide some system to evaluate whether a previous decision by the patient was one they would continue to assert in their present circumstances. On the other hand, we may wish to require only an express contemporaneous request and not statements made in advance or by others. There is legal precedent for this, as those who are not competent cannot, for example, get married, irrespective of whether or not they had written an advance directive or a surrogate would agree on the individual's behalf. We might decide that the problem of whether our future selves agree with our present selves about such treatment is too fraught with difficulty for a general rule which allows end-of-life treatments in these cases. In general, we may also decide that autonomy claims become less strong the further away from the decision we get. We might also have concerns about the types of treatment available and not wish to allow all the kinds of practices we might find acceptable in the cases of competent patients. My own feeling is that those who are not competent should be ineligible for assisted dying practices. The differences in the way that various ethical principles work (e.g. autonomy and the value of life) do not provide sufficient grounding for treating these cases like those of competent patients and the practical problems associated with regulation are too great. Thus, non-voluntary euthanasia would not be acceptable even though other practices (such as the withdrawal and withholding of treatment) should continue to be acceptable.

Furthermore, we have the issues involved in the specific case of Anthony Bland, where he had not created an advance directive nor had he requested that someone act as a surrogate. In the case itself, most people seem to think the correct decision was reached. I would agree with that conclusion, although I again find it tricky to articulate a particular rationale as to why. We cannot rely on autonomy interests to back it up, nor is it easy to rely on value of life determinations (since, under my view, the individual's feelings about their own life carry considerable weight and we do not know what Anthony Bland thought about life in PVS). Conceptions of harm, beneficence and non-maleficence seem to offer only minimal help. If forced, my opinion about Anthony Bland probably relies on the fact that, presuming the doctors were correct about his physical state, there was no possible recovery or improvement. There was, quite simply, nothing that could be done for him. Relying on that as a general principle, though, is disquieting at the very least. It is unclear as to who gets to make those sorts of decisions and their expertise for being able to do so. Moreover, unless very carefully limited, the prospects for abuse are quite high. The reason argued earlier that quality of life judgements made by individuals do not lead to a slippery slope is because other interests are in play which limit unfettered decisions about whose lives are worthy and whose are not. Removing those limitations raises those issues again. Furthermore, even if we could be sure that these decisions would stay within their specified boundaries, we would need to return to Lord Browne-Wilkinson's hypothetical. Why couldn't the doctors just provide Anthony Bland with a lethal injection? Ethically, the principles which allow us to justify assisted dying in competent patients are not present in this sort of case any more than they are in other cases where a patient is incompetent. Indeed, while we could argue that there are some limited autonomy rights for patients who have created an advance directive for assisted dying but who are now incompetent, this is not possible for Anthony Bland. Regulatory problems provided greater reason for refusing to allow assisted dying for Anthony Bland. The result, however, is not radically different using the withdrawal of treatment. Withdrawing treatment was guaranteed to kill Anthony Bland in the same way that a lethal injection would have. This is true but I see no way around the issue. There is little distinguishable way to allow Anthony Bland to have a lethal injection without applying the same rationale to everyone. This, though, would be going too far. It is thus a case where Anthony Bland is being subject to treatment merely at the expense of adverse effects on others but I think it is the one limited case where we need to do so.

That leaves us only with the final question about whether doctors and other health-care practitioners are actually necessary. There are jurisdictions where doctors have no special privileges in relation to the sorts of end-of-life decision we have been considering. Switzerland, for example, does not treat doctors any differently from others and the new prosecutorial guidelines in the UK seem to actively discourage doctors from participating. These might provide some support for the claim that the involvement of health-care workers in these sorts of end-of-life decision is non-essential. From the perspective of expertise about the sorts of interest involved at the end of life, it is true that doctors or other health-care professionals are unlikely to have special qualifications outside purely medical concerns. There is nothing in the requisite training of doctors, nurses or others which provides them with special insight or expertise in determining the value of life, whether a particular practice is harmful or whether decisions are autonomous or not. On that basis, then, there is no reason to prefer health-care professionals over others. I do not think, however, that this is the benefit of requiring the involvement of health-care workers. It is not because they have special expertise that they are important. They are important, instead, because of the vital duties they have in relation to patients. Due to professional codes of conduct and the like, they are required to act in particular ways in relation to patients which are not always mirrored in our general ethical codes. Doctors and nurses, for example, are required to act in their patient's best interests. They are thus expected to put the desires and wishes of the patient ahead of their own, at least within the context of treatment. That is not something we are generally required to do in our ordinary everyday lives. We may choose to act in ways consistent with those duties, of course, but there is no specific demand that we do so. The lack of specific fiduciary duties (among others) means that health-care professionals are particularly well placed to act in these sorts of case. That does not mean that we could not replicate these duties in others, eliminating the primary need for the involvement of doctors, nurses and other health-care staff. How we would do so is not especially clear, nor does it seem to be imperative, unless doctors and other health-care workers refuse to participate. If that were to occur, we may need to create a position for those tasked with helping others in end-of-life decisions but unless that problem presented itself (and it does not appear likely based upon the evidence we have), utilising the protection afforded by the existing duties of health-care professionals seems the most ideal.

4   Final conclusions

I do not think, however extensive this book (or any other one) is or could be, that we can definitively solve all of the issues surrounding end-of-life treatment. There are too many variables in relations to patients, medical conditions and treatment options for one set of ethical principles and legal requirements to cover every possible case. What we can strive to do is to provide clear, consistent arguments about the best ways to approach these concerns in an effort to minimise the number of problem cases and provide some semblance of a framework for making tough decisions. We cannot eliminate the fact that those decisions are often difficult, troubling and controversial. What I have attempted to provide within this book is a possible way forward. It does not answer all of the potential questions that people may have nor does it provide us with the easiest of answers. The ethical principles used here are often more complex than we have grown used to and they do not always lead to firm conclusions. To return to what I said at the beginning of both the book and this chapter, these issues are messy. There is no way anyone can provide firm conclusions to these issues in a way which removes all of those factors because so many of them are personal and individual. We must accept that disagreements are likely and no ethical and legal structure will eliminate them. The best we can have is a roadmap to help us through the increasingly difficult maze of these questions. That map should include a strong ethical framework which includes a number of different interacting principles as well as a firm understanding of the types of problem which develop in the regulation of human behaviour by the law. We need greater empirical evidence about what people are doing, what they want to be able to do and the effects of these decisions as well as greater discussion about the role of various principles both in our day-to-day lives and in medical care. We are all likely to face the problems at the end of life sometimes over our lives. The issues surrounding dying are impossible to avoid. We may, if we explore the ethical and regulatory issues, be able to reduce them even if we cannot avoid them entirely. In the end, if we can make the dying process even a bit less bad than it is – a bit less painful, a bit less dehumanising, a bit less debilitating, a bit less problematic – hopefully, we can then proceed to really explore what the concept of a 'good death' really means. Death is inevitable, a bad death is not. Maybe if we can provide the support to individuals to avoid a bad death, we can begin to focus on helping them not to extend the dying process, but to live, even in the face of dying.

Bibliography

Anderson, J. and Gallup, G., 'Self Recognition in *Saguinus*? A Critical Essay' (1997) 54 *Animal Behaviour* 1563–1567

Anonymous, 'A Piece of My Mind' (8 January 1988) 259(2) *JAMA* 272

Ashworth, A., 'Taking the Consequences', in S. Shute, J. Gardner and J. Horder (eds.), *Action and Value in Criminal Law* (Oxford: Clarendon Press, 1993), pp. 107–124

Battin, M. P., *Ending Life: Ethics and the Way We Die* (Oxford University Press, 2005)

Battin, M. P., Francis, L. P. and Landesman, B. M. (eds.), *Death, Dying and the Ending of Life* (Aldershot: Ashgate Publishing, 2007), vol. I

Death, Dying and the Ending of Life (Aldershot: Ashgate Publishing, 2007), vol. II

Battin, M. P., van der Heide, A., Ganzini, L., van der Wal, G. and Onwuteaka-Philipsen, B. D., 'Legal Physician-Assisted Dying in Oregon and the Netherlands: Evidence Concerning the Impact of Patients in "Vulnerable" Groups' (2007) 33 *Journal of Medical Ethics* 591–597

Beauchamp, T. and Childress, J., *Principles of Biomedical Ethics* (6th edn) (Oxford University Press, 2009)

Bennett, J., 'Morality and Consequences', in *The Tanner Lectures on Human Values II* (Salt Lake City, UT: University of Utah Press, 1981), pp. 66–68

'Negation and Abstention: Two Theories of Allowing' (1993) 104 *Ethics* 75–96, reprinted in B. Steinbock and A. Norcross (eds.), *Killing and Letting Die* (2nd edn) (New York: Fordham University Press, 1994), pp. 230–256

Beyleveld, D. and Brownsword, R., *Human Dignity in Bioethics and Biolaw* (Oxford University Press, 2002)

Biggs, H., *Euthanasia: Death with Dignity and the Law* (Oxford: Hart Publishing, 2001)

Blackstone, W., *Commentaries on the Laws of England*, 4 vols. (Oxford: Clarendon Press, 1765–1769), vol. IV

Bostrom, N., 'Dignity and Enhancement', in E. D. Pellegrino, A. Schulman and T. W. Merrill (eds.), *Human Dignity and Bioethics* (University of Notre Dame Press, 2009), pp. 173–206

Cantor, N. L., 'On Kamisar, Killing and the Future of Physician-Assisted Death' (2003–2004) 102 *Mich. L. Rev.* 1793

Cassidy, S., 'The Formal Problem of the Epilogue in "Crime and Punishment": The Logic of Tragic and Christian Failures' (1982) 3 *Dostoevsky Studies* 171

Chin, A. E. *et al.*, 'Legalized Physician-Assisted Suicide in Oregon: The First Year's Experience' (1999) 340 *New England Journal of Medicine* 577–583

'Oregon's Death with Dignity Act: The First Year's Experience' (1999), Department of Human Resources, Oregon Health Division, Center for Disease Prevention and Epidemiology

Chochinov, H. M. and Schwartz, L., 'Depression and the Will to Live in the Psychological Landscape of Terminally Ill Patients', in K. Foley and H. Hendin (eds.), *The Case against Assisted Suicide* (Baltimore: Johns Hopkins University Press, 2002), pp. 261–277

Cohen, J., 'European Public Acceptance of Euthanasia: Socio-demographic and Cultural Factors Associated with the Acceptance of Euthanasia in 33 European Countries' (2006) 63 *Social Science and Medicine* 743–756

Dancy, J., 'Intuitionism', in P. Singer (ed.), *A Companion to Ethics* (Malden, MA: Blackwell Publishing, 1991), pp. 411–420

D'Arcy, E., *Human Acts: An Essay in Their Moral Evaluation* (Oxford: Clarendon Press, 1963)

de Haan, J., 'The New Dutch Law on Euthanasia' (2002) 10 *Medical Law Review* 57–75

Deliens, L. *et al.*, 'End-of-Life Decisions in Medical Practice in Flanders, Belgium: A Nationwide Survey' (2000) 356 *The Lancet* 1806–1811

Dennett, D. C., 'Commentary on Kraynak', in E. D. Pellegrino, A. Schulman and T. W. Merrill (eds.), *Human Dignity and Bioethics* (University of Notre Dame Press, 2009), pp. 83–88

De Veer, M. and van den Bos, R., 'A Critical Review of Methodology and Interpretation of Mirror Self-recognition Research in Nonhuman Primates' (1999) 58 *Animal Behaviour* 459–468

Devlin, P., *The Enforcement of Morals* (Oxford University Press, 1965)

Director of Public Prosecutions, *Policy for Prosecutors in Respect of Cases of Encouraging or Assisting Suicide* (London: Stationery Office, 2010)

Dworkin, G., 'Paternalism' (1972) 56 *The Monist* 64–84

The Theory and Practice of Autonomy (Cambridge University Press, 1988)

Dworkin, G., Frey, R. G. and Bok, S., *Euthanasia and Physician-Assisted Suicide: For and Against* (Cambridge University Press, 1998)

Dworkin, R., *Life's Dominion* (New York: Vintage Books, 1994)

Emanuel, E. J., 'Euthanasia and Physician-Assisted Suicide: A Review of the Empirical Data from the United States' (2002) 162 *Archives of Internal Medicine* 142–152

Enoch, D., 'Once You Start Using Slippery Slope Arguments, You're on a Very Slippery Slope' (2001) 211 *Oxford Journal of Legal Studies* 629–647

Erin, C. and Ost, S. (eds.), *The Criminal Justice System and Health Care* (Oxford University Press, 2007)

Feinberg, J., *Harm to Others: The Moral Limits of the Criminal Law* (New York: Oxford University Press, 1984), vol. I

Feldman, D., 'Human Dignity as a Legal Value: Part One' (1999) *Public Law* 682–702

Finnis, J., '*Bland*: Crossing the Rubicon' (1993) 109 *LQR* 329–337

'The Fragile Case for Euthanasia: A Reply to John Harris', in J. Keown (ed.), *Euthanasia Examined* (Cambridge University Press, 1995), pp. 46–55

Natural Law and Natural Rights (Oxford University Press, 1980)

'A Philosophical Case against Euthanasia', in J. Keown (ed.), *Euthanasia Examined* (Cambridge University Press, 1995), pp. 23–35

Fischer, J. M., *My Way: Essays on Moral Responsibility* (New York: Oxford University Press, 2006)

Fischer, J. M. and Ravizza, M., *Responsibility and Control: A Theory of Moral Responsibility* (New York: Cambridge University Press, 1998)

Foley, K. and Hendin, H., 'The Oregon Experiment', in K. Foley and H. Hendin (eds.), *The Case against Assisted Suicide* (Baltimore: Johns Hopkins University Press, 2002), pp. 144–174

Foot, P., 'Killing and Letting Die', in J. L. Garfield and P. Hennessey (eds.), *Abortion: Moral and Legal Perspectives* (Amherst, MA: University of Massachusetts Press, 1984), pp. 177–185

'The Problem of Abortion' (1967) *Oxford Review* No. 5, reprinted in B. Steinbock and A. Norcross (eds.), *Killing and Letting Die* (2nd edn) (New York: Fordham University Press, 1994), pp. 266–279

Frey, R. G., 'The Fear of a Slippery Slope', in G. Dworkin, R. G. Frey and S. Bok (eds.), *Euthanasia and Physician-Assisted Suicide* (Cambridge University Press, 1998), pp. 43–63

Gailey, E., *Write to Death: News Framing of the Right to Die Conflict, from Quinlan's Coma to Kevorkian's Conviction* (Westport, CT: Praeger Publishers, 2003)

Gardner, J., 'Nearly Natural Law' (2007) 52 *American Journal of Jurisprudence* 1–22

Gilligan, C., *In a Different Voice: Psychological Theory and Women's Development* (Cambridge, MA: Harvard University Press, 1982)

Glover, J., *Causing Death and Saving Lives* (London: Penguin Books, 1977)

Gormally, L., 'Walton, Davies, Boyd and the Legalization of Euthanasia', in J. Keown (ed.), *Euthanasia Examined* (Cambridge University Press, 1995), pp. 113–140

Griffiths, J., Bood, A. and Weyers, H., *Euthanasia and Law in the Netherlands* (Amsterdam University Press, 1998)

Griffiths, J., Weyers, H. and Adams, M., *Euthanasia and Law in Europe* (Oxford: Hart Publishing, 2008)

Grimshaw, J., 'The Idea of a Female Ethic', in P. Singer (ed.), *A Companion to Ethics* (Malden, MA: Blackwell Publishing, 1991), pp. 491–499

Harris, J., 'Euthanasia and the Value of Life', in J. Keown (ed.), *Euthanasia Examined* (Cambridge University Press, 1995), pp. 6–22

'The Philosophical Case against the Philosophical Case against Euthanasia', in J. Keown (ed.), *Euthanasia Examined* (Cambridge University Press, 1995), pp. 36–45

The Value of Life (London: Routledge, 1985)

Harris, J. and Holm, S., 'Abortion', in H. LaFollette (ed.), *The Oxford Handbook of Practical Ethics* (Oxford University Press, 2003), pp. 112–135

Hart, H. L. A., *The Concept of Law* (2nd edn) (Oxford University Press, 1994)
Law, Liberty and Morality (Stanford University Press, 1963)
Hendin, H., *Seduced by Death: Doctors, Patients and Assisted Suicide* (New York: W. W. Norton & Co., 1998)
Hendin, H., Foley, K. and White, M., 'Physician-Assisted Suicide: Reflections on Oregon's First Case' (1998–1999) 14 *Issues in Law and Medicine* 243–270
Hobbes, T., *Leviathan* (London: The Fontana Library, 1962 [original publication 1651])
Holmes, O. W., 'The Path of the Law' (1897) 10 *Harvard Law Review* 457–478
House of Lords Select Committee on the Assisted Dying for the Terminally Ill Bill, *Report [HL Paper 86-I]* (London: Stationery Office, 2005)
Huxtable, R., *Euthanasia, Ethics and the Law: From Conflict to Compromise* (Abingdon: Routledge-Cavendish, 2007)
Kass, L. R., 'Defending Human Dignity', in E. D. Pellegrino, A. Schulman and T. W. Merrill (eds.), *Human Dignity and Bioethics* (University of Notre Dame Press, 2009), pp. 297–331
'Neither for Love nor Money: Why Doctors Must Not Kill' (1989, Winter) 94 *Public Interest* 25
Keown, J., *Euthanasia, Ethics and Public Policy: An Argument against Legalisation* (Cambridge University Press, 2002)
Keown, J. (ed.), *Euthanasia Examined* (Cambridge University Press, 1995)
Publication Review: R. Dworkin, Life's Dominion – *An Argument about Abortion and Euthanasia* (1994) 110 *LQR* 671–675
'Restoring Moral and Intellectual Shape to the Law after *Bland*' (1997) 113 *LQR* 482–503
'Restoring the Sanctity of Life and Replacing the Caricature: A Reply to David Price' (2006) 26 *Legal Studies* 109–119
Kinnell, H. G., 'Serial Homicide by Doctors: Shipman in Perspective' (2000) 321 *BMJ* 1594–1597
Koontz, D., *Watchers* (New York: Berkley Books, 1988)
Kramer, M., 'What Good Is Truth?' (1992) 5 *Canadian Journal of Law and Jurisprudence* 309–319
Krant, M., *Dying and Dignity: The Meaning and Control of a Personal Death* (Springfield, IL: Charles C. Thomas, 1974)
Kraynak, R. P., 'Human Dignity and the Mystery of the Human Soul', in E. D. Pellegrino, A. Schulman and T. W. Merrill (eds.), *Human Dignity and Bioethics* (University of Notre Dame Press, 2009), pp. 61–82
Kuhse, H., 'Is There a Tension between Autonomy and Dignity?' in P. Kemp, J. Rendtorff and N. M. Johansen (eds.), *Bioethics and Biolaw*, vol. II: *Four Ethical Principles* (Copenhagen: Rhodes International Science and Art Publishers and Centre for Ethics and Law, 2000), pp. 61–74
Kuhse, H. and Singer, P., *Should the Baby Live?* (Oxford University Press, 1985)
Kuhse, H., Singer, P., Baume, P., Clark, M. and Rickard, M., 'End-of-Life Decisions in Australian Medical Practice' (1997) 166 *Medical Journal of Australia* 191–196

Lasson, K., 'Torture, Truth Serum, and Ticking Bombs: Toward a Pragmatic Perspective on Coercive Interrogation' (2008) 39 *Loyola University Chicago Law Journal* 329–360

Lee, P. and George, R. P. 'The Nature and Basis of Human Dignity', in E. D. Pellegrino, A. Schulman and T. W. Merrill (eds.), *Human Dignity and Bioethics* (University of Notre Dame Press, 2009), pp. 409–433

Lewis, P., *Assisted Dying and Legal Change* (Oxford University Press, 2007)

Lillehammer, H., 'Voluntary Euthanasia and the Logical Slippery Slope Argument' (2002) 61 *Cambridge Law Journal* 545–550

Lloyd, G. E. R. (ed.), *Hippocratic Writings* (London: Penguin Books, 1978)

Locke, J., *Two Treatises of Government* (Cambridge University Press, 1960 [original publication 1690])

Macklin, R., 'Dignity Is a Useless Concept' (2003) 327 *BMJ* 1419–1420

Magnusson, R., *Angels of Death: Exploring the Euthanasia Underground* (New Haven, CT: Yale University Press, 2002)

Marzen, T. J., O'Dowd, M. K., Crone, D. and Balch, T. J., 'Suicide: A Constitutional Right?' (1985) 24(1) *Duquesne L. Rev.* 17–56

Meier, D. *et al.* 'A National Survey of Physician-Assisted Suicide and Euthanasia in the United States' (1998) 338 *The New England Journal of Medicine* 1193–1201

The Merriam-Webster Dictionary, New Edition (Springfield, MA: Mirriam-Webster, Inc., 2004)

Mill, J. S., *On Liberty* (Oxford University Press, 1991 [original publication 1859])

Mitchell, K. and Glynn Owens, R., 'National Survey of Medical Decisions at End of Life Made by New Zealand General Practitioners' (2003) 327 *BMJ* 202–203

New York State Task Force on Life and the Law, *When Death Is Sought: Assisted Suicide and Euthanasia in the Medical Context* (New York, 1994)

Nietzsche, F., *Thus Spoke Zarathustra* (London: Penguin Books, 1961 [original publication 1883–1885])

Noddings, N., *Caring: A Feminine Approach to Ethics and Education* (Berkeley: University of California Press, 1978)

Norcross, A., 'Introduction to the Second Edition', in B. Steinbock and A. Norcross (eds.), *Killing and Letting Die* (2nd edn) (New York: Fordham University Press, 1994), pp. 1–23

Nussbaum, M., 'Human Dignity and Political Entitlements', in E. D. Pellegrino, A. Schulman and T. W. Merrill (eds.), *Human Dignity and Bioethics* (University of Notre Dame Press, 2009), pp. 351–380

O'Neill, O., *Autonomy and Trust in Bioethics* (Cambridge University Press, 2002)

Onwuteaka-Philipsen, B. D. *et al.*, 'Euthanasia and Other End-of-Life Decisions in the Netherlands in 1990, 1995, and 2001' (2003) 362 *The Lancet* 395–399

Oregon Department of Human Services, *Annual Reports on Oregon's Death with Dignity Act* (Portland, OR: DHS)

Otlowski, M., *Voluntary Euthanasia and the Common Law* (Oxford University Press, 2000)

Pattinson, S., *Medical Law and Ethics* (London: Sweet and Maxwell, 2006)

Pellegrino, E. D., Schulman A. and Merrill, T. W. (eds.), *Human Dignity and Bioethics* (University of Notre Dame Press, 2009)

Plotnik, J. M., de Waal, F. B. M. and Reiss, D., 'Self-recognition in an Asian Elephant' (2006) 103 *Proceedings of the National Academy of Sciences of the United States of America* 17053–17057

Posner, R., *Aging and Old Age* (University of Chicago Press, 1995)

Price, D., 'Fairly *Bland*: An Alternative View of a Supposed New "Death Ethic" and the BMA Guidelines' (2001) 21 *Legal Studies* 618–643

'My View of the Sanctity of Life: A Rebuttal of John Keown's Critique' (2007) 27 *Legal Studies* 549–565

Quill, T., 'The Ambiguity of Clinical Intentions' (1993) 329 *New England Journal of Medicine* 1039–1040, reprinted in M. P. Battin, L. P. Francis and B. M. Landesman (eds.), *Death, Dying and the Ending of Life* (Aldershot: Ashgate Publishing, 2007), vol. II, pp. 15–16

'Death and Dignity: A Case of Individualized Decision Making' (1991) 324 *New England Journal of Medicine* 691–694

Quine, W. S., 'Actions, Intentions and Consequences: The Doctrine of Doing and Allowing' (1989) 98 *Philosophical Review* 287–312, reprinted in B. Steinbock and A. Norcross (eds.), *Killing and Letting Die* (2nd edn) (New York: Fordham University Press, 1994), pp. 355–382

Rachels, J., 'Active and Passive Euthanasia' (1975) 292 *New England Journal of Medicine* 78–80, reprinted in M. P. Battin, L. P. Francis and B. M. Landesman (eds.), *Death, Dying and the Ending of Life* (Aldershot: Ashgate Publishing, 2007), vol. II, pp. 5–8

The End of Life (Oxford University Press, 1996)

'More Impertinent Distinctions and a Defense of Active Euthanasia', in T. A. Mappes and J. S. Zembaty (eds.), *Biomedical Ethics* (New York: McGraw Hill, 1981), pp. 355–359, reprinted in B. Steinbock and A. Norcross (eds.), *Killing and Letting Die* (2nd edn) (New York: Fordham University Press, 1994), pp. 139–154

Reiss, D. and Marino, L., 'Mirror Self-recognition in the Bottlenose Dolphin: A Case of Cognitive Convergence' (2001) 98 *Proceedings of the National Academy of Sciences of the United States of America* 5937–5942

Rescher, N., *Welfare: The Social Issue in Philosophical Perspective* (University of Pittsburgh Press, 1972)

Rolston III, H., 'Human Uniqueness and Human Dignity: Persons in Nature and the Nature of Persons', in E. D. Pellegrino, A. Schulman and T. W. Merrill (eds.), *Human Dignity and Bioethics* (University of Notre Dame Press, 2009), pp. 129–153

Rubin, C., 'Human Dignity and the Future of Man', in E. D. Pellegrino, A. Schulman and T. W. Merrill (eds.), *Human Dignity and Bioethics* (University of Notre Dame Press, 2009), pp. 155–172

Schulman, A., 'Bioethics and the Question of Human Dignity', in E. D. Pellegrino, A. Schulman and T. W. Merrill (eds.), *Human Dignity and Bioethics* (University of Notre Dame Press, 2009), pp. 3–18

Seale, C., 'Investigating End-of-Life Decision Making in U.K. Medical Practice', Address at Institute of Medical Law, University of Birmingham, 22 March 2006

'National Survey of End of Life Decisions Made by U.K. Medical Practitioners' (2006) 20 *Palliative Medicine* 3–10

Singer, P. *Animal Liberation: Towards an End to Man's Inhumanity to Animals* (London: Paladin, 1977)

'Famine, Affluence and Morality' (1972) 1 *Philosophy and Public Affairs* 229–243

Practical Ethics (2nd edn) (Cambridge University Press, 1993)

Smith, J., *Sixth Report – Shipman Inquiry: The Final Report* (Crown Copyright, 2005)

Smith, S. W., 'Dignity: The Difference between Abortion and Neonaticide for Severe Disability', in C. Erin and S. Ost (eds.), *The Criminal Justice System and Health Care* (Oxford University Press, 2007), pp. 175–188

'Evidence for the Practical Slippery Slope in the Debate on Physician-Assisted Suicide and Euthanasia' (2005) 13 *Medical Law Review* 17–44

'Fallacies of the Logical Slippery Slope in the Debate on Physician-Assisted Suicide and Euthanasia' (2005) 13 *Medical Law Review* 224–243

'Precautionary Reasoning in Determining Moral Worth', in M. Freeman (ed.), *Law and Bioethics, Current Legal Issues* (Oxford University Press, 2008), vol. XI, pp. 197–212

'Some Realism about End of Life: The Current Prohibition and the Euthanasia Underground' (2007) 33 *American Journal of Law and Medicine* 55–95

Specter, M., 'The Dangerous Philosopher', *The New Yorker*, 6 September 1999, pp. 46–55

Spiegelberg, H., 'Human Dignity: A Challenge to Contemporary Philosophy', in R. Gotesky and E. Laszlo (eds.), *Human Dignity: This Century and the Next* (New York: Gordon & Breach, 1970), pp. 55–56

Steinbock, B., 'The Intentional Termination of Life' (1979) 6 *Ethics in Science and Medicine* 59–64, reprinted in M. P. Battin, L. P. Francis and B. M. Landesman (eds.), *Death, Dying and the Ending of Life* (Aldershot: Ashgate Publishing, 2007), vol. II, pp. 9–14

Steinbock, B. and Norcross, A. (eds.), *Killing and Letting Die* (2nd edn) (New York: Fordham University Press, 1994)

Sulmasy, D. P., OFM, 'Dignity and Bioethics: History, Theory and Selected Applications', in E. D. Pellegrino, A. Schulman and T. W. Merrill (eds.), *Human Dignity and Bioethics* (University of Notre Dame Press, 2009), pp. 469–501

Swift, Z., *A System of the Laws of the State of Connecticut* (Windham: John Byrne, 1796)

Sykes, N. and Thorns, A., 'Sedative Use in the Last Week of Life and the Implications for End-of-Life Decision Making' (2003) 163 *Archives of Internal Medicine* 341–344

'The Use of Opioids and Sedatives at the End of Life' (2003) 4 *The Lancet Oncology* 312–318

Tasioulas, J., 'Mercy' (2003) 103 *Proceedings of the Aristotelian Society* 101–132

Thorns, A. and Sykes, N., 'Opioid Use in the Last Week of Life and Implications for End-of-Life Decision-making' (2000) 356 *The Lancet* 398–399

Tooley, M., *Abortion and Infanticide* (Oxford: Clarendon Press, 1983)

Unger, P., *Living High and Letting Die* (Oxford University Press, 1996)

van der Heide, A. *et al.*, 'End-of-Life Decision-making in six European Countries: Descriptive Study' (2003) 361 *The Lancet* 345–350

'End-of-Life Practices in the Netherlands under the Euthanasia Act' (2007) 356 *New England Journal of Medicine* 1957–1965

van der Maas, P. J. *et al.*, 'Euthanasia and Other Medical Decisions Concerning the End of Life' (1991) 338 *The Lancet* 669–674

'Euthanasia, Physician-Assisted Suicide, and Other Medical Practices Involving the End of Life in the Netherlands, 1990–1995' (1996) 335 *New England Journal of Medicine* 1699–1705

Volokh, E., 'The Mechanisms of the Slippery Slope' (2003) 116 *Harvard Law Review* 1026–1137

Warren, M. A., *Moral Status* (Oxford University Press, 1997)

Wienrib, E. J., 'The Case for a Duty to Rescue' (1980) 90 *Yale Law Review* 247–293

Willems, D. *et al.*, 'Attitudes and Practices Concerning the End of Life' (2000) 160 *Archives of Internal Medicine* 63–68

Wolff, R. P., *In Defense of Anarchism* (New York: Harper & Row, 1970)

Index

active euthanasia, definitions, 12
active voluntary euthanasia (AVE), 13
  vs. physician-assisted suicide (PAS),
    304–05
actual causal pathway, 89
Adams, John Bodkin, 207–08
Adams, M., 1, 173, 245, 247–48
Agatha example from John Keown, 51
  lack of information about uniqueness
    as individual, 70, 71
Agent's Rights Principle, Mary Anne
    Warren, 39, 40, 48, 146
AIDS patients, and PAS/voluntary
    euthanasia, 200
Alexander, Leo, 266–67
anencephalic infants, 329–30
  capacity for rationality, 135–36
  human dignity, 136
Angels of Death (R. Magnusson), 1,
    178–80, 191, 210, 214–15, 216,
    220, 222, 223, 224–25, 236,
    241–42
Anti-Cruelty Principle, 1
  Mary Anne Warren, 39, 47, 146
aspirations, 119
  vs. legal obligations, 168–69
assisted dying
  and patient communication,
    191–92
  definitions, 13
  demographics of those choosing, 200,
    202, 237
  model regime, 327–28
  prioritising over euthanasia, 328–29
  prohibition and suicide reduction,
    187–94
  requests for, 149
  under preferred ethical approach,
    161–62
assisted suicide
  definitions, 11, 13, *see also* physician-
    assisted suicide (PAS)

Australia
  attitudes toward euthanasia, 283–84
  euthanasia practices survey, 173–74
autonomous decisions
  and prior interaction with others,
    104–05
  interference with, 112–15
  preconditions for, 107–09
  which limit future uses of autonomy,
    105–07
autonomy
  concept of, 95–109, 114–15
  definitions, 97, 98, 109, 148–49
  preferred approach, 148–52, 329–30
  regulation of, 110–15, *see also* respect
    for autonomy of others
autonomy by concert, 110–11
Ayers Rock, *see* Uluru/Ayers Rock

Bamiyan Buddhas, 38
basic goods, John Finnis, 51, 54–55
Battin, Margaret P., 1, 185, 200
Beauchamp, Tom L., 97–98, 117, 320
  Principles of Biomedical Ethics, 118–19,
    121–23, 148–49
Belgium
  attitudes toward euthanasia, 283–84
  euthanasia practices survey, 174
beneficence, 117, 122–25, 127,
    152, 321
Bertha example from John Keown, 52
  lack of information about uniqueness
    as individual, 70–71
Beyleveld, Deryck, 23, 131, 132, 137
Biggs, Hazel, 130
bioethicists, counter-intuitive statements
    by, 5
bioethics
  controversial nature of, 3–4
  importance of usefulness, 6
biographical life, 63
  evaluating, 63